The Allure of Authors

Author Studies in the Elementary Classroom

CAROL BRENNAN JENKINS

HEINEMANN
Portsmouth, NH

To my parents, Mary and Patrick Brennan,
with endless love and gratitude

Heinemann
A division of Reed Elsevier Inc.
361 Hanover Street
Portsmouth, NH 03801-3912
http://www.heinemann.com

Offices and agents throughout the world

Library of Congress Cataloging-in-Publication Data
CIP is on file with the Library of Congress.
ISBN 0-325-00001-8

Editor: William Varner
Production: Melissa L. Inglis
Cover design: Linda Knowles
Manufacturing: Louise Richardson

Printed in the United States of America on acid-free paper

Docutech RRD 2006

Contents

Preface
Acknowledgments

1   THE ALLURE OF AUTHORS   1
In the Words of Readers
Why Conduct Author Studies?

2   HISTORICALLY SPEAKING: THE PLACE OF AUTHOR   23
Three Cynthia Rylant Author Studies
Taking Stock: Beliefs About Author Studies
Historical Roots of the Three Author-Study Perspectives
Radical Theories About Literature
Concluding Comments

3   THE AUTHOR STUDY AS MULTIPLE RESPONSE: FEATURED AUTHOR: 43
     CAROLYN COMAN
Principle One: Readers Respond in Multiple Ways to an Author's Works
Principle Two: Aesthetic Engagement Must Precede Critical and Biographical
     Response
Principle Three: Critical Response Deepens and Extends the Literary Experience
Deciding When to Teach Which Literary Element
Teacher Knowledge and the Literary Elements
Principle Four: Biographical Response Heightens and Intensifes the Literary
     Experience
Principle Five: Children Are Drawn to Meaningful Endeavors and Learn Best
     Through Interaction with More Knowledgeable Others
Concluding Comments

AUTHOR RESPONSE: CAROLYN COMAN ON AUTHOR STUDIES   *81*

4 PICTURE-BOOK AUTHOR STUDY: FEATURED AUTHOR: MEM FOX 83
Classroom Context
Mem Fox Author Study
Concluding Comments

5 DESIGNING AN AUTHOR STUDY 112
Choosing an Author
Savoring the Author's Literature
Researching Biographical and Autobiographical Links
Organizing Learners: A Continuum of Literature-Based
    Perspectives
Establishing a Tentative Timeline for the Author Study: Expect the Unexpected
Journeying Without a Detailed Road Map
Author-Study Culmination
Concluding Comments

6 CHAPTER-BOOK AUTHOR STUDY: FEATURED AUTHOR: AVI 129
Designing and Implementing a Chapter-Book Author Study
Classroom Context
The Avi Author Study
Concluding Comments

AUTHOR RESPONSE: AVI ON AUTHOR STUDIES 167

7 NONFICTION AUTHOR STUDY: FEATURED AUTHOR: JOANNA COLE 174
Designing the Joanna Cole Author Study
Implementing the Joanna Cole Author Study
Third Graders Write and Illustrate The Magic School Bus Goes to the Vernal
    Pool
Concluding Comments

AUTHOR RESPONSE: JOANNA COLE ON AUTHOR STUDIES 216

8 THE ENDLESS POSSIBILITIES OF AUTHOR STUDIES 220
Patricia Polacco
Mildred Taylor
Kathryn Lasky
Concluding Comments

AUTHOR RESPONSE: KATHRYN LASKY ON AUTHOR STUDIES 256

References 261
    Professional References
    Children's Literature References

Index 272

Preface

A few years ago, I had the pleasure of working with a group of energetic and engaging teachers in Carlisle, Massachusetts. During one of our workshops on literature-based learning, a teacher shared an "Arthur" story that one of her second graders had written as part of an author study on Marc Brown. No sooner had she finished reading the story than the questions began: "Do you have a videotape of Marc Brown talking about the *Arthur* books?" "Did you find any autobiographical material on Marc Brown?" "How many *Arthur* books did you read?" "How did you start the author study?"

Lively discussion about author studies ensued. One teacher explained that he began his author study on Katherine Paterson by having his fifth graders watch a videotape in which Paterson talks about the personal tragedy that inspired *Bridge to Terabithia* and about her writing habits. Another noted that she read Kevin Henkes's books to her first graders and focused on story themes, and wondered where she might find biographical information on Henkes. Intrigued by these and other ideas, I offered to check the literature and to share ideas about author studies during our next session. Surprisingly, I found no books about author studies and very few articles. So began this book.

The Allure of Authors explores the place and power of author studies in the elementary classroom. It springs from author studies that I implemented with children across various grade levels. Indeed, it is their energy, enthusiasm, and insight that gives life to this book.

Chapter 1 explores the reasons for readers' fascination with particular authors. Third and fifth graders, surveyed about their favorite authors, explain why they return time and again to these authors. Not surprisingly, their reasons align closely with the testimonials of acclaimed writers who have written about the import of authors in their own lives. The chapter then turns to a discussion about why author studies belong in the curriculum. It makes the case that when we bring author studies into the classroom, we not only honor children's fascination with certain authors but also spark an expansive range of new learnings.

In Chapter 2, three prominent author-study models are examined against the backdrop of major literary movements that have waxed and waned over the centuries. The theoretical assumptions of each of these perspectives that have influenced, consciously or unconsciously, the design and implementation of author studies are explored. Chapter 3, while acknowledging the contributions of each perspective, advocates a merging of what is best about each of these perspectives. It presents the principles of the author-study model advocated in this book—*author study as multiple response*. It is my belief that author studies that invite children to respond aesthetically, critically, and biographically to an author's body of work significantly expand their literary and literacy understanding. This chapter emphasizes the importance of teacher knowledge; research on children's literary understanding along with snapshots of an author study implemented with sixth graders on the life and works of Carolyn Coman buoy this chapter.

Chapter 5 addresses the practical aspects of designing and implementing an author study—aspects such as choice of author (Who chooses the author? Which authors work best?); the timeline of an author study; issues of teacher versus child control; and ways of sharing an author's literature with readers (whole class? literature circles? independent reading?).

Chapters 4, 6, and 7 merge theory and practice, demonstrating the multiplicity of response that readers bring to an author's works and emphasizing the importance of moving from aesthetic to critical and biographical response. Chapter 4 profiles an author study conducted with third graders on Mem Fox. Chapter 6 presents an Avi author study implemented with fifth graders. Chapter 7 explores a nonfiction author study using the works of Joanna Cole.

Chapter 8 offers suggestions for author studies on the lives and works of Patricia Polacco, Mildred Taylor, and Kathryn Lasky. For each author, one critical aspect of her literature, along with autobiographical connections, are explored in detail.

Gracing this book, also, are the voices of four of the acclaimed children's authors profiled in these chapters: Avi, Joanna Cole, Carolyn Coman, and Kathryn Lasky. Each author shares his or her thoughts about the viability of author studies. These author responses follow the chapter in which the author is featured.

Acknowledgments

Joy is the word that comes to mind when I think about the children who participated in the author studies that illuminate this book. They brought an intellectual and emotional exuberance to these author studies, offering engaging ideas at every turn. It was from continual collaboration with these young minds that I learned what it takes to make an author study take flight. Their unbridled enthusiasm for life, learning, and literacy made me long for my own classroom. Many thanks to each and every child.

I am deeply indebted to the classroom teachers who allowed me to live and learn in their classrooms: Maura Albert, Alice Earle, and Joanna McCarthy. Their classrooms are havens of learning and laughter, of genuine caring and high expectation, and of educational adventure. Their belief in children, their commitment to caring classrooms, and their expertise in literacy development ensured the success of the author studies that are showcased in this book. I am grateful to Maura, Alice, and Joanna for their generosity of spirit and for their willingness to share their children with me.

Heartfelt gratitude is extended to the award-winning authors—Avi, Joanna Cole, Carolyn Coman, and Kathryn Lasky—who gave so graciously of their time to share their thoughts about author studies. I thank each of you for your passionate concern about children, your honesty, and your good will. Most of all, I thank you for gracing readers' lives with literature worthy of author study.

To my friends and colleagues at Boston University who have seen me through the highs and lows of this writing venture with good humor and genuine caring, I send sincere gratitude. I thank Dean Edwin Delattre for his intellectual guidance, unfailing support, and friendship. I thank my mentor, Judith Schickedanz, whose knowledge of and passion about literacy and children continue to lift me to new intellectual heights. I thank Associate Deans Joan Dee and Boyd Dewey, Thomas Culliton, Stephan Ellenwood, and Burleigh Shibles for their daily words of encouragement, warm friendship, and wisdom. To Judy Chambliss, who picks up the pieces of my life on a regular basis with her patient counseling and deep compassion, I am indebted. To Christine LaRosa and Amanda Romero, many thanks for the computer searches, for tracking down resources, and for keeping some semblance of sanity in life.

I extend sincere gratitude to Bill Varner, Acquisitions Editor, who believed in this book, and who offered continual support and encouragement. I also thank Melissa Inglis, Production Editor, for her magical touch and for her gentle nature; she transformed this unwieldy manuscript into a readable text with masterful skill.

Endless love and gratitude to my family, especially to my parents, Mary and Patrick Brennan, whose words of encouragement and wisdom continue to sustain me. From my earliest years, I watched my parents live the virtues of hard work, compassion, and service to others. They are what I aspire to be. To my brother, Tom, thank you for going the distance with me. We're going to make it, buddy. And to my sister, Maureen, whose life and death ripple through the pages of this book, know that you are always with me.

To Ted, my husband and best friend, who fills my life with hugs, laughter, and walks on the beach, and who has championed my passionate interest in children with unconditional love and understanding, I send my deepest gratitude and love. I couldn't do this without you.

1

The Allure of Authors

In *The Call of Stories*, Robert Coles (1989) writes poignantly about his parents' affaires de coeur with particular authors. "He was a great admirer of the Victorian trio, Dickens, Eliot, Hardy. . . . Though my father did not dislike the Russians, he never took to them with the passion my mother felt. She read and reread Tolstoy all through her life—*Anna Karenina* three times, short stories such as "The Death of Ivan Ilyich" and "Master and Man" repeatedly, and *War and Peace* twice" (p. xiv). Smitten with these authors, Coles's parents read their works aloud to each other each evening—a practice that their sons found peculiar. When Robert asked about this ritual, his father explained that novels are "reservoirs of wisdom. . . . Your mother and I feel rescued by these books. We read them gratefully. You'll be grateful one day to the authors" (p. xii). That day arrived when Coles, a junior in a college English course, succumbed to the works of poet/physician William Carlos Williams. Within a year, Coles relinquished his plans to teach English in order to pursue a career in medicine.

Coles's account illuminates not only our passionate need for story but also our yearning for sustained engagement with particular authors. What is this power that certain authors hold over us? In what ways do they influence our lives? Are all readers—children and adults—drawn to certain authors? It is the intent of this chapter to explore these and other questions. While ample research exists on the primacy of literature in our lives, the primacy of the authors themselves has escaped scrutiny. Indeed, literary biographies that examine the life and times of an author against the backdrop of his or her literature abound, but the stories of readers summoned by particular authors are untold. It is the intent of this chapter to explore these stories. To do so, it turns to the testimonials of prominent literary figures who have written passionately about the authors in their lives. It also turns to the words of young readers who talk about their enchantment with favorite authors.

In the Words of Readers

To explore the dimensions of readers' fascination with particular authors, I asked thirty-two third graders and nineteen fifth graders to complete informal questionnaires. These questionnaires were analyzed to identify common patterns of response among readers. These patterns were translated into coding categories that were used to code each student's statements. Analysis of these surveys yielded four dimensions with regard to the allure of authors: emotional sustenance, wisdom, delight with craft, and intrigue with the author as person and writer. Not surprisingly, much compatibility was noted between the testimonials of acclaimed writers and of these readers.

Moved by Authors

In the *Call of Stories*, Robert Coles (1989) talks movingly about both his literary and personal relationship with William Carlos Williams, a physician who tended poor immigrants by day and who wrote poetry about these life-sustaining encounters by night. As Williams explained to Coles:

> I don't know what I'd do without those patients! Everyone thinks that doctors are good people because they help other people who are sick. But if you ask me, the people who are sick are helping us all the time—if we let them help. . . . A kid is telling me . . . "I got a real jab of pain, and it was like a knife, pushing itself from the skin right through and through to the bone, that's right, the bone. I could see stars, that's how hard the pain was. I thought God was trying to get me to kneel and plead with Him to come get me, and I mean right away." Do you see what I'm trying to say? I can't hear a kid talk like that and not be sprung—sprung right out of my own damn self-preoccupations. . . . I wouldn't walk away from those talks for anything; I come away from them so damn stirred myself—I needed to walk around the block once or twice to settle down . . . so I can stop and think. It's like reading Tolstoy; you can't just breeze through his stories, even if his writing is so "easy," it just envelops you. You get stopped in your tracks by something he says, and it takes time to let it work its way through your head and your heart, both of them. (pp. 104–105)

The statement "I come away . . . so damn stirred myself" captures the impact of William Carlos Williams's poetry on Coles. In reading Williams's most famous poem, *Paterson*, Coles found himself sorrowed by the pain of terminal illness, despaired by social injustices that plagued the poor, aroused by extent of human caring, and buoyed by the resilience of the human spirit.

Coles is only one of many writers who has been emotionally rescued by particular authors. Of the ancient poet Homer, Helen Keller (1965) wrote, "When I read the finest passages of the *Iliad*, I am conscious of a soul-sense that lifts me above the narrow, cramping circumstances of my life. My physical limitations are forgotten—my world lies upward, the length and breadth and the sweep of the heavens are mine" (p. 65). Maya Angelou (1969) acknowledged that while other writers touched her heart and mind, only Shakespeare spoke to her young and broken soul. In *I Know Why the Caged Bird Sings*, Angelou wrote, "I met and fell in love with William

Shakespeare. He was my first white love" (p. 11). Katherine Paterson (1990), too, expressed her gratitude to Gerard Manley Hopkins (who was to become the namesake of Gilly Hopkins): "Through the thirty-six years since that January morning I've gone back again and again to my slender volume of Hopkins's poetry for inspiration, for nourishment, and for comfort" (p. 150).

Young readers, surveyed about their favorite authors, also speak to the emotional charge that authors spark. Nineteen fifth graders responded to the questions presented in Figure 1-1. Lyra, an avid reader, acknowledged the affective pull of her favorite authors as did three other fifth graders:

> Dear Joanna Hurwitz,
> I have read so many of your books. They were excellent. My favorite one is *The Rabbi's Girls*. When I read it, I felt myself in the book and could feel all the emotions of sadness and happiness in the book. I would like to meet you someday.

> Dear Lois Lowry,
> I really like the book *Number the Stars* because it shows people that killing is bad. Somebody I know (who died last year) was Jewish and his family was captured in the war and he was the only one in his family to escape. I thought about him when I was reading your book and just felt so sad and upset.

> Dear Scot O'Dell,
> I love your books, especially *Island of the Blue Dolphins*. When I read it, it made me feel like I was really in the book. It seems like it is a true story. I also like *Thunder Rolling in the Mountains*, I thought it was very sad though.

Thirty-two third graders also wrote about a favorite author. Samantha's generic response, in Figure 1-2, is highly representative of this age group. Half of the third graders chose favorite authors because they wrote books that were "funny" or "scary." The basic human emotions of laughter and fear characterized the third graders' attraction to certain authors.

Instructed by Authors

Robert Coles sought out William Carlos Williams's work because it not only inspired him but also accorded the moral compass that would guide his own work as a psychiatrist. Coles recognized that Williams's medical practice, and subsequently his poetry, were as much about moral responsibility as they were about physical and spiritual healing. As Coles (1989) wrote:

> All through his greatest work, the long poem, *Paterson*, he poses one of the oldest dilemmas: the sad commonplace that ideas or ideals, however erudite and valuable, are by no means synonymous with behavior, that high-sounding abstractions do not necessarily translate into decent or commendable conduct.... As Williams once reminded me about Nazi Joseph Goebbels and Williams' own friend Ezra Pound: "Look at the two of them, one a Ph.D. and smart as they come, and the other, one of the twentieth century's most original poets, also as brilliant as they come in certain ways—and they end up peddling hate, front men for the worst scum the world has ever seen." (pp. 108, 195)

Name _Lyra Brennan_

1. Do you have ~~a~~ *some* favorite author? (Yes) No

2. If you have a favorite author, write his or her name on the line.
③ _Avi, ②Roald Dahl,①Jane Yolen,①Jaqueline Woodson_

If you have a second favorite author, write his or her name on this line.
⑤Margaret Mahy ④Ida Vos ②Karen Hesse

3. If you don't have a favorite author, tell me why on the <u>back of this sheet</u>.

4. What are some of the books you have read that were written by your first favorite author. (You don't have to remember the full title.)

The True Confessions Char Do, Matilda, The Devils Arithmatic
I had — _Melanin Sun, The Girl with the Green Ear,_
Hide and Seek, Music of Dolphins, Letters
From R.ifka

5. If you were going to write a letter to your favorite author to tell him or her why he or she is your favorite author, what would you write? Try to write three different ideas about why you are interested in this author's books.

Dear _Jane Yolen_

because she _That book the "Devils Arithmatic" was_ sadness
her aunt _touching and fantastic I cried so_ happiness
of a friend _much. It had a little bit of everything_ scar
because _Wonderful job!_
of the terror
of the Holocaust _Dear Karen Hesse, I loved your_
Perfect _book. It was very touching. It was a_
perfect book for me because lots of times I feel I
am differ.

6. What would you say to convince a friend that your favorite author is a great author and that he or she should read some books by this author?

Trust me Jane's books are awesome!
You will become interested in seconds.
Some _~~We~~ are tear jerkers though. She's a_
FANTASTIC writer

FIGURE 1-1 *Lyra's (Grade 5) responses to the author-study questionnaire*

4

Name Samantha

1. Do you have a favorite author?   (Yes)   No

2. If you have a favorite author, write his or her name on the line.

Rhol Dahl

If you have a second favorite author, write his or her name on this line.

_____

3. If you don't have a favorite author, tell me why on the back of this sheet.

4. What are some of the books you have read that were written by first your favorite author.

fantastic Mr. fox,
The twits, gorges magical
medince.

5. If you were going to write a letter to this author to tell him or her why he or she is your favorite author, what would you write?

Dear mr Dahl,
I like your books because
their funny and because you
make the charactars
in a funny way, solve stuff

6. What woud you say to convince a friend that your favorite author is a great author and that he or she should read some books by this author?

I think you Should read
books by this author because
he's funny and I think you
would Enjoy him

FIGURE 1-2 *Samantha's (Grade 3) responses to the author-study questionnaire*

Coles took counsel in Williams's conviction that ultimately a doctor's worth resides not only in medical knowledge but in moral actions. It is this core truth that continues to anchor Coles's own practice and writing. Authors such as Avi, an award-winning children's author, and Chukovsky, the Russian poet, also acknowledge the teaching power of their literature:

> If we—in the world of children's literature—can help the young stand straight for a moment longer than they have done in the past, help them maintain their ideals and values, those with which you and I identify ourselves, help them demand—and win—justice, we have added something good to the world. (Avi in Collier and Nakamura, 1992, p. 2507)

> The goal of every storyteller consists of fostering in the child, at whatever cost, compassion and humanness, this miraculous ability of man to be disturbed by another being's misfortune, to feel joy about another being's happiness, to experience another's fate as your own. (Chukovsky, 1965, p. 138)

Plato wrote about this goal four thousand years ago. He understood the power of story not only to move us intellectually and emotionally but also to instill moral sensibility. He especially understood the power of story to teach children the enduring lessons of a moral life, observing that children not only delight in story but also appropriate the actions of characters during play. Plato believed that if children were immersed in tales of virtuous activity, they would act in virtuous ways, at first in play, and then in life (Bloom, 1968). Plato's wisdom is confirmed in classrooms every day as this interview with Shane, a fifth grader, illustrates:

CAROL: Think about a great story that you have read lately. What makes this story great in your opinion?

SHANE: I read *The Client* by John Grisham. You probably don't believe me. Adults don't think kids can read and comprehend Grisham's books but I can. Grisham is my favorite author and my mother's too.

CAROL: You're such a good reader that I'm sure you can. Why is *The Client* a great book?

SHANE: It's great because it showed people the consequences of lying. See, Mark, he's an eleven-year-old kid who got into big trouble for not telling the truth. Mark and his little brother saw this lawyer guy named Romey try to kill himself. Mark tried to stop him by pulling out the hose out from the car's pipe. . . . But Romey woke up and blew his head off with a gun. Mark and his brother saw the whole thing. They ran home but the brother went into like a trance. He was in shock. His mother came home and called the ambulance but Mark doesn't tell her the truth about what happened. Then the police came and soon Mark's telling one lie on top of another. He doesn't even tell the doctor at the hospital the whole truth. And his brother might never come out of the trance because Mark hasn't told the doctor the truth.

CAROL: Why do think Mark didn't tell the truth?

SHANE: 'Cuz he was smoking with his little brother when he saw Romey's car and he didn't want to get in trouble for smoking.

CAROL: It sounds as if he paid a big price for lying.

SHANE: He did but I like stories that teach you something. When I write, I try to do the same thing. Like I wrote this story about a kid who wrote a report on George Washington and then boasted about how awesome the report was to all the kids in school. He boasted so much that the other kids stole the report and made him sweat it out.

CAROL: How did the story end?

SHANE: The kids slip the report in his pocket on the day it is due and then tell him that they stole it because he was bragging so much. So the lesson is that you're not going to have any friends if you're a brag or a show-off.

CAROL: Has a similar bragging situation ever happened to you or to one of your friends?

SHANE: No. I don't have any friends who do that but I know some kids who do. There are some kids who are so smart that they think they'll ace every report, and they usually always do, but you still shouldn't go around saying it. I wouldn't want to be friends with someone who shows off. Once I went fishing with some kids and Billy caught two rainbow trout. The rest of us only caught some small fish. Billy bragged about his fish all day. It was so annoying.

While Plato would argue strenuously against exposing children to stories that contain violent and immoral actions, he would acknowledge the clear moral lesson that Shane not only absorbed from Grisham's work but also "played out" in his own story. Shane's piece, however, is not a mere replay or imitation of John Grisham's. Rather, it is Shane's attempt to connect the story to his own life, to make personal sense of Grisham's message.

In *Books That Made a Difference*, Gordon and Patricia Sabine (1983) solicited testimonials that attest to the teaching power of literature:

- Ruby Bridges, the six-year-old black child, who was caught in the firestorm of 1960's desegregation movement, walked daily through angry crowds of white protesters to attend school—by herself because white parents had pulled their children. The story that sustained her through this year-long ordeal was "Tar-Baby." Bridges writes: "When people struck out at Tar-Baby, they got stuck to him. Because of their striking out, they were the ones who got hurt. . . . Now as I look back on it, maybe the story of Tar-Baby is what gave me the courage to go on, because it was a lonesome year, a very lonesome one, and I didn't understand why it had to be like that. It took some doing to stay there all year long. But I did, and that sort of had a happier ending that I was expecting, too." (p. 46)
- Author Studs Terkel shared the lesson he learned from Twain's *The Adventures of Huckleberry Finn*: "In the words of Martin Luther King, that there is something beyond the written law; there is the law of human decency." (p. 113)

Given the moral acuity of these and other testimonials in *Books That Made a Difference*, it was surprising to find that only a few students mentioned the teaching power of literature. This curious finding may be tied to the moral relativism that has permeated American classrooms since the 1960s (Ryan, 1997). Moral relavitism purports that values are a personal matter—what is right for me may not be right for you—and that one's values are not to be judged by others, including the teacher. This belief causes many teachers to steer clear of the moral import of story and to concentrate instead on the critical dimensions of the literary experience. Hence, it is not surprising that readers approach literature in terms of characters and plot, rather than in terms of what they carry away in their hearts and minds.

This tide of moral relativism is beginning to turn. Coles's publication of *The Moral Life of Children* coincided with the public's concern about disturbing trends in youth violence, teen pregnancy, and drug abuse. By the 1990s, Coles and others (Bennett, 1993; Kilpatrick and Wolfe, 1994) called for the restoration of moral education in the schools and, with it, literature that promotes character development. However, as with all deeply embedded belief systems, change comes slowly. Only two of the nineteen fifth graders acknowledged the teaching power of their favorite authors on their surveys:

I really like the book *Number the Stars* because it shows people that killing is bad.

In *Shiloh* you [Phyllis Reynolds Naylor] show you shouldn't abuse your dog.

This finding, however, should not be interpreted that readers are oblivious to story's moral force. In literature conversations with children across grade levels, I have found time and again that readers, when asked *directly* to talk about what they have learned from an author, do so with insight. A case in point is Lyra, whose questionnaire is presented in Figure 1-1. When asked to talk specifically about what she internalized from Avi's literature, she not only pinpoints these learnings but also connects them to her own life:

CAROL: Do you think there are any messages in Avi's books?
LYRA: Sure. I can think of plenty, like "Trust yourself" and "Do the right thing" and "Face your fears."
CAROL: Give me an example of a book that sends the message "Do the right thing."
LYRA: In the *Fighting Ground*, he [Jonathan] had to figure out the right thing to do. He wasn't sure but he thought, "I'm not going to just do what the Hessians do or what the Corporal does. I have to trust my feelings and do what I think is right."
CAROL: Do you think it's important to do the right thing?
LYRA: Yeah. It's not always easy but it's always right.

8

CAROL: Can you think of a time when you had to do the right thing and it wasn't easy?

LYRA: This happened recently. The principal told us to report on anybody who was standing up on the bus because it's not safe. The next day, one kid was standing up and swearing and throwing stuff, and I got the courage to report him.

CAROL: Why did it take courage?

LYRA: Because I felt that everyone would be calling me "Tattletale, Tattletale."

CAROL: And did anybody accuse you of being a tattletale?

LYRA: The kid I reported started calling me names and his friends too, but I told him I didn't care what he thought because he was doing the wrong things. And my friends said, "Good job, Lyra," so that made me feel good.

CAROL: And what about the message "Face your fears?"

LYRA: Well, in *Poppy*, the message was face your fears. It's good to obey but if you need to do something that is the right thing and if it's safe enough, go right ahead; follow your dreams. Go to the top of that hill! One time, a couple of years ago, a kid said he was going to beat me up. I don't remember why but I was scared. I wanted to fake being sick but I didn't want to get in trouble so I went to school and, lucky for me, the kid left me alone.

CAROL: Do you think the theme "Face your fears" runs through any of Avi's other books?

LYRA: Yeah, a bunch of his books. In the *Fighting Ground*, he has to face his fears about the Hessians at the end and try to save them and definitely Charlotte Doyle has to stand up to that awful Captain.

Thus, while children may not offer "lessons learned" as their primary attraction for certain authors, there is no doubt that these authors make a moral impression. This also proved true for the third graders, none of whom chose to write about the truths they intuited from favorite authors. For example, in a conversation with a group of Matt Christopher fans, Cayton volunteered, "Well, like in *Face Off*, Greg isn't a good skater but he helps his team so I think it's supposed to tell you that it doesn't matter if you're bad or a beginner at hockey. Even if you're not good, you can still play." John shared that "In the *Hockey Machine*, Steve goes with Kenneth to this place in Indiana without telling his parents and he tries to join a team but they won't let him on the league without his parents' permission. So I think the moral there is that you shouldn't go with someone you don't know because it's dangerous because if he [Steve] tries to escape he has to stay in this room like a prison for forty-eight hours."

Thus far, we have explored two dimensions of the allure of particular authors: a) their ability to jar us emotionally, and, in the process, to heighten our compassion and humanity, and b) their ability to teach us, to give us a standard by which to assess our lives. Now we turn to the most prominent dimension noted across young readers—the ability of authors to delight us with their gift for language and for storytelling.

Delighted by Authors

Reverence for Language

Authors lift us not only with their life-affirming sensibilities but also with their reverence for language. Cynthia Rylant's (1985) passion for James Agee and his work traverses multiple spheres:

> Today, I protect the books I love like a mother lioness. I have a copy of a book by James Agee. It's called *Let Us Now Praise Famous Men*. It and his other book, *A Death in the Family*, are most responsible, I think, for my writing. How I write, what I write. . . . I often keep one of those books by my bed. When I need solace and there is none, I reach for Agee. When I can't write and think I won't ever again, I reach for Agee. And though James Agee died a young man in 1955, leaving behind only a few works, he seems as much a part of my life sometimes as my husband or my children. (p. 462)

Rylant's words—"how I write"—bring to mind those of Aristotle (1991): "The next task is to speak of style. For it is not sufficient to have a grasp of what one should say, but one must also say these things in the way they should. . . ." (p. 216). Aristotle, in fourth century B.C., identified three elements of style—word clarity, vividness of metaphoric language, and rhythm—as central to the charm and intellectual acumen of rhetoric.

Word clarity preoccupies all writers:

> Mark Twain: "The difference between the right word and the almost right word is the difference between the lightning bug and lightning." "When you catch an adjective, kill it." (Charlton, 1997, pp. 76–77)

> Ernest Hemingway revised the ending of *Farewell to Arms* thirty-nine times; his greatest problem: "Getting the words right." (Atwell, 1987, p. 56)

> Mem Fox: "Getting the idea may be difficult, but actually writing it down is such torture that my shoulders ache with the tension of trying to choose the right words to put in the right places." (1990, p. 151)

Aristotle, so taken with the arresting images in Homer's epic poems, *The Iliad* and *The Odyssey*, proclaimed: "But the greatest thing by far is to have command of metaphor. This alone cannot be imparted by another; it is the mark of genius, for to make good metaphors implies an eye for resemblances" (p.104). While the bold simile or striking metaphor often constitute the essence of literary imagery, any entrancing sweep of language that appeals to the senses evokes images. C. S. Lewis (1955) writes about the "enormous bliss" he experienced as a young boy in reading the works of Beatrix Potter—a bliss that was tied not only to story but to Potter's ability to evoke the beauty of autumn:

> The second glimpse [of blissful sensation] came through *Squirrel Nutkin*; through it only, though I loved all of the Beatrix Potter books . . . it administered the shock, it was a trouble. It troubled me with what you can only describe as the Idea of Autumn. It sounds fantastic to say that one can be enamored of a season, but that is

something like what happened . . . the experience was one of intense desire. And one went back to the book, not to gratify the desire (that was impossible—how can one possess Autumn?) but to reawake it. And in this experience also there was the same surprise and the same sense of incalculable importance. It was something quite different from ordinary life and even from ordinary pleasure; something, as they would now say, "in another dimension." (pp. 16–17)

Aristotle's third element of style, rhythm, concerns not what is said but how it is said—the flow of language, the cadence of sounds. In discussing his writing, Avi (1982) notes:

And I'm not just thinking of plot and character but of words, rhythm, that slender, silken, but always *spoken* thread that beads your vision. . . . I respond to my work as a listener, seeking that right voice, tone, flow. I read my books aloud so I can hear them. (p. 20)

This dimension of language, which often operates at an unconscious level, delights readers, young and old. For example, in *Night Noises*, Mem uses a medley of *r*'s and *t*'s to effect the rat-a-tat-tat of the stormy night in the line "Wind and *r*ain *r*a*tt*led at the windows, and *t*rees banged against the *r*oof." This sound device of repeating a consonant or two, called consonance, is bolstered by the onomatopoetic words, *rattle* and *bang*. Assonance—the repetition of similar vowel sounds— is realized in the opening line of *Night Noises*, rendering a soft, lilting introduction to the main character: "Lily Laceby lived in an old cottage in the hills."

Interestingly, whereas none of the fifth graders mentioned their delight with an author's use of language, several of the third graders did. For example:

I like your books [Eve Bunting] because I can pitchure most things in my head of what you wrote.

He [Marc Brown] can put good words into good sentences.

Literary Elements

The best stories touch the deepest chords of our humanity. As Katherine Paterson (1990) eloquently explains:

What I think I am doing when I write for the young is to articulate the glorious but fragile human condition for those whose hearts have heard but whose mouths, at the ages of five or ten or fourteen, can't yet express. But the truth is that I can't really express it either. So what happens is a reciprocal gift between writer and reader: one heart in hiding reaching out to another. We are trying to communicate that which lies in our deepest heart, which has no words, which can only be hinted at through the means of a story. And somehow, miraculously, a story that comes from deep in my heart calls from a reader that which is deepest in his or her heart, and together from our secret hidden selves we create a story that neither of us could have told. (pp. 152-153)

Paterson and other storytellers accomplish this "heart calling" by creating characters about whom readers care deeply, characters with complex human emotions.

Thrust into a series of events that trigger internal conflict and ultimately test their moral fiber, these characters enter our consciousness and stretch our humanity. It is, then, through character, plot, and theme that authors bring readers inside:

> . . . the enduring lessons in the human condition—that individuals and institutions are everywhere fallible; that justice is hard to achieve and equally hard to maintain; that temptations to intemperance are not of recent invention; that ignorance and cowardice militate against civility; that love is more demanding and can lead to greater heartache and greater fulfillment than selfishness and indifference; that the price of freedom is eternal vigilance; that evil sometimes prevails over good; and that disappointment can sometimes be tempered with humor. (Delattre, 1988, p. 12–13)

Thirteen of the nineteen fifth graders chose favorite authors because of their artistry with critical elements such as character and plot:

> Also your books [Robert Newton Peck] are cool because they are about a smart kid with no commonsense and a regular kid getting in trouble together.

> I really like your book [Avi] because they keep on the edge of your seat and you have to force yourself to stop reading.

> Mildred Taylor I really like your books. I especially like the characters. I like Little Man especially because he likes to be neat but it doesn't work because he always gets messy.

As Samantha's questionnaire reveals (Figure 1-2), third graders also have a strong affinity for good storytelling. Twenty of the thirty-two readers chose authors who crafted funny or scary plots and who created funny characters. Other examples include:

> Your books [Judy Delton] are very good because somthing bad always happens in them and they end coming out good!

> I like your books [Judy Blume] because you make them funny and nice because in the *Fourth Grade Nothing* Peter though he was going to be in the comersel but insted Fudge went on the comersel.

In sum, these informal data suggest that readers, first and foremost, want a good story. Indeed, writers themselves concede that story is their first mission:

> Avi: "In short, I want my readers to feel, think, sometimes to laugh. But most of all I want them to enjoy a good read." (Collier and Nakamura, 1993, p. 2502)

> Jane Yolen: ". . . the first axiom of writing books, and especially writing books for children [is to] ALWAYS REMEMBER, YOU ARE A STORYTELLER. Not a preacher. Not a prophet. . . . If you are someone who has real morals and moral value in your life, they will come out all unbidden in your writing." (1973, p. 7)

However, as these comments reveal, a good story is more than plot and character:

> For stories that have endured, the stories to which we turn as we seek to shape our own lives, are all beautiful in this three-fold sense. Simple with "nothing lacking, nothing superfluous." Harmonious with elegant symmetry—each element—character, plot, theme, setting—in balance. Brilliant in that the story is told with clarity and sheds light on the breadth of human experience. (Paterson, 1997, p. 11)

Intrigued by Author as Person

One unexpected finding surfaced across a few of the surveys. A handful of readers were drawn to certain authors because their works are or appear to be autobiographical. Two fifth graders and a third grader offered the following responses:

> Dear Robert Newton Peck, . . . I have read the entire Soup series and I think you write very creatively. It seems like maybe when you were a child these things might of happened to you. . . .

> Dear Julie Edwards, I really like your books . . . Did your acting career inspire any of your stories? . . . I know you're real name JULIE ANDREWS.

> I like Eve Bunting because she write from her experences like riots

For these readers, a fascination with the person behind the story takes hold because something acutely gripping in knowing that fiction has its seeds in real life. Indeed, many authors concede that their own lives penetrate their work. Some say their literature springs from childhood experiences:

> Isaac Bashevis Singer: "Writers always go back to their young days, to their young lives. If a writer writes about his life, and he is serious, he will go back there, just like a criminal goes back to the place of his crime." (Murray, p. 87)

> Ross MacDonald: "I don't think people become writers, for the most part, unless they have experienced a peculiar distancing, which generally occurs in childhood or youth and makes the direct satisfactions of living unsatisfactory, so that one has to seek one's basic satisfactions indirectly through what we can loosely call art. What makes the verbal artist is some kind of shock or crippling or injury which puts the world at one removed from him, so he writes to take possession of it. . . . We start out thinking we're writing about other people and end up realizing we're writing about ourselves." (Murray, p. 7)

Others believe story spins out of life's most jarring moments:

> F. Scott Fitzgerald: "Mostly, we authors must repeat ourselves—that's the truth. We have two or three great moving experiences in our lives—experiences so great and moving that it doesn't seem at the time that anyone else has been caught up and pounded and dazzled and astonished and beaten and broken and rescued and illuminated and rewarded and humbled in just that way ever before." (Murray, p. 84)

Elie Wiesel: "Writing is a duty for me as survivor. I entered literature through silence; I seek the role of witness, and I am dutybound to justify each moment of my life as a survivor." (Murray, p. 8)

Lest we assume, though, that all fiction is a window on an author's life, we need to heed the words of Joyce Carol Oates: "My writing is full of lives I might have led. A writer imagines what could have happened, not what really happened."

This intriguing conundrum of whether literature draws its life force from the author's lived experiences or from the author's fertile imagination is one that will be explored in detail in the following chapter.

Readers Without Favorite Authors

While all thirty-two of the third graders identified a favorite author, four of the nineteen fifth graders acknowledged no such favorite. As Biz's questionnaire (Figure 1-3) reveals though, this was not from lack of trying. Two fifth graders noted that they liked all kinds of books; one pointed out that "If you have a favorite author and you read all their books there be will nothing left to read." Kyle wrote that he doesn't have a favorite author "because most authors write stories with the same plot—character leaves home, gets in trouble, returns home, happy ending." When I asked whether he thought that many books, regardless of author, followed this storyline, he replied, "Not *Seven Spiders Spinning*—all of them die except one and he gets captured in a lunch box."

These free-spirited readers are telling us that literature is a deeply personal encounter—one that they prefer not to have restricted. They force the question about whether it is sanguine to require students to pursue one author. It is a question, of course, that transcends author studies. As we design our literature-based reading programs, we wrestle with questions about student versus teacher control. For example, if we accord children total control of their reading lives in the classroom, when will they come together as a community of readers to explore aesthetic renderings and critical insights? Yet, if we impose literature, how will children learn to choose literature? As will be explored more fully in Chapter 5, most teachers believe that a strong literature program needs to provide children with multiple literary experiences—personal, group, and whole class—as well instructional encounters that stretch them intellectually and emotionally. It is this perspective of balance that allows author studies to fill one dimension of a literature program.

Why Conduct Author Studies?

As the previous testimonials reveal, children attach themselves to authors without direction from us. They return, time and again, to these authors for many of the same reasons that we return: emotional sustenance, wisdom, appreciation of the author's craft, and intrigue with author as person and as writer. However, while this authorial experience is emotionally and intellectually gratifying, I

Name **Biz Kohn**

1. Do you have a favorite author?   Yes   (No)

2. If you have a favorite author, write his or her name on the line.

_____

If you have a second favorite author, write his or her name on this line.
Avi and Wilson Rawls

3. I don't have a favorite author because I read alot of different books written by alot of different authors so I can't decide which I like best.

4. What are some of the books you have read that were written by your ~~first~~ second favorite author. (You don't have to remember the full title.)
Poppy, Something Upstairs, The Fighting Ground.

_____

5. If you were going to write a letter to your favorite author to tell him or her why he or she is your favorite author, what would you write? Try to write three different ideas about why you are interested in this author's books.

Dear Avi,
    I love your books because you always write about different thing so I never get bored o your books. You seem really nice and I would love to meet you
            Sincerely,
                Biz Kohn

6. What would you say to convince a friend that your favorite author is a great author and that he or she should read some books by this author?
Avi is so cool. He writes about everything. All of his books are exciting. You really should read one. You'll be at the edge of your seat the whole time. His plots are excellent. One thing happens after another, there are no boring spots.

FIGURE 1-3   *Biz's (Grade 5) responses to the author-study questionnaire*

suspect that most readers don't take the time to examine the full expanse of this experience. For example, my private reading of Dostoevsky's *Crime and Punishment* paled in comparison to a collegial reading of this masterpiece. Communal study of an author is a decidedly different experience—one that brings intuitive thoughts and feelings to a conscious level. While readers may be aware of themes that course through an author's work, deliberate contemplation of these themes may not occur. When lived-through experiences and universal themes are shared with other readers, heightened understandings of life and literature unfold. It is then that readers return to beloved authors or new authors with renewed insight and appreciation.

It is this conviction about the life-enhancing power of author studies that drives this book. Perhaps the best endorsement for implementing an author study is found in words of the children themselves. At the end of the Mem Fox author study (described in Chapter 4), seventeen third graders completed a questionnaire (Figure 1-4). When asked if they enjoyed the author study, all seventeen replied affirmatively. As to their most favorite activity, writing the research reports on Australian animals garnered the most votes. Acting out the Mem Fox books and making a video to send to Mem tied for second place, followed by performing a Readers' Theatre for a kindergarten class. Sixteen of the seventeen third graders noted that there wasn't any part of the author study they didn't enjoy; one child said she didn't like doing the reports. With regard to favorite books, *Koala Lou* ranked first, followed by *Possum Magic* and *Wilfrid Gordon McDonald Partridge*.

In response to the question "Do you think it is a good idea to study the books of one author?" every child circled, "Yes"; their reasons are summarized in Figure 1-5 on page 19. By far, the most popular reason for doing author studies was the autobiographical dimension. As will be revealed in Chapter 4, autobiographical hunches about Mem surfaced on the second day of the author study and continued throughout. The third graders were fascinated to learn about the events in Mem's life that permeated her books. The extent of their sincerity is captured in Kevin's letter (Figure 1-6, page 19), which was written after completion of the questionnaire because, in Kevin's words, "I forgot to say some things in my answers."

The last two comments in Figure 1-5 are also tied to biographical response. The child's comment about learning "how that author writes" springs from the Mem Fox video that the students watched on the final day. It appears that this child absorbed details about Mem's love of words, and her struggle to find the right words. I suspect the final comment by another child about watching authors change over time emerged not from the author study per se, but from the portfolio process in which the third graders were involved at the time. At the end of the school year, the third graders were asked to write how they have changed as writers over time. I suspect this child reasoned that if she had changed as a writer, so too must have Mem Fox.

Four youngsters acknowledged the power of author studies to spark further

Name **Alexis Regan**

MEM FOX AUTHOR STUDY SURVEY

1. Did you enjoy studying the books of Mem Fox?   (YES)   NO

2. What was the best part about studying Mem Fox's books?

Working as a team, and trying our best. Anl Do the plays and vidoes

3. Read each of the activities (listed below) that we did while studying Mem Fox. Write number 1 next to your most favorite activity. Write number 2 next to your second favorite activity. Write number 3 next to your third favorite activity.

_____listening to Mem Fox books   **3**_____making the video to send to Mem Fox

_____acting out Mem Fox books   _____writing about the messages of *Koala Lou*

1_____writing research reports   **2**_____studying about Australian animals

_____performing *Hattie and the Fox* for the kindergartners

_____sharing a memory after reading *Wilfred Gordon McDonald Partridge*

_____watching the Mem Fox video

4. Was there any part of the author study that you didn't like? Tell what you didn't like and why. **NO**

FIGURE 1-4   *Alexis's (Grade 3) responses to the author-study survey*

5. Place a **star** next to your favorite Mem Fox book. Place a **check** next to your second favorite book. Place a **circle** next to your third favorite book.

_☆_Possum Magic   _✓_Koala Lou   ____Sophie

____Time for Bed   _○_Tough Boris   ____Night Noises

____Hattie and the Fox   ____Wilfrid Gordon McDonald Patridge

6. Why is the book with a star next to it your favorite? It inculded a lot of amagiation, and cre-atuvness.

7. Do you think it is a good idea to study books of one author? (YES) ▓
Why? Give 2 reasons if you can. The reasons yes: So you can learn a lot about real person the did the book. So you can compare his/her books wich one you like better

8. If you happen to notice a new Mem Fox book in a library or in a bookstore, will you pick it up and read it? (YES)   NO

Tell why or why not? I like reading and I know shes a great author

9. If you had to give one piece of advice to teachers about doing author studies, what would you tell them? Make sure they use team work

THANKS SO MUCH!

FIGURE 1-4   (*Continued*)

Reasons to Do an Author Study	Frequency of Response
"It's a good idea to study one author becaues you learn more about the author and you learn about what ther like in real life."	14
". . . and it could turn out that you like that auther and want to read his or her books more often."	4
"You should study about the same author and after you fineshed you can compare to see if the message is the same, in the books."	3
"It's a good idea to study about one auther because it could be intreasting and you could learn about animals . . ."	2
"Because they are fun!"	2
"You can learn how that auther writes."	1
"You can watch them [authors] change over time . . ."	1

FIGURE 1-5   *Third graders explain why author studies are worthwhile*

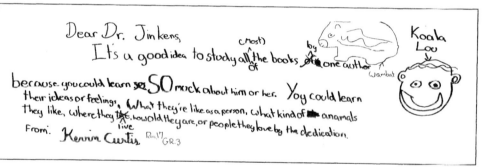

FIGURE 1-6   *Kevin's (Grade 3) thoughts about the Mem Fox author study*

interest in reading. For young readers new to the world of literature, and for reluctant readers, this realization can be immensely satisfying.

The critical dimension of "comparing" Mem's works was also cited by the third graders in Figure 1-5 as a reason for studying one author. During the author study, the children were asked to think about "messages" that Mem might be trying to convey to readers. These themes were discussed in terms of their own lives. In addition, the third graders acted out three of Mem's books and the audience identified each book's message. They also compared two of Mem's books in a Venn Diagram activity. Another critical dimension was tied to the interdisciplinary opportunities afforded by the author study. Two children, taken with the Australian animals in Mem's books, saw author studies as an avenue for extended science study.

While the third graders affirmed the centrality of biographical and critical response to an author's works, aesthetic response is curiously absent. I say *curiously* because as the third graders' written responses presented in Chapter 4 reveal, they were moved deeply by Mem's books, especially by *Koala Lou* and *Wilfrid Gordon McDonald Partridge*. However, glimpses of aesthetic response were noted in four of the third graders responses to the sixth question in Figure 1-4. For example, Kevin wrote that he chose *Koala Lou* as his favorite book because "it reminds me of me and my mother." Brittany wrote, "I like *Koala Lou* because some of it reminds me of myself." I suspect that if I had asked this survey question: "Did you find things in Mem's books that reminded you of things in your life? If so, tell me about them" their responses would have resonated with affect. One poignant piece of evidence to support this speculation is a letter from Kevin's mother—written one year after the author study (Figure 1-7).

In response to the final question in Figure 1-4, the children had plenty of advice for teachers about doing an author study; a sampling of their ideas is presented in Figure 1-8.

The third graders' embrace of this author study called to mind the author encounter that the kindergartners in Vivian Paley's classroom experienced. In *The Girl With the Brown Crayon*, Paley (1997) illuminates the yearlong literary rendezvous of Reeny, an African American five-year-old, and her classmates with Leo Lionni and his works. The rendezvous evokes intense intellectual and emotional response. It begins with Reeny's discovery of Lionni's *Frederick* and her declaration that "That brown mouse [Frederick] seem to be just like me! Because I'm always usually thinking 'bout colors and words the same like him." However, when Lionni leaves readers with conflicting messages about the simultaneous importance of individuality (*Frederick*) and of conformity (*Tico and the Golden Wings*), Reeney suggests that the class write to invite him to class to see if he "wants to change his mind about Tico's friends" (p. 24). But when Lionni responds that he cannot visit because he is not well and too old to travel, Reeny literally sobs, "We had questions . . . it's not fair . . . I'm not listening to him" (p. 37). It is only when Reeny decides that Lionni is "too old, like great-grandam. Old. She can't go out nowhere" (p. 41) that the author study resumes. Reeny, however, continues to bring a critical eye to Lionni's work, refusing to accept Lionni's proposition that when Little Blue and Little Yellow merge and turn green their parents don't recognize them: "That's a lie. A mommy and a daddy hasta remember their own child." Nor does she accept the notion that these "people" circles as she calls them can "change colors. Me and Cory [a white child] hug and we don't change colors" (p. 41). Once again Reeny reconciles with Lionni, explaining Lionni's "mistakes" to the class, "See, here's what it is. He's old. And he doesn't feel too good. He made a mistake, that's what happened. It's only a mistake" (p. 41). In

July 29, 1998
Page 1

Carol Jenkins

Dear Dr. Jenkins:

Enclosed please find the Student Permission Form and the Photographic Release for use of Kevin's name, writing samples, and photographs. Should you need any additional documentation please feel welcome to contact us.

We very much enjoyed receiving the excerpts you provided. It is a rare occasion when we get such a glimpse into Kev's exploits at school. Kevin did, however, keep us well informed about your work with Mrs. Earle's class. He was totally engaged in the author study and spoke with great enthusiasm about the activities you structured around Mem Fox's work. I believe your project was one of the highlights of Kevin's third grade year.

Thank you for introducing Kev (and the rest of the family) to Mem Fox. Kevin was, and is, smitten with her characters. So much so that we still say " I love you, Koala Kev" and "I love you, Koala Mum".

We will watch for publication of your book and when it is available, we would be honored to buy a copy for Kevin's memorabilia collection. Best of luck with your undertaking.

Sincerely yours,

Helen L. Curtis

Helen L. Curtis

Enclosures (2)

FIGURE 1-7   *Kevin's mother's letter*

Third Graders' Advice to Teachers About Doing Author Studies

"Have the kids do fun projects like animal reports and making a movie."

"Send the author something."

"Study one author at a time."

"Make sure they use team work."

"Be sure to pick authers the kids like."

"Do an author thats well-known but not so well known that the kids would know a lot about him or her."

"Help them learn as much as you can each day."

"Have an Athor study because thy're fun!"

FIGURE 1-8   *A sampling of third graders' suggestions for teachers implementing author studies*

between these confrontations with the author, Reeny writes her own Lionni stories, merging all the Lionni characters and, with her peers, acts out these stories, paints Lionni scenes, creates Lionni raps, and designs a collage as a gift for Lionni. As Paley writes, "The characters enter our stories, our play, and our ordinary conversations" (p. 49). In sum, it's all there—aesthetic response, critical response, and biographical response—driven by the heart and mind of this five-year-old. *The Girl With the Brown Crayon* is a glorious testimony to the magnetic pull of an author and his works.

2

Historically Speaking: The Place of Author

At the turn of the century, John Dewey (1909/1933) distinguished between classroom practice that is belief-based and classroom practice that is random and atheoretical:

> In the first place, it [reflective thought] is valuable for it emancipates us from merely impulsive and merely routine activity. . . . Put in positive terms, thinking enables us to direct our activities with foresight and to plan according to end-in-view, or purposes of which we are aware. . . . By putting the consequences of different ways and lines of action before the mind, it enables us to *know what we are about* when we act. *It converts action that is merely appetitive, blind, and impulsive to intelligent actions.* (p. 17, italics original)

Successful implementation of author studies demands that we "know what we are about." As you read each of the following author-study profiles on Cynthia Rylant, reflect on the theoretical assumptions that anchor each profile, and decide which, if any, approximate the way in which you approach an author study.

Three Cynthia Rylant Author Studies

Ms. Farley's Author Study on Cynthia Rylant

Ms. Farley, a fifth-grade teacher, opens her Cynthia Rylant author study by reading the first chapter of Rylant's autobiography, *But I'll Be Back Again*, to her students. When she finishes the chapter, she asks the children to help her fill in the timeline that she has attached to the board. For example, she asks what happened to Cynthia at the age of four. Students reply that Cynthia and her mother left her alcoholic father and moved to Cynthia's grandparents' home in West Virginia. Ms. Farley records this information under the timeline; above the timeline, she writes 1958, explaining that 1958 was the last time that Cynthia would ever see her father. Ms. Farley asks about the other traumatic event that happened to Cynthia in 1958. They reply that Cynthia's mother left her with her grandparents so she could enroll in nursing school. Ms. Farley records this information and solicits reactions to the sorrows that young Cynthia endured. Ms. Farley then writes 1960 on the timeline and asks about Cynthia's life with her grandparents. The fifth graders recall the warmth and love with which her grandparents, aunts, uncles, and cousins surrounded Cynthia. They recall some of Cynthia's memories: getting into trouble in the johnny-house with her cousins, taking baths in a metal tub, and having ticks burned off her skin. Ms. Farley tells the class that tomorrow she will read two of Cynthia Rylant's books, *When I Was Young in the Mountains* and *The Relatives Came*, in which Cynthia relives episodes from these four special years in her life.

Later in the week, Ms. Farley reads the next chapter of *But I'll Be Back Again*, which begins with Cynthia's mother's return and their move to a nearby town called Beaver. After life details are logged on the timeline, Ms. Farley shares many of Cynthia Rylant's autobiographical poems in *Waiting to Waltz*, which recall her life in Beaver. The following week, after another chapter of *But I'll Be Back Again*, Ms. Farley reads the chapter book *A Blue-Eyed Daisy*, which weaves in many events and characters from Cynthia's adolescent life.

And so the author study continues. Ms. Farley unfolds the details of Cynthia's life and then brings them to life by reading or having the children read her works. The thrust of the author study is to search and to reflect on the parallels between Cynthia's life and her literature. By the end of the author study, an elaborate timeline of Cynthia's life has been created by the class.

Mr. Underwood's Author Study on Cynthia Rylant

Mr. Underwood, a fifth-grade teacher, passes out copies of *Missing May* and asks the students to examine the title and the front cover of this Newbery winner, and to respond to the question "What do you think this story might be about?" As the fifth graders offer ideas, he maps them on the board. Responses range from "The grandmother, May, is on a plane and the grandfather and two kids are missing her" to "The three characters go on adventure together because their shadows start out separately and then they merge into one shadow." Mr. Underwood asks students to listen to see if any of their predictions are confirmed (in part or in full) as he reads the first three chapters. The fifth graders confirm partial predictions, and give supporting evidence; they decide that some predictions still may come true. Mr. Underwood then asks for new predictions, which he adds to the map. He assigns chapters 4 and 5 for homework. The children move through the remainder of the book in a similar fashion, making predictions, confirming and/or rejecting them, and making new ones. After the book is finished, students complete a story map of the plot structure (setting, characters, problems, attempts, resolutions).

Mr. Underwood then asks the fifth graders, working in groups, to answer the question "What are the topics about which Cynthia Rylant writes in *Missing May*?" They generate themes such as death, fear of losing someone, and caring for one another. Mr.

Underwood, then, teaches a series of minilessons on theme, helping students understand the importance of theme, the difference between explicit and implicit themes, and the difference between primary and secondary themes. He explains that they will use their new knowledge about theme as they choose another of Cynthia Rylant's books (*A Blue-Eyed Daisy*, *A Kindness*, *A Fine White Dust*, and *The Van Gogh Cafe*) and join a literature circle. As they read, they keep track of the Rylant themes in their literature logs. Mr. Underwood meets periodically with each circle to discuss theme ideas. If students finish their book early, they are encouraged to read some of Cynthia Rylant's picture books, which are on display, and to keep track of themes.

The author study ends with an examination of these themes across books. As a class, the fifth graders use their literature logs to compile all of Rylant's themes. Then, working in teams, the fifth graders create a large grid. Across the top of the grid, they list the class-generated themes. On the side of the grid, they list Rylant's five chapter books. Each team then decides whether each theme listed at the top of the grid applies to the first book on the list. If it does, they discuss whether the theme is explicit or implied, and primary or secondary, and record decisions on the grid. Upon completion, the class compares and then analyzes the results to answer questions such as: Which theme occurs most frequently? Does Rylant primarily incorporate explicit or implicit themes in her books?

With the exception of discussing themes that are important to Rylant, Mr. Underwood gives no attention to Cynthia Rylant, the person behind the book.

Ms. Cassidy's Author Study on Cynthia Rylant

Ms. Cassidy notices that some of her fifth graders have been choosing to read Cynthia Rylant's books during reading workshop. She organizes a display table of Cynthia Rylant's books to increase student interest. Following their lead, she suggests a Cynthia Rylant author study. Ms. Cassidy opens the first day by reading the first three chapters of *A Blue-Eyed Daisy* and asks the fifth graders to join her in writing a personal evocation. Ms. Cassidy then shares her own response.

> As I read about the time that Ellie spent with her dad hunting, I tried to remember a special time that my dad and I spent together—just the two of us—when I was young. But I could only remember only family events—trips to the beach or to the park. With five children, I think it is fair to say that my father did his best to keep us entertained. I have to admit, though, I felt a little pang of jealousy when I read about the hunting trip Ellie took with her dad. It made me wonder if I would be closer to my dad today if we had spent special times together. But then I realized that it is never too late to strengthen our relationship. I just need to take the first step.

Ms. Cassidy asks if anyone else wrote about this hunting episode. Ted shares that Ellie's father reminded him of his Uncle John. He explains that his Uncle John went on a hunting trip with his buddies, but when it came time to kill a deer, he couldn't do it. He said it made no sense to kill an innocent creature. John's buddies gave him a hard time but he didn't care. The fifth graders ask Ted questions; others share their fathers' hunting tales. With time running short, Ms. Cassidy comments on the power of books to help us relive events in our own lives and to reflect on these events. She then asks the fifth graders to share their written responses with a partner. Over the next week, students read and respond aesthetically to the remaining chapters of A Blue-Eyed Daisy.

Ms. Cassidy then previews each of Cynthia Rylant's four remaining chapter books and asks the fifth graders to sign up to read the book of their choice. Members of each group independently read their book during reading workshop. Upon completion, students gather in their book clubs and share favorite scenes. Each group, then, decides which scene it wants to act out for the class. Students who finish the group book early are encouraged to start another Rylant book. For each book read, they complete a response activity from a list of options (e.g., write a letter to a character telling him or her why you agree or disagree with an action that the character has taken).

Ms. Cassidy ends the author study with a film in which Cynthia Rylant talks about her life and about her work. After the film, students are asked to write and share a personal response. Ms. Cassidy then suggests a culminating project: a Cynthia Rylant quilt. The fifth graders receive a quilt patch on which they will illustrate an aspect of Cynthia's life or literature that they believe to be memorable and significant.

Taking Stock: Beliefs About Author Studies

If you approach author studies in a fashion similar to Ms. Farley, you subscribe to the perspective of *author study as literary biography*. You seek to help young readers understand that much of what authors write about is anchored in their own lives. In essence, you work to show them the inextricable link between the author's life and her literature. If, on the other hand, you align yourself with Mr. Underwood's approach to author studies, you adopt the perspective of *author study as critical response*. You believe that the best way to study an author is to study the author's craft. You direct children to examine the themes that undergird his or her books, the symbolism that enriches the works, the credibility of characters, and so forth. The degree to which the author's life spills into his or her works is of little interest because it is the works that stand the test of time, irrespective of the author's intentions. If you frame your author studies as Ms. Cassidy does, you espouse the perspective of *author study as aesthetic response*. You accord the reader the central place in the author study. You care most about the reader's response to the body of work and give only minimal attention to the author.

These three author-study perspectives have a rich historical tradition. From the sixteenth to the nineteenth century, literary biography dominated the field of literary theory. Readers examined the life and times of an author and interpreted the corpus of his or her works through the lens of biographical data. The twentieth century, however, gave rise to new literary movements such as New Criticism and Structuralism, which severed the author from his or her work and which asked readers to focus solely on the text—its structures, imagery, ambiguities, and so forth. Moreover, the reader's thoughts and feelings were considered irrelevant to any interpretation of the text. It wasn't until the embrace of reader response theory in the 1980s that the reader was returned to the literary equation. In the words of Louise Rosenblatt (1938):

> The joys of adventure, the delight in the beauty of the world, the intensities of triumph and defeat, the self-questionings and self-realizations, the pangs of love and hate—indeed as Henry James has said, "all life, all feeling, all observation, all vision"—these are the province of literature. . . . No matter how much else art may offer, no matter how much the writer may be absorbed in solving the technical problems of his craft, in creating new forms of esthetic experience, the human element cannot be banished. (p. 6)

In this perspective, it is the reader in continual transaction with the text that defines the literary experience (Rosenblatt, 1938, 1978; Iser, 1978; Fish, 1980).

This chapter surveys this historical backdrop against the current implementation of author studies in elementary classrooms. It explores how the theoretical assumptions of each of these three perspectives—*author study as literary biography, author study as critical response,* and *author study as reader response*—have influenced, consciously or unconsciously, the current design and implementation of author studies in the classroom.

Historical Roots of the Three Author-Study Perspectives

Author Study as Literary Biography

In the history of modern literary theory, particularly during the nineteenth century Romantic period, literary biography reigned. Literature was viewed as the embodiment of the writer's life and times—his or her relationships with family and friends, the influences and experiences that shaped his or her early life, and the social/historical context in which he or she lived. Thus, to study *David Copperfield* was to study Charles Dickens's despair and humiliation when, at the age of twelve, he was forced to work in a rat-infested blacking warehouse. In Dickens's words, "No words can express the secret agony of my soul as I sunk into this companionship . . . and felt my early hopes of growing up to be a learned and distinguished man crushed in my breast" (Johnson, 1969, p. 44). To study *Little Dorrit* was to study Dickens's outrage at the abysmal conditions of the debtors' prisons where his father was jailed during his early life. To study *Oliver Twist* was to study Dickens's vehement protest of the Poor Law of 1834, which relegated paupers to lifelong servitude if they survived the wretched warehouse conditions (Hibbert, 1969). From the standpoint of the literary biographer, "The work of Dickens' whole career was an attempt to digest these early shocks and hardships, to explain them to himself, to justify himself in relation to them, to give an intelligible and tolerable picture of a world in which such things could occur" (Wilson, 1941, p. 8). Thus, from the perspective of literary biography, to read Dickens without intimate knowledge of his childhood suffering is to not read Dickens at all.

It is this perspective that Ms. Farley, the first teacher described at the beginning of this chapter, espouses. She believes that the best way for children to know and to appreciate Cynthia Rylant's literature is through the pursuit of her life. Of course, the ability of literary biography to shed light on works of art depends on the authenticity and availability of the biographical, autobiographical, and historical evidence. In the case of Rylant, her autobiographical pieces and biographical publications permit readers to juxtapose her life and literature with a good degree of certainty. Like Dickens, Rylant (1989) acknowledges the pull of her life in her books:

> They say that to be a writer you must first have an unhappy childhood. I don't know if unhappiness is necessary, but I think maybe some children who have suffered a loss too great for words grow up into writers who are always trying to find those words, trying to find a meaning for the way they have lived. Painters do that. And composers. Everything they have lived is squeezed onto canvas or is penned between the bars of a page of music. It is as if we, as children, just *felt* the life, then after we grew up we wanted to *see* it. So we create stories and paintings and music, not so much for the world as for ourselves. (p. 5)

Rylant (1989) is forthright, for example, in telling us that her abandonment at the age of four by her alcoholic father left an indelible ache that fueled much of her writing. "I did not have a chance to know him or to say good-bye to him, and that is all the loss I needed to become a writer" (p. 7). This child who also was abandoned by her mother for four years, who was raised by her gentle, loving grandparents, who was convinced by the Baptist preachers that every bone in her body was "soaked in sin," was reborn in books such as *When I Was Young in the Mountains, A Fine White Dust,* and *Missing May.*

Coming to know an author also means coming to know his or her writing habits. Dickens wept uncontrollably when he killed Little Nell in *The Old Curiosity Shop* (Kaplan, 1988). He suffered a recurrence of painful childhood spasms while writing *David Copperfield,* reliving the nightmare of his warehouse experiences (Hibbert, 1967). Writing was so physically and emotionally demanding that Dickens often walked the London streets at night to distance himself from his beloved characters. Writing was a slow, laborious process of revision upon revision with meticulous attention to detail. He had little respect for writers "who suppose that volumes are to be tossed off like pancakes, and that any writing can be done without the utmost application, the greatest patience, and the steadiest energy of which the writer is capable" (Wagenknecht, 1957, p. 28). Dickens was a highly disciplined writer who needed absolute silence, and who adhered to a set daily writing schedule, regardless of productivity. "Sometimes I have to coax it; sometimes I do little else than draw figures or make dots on paper, and plan and dream till perhaps my time is nearly up. But I always sit there, for that certain length of time" (Wagenknecht, 1957, p. 28). Somehow, knowing that Dickens struggled to get his thoughts on paper, as most of us struggle, increases his humanness and strengthens our bond to him. We take comfort in fact that writing challenges even the best literary minds.

But not all. For Cynthia Rylant (1990), writing "comes quick and clean and nearly perfect the first time I sit down with a pen in hand" (p. 19). Rylant wrote *When I Was Young in the Mountains*, cover to cover, in one hour with no revision. Two months later it was published. Rylant believes that "writers are born with the word in their blood and the plain truth is not everybody can be a writer" (p. 18). Not surprisingly, her view on writing emerges from her own experiences. With no library in town, she grew up on comic books. With the exception of a story she wrote about the Beatles, she never wrote. It wasn't until college that she entered a library for the first time, where she entered the world of children's books and she knew she wanted to write for children. Her store of life experiences fed her writing soul and the books just "came"—no struggle, no rewrites, no self-doubt.

Literary biography has enormous appeal. To know that Dickens and Rylant lived the lives of their characters, endured tragedies that no child should have to endure, numbs us. To know that these authors clung tenaciously to life in the midst of many travails restores us. The search, then, for the author's life in his or her literature not only illuminates the works, but also heightens our intrigue with the author. Because we have come to know the author, to know what matters to him or her and why it matters, we are drawn, like magnets, to his or her life and literature.

Literary biography, however, is not without its limitations. Critics charge that great literature is not a mere copy of life. Rather, great literature transcends life. Such literature stands on its own merit, irrespective of an author's intentions. Reading works of art for the sole purpose of finding the author reincarnate reduces literature to mere autobiographical renderings and violates its significance. Furthermore, critics argue, while a real event in an author's life may trigger a story, the event is often transformed to fit the fictional account. For example, *A Fine White Dust* has its origins in Cynthia Rylant's (1989) teenage encounter with a Baptist preacher who convinced her (and others) "to walk down the aisle in church and confess to the preacher and to everyone watching that I was an outright unsaved sinner" (p. 30). In *A Fine White Dust*, Pete, mesmerized by a charismatic preacher, not only walks the aisle to salvation but also vows to run away with this preacher to help him save other damned lives. Hence, Rylant takes a life episode and magnifies it to the point that it spirals out of her life and into her literature. As autobiographical as much of her work is, Rylant (1989) acknowledges this transformational dimension: "Writing stories has given me the power to change things I could not change as a child. I can make boys into doctors. I can make fathers stop drinking. I can make mothers stay" (p. 10). Put another way, "A work of art may rather embody the 'dream' of an author than his actual life, or it may be the 'mask,' 'the antiself' behind which his real person is hiding, or it may be a picture of the life from which the author wants to escape" (Wellek and Warren, 1949, p. 70). Indeed, in his most autobiographical work, *David Copperfield*, Dickens portrays David's mother as warm and loving, the mother Dickens wanted but never had. The untimely death of David Copperfield's mother leaves him an orphan, an event that perhaps fictionalizes the deep-seated feelings of abandonment that Dickens experienced in his early life. Dickens and Rylant, then, shuttled back and forth between fact and fiction and demonstrated that "the relation between the private life and the work is not a simple relation of cause and effect" (Wellek and Warren, 1949, p. 70).

Author study as literary biography, then, is the pursuit of the interplay of a writer's life and his or her works. It places the author at the center of the literary experience and turns readers into detectives who comb through details of the author's life in order to find their literary counterparts. Author study as literary biography seeks not to judge the quality of a literary work but rather to shed light on its roots, to pierce the soul of the writer whose art embraces us.

Author Study as Critical Response

The New Critics

D. H. Lawrence's quip, "Trust the tale, not the teller," foreshadowed the fall of literary biography and the rise of a literary movement called New Criticism, which dominated literary theory from the 1930s to the late 1950s (Beach, 1993). New Critics such as John Crowe Ransom and T. S. Eliot took exception to maudlin sentimentality of the nineteenth century Romantic critics who wallowed in issues of authorship and morality. They viewed literature as a self-contained, autonomous objet d'art. Like a Grecian urn, literature was to be scrutinized for its intricate form and appreciated for its inherent richness and complexity. The New Critics rejected the idea of literature as camouflaged autobiography. To read T. S. Eliot's *The Waste Land* with the intent of discovering T. S. Eliot, the person, was considered scurrilous. The New Critics purged not only the author from the literary experience but also the reader. It mattered not what the reader's emotional response was to *The Waste Land*. What mattered was the reader's ability to engage in a "close reading" of the text—a critical, objective dissection of the work. Readers were taught to search for internal incongruities in the text, to resolve them with metaphorical devices such as ambiguity, paradox, and irony, and ultimately to restore harmony and balance to the piece. To illustrate the intricacy of a "close reading," a synopsis of Wilfred Guerin and associates' (1992) critical analysis of the following poem is offered:

> A slumber did my spirit seal;
> I had no human fears;
> She seemed a thing that could not feel
> The touch of earthly years.
>
> No motion has she now, no force;
> She neither hears nor sees;
> Rolled round in earth's diurnal course,
> With rocks, and stones, and trees.

In the opening stanza, the narrator (a parent? a lover?) recalls an image of a female (a child? a lover?) untouched by earthly concerns. Then suddenly, in the second stanza, she dies.

> But there is a huge gap, and at once a leap beyond that gap, between the first and second stanza. . . . Somehow the child or woman has died. She already has been buried. The "slumber" of line one has become the eternal sleep of death. The "seal" of the "spirit" has become the coffin seal of the body. Even more poignantly, the life of the dynamic person in lines three and four, where sense perceptions of touching and feeling seem to be transmuted into ethereal or angelic dimensions, is now the unfeeling death of one who has no energy, no vitality, no sense of hearing or seeing. She is no more or no less than a rock or a stone or a tree fixed to the earth. The final irony, that paradox, is that the once motion-filled person is still in motion—but not the vital motion of a human person; she now moves daily a huge distance, a full turn of the earth itself, rotating with a motion not her own, but only that of rocks and stones—gravestones—and rooted trees. . . . In the third line the word "thing" at first seems to be a noncommittal, simply denotative word: perhaps the poet was not even able to think of a better word, and used a filler. But in retrospect the female figure now is indeed a "thing" like a rock or a stone, a mere thing—in truth, dust . . . . (Guerin, Labor, Morgan, Reesman, and Willingham, 1992, pp. 63–64)

For New Critics, the study of this poem ("A Slumber Did My Spirit Seal") was the study of paradox and irony. The poem's meaning was inscribed in the poem itself, not in the heart of its poet (Wordsworth), nor in his life experiences. The reader's mission was to read closely, critically, and dispassionately.

By the late 1950s, however, literary critics such as Northrop Frye decried the restrictive tightness of the New Critics and called for a broader-based system of criticism that focused on the structural dimensions of literature. With the publication of *Anatomy of Criticism*, Frye (1957) proposed an approach to literary analysis, often called myth or archetypal criticism, which entailed the structural dissection of text through classification, description, and subdivision. Building upon Aristotle's *Poetics*, Frye assigned any given work (from the classics to detective stories) to one of five fictional modes: myth, romance, high mimetic, low mimetic, and irony. Modes are defined in terms of "the hero's power of action" (Frye, 1957, p. 33). For example, a story containing a divine hero such as Apollo who is superior to human beings and nature is classified as myth; a story containing a hero such as Odysseus who is superior to humans but not to the laws of nature is classified as high mimetic; a story containing a hero who is neither superior to humans nor to nature—an ordinary human being like Robinson Cruso—is classified as low mimetic. Each mode is subject to further subdivision; for example, myth can be tragic or comic, sophisticated or naive. In addition to mode classification, each story is assigned to one of four archetypal narratives (comedy, romance, tragedy, and irony) and assessed for patterns of symbolism. These literary modes, Frye pointed out, parallel the development of literature across the centuries with myths predominating in the pre-medieval period, chivalrous romantic tales marking the medieval period, and so forth.

Frye traced all stories back to the Bible and believed that because literary works beget literary works, there is no place for value judgments, for literary criticism, per se. What is needed, according to Frye, is a unified structure of knowledge that describes "what literature as a whole is all about, an imaginative survey of the human situation from the beginning to the end, from the height and depth, of what is imaginatively conceivable" (1957, p. 102). While Frye's intricate scheme of literary analysis penetrated many college classrooms in the 1960s, it was attacked on a number of fronts for its reduction of literature to the smallest common denominator, its rejection of the author as transmitter of wisdom, and its total indifference to literary quality (Daiches, 1981; Wellek, 1982).

Frye was not the first to attempt a structural analysis of story. In the 1920s, Vladimir Propp noticed the structural similarities of Russian folktales. Using the elementary linguistics principle of sentence syntax (sentence = subject + predicate), Propp proposed a basic story syntax: narrative = characters + typical actions. Propp identified seven character roles (hero, villain, helper, . . .) and thirty-one narrative functions (actions), the last seven of which are:

25. A difficult task is proposed to the hero.
26. The task is resolved.
27. The hero is recognized.
28. The false hero or villain is exposed.
29. The false hero is given a new appearance.
30. The villain is punished.
31. The hero is married and ascends to the throne. (Propp, 1968)

Propp demonstrated that the thirty-one functions occur in folktales in a sequential order, although no story contains all functions. While Propp's analysis was restricted to folktales, applicability to other story genres is evident. Propp's theory about narrative as a structure of discreet units that have significance only when they are placed in tandem is further refined by Levi-Strauss, a structural anthropologist. Levi-Strauss (1968), building on Propp's theory about the interdependence of structural units, proposed that the rules that govern narrative syntax are deeply embedded in the human mind. The study of myths was not the study of the myths' content per se, but rather the study of the universal mental operations of the human mind (Guerin et al., 1992).

The Structuralists

The work of Propp and Levi-Strauss ushered in the literary movement of the 1960s known as Structuralism, and with it the continued primacy of the text, and the excoriation of the author and of the reader. Neither the author nor the reader was viewed as the source of meaning. In addition to establishing the "grammar" or underlying rules of literature, Structuralists, such as Saussure, investigated the linguistic rules that govern language. According to Saussure, language is a system of signs made up of signifiers (words) and signifieds (meanings). Each sign is defined by its difference from other signs; the word *date* carries meaning only because it is not *late*, *rate*, or *land*. Because *date* has multiple meanings (a calendar time, a romantic other, a fruit), there is no one-to-one correspondence between signifers and signifeds, although Saussure admits that certain signifers are attracted to certain signifieds, affirming a certain linguistic stability. As we will see in a later section, Saussure's work was turned on its head by the poststructuralists (also known as deconstructionists).

In many ways, the literary movements of New Criticism and Structuralism were a response to the twentieth-century preoccupation with science as the font of truth. Proponents of these movements sought to transform literature into a science—a self-enclosed, autonomous, objective system amenable to scientific inquiry. The theories of the New Critics and Structuralists flourished consecutively in college classrooms from the 1930s through the 1970s, and vestiges of their practices filtered down to elementary classrooms.

The Influence of Structuralism in the Elementary Classroom

The early work of Propp on story narratives was revisited in the 1970s by educational researchers who sought to redefine the basic structure of story (Mandler and Johnson, 1977; Rumelhart, 1975; Stein and Glenn, 1979). Their efforts resulted in the creation of story grammars—sets of rules that describe a story's structure. These grammars proposed that well-developed stories contain key story grammar elements such as:

- Characters who live in a particular place and at a particular time;
- A problem or tension point encountered by the main character, along with the character's response to the problem;
- The character's plan of action and attempt(s) to solve the problem;
- Outcomes of attempts—successes or failures; and
- A resolution to the problem and a reaction from the character. (Stein and Glenn, 1979)

As researchers discovered, these story grammars exist not only in the text but also in the mind of the listener/reader. Children as young as four years old who have been immersed in stories intuitively understand that stories are created according to a specific set of rules (story grammar elements). They use this schema knowledge to understand stories and to generate stories of their own—both oral and written—with increasing levels of competence, complexity, and sophistication over time (Golden, 1984; McKeough, 1984).

It is these story grammar understandings that Mr. Underwood, the second teacher described at the beginning of this chapter, puts into practice in his study of Cynthia Rylant. When he stops periodically to ask students to predict an upcoming event in *Missing May*, he does so with the knowledge that fifth graders possess a sophisticated mental schema for story and are adept at predicting a character's attempt or the resolution of a particular episode (Whaley, 1981). When he asks his fifth graders to complete a story map of *Missing May*, he is confident that they will be able to diagram the major episodes.

In addition to story structure, Mr. Underwood attends to the themes that illuminate Cynthia Rylant's books. Such attention would be applauded by Rebecca Lukens, who published *A Critical Handbook of Children's Literature* in 1976. An advocate of a structural approach to literature, Lukens writes,

> We may have felt amused and touched when we read *Charlotte's Web* by E. B. White, but how do we discuss or decide its literary worth beyond these vague feelings? Why train children to make critical judgments? Because, although the techniques of judgment may in themselves be ordinary, such increased consciousness of them is in itself valuable training. . . . This knowledge helps us to discover the reasons for our emotional responses. It sharpens our perceptions and increases our enjoyment of reading. (p. xii)

Mr. Underwood's pursuit of Rylant's themes stems from his belief that critical interpretation and analysis of text is essential if young readers are to understand the layers of meaning inherent in stories and to appreciate the art and craft of writing. For it is through critical analysis of themes and subthemes in Rylant's books that children contemplate the gift of friendship, the ache of betrayal, and the place of spirituality. Of course, exploration of theme is just one of the literary elements that graces Rylant's works. For example, when children discover that Cynthia Rylant essentially situates all of her characters in small Appalachian towns, they realize that such settings are integral to the portrayal and development of her characters. In addition, children come to understand the power of point of view when they analyze the impact of Cynthia Rylant's decision to allow Peter and Summer to narrate their tales. The first-person narration in *A Fine White Dust* allows readers direct access to Peter's innermost thoughts: his obsession with the preacher, his decision to run away with the preacher, and his devastation when the preacher jilts him. However, we do not know what the preacher thinks or feels or why he abandons Peter. First-person narration is seductive. We experience life events with the same intensity that the character does, causing us to care deeply about what happens to him or her. Cut off from the thoughts and feelings of other central characters, however, we sometimes are left with more questions than answers.

To conclude, author study as critical response centers on the vitality of the text—its structural attributes, its literary qualities, and its layers of meaning. The task of the reader, under the direction of a knowledgeable teacher, is to search the text through repeated readings for its internal coherence and unity. No attention is given to the author's life and times. In this author-study perspective, we come to know the author only through the themes he or she chooses to explore, regardless of original intentions.

Author Study as Reader Response

In 1938, when the New Critics were touting literature as an objet d'art to be scrutinized with dispassionate intensity, Louise Rosenblatt countered:

. . . any sensitivity to literature, any warm and enjoyable participation in the literary work, will necessarily involve the sensuous and emotional responsiveness, the human sympathies, of the reader. We shall not further the growth of literary discrimination by a training that concentrates on the so-called purely literary aspects. We go through empty motions if our primary concern is to enable the student to recognize various literary forms . . . to detect recurrent symbols, or to discriminate the kinds of irony or satire. Acquaintance with the formal aspects of literature will not in itself insure esthetic sensitivity. One can demonstrate familiarity with a wide range of literary works, be a judge of craftsmanship, and still remain, from the point of view of a rounded understanding of art, esthetically immature. . . . Knowledge of literary form is empty without an accompanying humanity. (1938, p. 52)

With the publication of *Literature as Exploration*, Rosenblatt boldly proposed that without the reader, there is no text:

A novel or poem or play remains merely inkspots on paper until a reader transforms them into a set of meaningful symbols. The literary work exists in the live circuit set up between the readers and text: the reader infuses intellectual and emotional meanings into the patterns of verbal symbols and those symbols channel thoughts and feelings. Out of this complex process emerges a more or less organized imaginative experience. (1938, p. 25)

However, it would take forty years for Rosenblatt's theory of transactional reading, also called reader response theory, and the theories of other reader response advocates such as Wolfang Iser (1978), Stanley Fish (1980), and David Bleich (1975) to be acknowledged by literary critics and embraced by educators.

Reader Response Theory

Reader response theory posits that text becomes a text only when a reader, at a specific moment in time, brings the aggregate of his or her life and literary experiences, attitudes, and values to the work. As the reader moves through the text, certain memories from this aggregate are activated. In 1890, William James called this phenomenon "selective attention," noting that in each of us there is "*some kind of consciousness always going on*. There is a stream, a succession of states, or waves or fields . . . of knowledge, of feeling, of desire, of deliberation etc. that constantly pass and repass, and that constitute our inner life" (pp. 245–246). This stream of consciousness pulls certain waves to the forefront and relegates others to the sideline. What is chosen depends on the reader's purpose. If the reader is reading for pleasure, he or she is likely to adopt what Rosenblatt calls the aesthetic stance. The aesthetic stance results in the evocation of private meaning, replete with personal thoughts and feelings. If the reader is reading the text to prepare for an exam, he or she will probably adopt the efferent stance, the stance resulting in retention of public meaning, replete with facts to be remembered, direction to be followed, and so forth.

To illustrate this continuum of efferent and aesthetic stance, I offer my personal response to the children's book *Sadako and the Thousand Paper Cranes* by Eleanor Coerr (1987) in Figure 2-1. This true story takes place in Japan ten years after the

As I read about Sadako's diagnosis of leukemia, I am pulled back in time to my sister's struggle with primary pulmonary hypertension, a respiratory disease that kills young women in their twenties within six months to a year. The only cure—a heart/lung transplant—is a highly experimental procedure in the early 1980s. Not wanting to explain to my husband who is sitting in the den with me why I am about to succumb to this children's book, not wanting to relive this moment with anyone, I escape to the bathroom. As I read the passage " 'Now I have only nine hundred and ninety to make,' Sadako said. With the golden crane nearby she felt safe and lucky. Why, in a few weeks she would be able to finish the thousand. Then she would be strong enough to go home," I cry uncontrollably. I remember so vividly the last two months of Maureen's life. Our daily visits to the hospital hardly brought a smile. She answered questions but did not initiate conversation. She wasn't angry or upset or sad. She wasn't anything. On numerous occasions, I begged the doctors to check the interaction of the drugs she was taking. Time and again, they assured me that she wasn't on any drugs that would cause her "zombie" state. I didn't believe them.

It wasn't until I read this passage in *Sadako*, five years after Maureen's death, that I realized that Maureen, during those final months, knew she was dying and had given up all hope. She folded no paper cranes, went through no dying rituals, made no requests, shared no fear or anger. She had resigned herself to dying and she had no intention of causing us any premature anguish or pain. She simply shut down. How her decision escaped us, I do not know. We knew she was very sick, but we didn't know—or perhaps couldn't accept—that the end was at hand.

Through a torrent of tears, I finish *Sadako* and grieve that I never had a chance to say good-bye, to tell her that she filled our lives with her goodness and her joie de vivre, to tell her that she would live on in me.

FIGURE 2-1   *My personal response to* Sadako and the Thousand Paper Cranes

bomb is dropped on Hiroshima. As the story opens, Sadako, an eleven-year-old girl, and her family attend the Peace Day ceremony to commemorate those who died in the war. Shortly thereafter, school begins and Sadako is chosen by her class to be on the relay team. The day of the race Sadako helps her team win, although the race leaves her dizzy. The dizzy spells continue until she collapses one day at school, is taken to the hospital, and is diagnosed with leukemia. Her best friend, Chizuko, brings Sadako a golden crane and reminds her of the ancient saying, "If a sick person folds a thousand paper cranes, the gods will grant her wish and make her healthy again" (pp. 35–36). Chizuko shows Sadako how to fold the cranes. Sadako folds 644 cranes before she dies.

My original intent in reading *Sadako and the Thousand Paper Cranes* was to determine whether it would fit into a unit on war I was preparing, and to compare and contrast it to other children's books of this time period. As I read the first few chapters, I took notes on life in Japan after war. However, I could not sustain this efferent stance. The centripetal force of *Sadako and the Thousand Paper Cranes* propelled me on a cathartic journey, on what Rosenblatt calls the "lived-through" experience. To read aesthetically is to relive life through the pages of a book. What I relive will not match what another reader relives; what I learn as a result of this encounter may not be what others learn. Aesthetic response is idiosyncratic and deeply personal. Rosenblatt (1991a) argues that teachers need to embrace the primacy of aesthetic stance when they ask readers to enter a book.

Adoption of the aesthetic stance does not preclude efferent understandings. In fact, Rosenblatt makes the point that much of our reading straddles the aesthetic/efferent midpoint of the continuum (Figure 2-2). Most literature affects us emotionally and intellectually, enabling us to evoke personal responses during the reading and to carry away efferent information after the reading. Critical analysis of the text has a place in reader response theory, but only after the affective encounter. In reference to a third-grade workbook that asked children "What facts does this poem teach you?" Rosenblatt points out, "Once the aesthetic reading of the text had been honored, it might be entirely appropriate to discuss the new information received

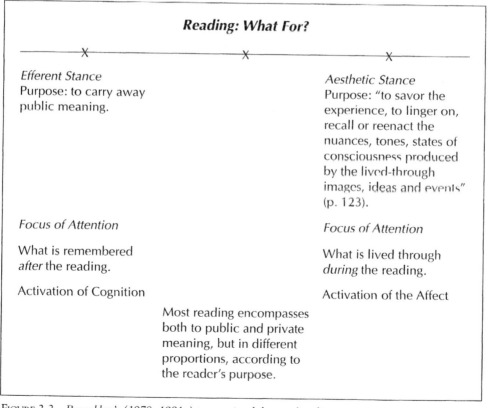

Reading: What For?

X ———————————— X ———————————— X

Efferent Stance
Purpose: to carry away public meaning.

Aesthetic Stance
Purpose: "to savor the experience, to linger on, recall or reenact the nuances, tones, states of consciousness produced by the lived-through images, ideas and events" (p. 123).

Focus of Attention

What is remembered *after* the reading.

Focus of Attention

What is lived through *during* the reading.

Activation of Cognition

Activation of the Affect

Most reading encompasses both to public and private meaning, but in different proportions, according to the reader's purpose.

FIGURE 2-2   *Rosenblatt's (1978, 1991a) transactional theory of reading*

through the experience. But that is not why or how the poems should have been read in the first place" (1991a, p. 122).

Criticisms of Reader Response Theory

As we have witnessed thus far, all theories are subject to critical review, and reader response theory is no exception. One criticism is that, in the end, a piece of literature can be shattered into thousands of interpretational bits—as many bits as there are readers. Critics ask, "Is any and every opinion acceptable?" The reply of the reader response theorists varies. Rosenblatt (1978) emphasizes the mutually inclusive nature of the reader-text relationship. She invokes the metaphor of text as musical score: While no two musicians play a Mozart concerto in an identical fashion, each remains true to the parameters of the score. So, too, are readers obliged to operate within the parameters of the text with the recognition that these parameters are expansive. Stanley Fish (1980), on the other hand, asserts that individual responses that remain within the textual boundaries are not enough. A communal effort is necessary in which readers communicate subjective responses and work to arrive at shared meaning. This does not mean that readers are in pursuit of *the* meaning of the text, for meaning is the domain of the community of readers.

Additional criticism concerns the absence of the author in reader response theory. To tackle this central issue, Rosenblatt explores the position of E. D. Hirsch, a hermeneutic theorist. Hermeneutics is the art of literary interpretation. Hirsch (1967) argues that, indeed, there may be more than one interpretation of any text—especially across centuries—but that any valid interpretation must operate within the sphere of the author's intentions. When an author writes a text, he or she intends the work to mean something. Although readers may not be able to access the author's *true* intent, the "aim of the discipline must be to reach a consensus, on the basis of what is known, that correct understanding of the author's meaning has probably been reached." Hirsch asserts that, although different people in different eras will assign differing levels of *significance* to a work of art, the work's *meaning* remains fixed.

Rosenblatt rejects outright any notion of authorial intention at the center of the reading transaction because the search for "the author's meaning" invalidates the reader. This does not mean, however, that readers are oblivious to the author when they read. At some point during the evocation process, Rosenblatt points out, most readers wonder about the author and his or her intentions, motives, and wishes. Pursuit of literary history or biography is natural response to these wonderings—an undertaking that Rosenblatt (1978) fully sanctions. Such pursuit expands the reader's engagement with the text. Such pursuit, however, is not to arrive at the author's meaning because it is erroneous to assume "that the author's reconstructed intention must be the only—and universally accepted—criterion of the sole 'meaning' of the text when it is read aesthetically" (p. 113). The life of a book is in the hands of the reader, not the author. There can be no substitute for the lived-through encounter. As Flannery O'Connor observed, "When this story is finished, and published, the fun is just beginning! I've often wondered what happens to some of my stories. They have a life, and those who read them are touched by that life—and you never know the new life that will result" (Coles, 1986, p. 59).

Convinced that reading, first and foremost, is aesthetic engagement and that a teacher's first responsibility is to help children "to savor the experience, to linger on, re-call or reenact nuances, tones, and states of consciousness produced by the lived-through images, ideas and events" (Rosenblatt, 1991a, p. 123), Ms. Cassidy engages her fifth graders in high levels of personal response to Cynthia Rylant's books. These re-sponses take the form of literature logs or dialogue journals as well as response projects (drama, art, music, bookmaking, advertisements . . .). If the fifth graders offer observa-tions about particular themes or symbols that they notice in the Cynthia Rylant books, Ms. Cassidy may pursue this line of critical study after—but only after—full attention has been given the affective dimension. If the children happen to read autobiographical material on Cynthia Rylant and to make connections between the author's life and her literature, these revelations are explored in terms of any personal significance they have for the children. Likewise, the film about Cynthia Rylant, which ends the author study, is shown more to amplify what the children have thought and felt about her works than to sketch the parallels between her life and her literature. Essentially, Ms. Cassidy, like many literacy teachers (Lionetti, 1992; Roberts and Nicoll, 1988; Tompkins and McGee, 1993) centers her author study on the evocation of personal meaning.

To conclude, author study as reader response insists on the primacy of the reader in transaction with the text. It is the reader who creates meaning, not the author or the text. Our mission as teachers is to bring children inside the works of a particular author for a highly personal rendezvous with characters and story events that will move hearts and will induce self-reflection. Essentially, it is our responsibility to help children understand that when "Books fall open, you fall in . . ." (McCord, 1986).

Radical Theories About Literature

Thus far, we have examined the three prominent literary theories that undergird cur-rent conceptions teachers hold about author studies (see Figure 2-3 on page 42). However, this is not to suggest that these are the only theories of literary criticism. Indeed, the last three decades have witnessed the eruption (or revival, in the case of Marxism) of three radical theories about literature. Because these political perspec-tives—deconstructionism, feminism, and Marxism—have not taken hold in main-stream elementary classrooms, and, by extension, have not influenced our thinking about author studies, only a brief overview of each approach is given.

Deconstructionism

In reaction to the work of the Structuralists who sought to establish language as a rule-governed system, the poststructuralists, also known as deconstructionists, argued that language was anything but systematic and that, in fact, language was "unruly, slippery, and therefore always suspect" (Beach, 1993, p. 41). While the Structuralists established a stable relationship between a signifier (a word) and its signifed (a word's meaning), the poststructionalists demolished this relationship. They demonstrated that because a signifier such as the word *head* can carry multiple meanings (body part, leader, vegetable mass, toilet, drug user . . .), and because these meanings change over time, it is impossible to assign stable meaning. If the dictionary offers twenty-one meanings for the word *head* and if each of these meanings, in turn, trigger different signifiers (for example, *leader* can signify the primary shoot of a plant, one who leads, an ellipse, an attachment to a fishing lure . . .), language becomes an endless chain of indeterminate meanings. And, without stable meaning, the deconstructionists posited there can be no truth or knowledge (Eagleton, 1983). Because language, including the language of texts, is so disorderly, contradictory, and incapable of carrying universal meaning, the texts, in the end, deconstruct. The deconstructionists charged that institutions—schools, religions, governments—use the language of distortion and falsehood to bring individuals in line with their prevailing ideologies. The goal of deconstructionism, then, is to undermine institutional authority (Beach, 1993) and to herald the demise of Western thought (Eagleton, 1983). Not surprisingly, literary critics of all persuasions have criticized deconstruction as "the new anarchy that allows a complete liberty of interpretation, and even of a self-confessed 'nihilism'" (Wellek, 1982). Its "antihumanism . . . cut off the literary work from the world, banished the author, devaluated the personal, ethical and emotional responses of the reader and ruled out traditional historical and biographical approaches" (Rosenblatt, 1991b, p. 59).

The deconstructionists' convictions about the oppressiveness and injustice of institutional authority course through two other prominent theories of literary criticism: feminist criticism and Marxism.

Feminist Criticism

This approach to literature is predicated on the belief that our male-dominated culture stereotypes and, in the process, marginalizes women, and that these stereotypes are both reflected and perpetuated in literary canon (which has systematically excluded the works of women). Feminist critics, enraged by this engendered power imbalance, work to eradicate these patriarchal prejudices, to redefine gender roles in both society and literature, and to promote the literature of women. This criticism found its way, in general, into elementary classrooms at the onset of the feminist movement. Concerned about the socialization of young children, feminists examined children's readers (e.g., the classic *Dick and Jane* basals and their successors). They discovered that females were portrayed as passive, dependent, emotional, and homebound, whereas males were portrayed as active, goal-oriented, unemotional, and world-oriented. In addition, they found that boys predominated as main characters and that only one biography in six was about a woman (Women on Words and Images, 1972). The response of publishers of basal programs and children's authors to this research was immediate. Within a decade, strong, independent, courageous female characters emerged as well as caring, nurturing males (Powell, Gillespie, Swearingen, and Clements, 1998). Although teachers incorporated this progressive literature into the curriculum, feminists argued that it was not enough. They posited that a true feminist curriculum must rock the political status quo. If children are to internalize values of this literature, they must participate in repeated and sustained conversations about gender roles—conversations that extend beyond the literature and into an analysis of the stereotypes that continue to permeate our culture and its contemporary music, film, and television (Wason-Ellam, 1997; Powell et al., 1998). Most important, children must come to understand that political activity is essential if the shackles of male dominance are to be broken. It is this level of feminist theory that has not been realized in most elementary classrooms. Resistance to this approach had been voiced by those taking exception to the maxim that all art is political as well as to the notion that all literature must be viewed through this reductionist lens (Silber, 1998; Vendler, 1990).

Marxist Criticism

To view literature from a Marxist perspective is to place literature in the context of history, economics, and politics of class struggle. Marxist critics comb literature for what they believe to be the insidious effects of capitalism in order to argue for a revolution to bring down capitalism. Literary criticism for Marxists is about "healing the terrible breach between the study of literature and the life that surrounds that study, between this hall, where we think about politics, and those streets which our thinking about politics and literature has so far helped to keep things as they are" (Levine, 1974, p. 435). Undoubtedly, the most prominent educator to advocate a "pedagogy of liberation" is Paulo Freire (1970, 1985). Firm in the belief that the poor remain poor because they are habituated to the economic dependence of the wealthy, Freire engaged adult illiterates in praxis (authentic dialogue for the purpose of reflecting on existing realities and for organizing to transform these realities) with the goal of challenging the dominant culture. Freire's concept of praxis is not restricted to adults; he, along with his disciples, educators Henry Giroux (1983) and Ira Shor (1992), urge teachers to help young children learn to "read the world, read the word" (Freire, 1984, p. 15). This construct of literary as political action, also known as critical literacy, has been embraced recently by literacy academics but with the goal of true democracy, not Marxist revolution. Educators such as Carole Edelsky (1994) and Patrick Shannon (1990, 1993) urge teachers to "tie language to power, tie text interpretation to societal structures, tie reading and writing to perpetuating or resisting" and to figure out "how systems of domination [e.g., government-backed corporations] are part of reading and writing. . . ." (Edelsky, 1994, p. 254). Shannon, for example, argues that we must discuss with children the political message embedded in books such as *If You Give a Mouse a Cookie* (Numeroff, 1985). The book, which opens with the title line and follows with "then he'll probably ask for a glass of milk," habituates children to think that we shouldn't give the poor "anything because they'll want more. . . . We'll have to feed them, house them. . . ." (Shannon, 1993). While isolated pockets of

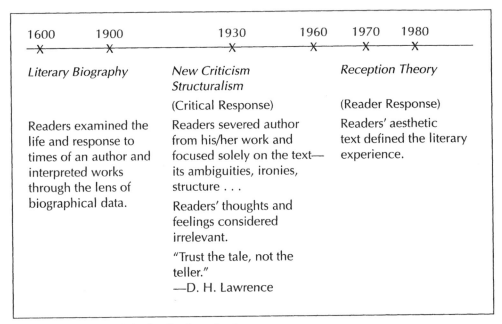

1600	1900		1930	1960	1970	1980
X	X		X	X	X	X

Literary Biography

Readers examined the life and response to times of an author and interpreted works through the lens of biographical data.

New Criticism
Structuralism

(Critical Response)

Readers severed author from his/her work and focused solely on the text— its ambiguities, ironies, structure . . .

Readers' thoughts and feelings considered irrelevant.

"Trust the tale, not the teller."
—D. H. Lawrence

Reception Theory

(Reader Response)

Readers' aesthetic text defined the literary experience.

FIGURE 2-3   *Historical sketch: The place of author*

teachers are implementing critical literacy, liberatory pedagogy has not taken hold in American classrooms, for the same reasons that feminist theory has not taken hold.

Concluding Comments

Over the last two decades, literature-based reading and writing programs have flourished in elementary classrooms across the country. One recent dimension of these literature-based programs has been the author study. In some classrooms, author studies emphasize the importance of the author by asking readers first to learn about the author and then to make life-literature connections as they read the author's books. In other classrooms, author studies begin and end with the works of the author, asking readers to examine the structural aspects of the texts such as themes, symbolism, and characterization and to appreciate the author's artistry. In yet other classrooms, author studies accentuate the personal journeys of readers as they travel through an author's body of work. This chapter has demonstrated that each of these perspectives—*author study as biography, author study as critical response, author study as reader response*—has a long and rich tradition within the field of literary theory and criticism. However, as the next chapter will reveal, if we are to respect the primacy of the literacy experience and to deepen children's literary understandings, we need to draw on the merits of each of these theoretical perspectives and to view *author study as multiple response.*

3

Author Study as Multiple Response: Featured Author: Carolyn Coman

More than two thousand years ago, Aristotle pointed out that the study of rhetoric involves three intersecting dimensions: the writer, the subject/text, and the listener/reader. To acknowledge one without the others, in Aristotle's view, is to diminish the literary experience. Yet, as the previous chapter revealed, it is this very preoccupation with one dimension or another of the Aristotelian triad that has characterized much of the history of literary theory and criticism, and in turn, that has influenced our thinking about author studies.

The thesis of this book is that while each perspective—*author study as literary biography*, *author study as critical response*, and *author study as aesthetic response*—has much to offer, no one perspective captures the whole literary experience. For example, to read Cynthia Rylant's works and not to know that, in her words, "So many of my books are directly connected to my real life, especially my childhood" (1989, p. 255), is to miss the life force behind her works. To read Cynthia Rylant and not to reflect on the poignant symbolism that enriches her stories is to miss layers of meaning and the artistry of her craft. To read Cynthia Rylant and not to savor the lived-through experience is to miss the literature itself. This book, therefore, argues for the dissolution of the boundaries among these author-study perspectives, and for the merging of theoretical assumptions and instructional practices. It advocates the perspective of *author study as multiple response*.

This chapter explores the domain of teacher knowledge that undergirds the perspective of author study as multiple response. It taps the research that seeks to address questions such as: What is the range of response that young readers bring to literature? Are young children capable of responding aesthetically to literature? What kinds of critical responses do children make to story? Do children make autobiographical connections between an author's life and his or her stories? This chapter presents the principles that guide the creation and implementation of author study as multiple response—principles that, in fact, apply to all literature study. When possible, each principle is anchored in the context of the research literature.

43

Infusing life into these principles are "snapshots" of a Carolyn Coman author study that was implemented with one section of Joanne McCarthy's sixth graders. With amazing vitality and humor, Joanne brings literature to life with four sections of sixth graders each day of the school year. Her literacy program is anchored in the best of children's literature; using the core literature model (Thompkins and McGee, 1993; see Chapter 5 for explanation), Joanne invites her sixth graders to probe the aesthetic and critical dimensions of story.

At the time of this author study, Coman had published two books. Her first book, Tell Me Everything, an ALA Notable Book, won much critical acclaim. In Tell Me Everything, twelve-year-old Roz is unable to comprehend her mother's recent tragic death. The only thing real about her mother's death is Nate, the boy who fell while hiking and whom Roz's mother tried to save before she fell of the mountain. For almost a year, Roz, obsessed with hearing Nate's voice, calls—but never talks to—Nate. The mere sound of his voice remains her only link to her mother. When Nate's family gets an unlisted number, Roz knows that she must find him to learn firsthand about her mother's death. She has to see Nate for herself—has to touch the scars of Nate's frostbitten toes—to reconcile her mother's death. Released from her torment, Roz returns home to bury her mother's ashes and to find her own identity, separate from but buoyed by her mother's unconditional love.

Coman's second book, *What Jamie Saw*, turns on the themes of child abuse, parental love, and determination, fear, and bravery. Nine-year-old Jamie witnesses his baby sister, Nin, being flung across the room by Van, his stepfather, and being caught miraculously by his mother, Patty. Jamie, Patty, and Nin leave their home and convince a friend to let them stay in his secluded trailer. There, they wait in terror for Van's reappearance. Fear translates into anger as Patty lashes out at Jamie, as Jamie kicks the drawer in which Nin is sleeping, and as Patty rams the trailer door, sealed shut during an ice storm. The waiting ends when Van appears while Patty is away. At the sight of Van's truck, Jamie hides Nin, then invites Van into the trailer with the hope that when his mother returns, she will see Van's truck and escape. Patty arrives home, terrified at the sight of the truck, and bursts into the trailer. With Jamie, who refuses to leave her side, Patty orders Van to leave and to never come back.

Coman won the Newbery Honor Book award for *What Jamie Saw* in 1996:

Coman's poetic prose is unsentimental and concise. The elements of plot and characterization meld into a finely balanced blend. This is a powerful story that probes with painful insistence at the insidious nature of fear and its consequences. (*Horn Book*, 1996)

With wrenching simplicity and mesmerizing imagery, Coman articulates nine-year-old Jamie's baffled, stream-of-consciousness of a violent act that robs him of his security, but not his innocence.... Shocking in its simple narration and child's-eye view, *What Jamie Saw* is a bittersweet miracle in understated language and forthright hopefulness. (*School Library Journal*, 1995)

Principle One: Readers Respond in Multiple Ways to an Author's Works

Until recently, research findings suggested that children are developmentally incapable of both critical and affective response to literature. In his landmark study, Applebee (1978) investigated the objective and subjective responses of six-, nine-, thirteen-, and seventeen-year-olds. When asked to tell about a favorite story, many six-year-olds responded by retelling the piece, complete with story dialogue. Most nine-year-olds offered more condensed synopses of the story. Both populations, however, focused on story action rather than on more abstract aspects such as theme or point of view. Applebee also investigated their subjective responses to a favorite story by asking the children to talk about what they liked and didn't like about the story. Applebee defined subjective response as "personal response . . . the recognition of the effect of the work on the reader or listener" (pp. 89–90). He found that most six-year-olds responded globally to a story ("It's good," or "It's nice") and defended their response by offering a story detail. The nine-year-olds approached the evaluation task more systematically and classified stories according to distinct attributes. Stories were described as "interesting," or "funny," and enjoyed "because they are about 'cowboys' or 'families,'" not because they are about "how families work" or "problems of good and evil" (p. 101). Applebee concluded that it is not until readers enter the formal operations stage around the age of eleven or twelve that they are able to think abstractly and subjectively about literature. Literature expert Bernice Cullinan and colleagues (1983) corroborated Applebee's findings. They examined fourth, sixth, and eighth graders' responses to Katherine Paterson's *Bridge to Terabithia* and Ursula LeGuin's *A Wizard of Earthsea*, and found that the fourth and sixth graders were preoccupied with story retelling and summarization. Only the eighth graders were able to judge the stories in the context of their own lives.

Recent investigations, however, have challenged this notion of cognitive limitations. Galda (1982) investigated the responses of three advanced fifth-grade readers to two stories matched for topic (*Bridge to Terabithia* and *Beat the Turtle Drum*), and found a range of response. Two of the fifth graders adopted a critical stance to the stories, critiquing plot and characters; the third student "entered the experience the text offered" (p. 16), adopting a personal stance. Thus, even when cognitive level is controlled, response will run the gamut from efferent (critical) to aesthetic. Furthermore, reader response is not age-dependent. Many (1991) found that grade level was not a factor in fourth, sixth, and eighth graders' ability to interpret stories or to adopt an aesthetic stance. For example, 40 percent of the fourth graders offered valid interpretations of story events; 16 percent also made connections between the stories and their own lives. Even children as young as first grade are able to evoke personal responses after listening to stories (McGee, 1992).

Multiple Responses of Sixth Graders to Carolyn Coman's What Jamie Saw

After reading the first two chapters of *What Jamie Saw*, the sixth graders were asked to respond to the following journal question: "What were your thoughts as you read the story?" Informal analysis of their responses corroborates research findings about the complexity of reader response. Three of the seventeen responses stall at the level of literal recall; fourteen span the aesthetic, critical, and biographical domains. Examples of these responses follow.

Literal Recall

Three sixth graders merely retold the story plot. An example of this most basic type of efferent response follows:

> Jamie saw his baby sister, Nin, get thrown across the room by Van. But luckily his mother caught her. Jamie was so frightened. His mother told him to come with her so he did. They went out to the car and Nin and Jamie sat and waited. His mother went in the house and brought out most of their belongings. When Jamie saw his bag of toys, he thought of Santa Claus. They went to a friend of his mother's house. . . . They stayed in Earl's apartment all night on a pull out couch. In the morning Jamie woke up, got dressed and went to find his magic tricks in the car. Magic was one of his favorite things to do.

Critical Response

Ten students responded to the journal question by addressing literary elements. Thoughts about the characters were prevalent. Catie, for example, offered global assessments of Jamie's mother, Earl, and Van (Figure 3-1). Other sixth graders offered similar character analyses and plot critiques:

> I think Van is an abusive stepfather and I bet he hurt Jamie and Nin before too.

> I can tell you that this boy has a rough time in his life. The mother is probably used to it when the little baby gets thrown by the stepfather.

> When his mother went to Earl's house, I thought she had an affair with him. I thought it [the story] was suspenseful.

> The book starts of pretty weird with a baby being thrown. There is a lot of tension in this story about what will happen next.

Aesthetic Response

Two sixth graders made personal connections to the story:

> I think that Jamie is unfortunate to have his parents divorced. My parents are divorced and I hate it. When I'm with my mother, I miss my dad and when I'm with my dad, I miss my mother. I wish they'd get back together or at least talk nicely to each other.

> Jamie must feel so confused about everything. I know what it feels like when you have to move from your house to someone's house you don't know too well. You don't feel like you belong anywhere and you wonder what will happen.

Biographical Response

Two students speculated about the autobiographical nature of the story:

> I wonder if the author was abused when she was little by her father or maybe it was her sister who was hurt.

> I think the author had a weird childhood. Maybe her father threw her baby sister across the room and frightened her and that's why she wrote this book.

Catie Smith Red 201

I was feeling scared in the first chapter. I wasn't sure if Van was going to hurt anyone else, or what he was going to do. But I'm glad that the mother had enough sense to get the kids & just get out of there. Earl seems like a nice guy. I really hope that Van doesn't find out where they are & try to take them away. I was thinking that Van was so mean, & I was wondering how anybody could do something like that to a poor little baby! I am really interested in what the rest of the book is going to be like.

FIGURE 3-1 *Catie's critical response to Chapter 1 in* What Jamie Saw

Although it is important to acknowledge that these written responses represent only the thoughts that children decide to make public, they do suggest a range of response, with critical response overshadowing all other responses. What accounts for this preponderance of critical response? I suspect that for most readers—both children and adults—critical response is our most immediate public reaction to literature. Case in point: When Carolyn Coman won the Newbery, I wrote her a congratulatory letter, an excerpt of which reads:

> *What Jamie Saw* is a treasure—jolting themes, riveting characters and a gripping pace. As the family cocooned themselves in the trailer, the tension escalated to the point that I worried more about Patty's state of mind than about Van's reappearance. . . . I loved your language play—not only the crisp metaphors but also the repetitive cadence. You stretched the boundaries of language in a way that I found intriguing. . . .

In essence, I shared my critical review of the book. Comparably, when someone asks, "So what did you think of this book?" our first impulse as readers is to offer a critique of plot, characters, and themes. We rarely share a personal response, "Remember that scene where . . . happened? It reminded me of an event in my life . . ." or speculate about a biographical connection.

Louise Rosenblatt (1978) argues that our affinity for critical response is a learned response. As students, we spent our school careers steeped in critical response—writing book reports, diagramming plot structures, and analyzing characters. Teachers asked only for those critical responses. Rosenblatt (1985) asserts that far too many teachers are still designing activities "that push the child in a nonaesthetic direction" (p. 42). For example, teachers ask children to read a story and then to complete a story map or to list all the adverbs in the piece—without any discussion of how the story touches children's lives. These teachers need to be awakened to the life-sustaining power of literature. However, with this awakening comes the realization that readers respond to literature in multiple ways and that we have a responsibility to evoke aesthetic response before critical or biographical response.

Principle Two: Aesthetic Engagement Must Precede Critical and Biographical Response

In Chapter 2, we explored Rosenblatt's conviction about the primacy of aesthetic response to literature. According to Rosenblatt (1978), "We peel off layer after layer of concerns brought to bear [in encounters with the text]—social, biographical, historical, linguistic, textual—and at the center we find the inescapable transactional events between readers and texts" (p. 175). In essence, her transactional theory posits that when readers encounter a piece of literature, they adopt either an aesthetic or efferent (critical) stance to the text in accordance with the purpose of the reading. With respect to children, though, Rosenblatt (1991a) believes that although "the mature, skilled reader usually selects the appropriate stance automatically, as with other skills . . . this act of selective attention must be learned by children" (p. 122) through indirect or direct teaching.

I doubt that Rosenblatt means *learn* in the sense that children are not in tune with their emotions and have to be taught how to summon these feelings. Rather, I suspect she means that children will only access their life experiences if we:

1. *Ask the right kinds of questions.* Instead of asking children "What are your thoughts about this story?" we need to say, "Think about something in the story that reminds you of something that has happened in your life. Write what happened, how you felt about it, and what you learned." At times, it is helpful to ask aesthetic questions specific to an event in the book. For example, for *What Jamie Saw*, I might ask: "After Patty and Jamie return home from the carnival—shaken by the appearance of a man who looked like Van—Patty screams at Jamie, 'What? Who're you looking at?' Angered by his mother's sarcasm, Jamie kicks the drawer in

which Nin is sleeping. What would you have done in this situation? Why?" If we want personal response, we have ask for it; otherwise, as we noted earlier, critical response will prevail.

2. *Model aesthetic response.* This may be what Rosenblatt means by indirect teaching. We need to share our life-literature connections to show how an event—primary or secondary—in a story evokes a personal memory. Unbelievable as it may sound, each semester I have undergraduate students tell me that they can't write a personal response to Lois Lowry's *Number the Stars* because they aren't Jewish, have no personal connection to the Holocaust, and have not experienced discrimination. I have to help these students understand that, for some readers, aesthetic response is anchored in the pivotal events of the story; for other readers, though, aesthetic response is grounded in the compelling themes that drive a story. I recall the scenes in *Number the Stars* in which a) Annemarie's father lies to the soldiers when they invade the family home; b) Annemarie's mother and uncle lie to her about Great-aunt Birte; and c) Annemarie lies to the soldiers in the forest. I ask the undergraduates, "How many of you have lied to protect someone about whom you care?" and "How many of you have been the recipient of a protection lie?" When students hear the questions, they begin to understand what aesthetic response is. However, the power of aesthetic response lies not so much in the accounting of the parallel event as in reflections about the event. The power resides in what we have learned about ourselves and about life as a result of this evocation. For example, we need to confront our experience with lying to protect, and ask if indeed there are situations in which lying is sanctioned. It is at this level of reflection that Rosenblatt might advocate direct teaching.

Minilesson: Activating Aesthetic Response

As previously noted, the majority of the sixth graders wrote critical responses to *What Jamie Saw*; only two wrote personal responses. No doubt the prevalence of critical response was tied directly to the broad question I posed to the sixth graders ("What were your thoughts as you read the story?"). Committed to having these students live the book before dissecting it, I shift the thrust of their engagement with the implementation of the following minilesson.

I begin by asking them to think about the aesthetic-bound question to which they will respond later in the session: "Think about something in the story that reminds of something that has happened in your life. Write what happened, how you felt about it, and what you learned." I then ask, "To which topics or events in *What Jamie Saw* do you think readers might make personal connections? Write down your ideas." Without discussion, I then read my personal response:

When I read the excerpt, "She [Jamie's mother] kept saying that, that lullaby, calling to Jamie, but he was still in bed, eye wide, watching and his body was frozen. . . . Only his eyes could move" (p. 10), I am jettisoned back to a night when I was home alone. As I am brushing my teeth, I hear a knock at the front door and then a rattling of the doorknob. The knocks turn to bangs and the knob rattling accelerates. I can't move. Bang, bang, bang—finally I jump into the bathtub, close the shower curtain, and grab the X-14 tile cleaner. Barely able to breathe, my only thought is, "If he breaks down the door and finds me, I'll spray him." After about five minutes, the banging ceases. I peek out the bathroom window and spy an unfamiliar car. Back into the bathtub. Finally I hear the engine start and the car departs. Knowing that I can't stay in the house, I bolt to the garage and drive to the police station. A police officer follows me home. The car is back. The police officer, flashing lights and using the blow horn, orders the would-be intruder out of the car. As my husband emerges with his hands held high, I want to melt into the car seat. My husband explains that he had to leave his car in the shop and take a rental. They laugh; I die.

As I think back, I realize that I, like Jamie, was paralyzed with fear—a fear that prevented me from thinking logically. Did I think to go to the front window to see who was banging? No. Did I think to call the police as soon as the knob rattling started? No. This experience taught me that when one allows fear to spin out of control, rational thought evaporates. I hope that if I am ever in a similar position again, I will concentrate on my range of options and act more wisely.

I ask, "How many of you have had an experience where you were so frightened you couldn't move?" Many hands go up. I ask, "How many of you wrote *fear* as a topic on your list?" No hands raise. We then talk about their list of ideas. Predictably, they offer the pivotal events of the story, such as child abuse, divorce, and parents not having enough money to buy Christmas presents. I ask them to guess why they think I didn't write about any of these events. Philip replies, "Maybe none of those things happened in your life."

"Exactly," I reply. I explain that, although I can imagine how painful it must be when parents divorce, I haven't experienced it myself and wouldn't be able to write about it easily. I explain that I had to think about other aspects of the story to which I could relate, such as Jamie's paralyzing fear.

I ask about other events in the story that most of us have experienced. They reply, "temper tantrums," "having a hobby you love," and "vomiting because you're so scared." As they are about to begin their responses, I remind them that sometimes a life event is so personal that they don't want to share it with teachers or peers, and that this is their prerogative.

As the two following responses reveal, many of the sixth graders latch onto the topics generated during our discussion:

This chapter [#6] reminded me of a time when my father got really mad at me because I forgot to do a small chore. I hate it when he gets mad at me, so I went outside to let him cool off. When I was out there I could see him through the window. He was still very mad. And he got worse because my sister was being bad. When I heard him yelling, I threw up. I went inside to get cleaned up. My father ask me what happened and I told him. He felt so bad he wasn't even mad anymore.

If I was Jamie, I would be shocked to hear my mother say that to me [Jamie's mother screamed at him for pulling a temper tantrum]. But I would understand what she's going through. There was one time when my mom broke up with her boyfriend and she was upset. She snapped at me. But I understood what she was going through so I waited a little while and asked her again.

Johnathan's response is particularly poignant—not only for what is said about the fire but for how it is said (see Figure 3-2). In comparing this response with Carolyn Coman's (1995) opening line of *What Jamie Saw*, it is evident that Johnathan absorbed the cadence of Carolyn's language:

When Jamie saw him throw the baby, saw Van throw the little baby, when Jamie saw Van throw his baby sister, Nin, then they moved. (p. 7)

As these three representative responses reveal, the sixth graders have no difficulty connecting their lives to the story. Absent from most of their responses, though, is the dimension of self-reflection. It is only through repeated demonstrations and ongoing discussion that readers learn the power of story to help us to look inward, offering a standard by which to assess our lives.

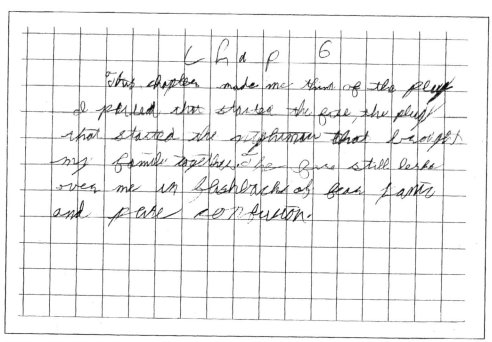

FIGURE 3-2 *Johnathan's aesthetic response to* What Jamie Saw

The Inevitability of Multiple Response During Aesthetic Discussions

To guide the aesthetic conversation of the final chapter of *What Jamie Saw*, I ask the sixth graders to respond in their journals to the following question: "Recall when Van showed up at the trailer on Christmas Eve and only Jamie and Nin were at home. If you were Jamie, what would you have done and why?" As they share responses, intense conversation ensues.

> JAN: I would do what Jamie did—let Van in the house because I would want to protect my mother too.
>
> JOHN: But how is letting Van in the house going to protect his mother? There's no way my mother would come home, see Van's car and then take off. She'd be crazy worrying that something would happen to us. She'd do what Patty did.
>
> STEPH: I wouldn't let Van in either. I'd call the police so that they'd be there when his mother would show up and they'd protect her.
>
> JAN: But the police might not get there in time. Then what would you do?

In the middle of this debate, Johnathan attempts to move the conversation in a different direction:

> I didn't like how the book ends. It had an ending like *Under the Blood Red Sun*. *What Jamie Saw* really didn't have an ending so it leaves the thought in your mind that you just ran into a brick wall—it stops there. There are so many questions that aren't answered like, "What happens to Van?" Same thing in *Under the Blood Red Sun*; it's about a Japanese boy during the bombing of Pearl Harbor. His grandfather and father were arrested just because they were Japanese and at the end, he just pretended his parents were there and that was it. You don't even know what happens to everybody.

Critical response infiltrates personal engagement with the story. Not wanting to lose the momentum, I thank Johnathan for his interesting observation and promise to return to it later in the session. I revive the debate by asking how many in the class would not let Van in and would call the police.

This kind of interplay between aesthetic and critical is standard fare when discussing a story; it is not restricted to the aesthetic and the critical. During a discussion of the symbolic meaning of magic in *What Jamie Saw* (see Principle Three), Catie interjected that, "If the story is based on personal experience, she [Carolyn Coman] might have had a magic set when she was a child" (Figure 3-3). Here the biographical intersects with the critical; five other sixth graders make similar comments on this worksheet.

In essence, these readers—like all readers—shuttle back and forth among the aesthetic, critical, and biographical dimensions of story (Figure 3-4). As facilitators, though, we want to achieve a sense of conversational coherence that inspires the continual refinement of thought. Consequently, we often have to walk the fine line

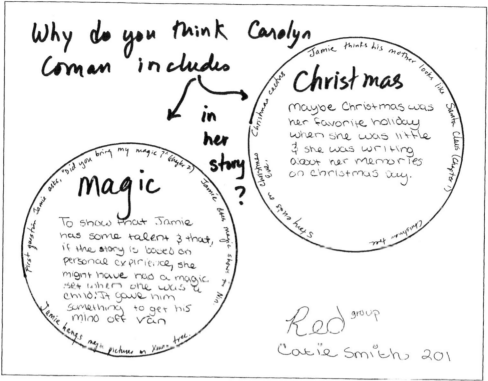

FIGURE 3-3   *Catie's interplay of critical and biographical response*

of keeping the conversation moving on the chosen path while acknowledging—but generally not pursuing—these interesting sidelines. Of course, when the conversation has peaked, exploration of such comments may be entirely appropriate.

As it turned out, we ran out of time and didn't pursue Johnathan's comment until the next session. I asked him to replay his thoughts about the story ending; there was much agreement that the ending left too many questions. I explained that the ending of *What Jamie Saw* is called an ambiguous ending. After a quick discussion of the term, I asked about their reactions to movies that have ambiguous endings. We generated one pro ("leaves the reader thinking") and many cons, with the unanimous decision that such endings are not satisfying. This is as far as I went with the element of story endings because I had already decided to pursue Johnathan's earlier insight about the symbolism in *What Jamie Saw* (see Principle Three)

Research on the Evocation of Aesthetic Response

In the author studies profiled in this book, numerous examples of children's aesthetic responses verify that literature carries the same emotional import for children as it

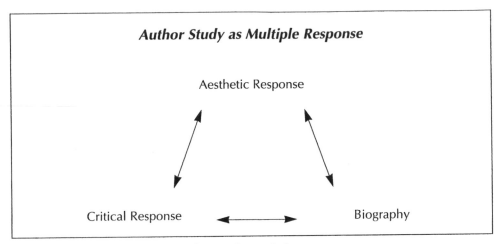

FIGURE 3-4 *Readers respond to an author's work in multiple ways*

does for adults. Literature permits readers of all ages to re-create past experiences, to transform present understandings, and to renew dreams for self and others. Such evocation is essential because it significantly increases levels of understanding (Cox and Many, 1989; Many, 1991). Children who "focused in their response on the lived-through experiences of the story were significantly more likely to interpret story events, to apply the story to life, and to make abstract generalizations than were students who responded efferently or with no single primary stance" (Many, 1991, p. 77). Consequently, we have an obligation to honor aesthetic response before critical and biographical response. Central to this obligation is an understanding of the current research on factors that contribute to the evocation of aesthetic response in children:

1. *Quality of Literature:* The literature used in the classroom influences the quality of response. For example, the exceptional quality of Natalie Babbitt's *Tuck Everlasting* evoked greater in-depth personal responses from fifth and sixth graders than other texts such as Louise Fitzhugh's *Harriet the Spy* (Eeds and Wells, 1989). Likewise, first graders offered more extensive personal responses to Judy Blume's *The Pain and the Great One* than to Pat Hutchins's *Rosie's Walk* or Yorinks's *Hey, Al* (McGee, 1992).

2. *Discussion Questions:* As already noted, the kinds of questions that we ask about literature influence response. Open-ended questions elicit stronger levels of discourse in that children talk among themselves, express feelings, ask questions, and connect life and literature (Kiefer, 1983). However, in my experience, even the open-ended question

"What do you think about the story?" yields a range of responses from aesthetic to efferent, with the majority of responses at the efferent level. An invitation such as "Share your thoughts and feelings about an event in this book that reminds you of an event in your life, and explain what you learned" yields stronger life-literature links.

3. *Children's Expectations:* Children's expectations about the purpose of literature discussions influence the quality of group talk. If children view book talk as a "gentle inquisition" (Eeds and Wells, 1989, p. 14)—talk for the sole purpose of checking literal understandings—critical talk will dominate (Wollman-Bonilla, 1994). On the other hand, if children view book talk as genuine sharing of personal response, engaging talk prevails.

4. *Peer Talk:* Group-constructed understandings often are broader and deeper than understandings constructed by individual readers. Peer collaboration enhances reader response (Golden, 1987; Helper and Hickman, 1982; Wollman-Bonilla, 1994).

These findings suggest that reader response is a complex phenomenon that is tied to the reader and his or her experiences with literature, the quality of the literature, and the classroom context. Hence, when implementing author studies, we need to find authors whose literature jars the soul, to share repeatedly our personal responses to this literature, to ask questions and to design activities that evoke life-literature links, and to provide multiple forums for peer construction of meaning.

Principle Three: Critical Response Deepens and Extends the Literary Experience

Central to this principle is the assumption, espoused by both literacy and literature experts alike, that children are capable of adopting a critical stance toward literature. In their widely acclaimed book, *Grand Conversations: Literature Groups in Action*, Peterson and Eeds (1990) advocate "the conscious contemplation of a work of literature" (p. 12) through analysis of the literary elements. Tompkins and McGee (1993), Raphael and Hiebert (1996), and others also recommend introducing children to the literary elements. Likewise, literature experts such as Rebecca Lukens (1995) and Cullinan and Galda (1994) encourage such analysis.

But what does the research tell us about the acquisition and development of literary elements such as character, plot, theme, point of view, and symbolism? Because the investigation of children's response to literature—both aesthetic and critical response—is still in its infancy, we have only small pockets of information. We have already noted that earliest empirical data suggested that children are not cognitively mature enough to attend to the objective and affective dimensions of story (Applebee, 1978). However, as with affective domain, recent investigations have disputed this notion of cognitive limitations with respect to critical response. We turn now to this research on children's understanding of literary elements such as plot, theme, character development, and so forth. We begin with the sixth graders in the author study on Carolyn Coman and their foray into the literary element of symbolism.

Literary Element: Symbolism

As previously mentioned, the sixth graders read the first two chapters of *What Jamie Saw*, and shared their plot and character responses. As the session was about to end, Johnathan raises his hand and says, "Santa Claus, magic, and the map of Texas."

I ask, "What about Santa Claus, magic, and the map of Texas?"

He replies, "They are in the story."

"And what about them?" I probe.

"They're just there in the story," he repeats. His response recalls Peterson and Eeds's (1990) observation:

> Symbols in the world of story function to put the reader in touch with meaning that cannot be stated directly—the extended metaphor of the work. Abstract meanings are made accessible to the mind and heart of the reader through symbols. Symbols exercise an unconscious influence on our interpretations. (p. 44)

Johnathan intuitively senses that Santa Claus/Christmas, magic, and the map carried symbolic meaning. In fact, his first two intuitions are realized in the story; his third intuition is not. While the map had the potential to symbolize Jamie's absentee father, Carolyn Coman chose not to further complicate the story with the issue of abandonment.

Is Jonathan's stream of symbolic consciousness typical for a sixth grader? Unfortunately, with the exception of Cullinan et al.'s (1983) study, research on symbolic literary understanding of elementary children appears nonexistent. This dearth of research is fascinating, given the extent of research on symbolic thought in preschool children. We know that the ability to create an arbitrary relationship between an object and idea emerges during a child's first year. A sixteen-month-infant will see pictures in a story and will go and retrieve the actual objects (Snow and Ninio, 1986). By age three, children experiment with symbolic representation when they scribble a picture and report that they have created "daddy" or "a kitty" (Kagan, 1981). In addition, three-year-olds "read" the print embedded in a McDonald's sign or a Coca-Cola sign by attending to the logo or its color (Masonheimer, Drum, and Ehri, 1984). With continued exposure to and experimentation with print, children continue to refine their knowledge about language as a symbolic system.

As part of an investigation into children's developmental responses to literature, Cullinan and colleagues (1983) asked fourth, sixth, and eighth graders to read *Bridge to Terabithia* and *Wizard of Earthsea* and then interviewed them about the symbolism in each book. They found that fourth graders were oblivious to the symbolic meaning of the bridge and the shadow. Sixth graders demonstrated a tentative awareness of the symbols; eighth graders offered multiple meanings. The researchers concluded that symbolic understanding is developmental.

It is, perhaps, because of this research that we find attention to symbolism in grades five and six, but not before. Teachers' testimonials suggest that children, at least in upper elementary grades, can begin to understand and appreciate the richness of literary symbolism (Smith, 1990; Peterson and Eeds, 1995). However, as previously noted, the fact that researchers have successfully challenged the rigidity of developmental theory suggests that we suspend judgment on the symbolic capabilities of young readers until further qualitative study is undertaken.

Minilessons on Symbolism

While I am eager to pursue Johnathan's symbolic intuitions, I hold off because we have only read two chapters of *What Jamie Saw* and I don't want to preempt the aesthetic reading of the book with early instruction in symbolism. So I record Jonathan's ideas on a chart, acknowledge the intrigue of his insight, and promise to return to his ideas after we have finished the book.

Upon completion of the book, I hand out a blank copy of the worksheet presented in Figure 3-3, recall Johnathan's ideas, and ask the sixth graders to complete it for homework.

I begin the following session with a matching game. I divide the students into groups, and hand each group a plastic bag with scrambled puzzle pieces; some pieces have pictures (e.g., a dove, skull and bones), some have words (e.g., *peace*, *poison*). Their task, to match the pictures and the words, is completed in a few minutes with 100 percent accuracy. I ask how they are able to do the puzzles so quickly. They reply that they see these signs everywhere. I ask why we use these signs, instead of the words. Tim notes, "A little kid might not be able to read the word *poison*, but if he knows the sign, he'll stay away from it." They extend this comment to adults or foreigners who can't read English. I ask if anyone knows another word for these signs. With no reply, I introduce the term *symbol* as an object, an event, or a person that has both literal meaning and figurative meaning. I hold up the poison symbol and ask its literal meaning. I then ask how they think the figurative meaning evolved. They sort out the death inference quickly and then inquire about how the dove got its figurative meaning. I explain that while there are probably multiple answers, the one with which I am familiar is biblical: Jesus descending to earth as a dove. I encourage them to ask family members about alternative ideas.

In the following session, I post the chart with Johnathan's symbolic ideas. I explain that, like the symbols we see around us, authors frequently use symbols to convey special meanings—meanings that they rarely explain to the reader. I ask Johnathan why he originally thought the map of Texas might have special meaning. "Maybe because it's about his real father?" he replies. I talk about the potential of the map to represent Jonathan's abandonment, but note that because the map is not carried through the story, it does not have the power of a true symbol.

We then turn to their homework assignment (Figure 3-3) and explore the magic symbol:

> CAROL: Why do you think Carolyn Coman included magic in the story?
>
> JAN: It tells about Jamie's hobby. It gives you something to know about the character.
>
> CAROL: Why did Carolyn pick magic as Jamie's hobby instead of, for example, football?
>
> EDDIE: Because football is so common and she wants Jamie to be unique.
>
> CAROL: Okay, but actually Jamie does have an uncommon hobby—card playing. Why does the magic seem so much more important to the story than the card playing?
>
> CATIE: [Reads her response, Figure 3-3.]
>
> CAROL: Perhaps, Carolyn included magic because it was her special hobby. You make a good point too about the magic being a distraction for Jamie. What do you think Jamie secretly wished he could do with his magic?
>
> MIKE: Make Christmas gifts appear for everyone.
>
> CATIE: Make a brand new house appear for his mother.
>
> JOHNATHAN: Make Van disappear.
>
> CAROL: Excellent ideas. If you had to describe Jamie's life throughout the story in one phrase—out of control, in control—which would you pick?
>
> TIM: Out of control. That's why he was always having temper tantrums.
>
> CAROL: If you had to describe Jamie's use of magic in one phrase—out of control, in control—which would you pick?
>
> JOHNATHAN: In control. He had charge of the magic and he gets attention by using it.
>
> CAROL: Yes, the magic is Jamie's way of staying sane in an insane situation.
>
> JOHN: While you were talking about how magic kept Jamie from going crazy, I was searching through my thoughts to see what made me cool off sometimes and it's my dog, Lucky. She always listens to me when no one else will. She acts like she knows what I'm saying.

I acknowledge John's aesthetic response (in the midst of this critical conversation) and promise to return to it at a later point so that others can share their coping strategies. I pull them back to the magic conversation and explain that Coman uses magic at two different levels:

> At the literal level, she includes magic because it helps us come to know Jamie and what his interests are. She also uses it because magic is fun; readers like to read about magic. And perhaps she was an amateur magician when she was Jamie's age. At a more abstract level, though, the figurative level, Carolyn uses magic to help Jamie cope with an unbearable situation and at the same time to give readers the hope that somehow the story will have a magical ending. Literary symbols enhance story meaning.

In the following session, we explore the symbolism of Christmas in much the same fashion. Within a minute, Johnathan notes, "Christmas is that magical ending we were talking about yesterday. The story had to end happy because it is Christmas time." The power of symbolism is taking hold.

Deciding When to Teach Which Literary Element

Because acclaimed books such as *What Jamie Saw* are rich in literary elements, our impulse is to teach all of the literary elements that mark a particular story. To do so, however, is to overwhelm students and, in the process, to diminish the literature. Although children bring tacit understandings about the critical dimensions of text, they are inexperienced in critical analysis. Because analysis of any one of the literary elements demands extended discussion across a number of minilessons and across an author's works, I suggest that you formally pursue only one new element per book. Of course, if a literary element has been introduced in a previous book, we should expect readers to apply their understandings to the new book.

The decision about which element to teach often emerges as children discuss a story. I knew the moment Jonathan mentioned "Santa Claus, magic, and the map of Texas" that I would pursue symbolism. First, it was a literary element that we had not studied previously. Second, the symbols were limited in number and highly accessible. And finally, such instruction would carry over to Carolyn Coman's other book, *Tell Me Everything*, a book packed with abstract symbolism. As previously noted, other instructional opportunities on critical elements—story endings and character development—emerged from the sixth graders' intuitive comments. While these elements were not formally pursued, instructional possibilities were noted for future books.

At times, of course, the curriculum dictates instructional decisions. For example, if coverage of the literary element of point of view was mandated, I could have created minilessons to explore the limited omniscient perspective of *What Jamie Saw*, comparing and contrasting it with first-person, omniscient, and objective narration. Discussions about the strengths and weaknesses of each perspective would enhance student awareness of authorial choices.

Thus, we have to attend to critical observations that students make, weigh them against other possibilities and against curricular expectations, and choose one element to study in depth. We have to remember that we have 180 days to teach children about the critical dimensions of story and that learning does not occur in steady increments, but in spurts bolstered by repeated demonstrations over time (Giacobbe, 1995).

Teacher Knowledge and the Literary Elements

Bringing readers and writers inside the critical elements of story requires much teacher knowledge. It is not enough, for example, to talk in a general way with children about character development. They deserve an age-appropriate, in-depth encounter with this literary element—one that extends children's current understandings and enables them to view story in a new light. We turn now to the research and practice of the major literary elements.

Critical Response: Plot

Of all the literary elements, story plot—the interplay of action and tension in a story's chain of events—has received the most attention from researchers. Children as young as four years old who have book experience possess a story schema or mental representation of story structure. They know that stories place characters in time and place, that characters take action, and that stories have resolutions. They use their story grammar knowledge to understand, to recall stories, and to create stories of their own (Golden, 1984; McKeough, 1984; Stein and Glenn, 1979; Whaley, 1981). By grade four or five, children begin to demonstrate a deeper understanding of the story grammar elements of setting, plot, and character, moving beyond the surface features of story to more subtle features such as character's reactions and motives (Stein and Glenn, 1979).

These story grammar findings have influenced instruction over the last two decades. Story maps that ask readers to identify the elements of a story plot are standard fare in classrooms. Literature experts, however, ask us to bring children beyond the broad sweep of story structure to the central element of conflict/tension that drives stories. Four prominent patterns of conflict follow (Lukens, 1995).

Character-Against-Nature

William Steig's books, *Amos and Boris* and *Brave Irene*, illustrate the tension that occurs when characters are forced to battle nature. Amos, a mouse, falls off his boat into the sea. As his strength is about to give out, he is rescued by a whale named Boris. And just as the sea has threatened Amos's life, so does land threaten Boris's life as he is washed up on the beach during a hurricane. In *Brave Irene*, it is not the sea that assails Irene but the "wounding wind" of a blizzard. It is in these survival stories and others such as *Island of the Blue Dolphins*, *Sign of the Beaver*, *Julie of the Wolves*, and *Hatchet* that characters' tenacity and resolve are put to the test.

Character-Against-Character

Readers have little difficulty recognizing the character-against-character conflict in *What Jamie Saw* as Jamie and his mother escape an abusive stepfather and live in fear of his return. The character-against-character pattern thrives on the tension between the protagonist and the antagonist, and usually ends in the triumph of good over evil. This tension propels books such as *Chrysanthemum*, *Mufaro's Beautiful Daughters*, *The True Confessions of Charlotte Doyle*, and *Jacob Have I Loved*.

Character-Against-Self

When story tension erupts from within the psyche of the main protagonist, the character-against-self conflict pattern is set in motion. In Carolyn Coman's book *Tell*

Me Everything, Roz disintegrates emotionally and only becomes whole again when she finds the inner strength to unravel the mystery surrounding her mother's death. Many of Cynthia Rylant's works also reflect this conflict pattern. In *A Fine White Dust*, tension mounts as Pete is forced to choose between his family and what he thinks is a religious calling. In *Missing May*, Summer struggles with renewed thoughts of abandonment as her Uncle Ob, grieving the loss of his wife, fears that he can no longer raise her. The character-against-self pattern often turns on moral confrontation and personal reckoning. This pattern, while prominent in chapter books, also occurs in picture storybooks such as *Ira Sleeps Over; Two Bad Ants; Sam, Bangs, and Moonshine;* and *Mirette on the High Wire*.

Character-Against-Society

This more abstract conflict pattern is made concrete in both of Lois Lowry's Newbery winners, *Number the Stars* and *The Giver*, as the main protagonists are pitted against the societal forces of evil. In *Number the Stars*, Annemarie and her family defy the Nazi regime in order to save their friends. In *The Giver*, Jonas destroys his dystopian community to save young Gabriel's life. Some authors, such as Mildred Taylor, write exclusively in this conflict pattern. In her trilogy, *Song of the Trees; Roll of Thunder, Hear My Cry; Let the Circle Be Unbroken*, Taylor resurrects the pain and injustice of racism that plagued but never broke her own family. This conflict pattern is prevalent in chapter books as well as in picture storybooks such as *Faithful Elephants, Rose Blanche, Amazing Grace,* and *The Great Kapok Tree*.

Categorization of these conflict patterns is not meant to suggest that all stories fall neatly into one of these patterns or that any one story contains only one pattern. In fact, many authors embed two or more of these conflict patterns. *What Jamie Saw* interweaves at least two patterns: the threat of the abusive stepfather's return (character-against-character) and Jamie's struggle to get his fears under control (character-against-self). Although the overarching pattern of *Roll of Thunder, Hear My Cry* is character-against-society, instances of character-against-character conflict propel the story forward. In addition, Cassie's struggle to find her inner strength and self-respect in the midst of this oppression adds the layer of character-against-self. And finally, the fire that threatens the very survival of the family infuses character-against-nature tension at the end of the story. Taylor's ability to thread all of the conflict patterns speaks to her superb talent as a writer.

In addition to conflict patterns, authors also use literary devices such as flashback and epilogue to compress or to expand time. While most stories for young children use a chronological narration in which events move forward in a sequential way, stories for upper elementary readers become more complex as authors manipulate time. In *Number the Stars*, Lois Lowry uses a flashback—a recounting of a past event that influences a present event—to introduce readers to Annemarie's older sister, Lise, who was killed by the Nazis three years before the start of the story. Lowry also uses an epilogue to fast-forward time: two years have passed since the war has ended when readers learn of Peter's execution by the Nazis and of Annemarie's continued devotion to her Jewish friend, Ellen. Experiences with books like *Number the Stars* prepare readers for the intricately woven tapestry of flashbacks in Carolyn Coman's *Tell Me Everything*. Roz's present is so steeped in her past that readers quickly come to expect the continual juxtaposition of time.

Although there is little research on readers' abilities to process varying levels of plot complexity, most literature experts believe that the more sophisticated a plot structure is, the less accessible the story is for readers in the upper elementary grades (Cullinan and Galda, 1981). Story endings are a case in point. One study found that when a group of fourth graders were asked to retell Paterson's *Bridge to Terabithia*, every child omitted Leslie's tragic death. When asked to talk about this observation in group discussion, "the children insisted the character had come back to life" (Cullinan et al., 1981, p. 645). Children expect stories to have happy endings, endings that are congruent with a "just world" (Jose and Brewer, 1984; Squire, 1964). When they don't, children may transform the stories to match their expectations. Ambiguous endings too tend to frustrate readers of all ages. The sixth graders in the Carolyn Coman author study responded much more positively to the ending of *Tell Me Everything* than to the ending of *What Jamie Saw*. Roz's decision in *Tell Me Everything* to bury her mother's ashes brought closure to the story as well as a ray of hope that Roz was ready to begin living again—without forgetting her past. On the other hand, sixth graders felt the ambiguous ending of *What Jamie Saw* left too many things unresolved: "What happens to Van? Does he get charged with child abuse?" "What happens to Jamie and his kicking problem? Does he get help to find out why he's doing it?"

Critical Response: Character Development

Whereas plot is the centrifugal force of story, character is its centripetal core. As Vincent McHugh notes:

> From first to last, the novelist is concerned with character. In the novel everything is character. . . . Each event must be focused on human consciousness. Without someone to look at it, there is no landscape; no idea without someone to conceive it, and no passion without persons. (Murray, 1990, p. 153)

William Faulkner, John Irving, S. E. Hinton, and many others concur that character is "everything."

What do children understand about character portrayal and development? What little research there is reveals that children bring certain expectations about characters to stories. When Applebee (1978) asked children what characters such as lions, wolves, rabbits, and witches were "usually like" in stories, he found that 41 percent of the six-year-olds expressed plausible expectations for about half of the characters. For example, they expected fairies to be good and witches bad; none, however, expected lions to be brave or foxes cunning. By age nine, though, 86 percent held such expectations. Implications for comprehension are obvious. When Bruce (1978) asked upper elementary readers to respond to the objectively told story "The Fox and the

Rooster," he found that children who had already developed the schema of fox as cunning and greedy but capable of being outsmarted had no difficulty comprehending this tale; children who had not developed this schema missed the fox's motives as well as the trickery aspect of the story.

In contrast to earlier studies that found that young children are not sensitive to characters' goals and motivations (Golden, 1984; Mandler and Johnson, 1977), Lehr (1991), using real literature and a variety of interview techniques, discovered that young children indeed "talked at length about characters and their internal motivations" (p. 49). She also found that while kindergartners did not expect characters to change over the course of a story, second and fourth graders did.

However, while children are able to get inside of the main protagonist's head, they have difficulty juggling the perspectives of multiple characters. Upper elementary readers tend to focus on the motives and reactions of main characters to the exclusion of other characters (Emery, 1993; Shannon, Kameenui, and Baumann, 1988).

Insights about children's understandings about character portrayal also have emerged from Donald Graves's (1989) analysis of children's fictional writing. Concerned about the aggressive, often violent, nature of children's fiction, Graves set out to discover what children do when they write fiction. He concluded that "first through sixth grade children's progress in writing fiction could be traced through their development of characters" (p. 778). Figure 3-5 presents a summary of how children reveal characters in their story writing. Young children tuck family, friends, and favorite book or TV characters into their stories. These characters exist only to serve the plot, to move the story action. Over time, however, these predictable characters give rise to invented characters. As Graves notes, "It is a very important moment when a child creates a character with a name no one else knows. A new name is the beginning of any dimension to a character" (p. 778). Unlike Superman, for example, whose character is defined before any story even starts, an invented character is free to evolve over the course of the story, limited only by the writer's imagination. Children bring these characters to life through use of dialogue and description. By grade five, many writers understand that it is the character's reactions and inner thoughts that mark the story.

Graves's findings align with the character revelation categories that Rebecca Lukens (1976, 1995) describes. She posits that we come to know characters by what they do and say, how they look, and what others say about them, including the narrator's comments. It is the effective synchronization of action, dialogue, appearance, and others' comments that results in character believability—characters that tap the expanse of our human complexity. Of course, authors cannot equally endow every character. Most stories contain both flat characters and round characters, who may be either dynamic or static.

Flat Characters

In *What Jamie Saw*, Van, the abusive stepfather, exemplifies a flat character. Readers know little about him other than his violent streak and his dejected persona. We

---

When Children Weave Characters into Their Stories

Generic Characters

First and second graders pluck characters for their stories directly from their story world: TV/movie characters, book characters, and so on. Characters are created to serve the plot. From the child's perspective, characters are pawns to be tossed and tumbled as the action demands.

Friend Characters

Equally popular in grades one to three is the inclusion of characters who have names of the writer's friends. Children, in the early grades, also include themselves in stories.

Invented Characters

A significant step forward occurs when children invent a "new" character, a character unknown to the writer and the reader. The introduction of a "new" character into a story can begin as early as grade two but is commonplace by grade four.

Characters Through Dialogue

While younger writers allow bits of their characters' personalities to emerge through dialogue, older children (generally grade three and up) create character profiles through supporting dialogue.

Characters Through Description

Physical description, in addition to dialogue, brings characters to life; generally grades 5 and up.

Characters Through Reactions

The final developmental swing occurs as writers come to understand that characters' personalities are best revealed through their actions and their reactions. Fifth graders (and up) allow characters to share their inner thoughts. They also enjoy creating characters who are older than themselves, and who engage in adult activities (e.g., driving).

FIGURE 3-5 *Graves's research (1989, 1991, 1994) on children's use of characters*

have no access to his thoughts or his motives. The Van we see at the beginning of the story is the Van we see at the end: "Again Jamie looked at Van and saw him as he had first seen him: skinny, stooped, but as drained as he'd been after he threw the baby, threw Nin" (Coman, 1995, p. 120). However, without Van there is no story, for it is the mere threat of his reappearance that drives the story action and that enables Jamie to face his fears. In Lois Lowry's *Number the Stars*, Kirsti, Annemarie's younger sister, is the quintessential flat character. She is a one-dimensional character who, throughout the story, bubbles with warmth and energy and who remains oblivious to the peril around her. She is portrayed as an egocentric youngster who does little more than yearn for pink cupcakes and cry about the fish shoes she must wear. Kirsti exists for the sake of the plot, providing comic relief for this tense story.

Round Characters

In contrast to Van, Jamie is a fully developed character. Readers are taken with his strong sense of allegiance to and caring for his mother and his baby sister, and are simultaneously concerned about his temper tantrums. We wonder if Jamie's outbursts are a response to the violence he has seen; we know they are a response to the fear that has infiltrated his life. In *Number the Stars*, Annemarie is the round character at the center of the story conflict. Through her actions, thoughts, and other characters' reactions to her, we come to understand her fear of the Nazi soldiers, to appreciate her devotion to her best friend, and to admire her bravery. It is their complex range of emotions and actions that make Jamie and Annemarie believable characters.

Dynamic Characters

What binds us to both Jamie and Annemarie are their gradual transformations from fearful, powerless children to individuals who face their fears, take risks for loved ones, and exhibit true courage. It is this journey of personal transformation that characterizes the dynamic character. As readers, we live this gradual metamorphosis and internalize the belief that we, too, have within ourselves the power to change.

Static Characters

Jamie's mother, Patty, is a fairly unchanging character in *What Jamie Saw*. From beginning to end, we applaud her remarkable strength and fierce determination to protect her children. Refusing to give into her fears, Patty leaves Van. She insists on staying at the trailer even after her friend warns that they will be sitting ducks for Van. Finding Van in the trailer, she confronts him for the last time. Patty begins as a strong, willful character who faces her fears and ends as an equally strong, willful character. In *Number the Stars*, Ellen remains static over the course of the story. As the target of Nazi persecution, Ellen essentially is locked into the stance of the passive, fearful victim. She is terrified when the soldiers invade the Johansen's apartment, fearful on the train ride, fearful at the wake for the fictional Aunt Birte. Ellen serves as an interesting contrast to the dynamic characters in Jane Yolen's *Devil's Arithmetic*, who shed their passive personas and survive the terror of the concentration camps through strong-willed determination and deliberate activism.

Critical Response: Theme

As noted earlier, Applebee (1978) found that children were not capable of abstracting story theme because of cognitive limitations. However, Susan Lehr's (1988) reconceptualization of Applebee's research design resulted in dramatically different findings. She probed children's sensitivity to story themes across three grade levels—kindergarten, second, and fourth. To ascertain the impact of literature on theme development, she asked children to listen to three storybooks (varied by grade level) and to choose the two books that "tell about the same idea." For example, the kindergartners listened to *Titch, The Carrot Seed*, and *New Blue Shoes*, selected the two books with a similar theme, and then drew a picture of the shared theme. The children also were interviewed about their responses. Lehr found that kindergartners identified similar themes in 80 percent of the realistic books. In addition, kindergartners who had high exposure to books generated concrete thematic statements about the matched books. Increasing levels of thematic abstraction were found for second and fourth graders, prompting Lehr to conclude that "thematic identification is a fairly early developmental strategy" (1988, p. 351) and that exposure to literature is highly correlated with thematic awareness. Lehr's work affirms that a sense of theme is alive and well in the minds of young children and that it deepens over time. It also makes clear that the richer the child's exposure to books, the greater the degree of thematic generalization.

Author studies offer a particularly viable context for the study of theme. Most authors write about the truths that they hold dear. One can't read Mem Fox without delighting in the joyful, and what she calls "conspiratorial," bond between grandparent and child. One cannot read Mildred Taylor without being pierced by the injustice of racism. One cannot read Cynthia Rylant without being saddened by the idea of abandonment. Young readers and writers need to explore the types of themes with which writers experiment (Lukens, 1995).

Primary Theme

As writers spin their tales, they search for the thread that will hold the story together. They search for what matters to them and then work to unfold this central truth through their characters and their actions. This truth constitutes a story's primary theme. Two interconnected themes swirl through *What Jamie Saw:* that child abuse is reprehensible and is not to be tolerated at any cost—even if it means homelessness; and that life at its core is family. In *Number the Stars*, Lois Lowry infuses her story with the central truth that human life is precious and must be protected, sacrifices notwithstanding.

Secondary Theme

Secondary themes have the potential to scaffold and, at times, expand a primary theme. In *What Jamie Saw*, readers learn that fear, unchecked, can paralyze a person, preventing him or her from taking actions. *Number the Stars* also ripples with secondary themes such as what friendship entails, what true courage is, and when lies protect.

Explicit Theme

Authors must decide whether their themes will be offered to readers in an explicit or implicit manner. In *What Jamie Saw*, Carolyn Coman forcefully tells readers about the pernicious nature of fear in the excerpt:

> "Oh, God, Jamie," she said, "we're afraid—just sick with fear. And it's so settled inside us that we don't even know what living feels like without it. That must be the

thing about fear, the trick of it—you forget that that's what it is because it just starts to feel like your life. We're afraid Jamie. That's all we are. And if we don't get past it, we'll be hiding from strangers and throwing up in the sink." (pp. 72–73)

In *Number the Stars*, one of the secondary themes is bravery. In fact, Annemarie's transformation from child to adolescent is tied to the virtue of bravery. Frightened by an encounter with Nazi soldiers at the beginning of the story, Annemarie is "glad to be an ordinary person who would never be called upon for courage" (p. 26). However, Annemarie is called upon to risk her life to save Ellen and her parents. She doesn't recognize her action as bravery because she is so frightened. Her uncle, however, explains, "That's all that brave means—not thinking about the dangers. Just thinking about what you must do. Of course you were frightened. I was too, today. But you kept your mind on what you had to do . . ." (p. 123). Lois Lowry explicitly hands readers her wisdom about the virtue of bravery.

Implicit Theme

Not stated, but implied in *What Jamie Saw*, is the important theme that parents are human and experience a range of complex emotions. While Patty's love for her children is unconditional and fiercely protective, at times she cannot find it within herself to offer Jamie the words of comfort that he wants to hear. In *Number the Stars*, the undercurrent of lying that runs through the story asks readers to accept that lying is justifiable, under certain circumstances.

Critical Response: Point of View

As authors write the first page of their stories, they may not know how their storylines will ultimately unfold or the extent to which certain characters will change. However, they must know who is going to tell the story and must hold this point of view constant. In deciding who will narrate a story, authors deliberate on the strengths and limitations of each of the following point-of-view possibilities (Lukens, 1995).

First-Person Point of View

The allure of first-person narration, with its use of the personal pronoun *I*, is powerful. As readers, we become one with the narrator. We know the narrator's every thought, every fear, every dream. It is as if the narrator says, "Here, take my diary and read it so you will know me and care about me." In *Missing May*, we empathize with Summer, who is forced to cope not only with the loss of her mother and her Aunt May but also with the fear of yet another abandonment by her grieving Uncle Ob. However, while we sink deeply into Summer's world, we bob on the surface of Ob's world. Because Summer tells the story, we learn about the unbearable grief that Ob is enduring, but because Ob doesn't talk to us, we don't feel his grief directly.

Omniscient Point of View

If Cynthia Rylant had chosen to pursue the omniscient point of view—the point of view of the all-knowing narrator, told in third person—for *Missing May*, readers would have entered Ob's pain at losing May, his obsession with contacting May, and his shattered dream. We also would have known why Cletus didn't take Summer's reproaches to heart, and why he believed in Ob's dream. The omniscient narrator would have filled in many of the gaps about which we can only speculate. But, in the process, we would have lost some of our intimacy with Summer. Books such as *Tuck Everlasting* by Natalie Babbit, *Charlotte's Web* by E. B. White, and *The Lion, the Witch and the Wardrobe*, by C. S. Lewis are superb examples of omniscient narration.

Limited Omniscient Point of View

When the all-knowing point of view is limited to one or two characters, often the main protagonist, and is written in the third person, the narration is considered limited omniscient. Carolyn Coman chose to tell both *What Jamie Saw* and *Tell Her Everything* from the limited omniscient perspective. While the words and actions of other characters enhance our understanding of the main protagonists, we are not privy, in any significant way, to their thoughts. For example, we don't know how Jamie's mother feels about deserting Van, about living in the middle of nowhere with two young children, and about not having enough money to buy Christmas presents.

Likewise, we don't know what Roz's uncle, Mike, thought when he found Roz missing or when he attended Roz's burial ceremony for her mother.

Objective Point of View

In "Silver Packages," one of Cynthia Rylant's short stories in *Children of Christmas*, Frankie awaits the yearly arrival of the Christmas Train and the silver package that a rich man tosses to him. He prays that the silver package will contain a doctor's kit. The first year, he receives socks and a cowboy holster set; the next year, mittens and a police car. Wishing as he might, Frankie never receives the doctor's kit. Frankie grows up, leaves the hills where he spent his childhood, and returns home in later years as a doctor to return the kindness that marked his childhood Christmases. This synopsis parallels Rylant's objective telling of this tale. Rylant does not give readers access to Frankie's thoughts, just to his actions and his words. It is up to the reader to fill in the blanks. A number of the other short stories in *Children of Christmas* also adopt this stark, objective narration.

Because authors such as Cynthia Rylant, Avi, and Lois Lowry experiment with a range of narration styles, their works are invitations to this aspect of their literary craft. Although research exists on the degree to which children understand the perspectives of characters in stories (Bruce, 1984; Shannon, Kameenui, and Baumann,

1988), we do not know much about children's understandings of authorial point of view. We don't know, for example, whether Lukens's (1995) speculation that "the objective or nearly objective point of view in some stories makes heavier demands on the imagination and the understanding of the reader" (p. 140), or Cullinan and Galda's (1994) assertion that first-person narration "can sometimes be too intense for many readers" (p. 226) holds true for young readers.

Principle Four: Biographical Response Heightens and Intensifies the Literary Experience

Author as Person

Recall the opening scenario at the beginning of Chapter 2 in which Ms. Farley uses Cynthia Rylant's autobiography to drive her author study. Each of Rylant's works is preceded by autobiographical information; the children assume the role of detectives, combing the works for biographical links. In my observations of and conversations with teachers, this approach—author study as biography—is by far the most popular. As this chapter has emphasized, though, launching an author study with biography compromises readers' personal encounters with the author's literature.

In my experience, when children first come to know an author's works, they show a much greater readiness to know the author. As the next chapter reveals, I implemented a Mem Fox author study at the end of the school year with third graders. In the fall, eight months prior to the author study, the children listened to *Night Noises* and watched the Mem Fox videotape (Trumpet, 1992) as part of their literature program. When the author study began in June, not one child mentioned the Mem Fox video. As they began to offer hunches about Mem Fox, no reference was made to the videotape. Even when they rewatched the video on the final day of the author study, only one child recalled seeing the video. (He thought he had seen it at home on *Reading Rainbow*.) Even more surprisingly, his recollection did not trigger awareness on the part of his peers. What should we make of this curious situation? It doesn't seem unreasonable to expect young children to hold some information about Mem Fox over the school year. After all, we strive to engage children in curricular experiences that nurture the active construction of knowledge with the goal of long-term retention. Indeed, I suspect that it is this lack of active construction that contributed to the lack of recall with regard to Mem Fox. Because the third graders didn't have an opportunity to come to know Mem Fox as a person through her literature, they didn't have a scaffold to anchor their new learnings from the videotape.

Although no research appears to have been pursued in the area of biographical response, informal data across the author studies in this book suggest that some young readers, of their own accord, do link authors' lives to their literature. Recall the responses of two sixth graders to *What Jamie Saw* after reading the first two chapters:

> I wonder if the author was abused when she was little by her father or maybe it was her sister who was hurt.

> I think the author had a weird childhood. Maybe her father threw her baby sister across the room and frightened her and that's why she wrote this book.

These speculations prompted other students to venture guesses about Carolyn Coman. Moreover, guesses continued to be offered over the course of our study of the book, even when discussions emphasized personal response. For example, during the discussion of Chapter 6, the sixth graders shared events in their lives that paralleled Jamie's—being so frightened that they vomited, being so angry that they threw temper tantrums. In the midst of these sharings, Mark announced, "I think that Carolyn Coman swore a lot as a kid or maybe she just likes swearing. She has a lot of swears in the book." Unsolicited biographical hunches also occurred during critical analyses. When the sixth graders were asked to speculate about Carolyn's repeated reference to magic and Christmas in *What Jamie Saw*, a number of biographical links were offered (Figure 3-3).

These and other biographical comments that children offered during the author studies profiled in this book suggest that children assume that works of fiction are autobiographical profiles—what happens to characters in stories is what happened to the author in real life. From where does this author awareness emerge? I suspect that the thrust of their authorial understandings comes from the message that the writing experts have urged us to pass along to young readers:

> Writing comes from the events in our daily lives. . . . The writer's first act is to listen and observe the details of living. (Graves, 1994, p. 36)

> Not so very long ago, we urged teachers to bring children's lives into the classrooms, because then writers wouldn't be able to hide behind excuses like, "I have nothing to write about" and "Nothing happens in my life." Now we realize that the reason to invite children's lives into the classroom has no less to do with finding topics for writing than with the fact that we cannot learn unless we're alive to our existence. . . . Literacy is inseparable from living. (Calkins, 1991, pp. 12–13)

Children are taught to record personal experiences in their writer's notebooks (Calkins, 1991) and to transform these experiences into fiction and nonfiction. It is not a big leap for children to internalize that published writers, also, dip into the well of life. However, as the sixth graders in the Carolyn Coman author study discovered, many authors not only transform a personal event during the creative process, leaving few autobiographical traces, but also turn to historical or current events for story creation.

The culmination of the sixth-grade author study—an interview with Carolyn Coman—brings much energy to the biographical phase of the study. After both of Carolyn's books have been read and discussed, the biographical hunches, generated over time but not formally analyzed, become the focal point. The students, working in groups, are asked to assess the strength of these hunches in conjunction with the literary clues across both books, and to generate and to substantiate new hunches. Because so many hunches are offered, we establish an "interview committee" comprised of one member from each table group to sort the responses and to present a slate of viable hunches to the class. I work with the committee to prioritize these hunches. Then, the interview questions are shared with the class and further discussion ensues. For example, some students have reservations about the hunch that Carolyn likes to swear. Mark, who suggested it early on, thinks we should keep the question; others think it might embarrass her. I suggest the compromise that Mark ask Carolyn about swearing after the official interview; he agrees. Figure 3-6 presents the hunches generated by the sixth graders along with Carolyn's illuminating and poignant responses.

Carolyn Coman Interview: Author as Person

JOHNATHAN: As we read your books, we wondered about you as a person. We brainstormed six hunches about you that we would like to share. After we read each hunch, can you tell us if our hunch is on the right track?

CHRISTINE: Family is very important to you. Patty, Jamie, and Nin are very close and love each other a lot. Roz is so close to her mother that she can't let go. Is this hunch on the right track?

CAROLYN: This is completely on the right track. No matter what I set out to do, I seem to end up writing about family. You take your family with you your whole life, for better or for worse. There are things about your family that help you and things that hurt you—things you have to get over and things that you save as you go along in life. I'm always interested in family, and probably will continue writing about it.

NICOLE: We thought you might have had family problems. Maybe your parents were divorced because of abuse. Maybe your family didn't have a lot of money and couldn't afford Christmas gifts. Maybe your mother died when you were young. Are any of these hunches on the right track?

CAROLYN: No, the families I write about are not my family. I made up these families. My mother did die five years ago when I was in my thirties, so I didn't lose her when I was twelve years old the way Roz did. My parents were not divorced and did not fight. I did not witness the kind of violence that Jamie saw. But I know of people who had situations close to the one in the books. I also read about these situations and I learn about them when I work with groups of children. Sometimes I remember little things I know about these children and I use them in stories. And then I elaborate on what I know. But I didn't know *that* much about these children so mostly I make up what happens to them in my stories. Almost everything I write comes from an emotion or feeling that I have inside myself, but the actual people and circumstances are not the ones of my family, of my parents. That's why I like fiction. It gives me freedom.

FIGURE 3-6 *Sixth graders interview Carolyn Coman about autobiographical connections*

NICOLE: You are a rather private person. The characters in your books keep to themselves. They have hardly any friends. For example, when Mrs. Desrochers comes to visit, neither Patty nor Jamie want her there in the beginning. Is this hunch on the right track?

CAROLYN: Yes, again. I am a very private person and I'm becoming more private. I have a lot of friends, but only a few very very close friendships. I tend to want a very deep connection with someone or not at all. I'm not someone who likes to go to parties. I don't like to make small talk with people. I really like to have heart-to-heart conversation. Part of me is a little bit of a hermit, and I have noticed that when I write my books, I tend to have people who are fairly isolated, who are not a part of a bigger community. That must be coming from my sense of myself. A lot of times when I'm writing a story and I give it to my friends to critique, they ask: "Well what about the character's friends. What do they do after school? What music do they listen to?" They want more of that side of my characters but that's not what I'm after. I'm more interested about what's going on inside my characters' heads and hearts. What they think, what they're feeling inside but maybe not saying out loud. That's what really interests me more than their social connections.

MATT: You are an emotional person. Your characters are very emotional. Jamie cries; Patty cries. Jamie kicks everything around him when he's upset. You'd probably cry watching *Bambi*.

CAROLYN: YES [laughing]! Not only did I cry watching *Bambi*, I could barely stand to read *Hansel and Gretel* to my daughter when she was a little girl, because the mother makes the father abandon these children and I just couldn't stand it. My daughter would say, "Mom, it's just a story, keep reading." Yes, I'm very emotional and I respond to certain things in a very heartfelt way. There are many things that I don't care about, but the things that interest me get me, and I feel deeply about them.

JOHNATHAN: You are determined and independent. Both mothers, Patty and Ellie, had to raise their families on their own. The fathers were irresponsible or abusive. Even when the odds were against them, these mothers did everything they could to protect and to love their children.

CAROLYN: These questions are blowing my mind! I've never had such intriguing questions, really. The hunch that I'm independent? Yes, that's quite true. And yes, I'm determined. It's really interesting to write stories and then to stand back, to look at what I've said, and then to get feedback from readers about how I portray, for example, the women and men in my books. When I write stories I have to be true to the characters. I tend to write about children and I definitely tend to write about strong women. The men in my stories do seem be more mixed, but there's Earl and there's Mike. There are strong and decent male characters even though some other male characters are troublesome and confusing. But they all came out of me. So your hunch about my being determined and independent is very accurate.

CHRISTINE: You are a religious person. Throughout *Tell Me Everything*, you mention Bible stories like Abraham and Isaac, and Jesus.

CAROLYN: I was so amazed when I was writing *Tell Me Everything* and those Bible stories started creeping in. I thought, "Where are these coming from?" I was not reading the Bible at the time and I was not going to church, but they kept coming up because I was raised Catholic. My mother was a very devout Catholic and I went to a strict convent school from second to eighth grade. It was an in-

FIGURE 3-6 (*Continued*)

tense experience that gave me a lot of religious training. So when I start to write, of course those experiences come up. Whatever is happening to you right now in your lives is going to come out of you in some way when you get older. I do consider myself a spiritual person. Spirituality is very important to me, but I make the distinction between being religious and being spiritual, perhaps because I'm not a member of a church anymore. But issues about who we are, about why we do what we do, about the meaning of what we do, are essential to me, so they are essential to my writing. And the answers that people have about these questions are considered spiritual or religious.

MATT: How much can readers guess about an author from his or her books?

CAROLYN: Well, with the exception of the part of my family in my books, you guessed a lot. So I think you can know probably the most important things about an author from what they write. Whenever you write anything, you reveal yourself. Whenever you write a story, you tell something about who you are, what interests you, what you think is funny. You write about your take on life. It just comes out no matter what you write. One of the reasons I like fiction is that I can reveal myself without losing my own privacy. I'm not telling you the facts of my life. I'm telling you the most important beliefs of my life. So I think that you can tell a great deal, but you can't assume that what authors write about in fiction is based on their own personal experiences.

JOHNATHAN: Did anything in your books happen in your life?

CAROLYN: A lot of the little details in my books are part of my life. In *Tell Me Everything,* there is a snow storm and then it starts to thunder. I experienced that storm when I lived in the North Country in New Hampshire. The details about a heron that flew across the road and looked like a dinosaur—that happened to me. I know the places of both *What Jamie Saw* and *Tell Me Everything. Tell Me Everything* takes place in Newburyport where I live now. There's a real graveyard in Newburyport where I spent a lot of time walking around while I was writing the book. And there is a little house at the entrance to the graveyard that I imagined Roz living in. I've never been in it, but it was the one I pictured when I wrote about it. So it's real in that sense. *What Jamie Saw* takes place in the North Country where I lived for five years. So there are lots of small details that I drew from my own experiences, but I put them into a story in a different way. When you write stories, it's a good idea to use a setting you know well so that you can describe it with authority and provide details that you know are true. That doesn't mean that you have to talk about what actually happened to you when you lived in these places but you can write about a place that's very real.

CHRISTINE: Which characters in your books are you most like?

CAROLYN: There's probably some of me in every character. A number of my friends, after reading *What Jamie Saw,* told me Patty has my voice, which surprised me because I don't hear that. But they said, "Oh no, that's how you talk to your kids—that's your tone of voice." Like Patty and Roz's mother, I have a fierce love for my children. But, in many ways, I'm not Patty at all. There's not a character whom I think is all me by any means. They may start out modeled on someone— me or someone else. Jamie started out modeled on a child in my daughter's fourth-grade class who had a lot going on in his life and was dealing with it in an original way. But then Jamie became Jamie, his own self, his own original character. So I think the characters stand on their own

FIGURE 3-6 (*Continued*)

> NICOLE: Do you have a favorite author, and what is it about this author that makes you want to read his or her books?
>
> CAROLYN: Well, I have many favorite authors. I go through spells of reading where I focus on one author or one subject for a while. In terms of books for children and young adults, one of my favorite authors is Brock Cole, who wrote a wonderful book called *Goats*. And there's a new author called Adam Rapp who has a book coming out called *The Buffalo Tree*. He's a great writer and he has a big heart. This question always makes me think I can't even begin to mention all the people whom I love so much, all the poets and the adult writers and the artists of picture books. One characteristic that I respond to, though, across the board is an author who uses language in a way that I love to read the words and think about how they sound. Another very important characteristic of a favorite author is that he or she is saying something that moves my heart because I am an emotional person. I look for something that reaches in and grabs my heart and makes me feel something.

FIGURE 3-6   (*Continued*)

Author as Writer

Biographical study includes the search not only for the life experiences, aspirations, and motivations of authors, but also their approach to writing. Figure 3-7 presents the questions sixth graders asked Carolyn Coman about her life as a writer. Carolyn's responses not only demystify the writing process and affirm what all writers know—writing is hard work—but also help students see the very human side of authors.

Note that Carolyn's response to the question "Where do you get your ideas?" in Figure 3-7 parallels Avi's (1982) response to the same question:

> The answer is everywhere. Ideas don't come whole cloth. They are amalgams of random thoughts, observations, moods, squeezed into shape by the way I look upon the world. For example, my book *Sometimes I Think I Hear My Name* is based on a) the particular living circumstances of a kid I knew; b) a remark about locale by a writer friend; c) a passing reference by my wife to the way some kids were living; d) the off chance remark of another friend of a parent, and e) a quote from Ross MacDonald, "Most fiction is shaped by geography and permeated by autobiography, even when it is trying not to be." (p. 18)

In essence, both Carolyn and Avi soak up the world around them and then infuse—directly or indirectly—life's savory bits into story. This phenomenon, known in the literary world as intertextuality, marks the links that writers forge between what they have seen, heard, or read and what they write. In the words of Bakhtin (1986), writers echo the "words of others . . . then assimilate, rework and reaccentuate" (p. 86).

74

Carolyn Coman Interview: Author as Writer

MATT: When we read *What Jamie Saw*, we decided that you made Jamie interested in magic for the following reasons: a) it made him a more interesting character, b) it served as an escape for Jamie during this scary situation, and c) the fact that Jamie kept doing the magic made us hope that the story would have a magical ending and everything would work out. Did you choose magic for any or all of these reasons?

CAROLYN: Interesting observations. I didn't choose magic so much as it chose me. In Jamie's case, I knew he was a quiet child who stayed to himself. The magic just came to me—almost out of nowhere. I didn't sit down and think, "Oh, I'm going to have Jamie do something that's going to distract him from what's going on." Jamie's a kid, and it just came to me that he would like magic. Afterwards, I was aware that the magic did serve the purposes you mentioned—that it did seem right for Jamie and for the story. But I didn't think about magic consciously at first; it was a gift of my imagination. The funny thing is, I don't like magic. I'm not very interested in it, and when I see magic shows, I don't like them. There's something about them that annoys me. And so, as a writer, I almost wished that it wasn't magic, but I knew that it was Jamie, and so I stuck with it. I sent away to a magic company for some magic tricks that I did with my son who was five or six years old at the time and I figured out how to do the tricks. I could see how much it captured my son's imagination, so that's why I stayed with it. But I think what you said about the uses of magic in the book are exactly true.

JOHNATHAN: The ending of *What Jamie Saw* reminded us of the book *Under the Blood Red Sun*, because we weren't really sure what happened to the characters. Why did you leave the ending this way?

CAROLYN: Well, this is a very interesting question that I have been asked a number of times by sixth-grade readers. And the fact that readers keep asking me this question tells me that you wanted more than I gave you. For me, this book is about a journey of going from a place of being really afraid to a place of not being so afraid; not completely safe, but safer. I wanted this book to be about an emotional journey. For me that journey ended at that point where Jamie, who had been so terribly afraid of facing Van alone, found the courage to face him and to protect his sister. Van had come and gone and done no harm to anybody and Patty had told him not to come back. And I said, "That's the moment." Everybody is a little bit safer and better off; it was as far as I could bring them. So that's where I stopped because I had done what I set out to do. When I was first writing the book, I wanted a magical ending where everyone would be happy and safe, where there would be enough money. I wanted Patty to be able to go back to school; I wanted the best for everyone because I love these characters. But I realized quickly that I could only get them to a certain point, and that's where I stopped. One of the best letters I got from a sixth grader said, "We didn't even find out what he got for Christmas," which I thought was brilliant! I'm really going to think about this when I write my next book. I had brought it far enough for me, but had I brought it far enough for my readers? So I really appreciate feedback like this. Probably I needed to put in a little bit more than I did. A bit of a mistake actually.

CHRISTINE: Before reading the ending, we made the prediction that Patty and Earl would get married so that Jamie and Nin would finally have a loving family. Are you planning a sequel to *What Jamie Saw*, and if so will our prediction come true?

FIGURE 3-7 *Sixth graders interview Carolyn Coman about her writing process*

CAROLYN: I'm not planning a sequel now. As I said, I did what I set out to do with *Jamie* and I've gone on to other stories and characters. I suppose it's possible at some point that I might start thinking again about what happened to Jamie and Patty, and it may come to me to write a sequel. It does seem to make sense that she and Earl would get together but, in my heart of hearts, I think they'll be friends for the rest of their lives but I don't think they'll get married. I think if that was to happen, it would have already happened.

NICOLE: Where did you get the name Nin for Jamie's little sister?

CAROLYN: Nin, I love that name! And I heard it twenty years ago. There's a writer named Jack Kerouac, a beat writer, and he had a sister named Carolyn whose nickname was Nin. I don't even know who told me that, but I had never heard the name before and I liked it. I like one-syllable names: Roz, Nin, Van, Earl. They are just down to earth, common, good sounding names. So I always wanted to use the name, Nin, and I got a chance in this story.

MATT: Did you write *What Jamie Saw* during Christmas time?

CAROLYN: No, it wasn't because of Christmas time. When I saw Patty come out holding a bag of toys I thought, "Oh just like Santa Claus," so I included it. And then it kept coming up over and over again in the book. But when I first wrote the book, it took place over a longer period of time and it was my editor who suggested that I condense it to make it happen in a shorter period of time so I backed it up to Christmas. The decision to stop the story on Christmas Eve really influenced a lot of things. So it was just that one image of Patty standing with a bag of toys that reminded me of Santa Claus and that set other things in motion.

JOHNATHAN: Where do you get your ideas for stories?

CAROLYN: Because I'm a storyteller, I feel free to use anything from anywhere. I eavesdrop on conversations. People tell me things and I use them. I read the newspaper. I use things my parents told me growing up. These are the ingredients of my work. I feel free to use any detail that is given me or that I hear or that I see as long as I do it respectfully—as long as I don't use it to make fun of people or invade their privacy or tell a secret that they don't want me to tell. What inspires me to write any story is to figure out what matters to me. With Roz, I wondered how a young girl makes sense of losing someone she loved so much. Grief is a big question. With Jamie, it was that sense of fear. How do you get over being really afraid? That's something I've asked myself as an adult. These are the kinds of questions that matter to me, that I think about and worry about.

NICOLE: Do you ever get writer's block and can't think of anything to write?

CAROLYN: I don't suffer from writer's block the way some writers do in that I don't go through long periods of time where I feel absolutely unable to write anything. My version of writer's block is that I go through periods of time where I write but don't like what I write. But I know I have to go through those times to get to the times where it's right. For example, the new book that I'm writing now, I had to write a whole version of it to find out what it really was about. And then I started over. I can usually write something, but it's not always clear to me what it is.

CHRISTINE: What is it about writing that makes you want to write?

CAROLYN: I have to write. If I don't write, I feel as if I start to die. It's that elemental. It's not that it's so much fun. I usually don't feel great about my work at the end of the day. Some days go well, but a lot of days are just a grind. But I do it because I

FIGURE 3-7   (*Continued*)

believe in something bigger. I know that if I sit with a story and really work on it, I will eventually say something that matters. When I was in sixth grade at that convent school, we had to write a lot of stories because there was a real importance placed on writing. It mattered to me even then to write good stories; I was willing to spend the time on my writing more than on subjects like math that I didn't like so much. So writing for me is just like breathing—I have to do it. And I'm lucky I have that, I really am. A lot of people don't have something that they feel so passionately about. This passion is a gift. But I have to show up and do the work. I just can't sit and wait for this genius gift to spring into my mind. I have to do it and do it and do it and write it and throw it out and write it again.

MATT: When you were writing *What Jamie Saw*, did you outline the whole story ahead of time or did you make it up as you went along?

CAROLYN: I never outline the whole story ahead of time, because I never know what it is. I do it as I go along. Every once in a while I get a sense, "Oh, maybe this thing is going to happen further down the road." I'll get an idea or an image but I still won't know where it fits. It's like a puzzle. Basically, I start with what I'm given. I start with an idea. I have a little boy. A very scary thing has happened that he's witnessed, and the story is going to be about his life as this moment unfolds. Then I just have to watch it. I do tend to start at the beginning and go pretty much in order to the end. I'm always in awe of writers who do get an idea, plot out an outline, and then sit down and write it out. I have a much messier, disorganized, unconscious way of writing. But I trust it. It's different for everybody, but that's my way.

JOHNATHAN: What kind of writing process do you use? Do you write your whole book and then go back and make revisions? Or do you keep changing things after you write a few pages?

CAROLYN: I do both. When I'm writing a chapter, I have to get it to a certain point before I can go on to the next chapter. So I'll write a whole chapter and then I'll fiddle with the words to a point where I feel that I've got the words and ideas right. I do this by reading the chapter out loud so that I can hear it. But after all the chapters are written, I have to stand back and look at the whole story and figure out the changes that need to be made. At this point, it's not so much word-by-word editing. Rather, I ask myself questions like: Do readers need to know this sooner? Do I need to tell more about this character here, and so forth. So I revise during and after the story.

CHRISTINE: Is there ever a time when you are writing that you ask yourself why you became a writer and not something else?

CAROLYN: Yes. But it's not a question of "not something else" because I don't know what else I would do, really. But there are days when I think, I must be out of my mind to want to do this because it's so hard and it matters so much and when I don't do it well, I feel kind of lost. But deeper than that is knowing that I'm really lucky to have something that I love that much.

FIGURE 3-7 (*Continued*)

Mem Fox (1992) is forthright about the pervasiveness of intertextual links in her own writing:

> . . . the rhyme scheme and the setting grabbed unconsciously from *The Rime of the Ancient Mariner* to use in my *Sail Away*; the last line of *Possum Magic*, "And she did," nicked quietly from the story of *The Little Red Hen*; a couple of phrases—"Now it came to pass" and "in peace and unafraid"—in *Feathers and Fools*, whipped straight from the Bible; the underlying theme of Pat Hutchins's *Rosie's Walk* lifted unwittingly for my *Hattie and the Fox*, and so on. (pp. 183–184)

Recent studies have traced the vitality of intertextuality in children's writing. When sixth graders were asked "Do you ever think of stories you've read when you are writing a story?" 90 percent acknowledged that they borrowed ideas from story plots they had read or heard, though rarely copying the plots verbatim (Carney, 1990). When third graders were asked about intertextual links between fairy tales they had heard and then wrote, only 61 percent verbalized intertextual links. However, analysis of actual stories revealed that every child had incorporated, to varying degrees, fairy tale leads, characters, or plot details into their own stories (Bearse, 1992). Even children as young as six not only respin tales that they have heard but also rework ideas of peers (Carney, 1992). These findings suggest that children understand intuitively that:

> Stories lean on stories, art on art. And we who are the tellers and the artists do what has been done for all the centuries of tellings: We thieve or (more politely) borrow and then we make it our own. (Yolen, 1991, p. 147)

There is no reason, however, to leave intertextuality at the intuitive level. Author studies allow us to bring children inside this most fundamental facet of the writing process.

Principle Five: Children Are Drawn to Meaningful Endeavors and Learn Best Through Interaction with More Knowledgeable Others

A central premise of any author-study design is the belief in the constructive powers of young minds and the commitment to engage these powers in a real-world curriculum. A century ago, John Dewey insisted that language instruction must spring from a "real desire to communicate vital impressions and convictions" (p. 66), and that "education must be conceived as continuing reconstruction of experience. . . ." (1897/1959). With the advent of the literature-based programs, Dewey's beliefs about authentic literacy instruction have been revived. As Cambourne (1988) writes, "Teachers need to create settings in which learners experience an urgent need to read and write in order to achieve ends other than learning about reading and writing" (p. 64).

Carole Edelsky (1991), a proponent of authentic curriculum, argues that in order for a literary event to be authentic, it must: a) engage learners in meaning making, b) be viewed as purposeful by learners and not as an assignment, and c) place the learner in the position of the subject, not the object, of the event. Essentially, the learner must decide how, when, and where the literacy event will occur. Edelsky insists that all three criteria are interconnected—omission of even one condition annuls the event's authenticity.

Edelsky is firm in her belief about the intellectual capabilities of children and in her trust in their seriousness of purpose. However, author studies cast from this perspective surrender the curriculum to children lock, stock, and barrel and, in the process, negate the place of the teacher.

The work of the social-constructivists in recent years has shown that literacy surges occur within the social context of the home and the classroom through interaction with more knowledgeable others: more capable peers and teachers. A significant aspect of this interaction is both formal and informal instruction. As Vygotsky (1962) writes, "What the child can do in cooperation today he can do alone tomorrow. Therefore the only good kind of instruction is that which marches ahead of development and leads it; it must be aimed not so much at the ripe as at the ripening functions" (p. 104).

The best author studies are those that turn on the continual collaboration of teachers and students. Children's ideas about authentic adventures need to be actively solicited and judged in terms of their educative values. If their ideas are viable and not in conflict with other instructional priorities, they should be embraced.

Concluding Comments

If an author study is to move, to enlighten, and to instruct young minds, it must respect the multiplicity of response that readers bring to an author's works. It must acknowledge the continual interplay of aesthetic, critical, and biographical thought that swirls during the act of reading. It also must address the pivotal question as to which dimension—the aesthetic, the critical, the biographical—receives attention during the author study. This chapter has attempted to answer this question by offering five principles to guide the creation and implementation of author study as multiple response:

1. Readers respond in multiple ways to an author's works.
2. Aesthetic engagement must precede critical and biographical response.
3. Critical response deepens and extends the literary experience.
4. Biographical response heightens and intensifies the literary experience.

79

5. Children are drawn to meaningful endeavors and learn best through interaction with more knowledgeable others.

The following chapter describes an author study on Mem Fox implemented in a third-grade classroom. It puts into practice, with varying degrees of success, the essential principles of author study as multiple response. This author study prioritizes aesthetic response because children need to "live" the literature before they analyze it for critical or biographical elements. Whenever feasible, this author study takes its lead from the children.

Author Response:
Carolyn Coman on Author Studies

I have to admit feeling a bit the impostor responding to Carol's chapters on her author's study involving my work. What I do is *write* the books! I am no expert in teaching them, critiquing them, and certainly no expert when it comes to educational theories. Nonetheless, what she says, and what she and the kids did in the classroom, make perfect sense to me, since the ways she suggests responding to reading resonate deeply with the way I write. I write first and foremost to make a deeper sense of things that matter to me, ideas and questions and personalities and relationships that have meaning to me, that I want to understand more fully, that I want to see transformed. I write to find connections that I believe are there (all the time, in everything) but that I can't see, somehow, without words and story. Without an initial caring and interest and connection, nothing at all could happen. A fully realized and satisfying story could never emerge from something I tackled purely as a critical exercise, or from a superficially camouflaged version of some event in my own life. I have to wander into material that is ripe, malleable, complex, human, there for the probing, and only then can I move on to the very hard and conscious work of shaping, honing, pushing forward, intensifying. And at that point, a critical vocabulary of structure and craft is extremely useful. What is driving my narrative? Is the character emotionally true? Is the voice authentic and consistent? These are among the many questions that must be asked—and answered—but that can only come once I have been sufficiently engaged by the story itself. (It was the same, for me, with punctuation: I learned punctuation—to the extent that I *did* learn punctuation—only when I understood that it helped people read what I'd written the way I wanted it read: pause *there*; stop *there*; understand that a character is actually saying these words. Then came the appropriate squiggles and marks—in more or less—the right place.)

There are all sorts of ways to enter into a book—as a writer *and* a reader—and I'm a big believer in doing whatever works. All I know is that it has to matter to you at some level. There has to be a point of connection—one that is nearly always available in fiction thanks to the embracing scope of humanity! When my daughter was in the ninth grade, she was assigned to read (as I had been, nearly thirty years earlier) *To Kill a Mockingbird*. When I asked her what she thought of it, she told me, "It's a book I could have loved, Mom." She was referring to the endless lists of questions she was forced to answer chapter by chapter proving only that she had read the words and retained certain information from each chapter. The approach had effectively killed the story for her, and she knew it.

Critical analysis helps me all the time as a writer, but it seems to me that it has to be used as a tool for understanding, in service to the content of the story, rather than an end unto itself. It was clear in the discussions and question-and-answer session I had with sixth graders that there had been a merger of the two that deepened and widened the conversation. Plus, the kids and I had a common language that made the discussion free-flowing: *plot, character, theme, symbol*—words that had meaning in terms of the story.

The students came at me and my stories from a bunch of different angles. Their hunches about me as a person based on what they saw in my stories were fun for all of us, and I shouldn't have been surprised at how on-target they were because, of course, my stories reveal me! They are of me, and everything and everyone that has shaped me. There are events and places and characteristics that I have borrowed, stored, stolen, and mixed in service to my story, and for anyone interested in looking for them, there are clues to be found, hunches to be made about me from them. Why make them? I guess because it's another connection, and sometimes it's fun, especially when the author can come in and hear the hunches and respond to them. (I'm always interested to see a picture of the person who wrote the book I'm reading, even though I'm private enough not to want my picture on my books!)

Sometimes I am conscious of the extent to which a story mirrors some aspect of my own life experience or personality. Sometimes I am not. Sometimes the connections are murky to me, and hard to express. I think the important part of this particular approach to an author's work is in helping the reader understand that writing, like all art, is a revealing act. We allow others to see and know us through the work that we create, at any age, at any level.

One of the reasons I write of and for children is that I find their thinking so interesting, funny, fresh. I am constantly amazed by what some children carry, shoulder, find ways of coming to terms with. Their own stories, and their responses to my stories, continually reinforce that belief. They need to be asked the great big questions that we wonder about ourselves, and listened to as they puzzle out some answers.

Opening a child to appreciating reading has to be among the most important work in the world, truly a gift that goes on giving. Since my father became blind a number of years ago, the books-on-tape he listens to daily, supplied free through the Library of Congress, have been a lifeline for him. They are as important to him as breath, his connection to lives and experiences and information that keeps him linked to the world. I'm thankful that Carol has turned her intelligence and insight to thinking about just what makes clear and good sense in exploring authors' works. In her study of my books, there was a way "in" for everyone. I'm flattered that she chose my small body of work to consider, and privileged to have seen the results.

CAROLYN COMAN

4

Picture-Book Author Study:
Featured Author: Mem Fox

In her autobiography, *Dear Mem Fox, I Have Read All Your Books Even the Pathetic Ones*, Fox (1992) writes:

> In my experience the best-loved picture books are so well written that they leave a lasting impression on the reader. . . . They have a passionate quality. By *passion* I mean a constant undercurrent of tension combined with compassion, which makes readers care desperately about the fate of the main characters. It's not easy to achieve, but I'm convinced that writing without passion is writing for oblivion. (p. 148)

Indeed, it is this passion that envelops us as we read Mem Fox's *Koala Lou*, *Possum Magic*, and *Night Noises*. We ache with Koala Lou when she is pricked by sibling jealousy and cheer on her efforts to rewin her mother's love. We commiserate with Grandma Poss's desire to protect Hush, but applaud Hush's decision to become visible. We celebrate Lily Laceby's long life and sing "Happy Birthday" to her along with her "two sons, her three daughters, her fourteen grandchildren, her thirty-five great-grand children, her great-great grandchild, Emily. . . ." These stories are even more compelling because they spring from Mem's life experiences (see Figure 4-11 on page 110).

This chapter profiles an author study on Mem Fox that was implemented with a classroom of third graders. It begins with a description of these third graders as readers and writers, and of the literacy program that nurtured their literacy engagement. It then replays each day of the author study and concludes with reflections that will be explored in finer detail in the next chapter.

Classroom Context

The children who participated in this author study at the end of the school year live in a literature-rich, literacy-intensive classroom. Their passion for and engagement with reading and writing manifests itself in cubbies filled with books, in their eagerness to talk about books with anyone who will listen, and in their pleas to continue writing even when writing time has ended. During writing workshop (Atwell, 1987; Calkins, 1991), these third graders choose their own topics, genres, and writing timelines. Each writing workshop usually opens with a ten- to fifteen-minute minilesson. These minilessons, which spring from the children's writing needs and interests, focus on wide array of topics such as the strategies and basic skills that experienced writers use, the writing process, the range of genres, and the literary elements. A half hour of sustained silent writing follows the minilesson. During this time, Alice Earle, the classroom teacher, confers with individual writers about current projects. The writing workshop often ends with partner sharing.

In daily reading workshop (Atwell, 1987), these third graders select their own books, keep reading logs, read at their own pace, and write dialogue journal entries—letters to Alice in which they are encouraged to adopt an aesthetic stance to literature (Rosenblatt, 1978). In addition to minilessons on the aesthetic stance that take place early in the year, the third graders are encouraged to consult a reference poster that contains personal response questions (e.g., "What did you think about or feel as you read the story?") while writing their dialogue journal entries. Alice writes back to each student, responding to comments and sharing her own thoughts. Minilessons, conferences with peers and with teachers, as well as group share time also are integral parts of the reading workshop. Although the third graders had read a wide variety of literature, they had not participated in an author study during the school year—until Mem Fox came their way at the end of the year.

Mem Fox Author Study

Armed only with the principles discussed in Chapter 3 and my first lesson, I decide to allow this journey into the literature and life of Mem Fox to take root with and to be sustained by the intellectual and emotional energy of these third graders. Admittedly, entering this author study without an instructional road map causes some trepidation, but belief in the constructive powers of the young mind propels me forward.

Day One: Koala Lou and Aesthetic Response

As the third graders gather on the rug, I place all of the Mem Fox books on my lap. I show each one by one and say, "If you've read this book, raise your hand." Hands shoot up for many of the books, especially *Koala Lou* and *Night Noises*, the two books that are in the classroom library. I express my delight that many have read some of Fox's books. I do so because it is important in any author study to ward off any grumbles that occur when children are asked to reread or to relisten to familiar books. I explain that one of the great joys of reading is to revisit a book more than once because, with each revisit, we discover something new about the story or about the author that we didn't notice during our first read. For example, I share that I had read

Koala Lou at least fifteen times before I noticed that the Bush Olympics in the story opens with the lighting of the torch.

I then tell the class that Mem Fox is one of my favorite authors and that I am eager to find out their thoughts about her books. We start our author study with *Koala Lou*, my favorite of Mem Fox's books. Prior to reading the book, I ask them "to think about something that happens in this story that reminds you about something that happened in your life. When I have finished reading the book, I'm going to ask you to write down what happened and how you felt about it." With the exception of pointing to the illustrations of Australian animals such as the emu, kookaburra, and platypus to ensure recognition, and of inviting students to read chorally the line "Koala Lou, I DO love you," I read the book from cover to cover without interruption. When the story is finished, I ask them to write their response. I also write my response to the story.

Prior to teaching the lesson, I had debated whether to model aesthetic response by sharing my piece before they began to write. Because this class already had much experience writing personal responses and because the assigned question specifically asked for a life connection, I decided to hold off. I was not disappointed.

I had predicted that most of their responses would focus on how it felt to lose a race. But I was wrong. When we shared responses, only four boys and Alice (the teacher) talk about a lost race. Eleven out of the seventeen talk about parental love. Four share positive actions they had taken to win their parents' attention and love (babysitting for a younger brother; doing better in a piano recital so Mom would say "Great job" instead of "Good job"). Seven others tie their search for parental affection to sibling rivalry. For example, Lenny prefaces the reading of his piece (Figure 4-1) with the comment, "This happened when I was in kindergarten."

When he finishes, I ask, "Who was in the picture frame?"

He replies, "Oh, just me."

Koala Lou confronted these third graders with the complex issues of parental love, of sibling rivalry, and of winning/losing and allowed many of them to look inside and then beyond themselves. I explain that just as *Koala Lou* helped them think through their feelings, so too it helped me do the same. I read my response (Figure 4-2).

As the session closes, we agree to continue our conversation about *Koala Lou* tomorrow. I line up all of the Mem Fox books and ask for suggestions about how we should proceed to read them. Students offer possibilities such as voting each time for the next book, reading them alphabetically, reading the Australian books, and reading them chronologically. Ultimately, they vote to read them in the order of publication.

As I am about to announce snack time, Kevin proposes that, after we read all of the books, we should vote on our favorite book and then write a letter to Mem Fox telling her the results. Amid unanimous support for the idea, I explain that because famous authors like Mem Fox receive many letters each month, we might want to do something extra to grab her attention. The floodgates burst open. Kate suggests that

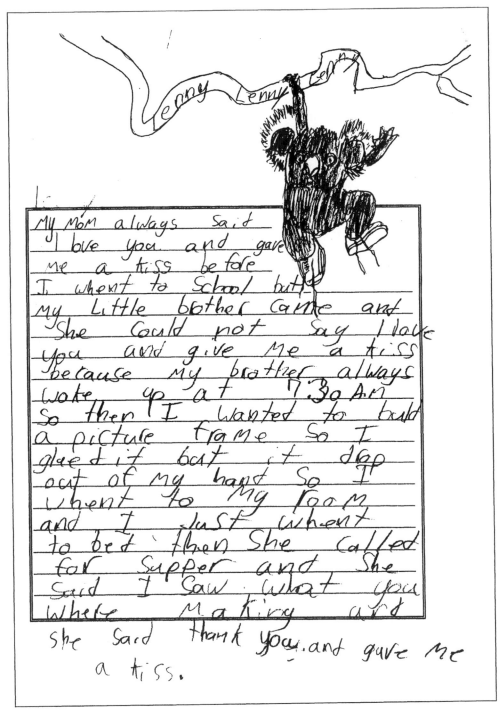

My mom always said
I love you and gave
me a kiss before
I whent to school but
my little brother came and
she could not say I love
you and give me a kiss
because my brother always
woke up at 7.30 Am
so then I wanted to build
a picture frame so I
glued it but it drop
out of my hand so I
whent to my room
and I just whent
to bed then she called
for supper and she
said I saw what you
where making and
she said thank you and gave me
a tiss.

FIGURE 4-1 *Lenny's personal response to* Koala Lou

When I read the part where Koala Lou is sad because her mother is too busy to say, "Koala Lou, I DO love you," I had a startling thought. I could not remember the last time my mother said, "Carol, I love you." Even when I reach back to when I was in third grade, I can't remember my mother saying those words. Then, I had an even more startling thought. I can't remember the last time I said those words— "I love you"—out loud to my mother. Oh, I've written the words on birthday cards and Mother's Day cards but I haven't said them to her.

I began to wonder, though, why, unlike Koala Lou, these startling thoughts didn't upset me. Then I realized that my mom and I don't need to say these words because in our hearts we know that our love is deep. We know this by the way we act toward one another, by the way we do caring things for each other. I also thought about the fact that my parents are Irish and do not express sentimental emotions. In many Irish homes, the only time you give your parents a hug is on special holidays like Christmas or Mother's Day. That's the way it is in my house.

FIGURE 4-2   *My personal response to* Koala Lou

we figure out Mem Fox's favorite animal by tallying the number of times that each animal is mentioned in her books and then doing a report on that animal. Kevin piggybacks on Kate's idea and proposes that the class break into teams to research different animals and then write poems because "Mem Fox might like poetry better than a report." Lenny suggests that we act out the poems and make a videotape. Molly proposes that we act out Mem's books and send her the videotape. During snack time, they continue to propose ideas—class books, dioramas, and so forth. They surround me with ideas that wouldn't have occurred to me—collaborative curriculum at its best. By day's end, they vote to make a video for Mem in which they talk about her books and show their animal reports.

Day Two: Koala Lou *and Critical Response*

As the morning bell rings, Tom bursts into the classroom with a fistful of *Wildlife Fact Files*. Each fact file is a four-page brochure on a particular animal that highlights the animal's habitat, habits, and so forth. Tom pulls out the file facts on the dingo, the wombat, and the kangaroo and tours the room with his treasures. Brittany hands me two printouts on the emu and the kookaburra from the *Microsoft Encarta* computer program that she has at home. Kate shows me a kangaroo book that she found in the classroom library. Alexis waves three fact cards she found in the classroom box of animal file cards. Their excitement is electric. I tell them I am thrilled with their first steps and encourage them to continue their search.

I begin the session by directing the students back to *Koala Lou.* I line up a series of objects: a stuffed koala, a small statue of an emu, a picture of Koala Lou's siblings, a branch, a headband, a whistle, a hat, and a handkerchief. I begin with the opening lines of the book: "Once there was a baby koala so soft and round that all who saw her loved her. Her name was . . ." I stop and they finish the sentence. I hold up the emu and say, "The _____ loved her." They fill in the blank. I ask, "Who else loved her?" Together, we move from object to object and retell the story. Their recall is so strong that they tell me I should have included other objects, such as a torch for the Bush Olympics. I begin with this retelling not because I want to check their comprehension—given the extent of their response yesterday, I know they understood the story plot—but because I want them to reexperience this splendid story.

After the reenactment, I share that I thought a lot about yesterday's personal responses and that their ideas inspired me to write some of the messages that I think Mem Fox might want us to think about when reading *Koala Lou*. I present the message tree (a blank version of Figure 4-3) and explain that I wrote what I thought is the "big" message of *Koala Lou* on the trunk, and some of the smaller messages on the branches. I explain that before I share my ideas, I want them to write their messages so that we can compare them.

Brock's message tree, presented in Figure 4-3, represents the degree of critical thought that these third graders brought to *Koala Lou*. Each child generates a minimum of two major themes; most generate three to five themes. Like Brock, more than half of the third graders pinpoint parental love and sibling rivalry as the essential themes. As Brittany puts it, "No matter how many brothers or sisters you have, your mother still loves you the same as your brothers and sisters. Don't think your mother hates you." Another group of five students link winning and losing to parental love as the primary theme. "Don't think parents hate you if you lose," writes Alexis. "You can't always win, no ones perfect." Nearly every child addresses these issues of sibling rivalry and of winning and losing as a primary or secondary theme. Other secondary themes include:

- "You don't have to do anything specail for your mom to love you."
- "Babies get more attention becaus they need more attention."
- "Try to win someone's love by trying to do the best at everything and making people proud of you."

The third graders are eager to hear what I have written on my message tree. I preface my remarks with the reminder that good readers think carefully about what authors might want us to learn from their stories. I explain that if we asked Mem Fox to complete the message tree, we'd know for certain what she wanted us to take away from *Koala Lou*. In the absence of her message tree, we have to make intelligent guesses that we can back up with evidence. As I read my messages, they delight in the degree of congruence. Although some of my messages have a slightly different twist, they note much similarity. Kevin then takes our conversation in a new direction with his comment that Mem Fox "might have had lots of brothers and sisters

FIGURE 4-3   *Brock's thematic response to Koala Lou*

and wanted attention. I think she was telling us she was sad." His comment represents our first hunch about Mem Fox. I compliment Kevin for suggesting a possible reason behind Mem Fox's messages about sibling rivalry. Two other children read their guesses about Mem Fox from their message trees: "She might have lost a race before," and "She might have had a hard time with her mother and father." The door to biographical study is now open. I share my delight and explain that as we read more of Mem's books, we may gather more evidence to support our hunches.

Day Three: Possum Magic *Invites More Biographical Response*

I introduce *Possum Magic* by passing out copies of the map of Australia that Mem Fox includes at the end of the book. Because the story includes so many unfamiliar Australian cities and Australian foods, I decide to use the map to facilitate their understanding. I explain that because the main characters in this book travel around Australia, it might be fun to track where they go as I read. Kevin barely has the map in his hands when he shouts, "Tasmania, there's Tasmania. I saw this show about the Tasmania Devil. . . ." Others who also saw this PBS program chime in with other facts. Kevin then provides a segue: "I wonder if there is a Tasmanian Devil in the book?"

Unlike *Koala Lou*, the reading of *Possum Magic* is highly interactive. We stop to identify and to speculate about the Australian wombat, kookaburra, dingo, and emu. We stop to trace the travels of Grandma Poss and Hush around Australia as they search for the ingredients of the magic potion. The third graders become as preoccupied with Australian food as they are with the animals. After the story is finished, they share their favorite part of the story:

"I like when they ate that yummy lamington."

"I like the part where Hush slides down the kangaroo's back."

"My favorite part is when they went all around Australia."

It is not until Alexis shares "the idea of being invisible" as her favorite part that a sustained conversation ensues. Lenny proclaims, "If I were invisible for a day, I would get into so much trouble." Before he has a chance to elaborate, Kenny pipes in, "I would haunt people." Not wanting to travel the road of mischievous imaginings, I interrupt and ask Alexis to explain her comment. Without any prompting, Alexis continues, "Maybe, Mem Fox wrote the book because she had some sort of experience about being ignored."

Caitlyn expands, "Maybe when she was on a trip or something and her family didn't pay any attention to her."

"Yeah, maybe she felt invisible," Alexis adds, "because her parents ignored her just like Koala Lou." The door to biographical response opens wider.

As the session closes, I decide to follow the children's lead on the two topics of intrigue—Hush's invisibility and hunches about Mem Fox. I tell them that I am fascinated with their thoughts on invisibility and ask them to write me a letter for homework in which they answer the following question:

> At the end of *Possum Magic,* Hush makes the decision to stay visible forever. If you were Hush, would you make the same decision or would you make the decision to remain invisible? Tell 3 reasons WHY.

I then attach a large piece of chart paper to the dryboard and write the words *Mem Fox* across the top. Under this heading, I write the subheading *Hunches* on one side and *Clues* on the other. I say, "Today, we did what readers often do when they read books. We formed some hunches about the author. For example, Alexis and Caitlyn offered the hunch that Mem Fox might have felt invisible because she might have been ignored by her family. I'm going to write down their hunch on the left side of the chart." I continue, "Now, it wouldn't be fair to Mem Fox if we went around making wild guesses about her. When we come up with hunches, we have to be able to offer evidence for our ideas. We have to find clues in her books that support our hunches. What clues did Alexis and Caitlyn use to create their hunch?" I record their responses on the chart. We then revisit earlier hunches that were made about Mem Fox by Kevin and others when they completed their message trees. I ask if anyone else has a new hunch about Mem Fox. Hands fly up. Molly thinks that Mem Fox loves animals, especially Australian animals. I write her hunch at the top of a new hunch chart. We talk about clues to support this hunch. I then explain that I will leave this hunch chart on the dryboard so that they can fill in their hunches and clues during free time. We break for snack time; within seconds, a group congregates at the chart.

Day Four: Australian Animals and Personal Response to Possum Magic

Today's before-school session is a replay of yesterday's—more *Wildlife Fact Files,* computer printouts, a *Ranger Rick* volume, a sister's report on the koala, and books are added to our resource library on Australian animals. When we come together, I share some nonfiction books that I bought when I was in Australia a few years ago. The third graders' fascination with Australian animals is so pronounced that they beg me to read *ABC of Australian Animals* by Steve Parish (1992). As I read the four lines of rhyming verses per page that accompany each animal photograph, they can hardly contain themselves. I stop at certain letters of the alphabet and ask them to predict the Australian animal. We are surprised in a few instances by Parish's choices. We predicted *dingo* for *d;* Parish chose *dancing duck.* We predicted *emu* for *e;* Parish chose *enchidna.* Upon completing the book, I ask how many would like to pursue Kevin's idea about doing an Australian animal report. All hands go up. We spend the next ten minutes brainstorming two lists: one of the Australian animals in Mem's books and one of possible nonfiction projects. The latter list yields ideas such as poster board displays, fact cards, brochures, poems, dioramas, and a class book. I add accordion books and flap books to the list and share examples. I ask them to come to class tomorrow with a decision about which animal they want to research. They ask if they can work with partners or teams. I tell them the decision is theirs.

The transition from Australian-animal mania to *Possum Magic* takes a few minutes. When they settle in, I show them the story grammar puzzle pieces that I have attached to the chart stand. On one side of the chart are five puzzle pieces that are labeled: *setting, characters, story problem, attempts to solve the problem,* and *resolution.* On the other side are five puzzle pieces that highlight story events or details (e.g., "Grandma Poss can't remember how to make Hush visible." "Australia."). I ask the children to work with a partner to match the events and the elements. They have no difficulty sorting the puzzle pieces. I return to the story problem and ask why Grandma Poss made Hush invisible in the first place. The response "to keep her safe from snakes and other trouble" prompts Kevin to say: "It's kinda like when my father makes me wear a mouthpiece in hockey. I know my father's trying to keep my teeth safe but I hate it because I can't talk with it in." This triggers other aesthetic responses about parental protection. There is much acceptance of the fact that parents make rules to keep us out of harm's way—rules that we may not like very much.

I then pose a question, "So if invisibility is the best way to protect the people you love, why does Grandma Poss change her mind and find a potion to make Hush visible?"

Alexis replies, "Because Hush is sad that she doesn't have a real life."

I ask them to take out the letters they wrote for homework. Then I ask for a show of hands: "How many of you would make the decision to stay invisible?" No hands go up. "How many of you would decide to stay visible as Hush did?" All hands go up; they share reasons:

"I couldn't order food from places."

"I couldn't be seen at my piano recitals or on stage."

"I would like to be like everyone else. If kids were playing, I would want to play too."

Although the notion of invisibility was irresistible to these third graders during yesterday's session, reason and affect prevail when faced with a final choice. Examination of their letters reveals that more than half of the children worried about being ignored if they were invisible. Many, like Brittany, whose letter is presented in Figure 4-4, surmised that they would feel sad and/or lonely and would miss being with family and friends. *Possum Magic* allowed them to taste the temptation of invisibility and to reject it in favor of family, friends, and the grandeur of life.

Having spent much of the session evoking aesthetic renderings, we turn to the more critical task of comparing and contrasting *Koala Lou* and *Possum Magic*. I present a Venn diagram, which is familiar to many students. I challenge them to tell me where I should place Alexis's comment about both Koala Lou and Hush, each in their own way being invisible, on the Venn diagram. "In the middle," they reply. They return to their table to complete their Venn diagrams; much conversation ensues. Alexis's Venn diagram, presented in Figure 4-5, is representative of the range of

Boston University

School of Education
605 Commonwealth Avenue
Boston, Massachusetts 02215

Curriculum and Teaching Department

Dear Dr. Jenkins,
  I would make the same decision as Hush, because:

1. No one can see me and might sit on me or something.

2. And If my mom didn't no I was invisible. she would panich.

and 3. Because I would fel lonly because noone could see me and they would know I was thee along as I say something of course. well these are my 3 resons why I don't want to be invisible.

Sincarly.
Brittany Costello

FIGURE 4-4 *Brittany's thoughts about invisible Hush in* Possum Magic

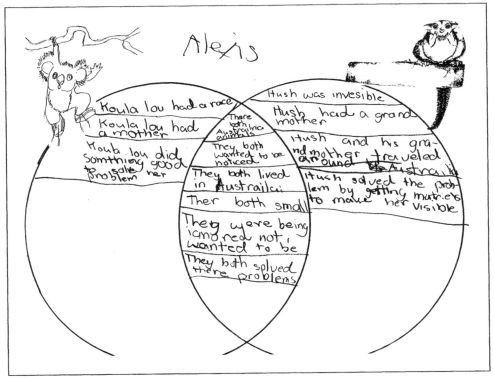

FIGURE 4-5   *Alexis's Venn Diagram*

ideas found across diagrams. Their comparisons center on the characteristics of the main protagonists. They attend to physical attributes (both have tails, both are small), conceptual attributes (both are marsupials, both are Australian animals), story grammar elements (both have problems to solve, both have happy endings), and character emotions (both are sad, both are ignored).

All in all, their ability to respond aesthetically and efferently to *Possum Magic* and *Koala Lou* lends credence to Louise Rosenblatt's conviction that most readers simultaneously attend to both dimensions of text (1991).

I had planned to end the session with their hunches but time ran out. I express my delight at finding the chart filled with ideas and promise to start tomorrow's session with their hunches.

Day Five: Autobiographical Renderings

I hang the chart of their original hunches and ask them to listen carefully to excerpts from Mem's autobiography to see if their hunches are correct:

1. *Mem might have had lots of brothers and sisters like Koala Lou and wanted attention. I think she was telling us she was sad.* Mem is the oldest of three girls. She was four years old when her sister, Jan, was born. Mem (1992) writes about Jan's birth:

   > I didn't feel put out at the time. It wasn't until her exceptional intelligence made itself apparent that I felt put out. She was five and I was nine when she explained loftily to me, her elder and her better, a piece of information about the Greek gods. I was impressed and reported the conversation to my parents. Almost immediately afterwards I felt an uncharacteristic dagger of self-doubt. Then jealousy. Then inferiority. I wasn't Jan's elder and better after all. I was her elder and lesser, and I've never recovered from that demeaning realization although I now suffer it more cheerfully. . . . Wondering whether or how much my parents love me is a foolish but continuing anxiety in my life, perhaps in all our lives. Is my father pleased with the way I've turned out? Is my mother proud of me? Do they think I'm absolutely and utterly terrific, or not? In my heart of hearts I believe that they do, but I had to write *Koala Lou* just to be sure. (pp. 25, 151)

2. *Maybe Mem Fox wrote the book [Possum Magic] because she had some sort of experience about being ignored. Maybe when she was on a trip or something, her family didn't pay attention to her . . . maybe she felt invisible.* Mem Fox (1992) was born in Australia but grew up in Africa, where her parents were missionaries. Her mother, however, wanted her girls to "understand that Australia was the most wonderful place on earth" (p. 28), so the family made yearlong visits there when Mem was seven, thirteen and eighteen years old. On the second trip, Mem's younger sister, Jan, whom Mem describes as "quiet, studious and self-contained," enraged Mem "by reading *War and Peace* on the long plane journey from Africa to Australia. We all knew she was clever, but I couldn't see why she had to be so ostentatious about it" (p. 26).

3. *She might have lost a race sometime.* Hush the Invisible Mouse, the original version of *Possum Magic*, was rejected by nine publishers over five years because it was considered to be, among other things, "too Australian." When finally accepted, the manuscript underwent major revisions and became a bestseller in no time. It was such a success that everyone thought it would be voted the Picture Book of the Year. Mem, expecting to win, bought an expensive dress for the big event. But *Possum Magic* came in second. Mem (1992) writes:

   > *Koala Lou* developed unconsciously out of my disappointment at *Possum Magic* not winning the Picture Book of the Year award, an event that hadn't been a disaster in world terms although I bawled like a baby at the time. Coming second with "highly commended" hadn't

been good enough. I wanted to hide for a while, to live through my failure alone. Writing *Koala Lou* was a catharsis. The pathetic little koala out on the limb in one of the final illustrations is none other than the author herself. (p. 149)

4. *She might have had a hard time with her mother and father.* Mem (1992) writes lovingly about her parents—about her father's gentleness, optimism, and work ethic and about her mother's friendliness, laughter, and physical and emotional toughness. "Unlike me, she abhors sentimentality" (p. 34).

The third graders conclude that three of their hunches are valid. When I ask for verification of their second hunch, they explain that Mem's parents probably showered Jan with praise for reading *War and Peace* and ignored Mem because she wasn't reading. I explain that because Mem doesn't actually tell us that she was ignored, we don't have clear evidence for this hunch. Our findings bring us to the conclusion that Mem sometimes writes about her life experiences but that other times may invent situations to convey her feelings.

We move to their new hunch chart (Figure 4-6). I ask the children who contributed ideas to read them. It becomes immediately apparent that I did a miserable job at explaining the difference between a hunch and a clue (and that I forgot to tell them not to repeat ideas). Under the hunch column, they include facts such as "She made Her secon book for her dauter clowy" and hunches that don't tie to the books they've read, such as "She's a generas person." I zero in on the plausible hunches and ask them to offer clues from Mem's books. Essentially, their hunches revolve around Mem's likes (Australia, animals, family) and around her personality (loving, gentle, caring). For example, for the hunch "She loves her family," Kevin notes, "She has family in all her books—mothers, kids, grandmothers but no fathers." The class is silent. Lenny suggests the new hunch that maybe Mem Fox's parents are divorced. I add it to the bottom of the list. I explain that, at a later point, we will watch a video about Mem Fox and discover which of our hunches are correct.

Day 6: Emus, Koalas, Kangaroos, Dingos, Kookaburras, and Wombats

The day to begin discussion about their research reports has arrived. Prior to starting this author study, I predicted that the third graders would initiate the study of Australian animals but I did not predict the extent of their fascination and excitement. I begin by asking if they have done any research projects in third grade; they talk about the reports they wrote on Native American homes. I ask what good researchers do. They reply that good researchers read many sources to get information, use highlighters to mark important information, take careful notes, and write reports in their own words and "don't just copy."

I show the book *Lolah: The Koala*, and explain that the authors, Jon Resnick and

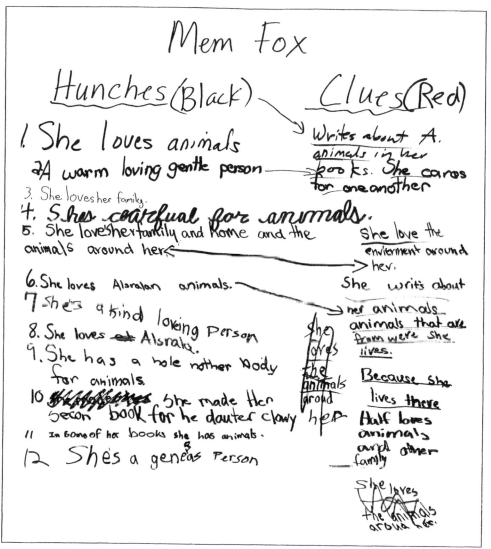

FIGURE 4-6 *Third graders' autobiographical hunches*

Jan Davis (1993), probably did all of the things that they just talked about—they read many sources, took notes, and so forth. I explain that these authors also did a fairly good job of organizing their information. For example, they put all the information about where koalas live in one section in the book. However, I note that they did not include any headings in their book. We talk about the ways headings help readers. I explain that if I had written this book, I would have used at least four headings. As I read each of my headings, I attach it to the chart pad:

FOOD: WHAT LOLAH EATS
HABITS: WHAT LOLAH DOES
DESCRIPTION: WHAT LOLAH LOOKS LIKE
HABITAT: WHERE LOLAH LIVES

I tell the children that, as I read *Lolah: The Koala*, I will stop periodically to ask them which heading the authors could have used. The reading of *Lolah: The Koala* is highly interactive. I interrupt the text to share my reactions and questions; they do the same. For example, when we learn that the male koala "makes loud 'snore-belches' to let others how where he is" (p. 11), we try to figure out how a snore-belch might sound. Their renditions elicit much laughter. Alexis promises to check her computerized encyclopedia program to see if the snore-belch is included.

The students are quick to identify the appropriate headings from my list. In fact, as I am reading, I hear them mumble "habitat," "habits". . . . When the book is finished, Brock comments accurately that the authors "split up" the description of what koalas look like on two different pages. We talk about this important observation. I then ask if they can think of another heading that the authors could have used at the end of the book. Molly correctly replies, "Why they are endangered."

I direct them back to the categories of description, habitat, and so forth, and ask if these categories would work if I were writing a book on dinosaurs or on sharks. "Yes," they reply and we talk about why. Tom asks permission to get his *Wildlife Fact Files* because he thinks the cards are organized in this fashion. He is excited to report that each *Fact File* uses these categories: "Food & Hunting," " Habits," "Breeding," "Koalas & Man," and "Did You Know?" We conclude that if many authors use these categories to organize information, we, too, can use them for our reports.

I remind the third graders that, earlier in the lesson, they told me that good researchers take notes as they read. I attach two worksheets called "Researcher's Notes" to the chart pad. Each worksheet contains two boxes, labeled "Habitat," "Description," and so forth. I ask them to help me fill in the description boxes with what we learned about koalas. Their recall is excellent. They remember that the male is twice as large as the female, weighs 12 kilos, and snore-belches. They remember that koalas have powerful hands and feet, cute noses, and sharp teeth. I ask them if we learned how tall koalas are, how much the female weighs, or about the color of their fur. They reply that they don't think so. I then ask how we obtain more information. I read excerpts from another book on koalas to illustrate the importance of using multiple sources. We add more physical attributes of the male and female koala to our worksheets.

I end the session by handing out copies of the "Researcher's Notes" worksheets and by urging students to record the information that they find from at least two different sources on the worksheet. We then decide who is going to investigate which Australian animal. With the exception of the wombat and kangaroo, the remaining animals have two to three researchers. Distressed that two animals are unaccounted for, a few children volunteer to take up their cause.

I explain that I will set aside a time tomorrow for researchers to work together. I encourage those who have resources on their animal to begin filling in their "Researcher's Notes" worksheets during free time and at home.

Day Seven: *Researchers in Action*

With the research groups established, I pass out assorted resources that have been collected over the past few days. As they read and take notes, Alice and I confer with groups and individuals, clarifying directions, reading difficult words, reminding them only to highlight important information that fits our research categories, and so forth. They tackle their task with a seriousness of purpose.

About fifteen minutes before the session ends, I call them to the rug to meet Wilfrid Gordon McDonald Partridge. The first time I heard Mem Fox read *Wilfrid Gordon McDonald Partridge* at a convention, I cried for my dad, whose short-term memory had already dissipated and whose long-term memory was lapsing on occasion. Because this book carries such an emotional wallop, I wasn't sure I could read it. Moreover, I had my doubts about whether children would respond to it as lovingly as I did. Essentially, at some level, I felt it was written more for adults than for children. However, because I couldn't imagine doing a Mem Fox author study without Wilfrid Gordon McDonald Partridge, I persevered. My judgment about this book couldn't have been more wrong. The children's response to *Wilfrid Gordon McDonald Partridge* surpassed their response to all of the other Mem Fox books.

I introduce *Wilfrid Gordon McDonald Partridge* and explain that Mem named the little boy in the story, Wilfrid Gordon McDonald Partridge, after her father. I read the story and ask for their thoughts. Alexis shares that her family "keeps pictures in albums from all the generations back so that everyone who lived will be remembered by this generation." Many concur that they have pictures of their great grandparents. Sean says that what he likes about the book is "that even though you're small like Wilfrid McDonald, whatever his name is, you can still help." We talk about Wilfrid's kindness toward Miss Nancy; the stories about how they have helped older people begin.

I bring closure to *Wilfrid Gordon McDonald Partridge* by asking the class to bring in one object, photograph, or drawing that holds a special memory and that they are willing to share.

Day Eight: **Wilfrid Gordon McDonald Partridge** *and the Evocation of Memories*

For the first time since the onset of the author study, Australian animals take a back seat to the third graders' "memory objects" during the before-school period. Stuffed animals, pictures, family mementos greet me. Some have brought in two or three objects. We assemble on the rug and I share the koala T-shirt that I am wearing along with the stuffed koala that were given to me by my Australian friend, Kay May. I talk about the wonderful morning I spent with Kay at Koala Park in Sydney. We then move around the circle and listen as the third graders share poignant memories:

> "This is a teddy bear and my aunt got it for me when I was four years old and I wanted to name it after her but she liked the name Sugarbear so that's what it's called."

> "This is a picture of me and my two brothers. I don't see my big brother any more because he lives with my aunt and when he was with me, he worked nights and went to school in the day and so I didn't really get to see him. I miss him."

> "This is the wallet that my dad gave me when he left the house after my mother and him got divorced. He lives far away now."

> "This [showing a blue bandanna] reminds me of my old dog. When we lived in Georgia, she got a haircut and wore this. Then when we moved up here, we had to put her to sleep because she couldn't walk she was so old."

I am so taken with the depth and sincerity of their responses that I share a memory that I have never shared before. I take a watch from my handbag and tell them that Lenny's memory about his dog reminded me of this watch, which I have carried with me every day for sixteen years. I explain that the watch belonged to my sister, Maureen, who died and whom I still miss very much. I share that I carry her watch because it reminds me of how fortunate I was to have Maureen in my life, even if only for a short time. This session speaks volumes about the capabilities of children to feel as deeply about life as adults do.

Day Nine: Readers' Theatre: Hattie and the Fox

I introduce *Hattie and the Fox* and explain that although Mem wrote this story for younger children, it is a great book for Readers' Theatre. I place the first page of the script on the overhead and ask if the class would like to participate (Figure 4-7). Energy is high, although most are not sure what Readers' Theatre is. When I explain, Kevin jogs his peers' memories about the Readers' Theatre that they did in health class earlier in the year. We talk about the structure of a script, what the role of the narrator is, and how dialogue of characters is arranged. I then ask them to read the script silently and to share any thoughts they have.

Kristen notes, "I think the moral of the story is 'Pay attention when someone is trying to warn you.'"

Kyle adds, "It's like the opposite of Peter and the Wolf." As students compare the two tales, stories about times in which some of them didn't heed a friend's or a parent's warning emerge. Aesthetic response is second nature to these third graders. They connect literature and life with ease.

I then assign character roles. Because I want everyone involved, I group students

---

Hattie and the Fox

Characters:

Hattie the big black hen	Horse
Sheep	Pig
Goose	Cow

NARRATOR: Hattie was a big black hen. One morning she looked up and said,
HATTIE: Goodness gracious me! I can see a nose in the bushes!
GOOSE: Good grief!
PIG: Well, well!
SHEEP: Who cares?
HORSE: So what?
COW: What next?
HATTIE: Goodness gracious me! I can see a nose and two eyes in the bushes!
GOOSE: Good grief!
PIG: Well, well!
SHEEP: Who cares?
HORSE: So what?
COW: What next?
HATTIE: Goodness gracious me! I can see a nose, two eyes, and two ears in the bushes!
GOOSE: Good grief!
PIG: Well, well!
SHEEP: Who cares?
HORSE: So what?
COW: What next?

FIGURE 4-7   *Readers' Theatre script for Hattie and the Fox (Fox, 1988)*

in threes. One group reads the goose's part, one group the pig's part, and so forth. I take the role of the narrator. Our dry run, as expected, is wobbly; readers aren't synchronized or expressive. I suggest that, before trying again, we do a little experiment. I hang a chart with the following three sentences on it:

The house is burning.

The house is burning?

The house is burning!

I ask them to read each sentence according to the punctuation mark; their renditions are excellent. We reread each sentence and talk about how each particular punctuation mark affects the pitch of our voices. I give scenarios such as "Suppose you look out your window and see your neighbor's house burning. Which pitch would you use?" They enjoy this interplay of meaning and the suprasegmental feature of pitch—so much so that Kevin invents a scenario that uses all three examples: "A guy who's been sleeping comes out of his house and another guy screams, 'The house is burning!' The sleepy guy says in a very sleepy voice, 'The house [yawn] is burning.' He then wakes up a little and says, " 'What, the house is burning?' " We express our delight at Kevin's cleverness.

I ask why Mem Fox wrote "Good grief!" instead of "Good grief?" or "Good grief." They decide that the exclamation point means that the goose is "excited but in an annoyed way—she's kind of frustrated with Hattie." We experiment with the line. They decide that the cow is bored and let their voices reflect this boredom while asking, "What next?" I ask each group to talk about their animal's attitude and to experiment. We tape record the second reread of the script. As they listen to the tape recording, I ask what they like about it and what they would like to change. They love how the horse group, of their own volition, added "Nei-ei-ei-gh, Nei-ei-ei-eigh," after "So what?" Other groups decide to follow suit. Students also comment that some groups need to work on synchronization and voice projection. I tell them that I am so pleased with their progress that, if they are willing to do further practice, they might be able to perform *Hattie and the Fox* for the kindergarten class in a few days. Their excitement affirms the research findings about Readers' Theatre—that it fosters active engagement with and enjoyment of literature, demands an interpretation of text, and increases fluency (Allington, 1983; Cunningham, 1979; Samuels, 1979).

We spend the last ten minutes or so on research report updates. Some students worked diligently over the weekend to complete their "Researcher's Notes" worksheets. They are eager to talk about final product possibilities. I promise to show them how to make a flap book and an accordion book. A few of the third graders, who completed major research projects as part of the school's enrichment program, offer to show classmates how to make brochures, poster board displays, and fact cards.

Day Ten: Literature as Drama

More *Wilfrid Gordon McDonald Partridge* memories open today's session as the children bring in additional artifacts. Their need to mark personal histories is strong. I ask them to explain what Mem Fox was trying to tell us when she wrote *Wilfrid Gordon McDonald Partridge*. "That memories are like gold, very precious," replies Lenny.

"Yes, memories are part of who we are," I add. Taking a manila folder on which I have traced a large wombat, I write the date and title of the book on the left side and the book theme we have just talked about on the right side.

"Let's see if you can identify the messages, also called themes, of the Mem Fox books that we have read to this point," I continue. "I am going to show you a message and I want you to identify the Mem Fox book." I show them only the message side of the folder (see third graders' version in Figure 4-9). They immediately guess *Possum Magic*; I open the folder to confirm their guess. We move chronologically through the messages of Mem Fox's other books. I place each wombat folder side by side and explain that together they represent a timeline of Mem Fox's books and that we will add three more books to the timeline today.

I remind the class that, when we started the author study, they had suggested that we act out some of Mem's books. I explain that I chose three books for dramatization: *Tough Boris*, *Sophie*, and *Time for Bed*. I set the following guidelines. Each group will:

1. Read its assigned book;
2. Decide how to share the book (have a narrator read while others act; act out the book; retell the story . . .);
3. Decide who has what responsibilities;
4. Rehearse;
5. Figure out the book's message and record it on the wombat folder.

I explain that their task is to perform the story so that the audience understands the story well enough to guess the story's message. My actors can't wait to get started. We talk about the importance of working quietly and of staying on task because our rehearsal time is limited.

The groups read their books quickly. Before planning their performance, two groups independently decide that they can't proceed without a list of characters and actors. Both groups work through equity issues ("But I'm hardly in the play!") with assistance. Such negotiations cut into rehearsal time and, at one point, I wonder if they will even get to rehearsal. But, with time reminders and a fair amount of on-task bedlam, they move ahead. The *Tough Boris* group are the first to ask about props. They remembered the headbands and other props that they had used during the Native American role plays and ask to use them. They turn headbands into eye patches, book bags into buried treasure chests, a large roll of brown paper towels into an anchor for the flag, and so forth. (The idea to use rulers for swords is vetoed.) The *Sophie* group follows suit, finding a "cane" for Grandpa, and so on.

Miraculously, when show time is called, the groups are ready. I remind everyone that, with only one rehearsal, we shouldn't expect perfection. We talk about what it means to be a respectful and appreciative audience. The *Sophie* group is the opening act. A narrator reads the story while the actors act. "Grandpa" steals the show and the audience has no difficulty generating messages for this intergenerational story: "Even though someone dies, they're always in your heart," and "You should always love your Grandpa." These messages corroborate the group's message: "Grandparents are special. You should pay attention to them."

Rather than assign a narrator, the *Time for Bed* group intuitively decides that story uses first-person narration. Even though there is no dialogue, the group decides that lines such as

"It's time for bed, little mouse, little mouse,
Darkness is falling all over the house."

should be read by the mother mouse. Thus, the mother animal in each scene reads her lines while coddling the baby animal. Members of the group take turns holding the book for the readers. Because there are many scenes and only six actors, there is much scurrying during the performance and continual consultation of the "who's who" list. Some of the actors remember to take on their animal's characteristics (slithering and hissing like a snake). The audience enjoys their performance and offers message statements such as, "Your parents always love you"; "Go to bed when you're told"; and "Go to bed and rest so you can have a nice day at school." The group concurs with these messages and share its own: "Everyone needs to rest."

Tough Boris, acted out by six boys, is the most physical performance. When the narrator reads, "He was tough. All pirates are tough," Boris turns from side to side to flex his muscles; the pirates turn from side to side to flex their muscles. When the narrator reads, "He was greedy. All pirates are greedy," Boris dives on the "treasure chest" (book bags) and the pirates follow suit. Unfortunately, their pirate rowdiness overshadows the final scene in which Boris cries when his parrot dies. Their exaggerated "boohoos" bring laughter instead of sadness from the audience (Figure 4-8).

FIGURE 4-8   *Brock as Tough Boris*

They redeem themselves, though, when they share their message chart (Figure 4-9). Clearly they understood Mem Fox's intention but couldn't resist the bravado.

I compliment the class on their ability to figure out the themes of Mem Fox's books. We talk about the challenges of acting (facing the audience, projecting one's voice, interpreting the author's message . . .) and about some of the changes they would make if they were to rehearse again.

I close the session by asking, "Now that we've read seven of Mem Fox's books, does anyone have any new hunches about Mem Fox as a person or as a writer?"

Alexis replies, "She had great experiences with her grandparents." When I ask for clues from her books, she says, "She writes about grandparents in *Sophie* and *Wilfrid Gordon* and *Possum Magic* and they are always loving and fun to be around." I record her hunch/clue on a new chart and encourage the class to record new ideas during free time. I reexplain the terminology, hunches and clues, using Alexis's example. I remind them to read the chart before adding their ideas to eliminate repetition. I reiterate that, on the last day of our author study, we will watch a videotape of Mem Fox and see how many of our hunches are true.

Day Eleven: More Biographical Response

Once again the hunch chart is filled with ideas. I begin by rereading Alexis's hunch about grandparents. I share that Mem Fox writes in her autobiography that she didn't really know her grandparents when she was growing up because they lived in Australia.

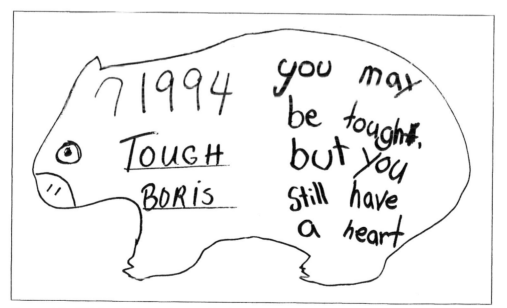

FIGURE 4-9   *Third graders write themes of books they role play*

It wasn't until Mem moved to Australia that she became close to her paternal grand-father (also Wilfrid Partridge), who was ninety years old at the time and living in an old age home. Mem visited him every weekend until he got so sick with pneumonia that he was unconscious most of the time. Mem writes about the nurse who told her, "'Hold his hand. He does know that someone's here even if he doesn't know it's you. It will give him comfort.' So I held his hand. My book *Sophie* arose directly from the throat-seizing sadness of this scene" (1992, p. 82). Mem goes on to write that Beverly Cleary is right when she said, "'If you lacked something as a child, give it to yourself in a story.' I think that's exactly what I've done" (p. 83). Once again, we understand that authors use both direct and indirect experiences to shape their stories as well as their dreams and hopes.

We move through other hunches in the same fashion. Some hunches I sub-stantiate; others I explain will be addressed by Mem Fox in her video. "What if we don't find out in the video?" asks Bobby. Kevin suggests that when we make our video for Mem, we should ask her about our hunches. The third graders love the idea.

With the announcement that the kindergartners are eager to see our *Hattie and the Fox* Readers' Theatre the next day, we rehearse our script a few times. By the second reading, the third graders have adopted a pulsating rhythmic beat: "Good grief! Honk, honk." "Well, well! Oink, oink." In addition, each group accompanies its animal sound with a body movement. For example, when the horses neigh, they shakes their heads; when the geese honk, they flap their wings. I suggest that, for the benefit of the kindergartners, each group holds a picture of its animal. I present the manila folders on which I have traced each animal across the two-page spread, and suggest that they attach their Readers' Theatre scripts to the back of the manila folders.

I turn over the role of narrator to Molly, who was absent on the introductory day. She suggests that we incorporate the fox (who has no lines) into our play. "When I read the line, 'I can see a nose in the bushes!'" she explains, "I'll tape a nose to a bush made out of construction paper." The idea of a story board is wildly popular. Molly volunteers to make the bush and the fox parts.

We spend our remaining time on the animal reports. I explain that, after our Readers' Theatre tomorrow, time will be set aside for sharing animal reports. Brock asks if he can share his flap book on the dingo now. His peers are eager to hear his re-port, so I ask him to share one heading of interest and the corresponding text. Before he begins, I ask him for his research material. He hands me the *Wildlife Fact File*, every line of which has been highlighted, and a Microsoft *Encarta* printout, also highlighted from top to bottom. As he reads his heading ("Food and Hunting"), I recognize the influence of the *Wildlife Fact File* and wonder if he has just copied the information. I am thrilled to find that his piece is in his own words and that it merges two sources of data. I highlight these two major understandings for the class, compli-menting Brock for his work as a nonfiction writer, and explain that I am looking for-ward to hearing more reports tomorrow.

Day Twelve: Readers' Theatre Performance

Excitement about their Readers' Theatre performance permeates the room as we move into final rehearsal. Because they had been encouraged to experiment with changes each time we rehearsed in the past, they continue to offer suggestions about how we might improve our reading of *Hattie and the Fox* . For example, Brad suggests that, instead of standing in our U-shaped formation, we scatter around the "stage" like in the book's illustration. I explain that while I love his idea, we are due in the kindergarten in twenty minutes and that we need to perfect what we've done to this point. Soon thereafter, we invade the kindergarten.

I announce the title and author, and the performance commences. Molly manipulates the story board with ease, and Kevin's performance of Hattie elicits much laughter. The kindergartners clap profusely. As we exist the room, the kindergartners are chanting, "Good grief! Honk, honk," "Well, well! Oink, oink." If only we had thought to involve the audience!

Upon returning to the classroom, the researchers bring their big poster boards, flap books, and brochures to the circle. To prevent information overload, I ask presenters to select one topic of interest and to tell or read that information. They are so excited about reports that it is difficult for them to stop at one piece of information.

I review the third graders' projects later in the day, and make two interesting observations. In general, children who created flap books or brochures resisted the temptation to copy text verbatim from one or more sources. However, children who created large display posters were much more inclined to cut and paste the actual text of various sources along with pictures and maps, despite the fact that they completed their "Researcher's Notes" worksheets. Of course, some children created reports that contained both their own text as well as excerpts of original sources. Alexis, Kevin, and Lenny's "expanded" flap book on the kangaroo, presented in Figure 4-10, is a wonderful example. In the flap book, they present basic information about the habitat, food, and sizes of kangaroos in their own words. However, because these children had accessed over thirty pages of Internet material on kangaroos—including EARTHWATCH Project results and aboriginal tales about kangaroos—they were determined to showcase some of this knowledge. The solution? Extend their flap book with the text and pictures of Internet sources.

In retrospect, these observations suggest that more instruction was needed to ready the third graders for nonfiction writing. I needed to demonstrate and redemonstrate each phase of the research, notetaking, drafting, and revising processes.

Day Thirteen: The Mem Fox Finale

The final day of our author study has arrived—the day we make a videotape to send to Mem Fox describing what we have been doing with her books as well as our unconfirmed hunches about her as a person. As always, the third graders are bursting with ideas. Given our time limits, I explain that I have choreographed our grand finale in the following acts:

FIGURE 4-10   *Kevin and Alexis's research report on kangaroos*

Act I: The children gather in assigned trios on the rug; back row in seats, front row on the floor. As a class, they read the huge cue card: "Hello, Mem Fox, from the third graders at the Kennedy School in Canton, Massachusetts."

Act II: While Tom holds up the first Hunches/Clues chart, Alexis reads a brief introductory letter: "Hi Mem, My name is Alexis. We have read many of your books and we love them. As we read, we made hunches about you that we'd like to share."

Act III: Each trio reads or tells one hunch and supporting clues that were generated in earlier sessions. For example:

Actor 1	Actor 2	Actor 3
We think you are a very caring person with a big heart	because the characters in your books care about each other	and even pirates cry. Grandma Poss cares about Hush; Koala Lou loves her mother.

Act IV: Alexis returns and continues with her letter: "Maybe you can tell us if our hunches are right. We made up a questionnaire [shows it]. Could you circle *yes* or *no* and send it back to us? Thanks from your fans in Canton!"

Tom adds a P.S.: "Mem, we also want to let you know that we had a great time acting out some of your books. I was a pirate in *Tough Boris*. Yesterday, we performed a Readers' Theatre of *Hattie and the Fox* for the kindergartners. We are including it here on the videotape so you can check out our performance.

Three takes and the videotape is completed. Of course, they beg to watch it. Because I felt it was important for them to meet Mem on video (The Trumpet Club, 1992) to assess their hunches, I promise to show our video on the last day of school. They are mesmerized by Mem Fox and are delighted to learn that she loves Australian animals; her family; words, especially alliterative phrases; and that, like Koala Lou, she wanted her mother to say, "I DO love you."

To cap off our author study, I had planned to act out *Night Noises* with Alice. *Night Noises* makes for a splendid finale because, like *Koala Lou*, it embodies the themes that Mem Fox holds dear. However, we have run out of time. I tell the children that I hope they will read *Night Noises* over the summer, if they haven't already, along with Mem Fox's latest books. I tell them that I will never be able to read another Mem Fox book without thinking of them and of our special time together.

Concluding Comments

I think it is fair to say that the third graders' degree of enthusiasm for and engagement with this author study sprang from their delight with Mem Fox and her works as well as from my willingness to listen to and to act on many of their ideas. Their investment in this curriculum endeavor was central to its success. While my decision to collaborate with the third graders on the direction of this author study is one that I defend wholeheartedly, I readily acknowledge that the pursuit of their ideas— the research reports, the plays, the communication with Mem Fox—compromised some of my ideas. For example, I had intended to integrate Mem's struggles as a writer—how beginnings and endings plague her, how she needs and at the same time detests reader feedback, how books like *Koala Lou* took forty-nine drafts and five years to complete, and so forth. However, once the author study took on a life of its own, I would have had to commandeer the time block for writing workshop in addition to that of the reading workshop in order to pursue my agenda. In retrospect, spreading the Mem Fox author study across both workshops would have permitted not only the study of Mem as a writer but also the study of nonfiction writing. As mentioned previously, the research and writing of the Australian animal reports was relegated essentially to free time and to homework. Although the children astounded me with the wealth of resources they had at their fingertips and with the knowledge they learned from this information, they needed more guidance

---

Mem Fox: Life-Literature Connections

Possum Magic 1983

Annotation: To protect Hush from snakes, Grandma Poss casts a magic spell to make her invisible. When Hush wants to become visible again, Grandma can't find the right spell. She then remembers it has to do with food. They travel around Australia, eating different foods until Hush is visible again.

Autobiographical Connection: Raising her children in Africa on a farm, Mem's mom worried about their encounters with wildlife. On one occasion, Mem's mom had to rescue her from a poisonous snake. Mem wrote *Possum Magic* to give her child a genuinely different Australian book (Fox, 1992).

Wilfrid Gordon McDonald Partridge 1984

Annotation: Wilfrid Gordon is a young boy whose favorite person at the old people's home is Miss Nancy. When Wilfrid learns that Miss Nancy has lost her memory, he brings her objects that make her cry, laugh, and feel warm, and Miss Nancy remembers.

Autobiographical Connection: Wilfrid Gordon McDonald Partridge is Mem's father's name. Mem didn't get to know her grandfather, also Wilfrid Partridge, until he was ninety years old and living in a nursing home in Australia. The setting and the characters of the story are based on people from his nursing home (Fox, 1992).

Hattie and the Fox 1988

Annotation: Hattie is a hen who spots a nose in the bush and warns the other farm animals, who pay no attention. Then she spots a nose and two ears, but no one pays attention. She continues to spot body parts until the fox leaps out of the bushes and frightens the animals.

Autobiographical Connection: Life on an African farm (where Mem's parents worked as missionaries) meant that Mem lived with the beauty of nature and all its creatures—cows, hens, chickens, cattle, snakes, donkeys . . . (Fox, 1992).

Koala Lou 1988

Annotation: Until her brothers and sisters come along, Koala Lou's mother tells her she loves her a hundred times a day. Soon, however, her mother is so busy she forgets to tell her she loves her. Koala Lou decides to enter the gum tree climbing race to rewin her mother's love. But Koala Lou comes in second. When she returns home her mother tells her how much she loves her.

Autobiographical Connection: As Mem writes, "When I ask myself why I'm now so driven to succeed, I come to the conclusion that it's partly an irrational and continual competition between Jan [her sister] and myself for parental approval" (1992, p. 36). Mem also shares that her mother "was tough. She would not say to

FIGURE 4-11 *Mem Fox: Life-literature connections*

me, 'I love you.' So I wrote a book in which a mother said that because I wanted that to happen" (Trumpet, 1992).

Night Noises 1989

Annotation: Lily Laceby, who is very old, lives with her dog, Butch Aggie. One night, Lily falls sound asleep. Butch Aggie hears noises outside and growls. As Lily dreams about her husband, her children, her wedding day, and her childhood, the noises get louder and louder until Butch Aggie barks so loudly that Lily wakes up. When she opens the door, family and friends shout "Happy Birthday" and Lily's ninetieth birthday party begins.

Autobiographical Connection: Mem named the old lady Lily after her husband's grandmother, who lived in a small village called Laceby in the north of England (Fox, 1992). Mem wrote *Night Noises* when her mother had a surprise seventieth birthday party. Mem got to know her grandfather when he was ninety (Fox, 1992).

Sophie 1989

Annotation: When Sophie is born, she curls her finger around Grandpa's finger. As Sophie grows taller, Grandpa grows weaker, but their love is strong. When Grandpa dies, Sophie has a baby who curls her finger around Sophie's finger.

Autobiographical Connection: When Mem's grandfather is so sick that he is unconscious, a nurse tells Mem, "Hold his hand. He does know someone is here, even if he doesn't know it is you." Mem writes, "My book *Sophie* arose directly from the throat-seizing sadness of this scene" (1992, p. 82).

FIGURE 4-11   (*Continued*)

and practice with notetaking and with transforming these notes into text. Writing workshop would have been the perfect solution.

As I fretted about these and other shortcomings (e.g., the books we didn't read), I recalled the sincerity and expansiveness of the third graders' assessment of the Mem Fox author study (see Chapter 1). I reminded myself that the best curriculum, glitches and all, is curriculum that turns on the ideas of both the children and the teacher, with the teacher attending to the whole and implementing those ideas that will move children forward as thinkers, readers, and writers.

5

Designing an Author Study

To think about the practical dimensions of designing an author study is to think about questions such as: Who chooses the author? Is any author appropriate for an author study? How do we locate biographical material? What is the timeline for an author study? This chapter addresses these and other questions by tracing the steps followed in designing the Mem Fox author study that was presented in Chapter 4. (Design issues specific to chapter-book author studies are addressed in Chapter 6; nonfiction author studies, Chapter 7.)

Choosing an Author

Prior to the author study on Mem Fox, I surveyed the third graders to ascertain their favorite authors. Their choices were as varied as we might expect for any group of readers. Single votes were cast for authors such as Mem Fox, Eve Bunting, Marc Brown, Eric Carle, E. B. White, Roald Dahl, Laura Ingalls Wilder, and Christopher Pike. Seven out of seventeen third graders chose R. L. Stine (four boys and three girls). I am certain that the third graders would have been delighted to pursue an author study on R. L. Stine, author of the *Goosebumps* series. Although many did not choose Stine as a favorite author, their reading logs attested to the popularity of his books. Knowing that choice increases ownership, I would have had a surefire start for my author study. However, in good conscience, I could not waste precious time on literature that offers little aesthetic and intellectual nourishment.

It's not that I object to children reading series books like *Goosebumps*. Series books fulfill a number of young readers' needs. First, elementary-age children are premiere collectors—baseball cards, troll dolls, beanie babies or whatever is in vogue; series books fulfill this need to collect. Second, series books eliminate the decision about what to read next. Knowing that the readability level of these series books is appropriate is a major consideration for the developing reader. Third, in the words of Avi, an acclaimed children's author:

It's important to give young writers series books such as *Goosebumps* or *The Babysitters Club*. They can imitate these books much better than they can imitate my books. Children get a very strong sense of structure from these formulaic books. Children are not going to get a sense of structure from my books. They're too complex; they're too different. If you read fifty *Babysitters Club* books, you know how to construct a Babysitter book. That's very important for the young writer. In essence, the structure of these book are much more transparent than the structure of my books and children will learn something from it. (1995)

The formulaic nature of these series books not only inducts young writers into story structure, but also holds great appeal for young readers. They enjoy the highly predictable plot structures, the sameness of characters, the built-in redundancy and the conventional themes (Mackey, 1990). It may well be that series books constitute one basic link to literacy. In an analysis of thousands of readers' autobiographies, Carlsen and Sherrill (1988) found that:

> The respondents also become momentarily addicted to both the series and comic books. Over and over accounts describe periods where such books became their steady reading fare   These materials seem to be as much a part of one's literary maturation as are the children's classics." (p. 16)

Series books, then, have a place in our classroom libraries. Children, as they have done for over one hundred years, are going to pursue series books, and to read up a storm in the process. However, although these books should be available for independent reading, they should not be the focal point of an author study. With shallow characters and contrived plots, these series books cannot evoke the range or depth of response that is essential to a successful author study. Although it can be productive to teach children how these formulaic texts work (and fail to work), such critical study can be done in lessons independent of an author study per se. In my opinion, when we ask children to rally around an author and his or her literature, we should do so with full knowledge that the literary experience will be of the highest quality. Children deserve no less.

Of course, this indictment of empty series books does not extend to the quality series books written by acclaimed authors—series such as the Ramona books by Cleary, the Anastasia books by Lowry, and the Alice books by Naylor. Each of these series books holds enormous appeal for young readers and offers a quality literary experience.

Thus, with R. L. Stine as a nonoption, I returned to the list of the third graders' favorite authors. Given the two-week time frame of the author study, I knew that I needed to pursue a picture-book author. Their list of favorite picture-book authors, already noted, was impressive. To choose among these authors meant weighing their work against the following criteria:

- Books that are age-appropriate and that sustain readers emotionally and intellectually;

- Books that evoke a range of aesthetic responses and that connect to children's lives;

- Books with memorable language, believable characters, engaging plots, and other critical elements that work together to offer universal themes; in other words, books of high literary quality;
- Availability of autobiographical and supporting biographical material.

If all four of these authors met the above criteria, I could have presented this list, perhaps read one book by each author, and asked the class to vote. However, I ruled out Marc Brown and Eric Carle because their works are more appropriate for first and second graders. Because I adore Mem Fox and because her work met the above criteria, she was my first choice. Eve Bunting also would have been a superb candidate. However, because her books expose readers to complex social issues such as the Los Angeles riots, homelessness, and illiteracy, I felt that they demanded the larger instructional context of the social-studies block.

Thus, after careful consideration of the children's choices, I made the decision about which author to study. By doing so, some educators would charge that I usurped the children's right to establish the boundaries of their literacy learning. I would counter, however, that whereas it is important to honor child-centered learning, it is equally important to allow teachers to bring their intellects and passions to the classroom. Child-centered curriculum should not abrogate the teacher's power and influence. Vygotskian theory (1978) suggests that we cannot expect children to view their learning with the same breadth and depth as we must view it. We need to solicit their ideas, assess the quality of their ideas as well as their understandings, and make decisions about how best to advance their learning. We follow their lead when it is judicious to do so; other times, we lead the way.

Savoring the Author's Literature

Having chosen Mem Fox, I had the delectable job of reading all of her works. Following Avi's (1991) advice, I read all of Mem Fox's books in chronological order so that I could "see the work as a whole, see the development, the evolution of ideas and themes" (p. 3). Grand advice, indeed, because I made a number of observations (e.g., Fox's refinement of early themes over time; her recent gravitation toward predictable books for very young children) that I might have missed if I had read the books in random fashion. With Post-its in hand, I read each story and jotted down any thoughts—aesthetic, critical, or autobiographical—that occurred to me. As I noticed patterns emerging, I recorded them in a notebook: episodes that triggered personal memories, critical dimensions of Mem Fox's craft such as the grandparent-child theme, and autobiographical hunches (e.g., given the prevalence of the grandparent, I suspected that Mem had a close and loving relationship with her grandparents). I made these observations not with the intention of sharing each and every one with the children, but rather with the intention of being ready to acknowledge and to extend similar observations that the third graders might offer. As was noted in Chapter 3, an effective author study is not about pursuing every personal response, dissecting every critical element of the author's craft, or speculating on every possible autobiographical hunch. Rather, it is about keeping the literature and the author alive by following the children's leads, when possible, with respect to this range of multiple response.

Researching Biographical and Autobiographical Links

In adherence to the principles of author study as multiple response (Chapter 3), I purposely chose not to begin my preparation of the Mem Fox author study with her autobiography. As readers, we too are entitled to the affective responses that take hold as we read children's books. Reading her autobiography before reading her works would have altered my reading experience. Rather than first reveling in Mem's stories, I would have been marking her literature-life links.

Upon consumption of her works, I laughed and cried my way through *Dear Mem Fox, I Have Read All Your Books Even the Pathetic Ones.* Rich in autobiographical detail and in life-literature connections, Mem's autobiography is an honest, moving, and hilarious self-portrait.

An Avalanche of Author Information

With the advent of literature-based programs in recent years has come enormous interest in children's authors, and the resulting avalanche of author information in the form of autobiographies, biographies, videotapes, convention speeches, and journal articles. Figure 5-1 offers a listing of acclaimed fiction authors who have written autobiographies or memoirs; Figure 5-2 presents a list of biographies of fiction authors. Scholastic's *Meet the Authors and Illustrators* series, written for children, also provides 120 biographical sketches of the major authors. Another excellent source of autobiographical statements and biographical information are the reference books *Something About the Author Autobiography Series* and *Major Authors and Illustrators for Children and Young Adults,* both published by Gale Associates. Available in most public libraries, these books contain personal data about family members, a career overview, a listing of the author's books, awards won, and a biographical piece that weaves in direct quotes from the author. Autobiographical information also may be found in the acceptance speeches of award-winning authors, published each year by *The Horn Book.* In addition, increasing numbers of authors are creating home pages for Internet users that offer autobiographical material. In a recent issue of *Book Links,* Roxanne Feldman (1998) compiled a list of Web sites that contain author home pages (Figure 5-3) as well as a list of publishers who offer home pages (Figure 5-4).

An excellent resource with respect to both autobiographical and critical

AARDEMA, VERNA
Aardema, V. (1992). *A bookworm who hatched.* Katonah, NY: Richard C. Owen.

ASCH, FRANK
Asch, F. (1997). *One man show.* Katonah, NY: Richard C. Owen.

BULLA, CLYDE
Bulla, C. R. (1985). *A grain of wheat: A writer begins.* Boston: David R. Godine.

BUNTING, EVE
Bunting, E. (1995). *Once upon a time.* Katonah, NY: Richard C. Owen.

BYARS, BETSY
Byars, B. (1991). *The moon and I.* New York: Messner.

CARLE, ERIC
Carle, E. (1996). *The art of Eric Carle.* New York: Philomel.

CLEARY, BEVERLY
Cleary, B. (1988a). *A girl from Yamhill: A memoir.* New York: Morrow.
Cleary, B. (1988b). *My own two feet: A memoir.* New York: Morrow.

COWLEY, JOY
Cowley, J. (1988). *Seventy kilometres from ice cream: A letter from Joy Cowley.* Katonah, NY: Richard C. Owen.

DAHL, ROALD
Dahl, R. (1984). *Boy: Tales of childhood.* New York: Farrar, Straus & Giroux.

DE PAOLA, TOMIE
de Paola, T. (1989). *The art lesson.* New York: Putman.
de Paola, T. (1993). *Tom.* New York: Putman.

EHLERT, LOIS
Ehlert, L. (1996). *Under my nose.* Katonah, NY: Richard C. Owen.

FOX, MEM
Fox, M. (1992). *Dear Mem Fox: I have read all your books even the pathetic ones.* San Diego: Harcourt.

FRITZ, JEAN
Fritz, J. (1982). *Homesick: My own story.* New York: Putnam.
Fritz, J. (1993). *Surprising myself.* Katonah, NY: Richard C. Owen.

GOBLE, PAUL
Goble, P. (1994). *Hau cola, hello friends.* Katonah, NY: Richard C. Owen.

GREENFIELD, ELOISE
Greenfield, E., & Little, L. (1979). *Childtimes: A three generation memoir.* New York: HarperCollins.

HELLER, RUTH
Heller, R. (1996). *Fine lines.* Katonah, NY: Richard C. Owen.

HOPKINS, LEE BENNETT
Hopkins, L. B. (1992).*The writing bug.* Katonah, NY: Richard C. Owen.
Hopkins, L. B. (1995). *Been to yesterdays.* Boyd Mills.

HOWE, JAMES
Howe, J. (1994). *Playing with words.* Katonah, NY: Richard C. Owen.

HYMAN, TRINA SCHART
Hyman, T. S. (1981). *Self portrait: Trina Schart Hyman.* New York: HarperCollins.

FIGURE 5-1 *Autobiographies of fiction authors*

KUSKIN, KARLA
Kushin, K. (1995). *Thoughts, pictures, and words.* Katonah, NY: Richard C. Owen.

LEWIS, C. S.
Lewis, C. S. (1985). *Letters to children.* New York: Macmillan.

LOWRY, LOIS
Lowry, L. (1998). *Looking back: A book of memories.* Boston: Houghton Mifflin.

LYON, GEORGE ELLA
Lyon, G. E. (1996). *A wordful child.* Katonah, NY: Richard C. Owen.

MAHY, MARGRET
Mahy, M. (1995). *My mysterious world.* Katonah, NY: Richard C. Owen.

MARTIN, RAFE
Martin, R. (1991). *A storyteller's story.* Katonah, NY: Richard C. Owen.

McPHAIL, DAVID
McPhail, D. (1996). *In flight with David McPhail.* Portsmouth, NH: Heinemann.

McKISSACK, PATRICIA
McKissack, P. (1997). *Can you imagine?* Katonah, NY: Richard C. Owen.

NAYLOR, PHYLLIS REYNOLDS
Naylor, P. R. (1978). *How I came to be a writer.* New York: Atheneum.

PAULSEN, GARY
Paulsen, G. (1990). *Woodsong.* New York: Simon & Schuster.

PEET, BILL
Peet, B. (1989). *Bill Peet: An autobiography.* Boston: Houghton Mifflin.

POLACCO, PATRICIA
Polacco, P. (1994). *Firetalking.* Katonah, NY: Richard C. Owen.

POTTER, BEATRIX
Potter, B. (1989). *The journal of Beatrix Potter: 1881–1897.* New York: Warne.
Taylor, J. (compiler) (1992). *Letters to children from Beatrix Potter.* New York: Warne.

RINGGOLD, FAITH
Ringgold, F. (1996). *Talking to Faith Ringgold.* New York: Crown.

RYLANT, CYNTHIA
Rylant, C. (1989). *But I'll be back again: An album.* Danbury, CT: Orchard.
Rylant, C. (1992). *Best wishes.* Katonah, NY: Richard C. Owen.

SAY, ALLEN
Say, A. (1994). *The ink-keeper's apprentice.* Boston: Houghton Mifflin.

SINGER, ISSAC BASHEVIS
Singer, I. B. (1969). *A day of pleasure: Stories of a boy growing up in Warsaw.* New York: Farrar, Straus & Giroux.

UCHIDA, YOSHIKO
Uchida, Y. (1991). *The invisible thread.* New York: Messner.

YEP, LAURENCE
Yep, L. (1991). *The lost garden: A memoir.* New York: Messner.

YOLEN, JANE
Yolen, J. (1991). *A letter from Phoenix Farm.* Katonah, NY: Richard C. Owen.

FIGURE 5-1   (*Continued*)

AVI
Bloom, S., & Mercier, C. (1997). *Presenting Avi.* New York: Twayne Publishers.
Markham, L. (1996). *Avi.* Santa Barbara: The Learning Works.

BURNETT, FRANCES HODGSON
Carpenter, A. S., & Shirley J. (1990). *Frances Hodgson Burnett: Beyond the secret garden.* Minneapolis: Lerner Books.

DANZIGER, PAULA
Krull, K. (1993). *Presenting Paula Danziger.* New York: Twayne.

DILLON, LEO AND DIANE
Preiss, B. (1982). *Chapters: My growth as a writer.* Boston: Little, Brown.

L'ENGLE, MADELEINE
Gonzales, D. (1991). *Madeleine L'Engle: Author of* Wrinkle in Time. New York: Dillon.
Hettings, D. (1993). *Presenting Madeleine L'Engle.* New York: Twayne.

HUGHES, LANGSTON
Walker, A. (1974). *Langston Hughes, American poet.* New York: Crowell.
Cooper, F. (1994). *Coming home: From the life of Langston Hughes.* New York: Philomel.

CARROLL, LEWIS
Bassett, I. (1987). *Very truly yours, Charles L. Dodgeson, alias Lewis Carroll.* New York: Lothrop.

NAYLOR, PHYLLIS
Sover, L. (1997). *Presenting Phyllis Reynolds Naylor.* New York: Twayne.

PATERSON, KATHERINE
Cary, A. (1997). *Katherine Paterson.* Santa Barbara: The Learning Works.

PAULSEN, GARY
Salvner, G. (1996). *Presenting Gary Paulsen.* New York: Macmillan.

POTTER, BEATRIX
Aldis, D. (1969). *Nothing is impossible: The story of Beatrix Potter.* New York: Atheneum.
Collins, D. R. (1989). *The country artist: A story about Beatrix Potter.* Minneapolis: Carolrhoda.
Taylor, J. (1987). *Beatrix Potter: Artist, storyteller, and countrywoman.* New York: Warne.

WHITE, E. B.
Collins, D. R. (1989). *To the point: A story about E. B. White.* Minneappolis: Carolrhoda.

WILDER, LAURA INGALLS
Blair, G. (1981). *Laura Ingalls Wilder.* New York: Putnam.
Giff, P. R. (1987). *Laura Ingalls Wilder: Growing up in the little house.* New York: Viking.
Greene, C. (1990). *Laura Ingalls Wilder: Author of the Little House books.* Chicago: Childrens Press.

YEP, LAWRENCE
Johnson-Feelings, D. (1995). *Presenting Lawrence Yep.* New York: Twayne Publishers.

FIGURE 5-2   *Biographies of fiction writers*

Children's Literaure Web Guide/Tell Me More
<http://www.acs.ucalgary.ca/-dkbrown/authors.html>

Fairrosa Cyber Library//Authors & Illustrators
<http://www.interport.net/-fairrosa/cl.authors.html>

Internet School Library Media Center's Index to Author and Illustrator Internet Sites
<http://falcon.jmu.edu/-ramseyll/biochildhome.htm>www.acs.ucalgary.ca/-dkbrown>

IPL's Ask the Authors
<http://www.ipl.org/ youth/askAuthor>

Kay Vandergrift's Learning About the Author and Illustrator
<http://www.scils.rutgers.edu/special/kay/author.html>

The Scoop's Interviews of Authors and Illustrators
<http://www.friend.ly.net/scoop/biographies/>

USM de Grummond Collection's Author/Illustrator
<http://www.lib.usm.edu/-degrum/newreg.htm#index>

Yahooligans Collection of Author and Illustrator Sites
<http://www.yahooligans.com/Art_Soup/Books_and Reading/Authors/>

FIGURE 5-3   *Accessing author Web sites (Feldman, 1998)*

Avon Books. *Avon Books*
<http://www.avonbooks.com>

Bantam Doubleday Dell. *Bantam Doubleday Dell Online*
<www.bdd.com/index.html>

HarperCollins. *HarperCollins Authors.*
<http://www.harpercollins.com/authors/index.htm>

Houghton Mifflin. *Houghton Mifflin.*
<http://HMCO.COM>

Little, Brown. *Little, Brown Books for Children—Featured Authors.*
<http://pathfinder.com/twep/lb_childrens/author/>

Penguin Putman. *Penguin Putman, Inc. Online Catalog.*
<http://www.penguinputnam.com/>

Random House. *Random House Children's Publishing Catalog Search.*
<http://www.randomhouse.com/kids/catalog/>

Simon & Schuster. *Simon Says Kids—Authors and Illustrators.*
<http://www.simonsays.com/kidzone/author_index.html/>

FIGURE 5-4   *Publishers' Web sites and author home pages*

dimensions of an author's works is the reference book *Children's Literature Review* (Gale Associates). In addition to presenting a full biographical statement and commentary by the author, *Children's Literature Review* offers a compilation of critics' reviews of the author's works. Critics' comments about the allure of characters, the staying power of plots, the effectiveness of narration, and so forth extend our own critical review of various works.

Journal Articles

Another source of data are the articles authors write for journals such as *Journal of Children's Literature*, *The New Advocate*, *The Reading Teacher*, and *Language Arts*. For example, an ERIC search of Mem Fox yielded five articles. These articles were particularly helpful because they were written after Mem's autobiography and offered insights about recently published books. For example, *Tough Boris* was written "with the deliberate purpose of giving boys permission to talk about crying" (Fox, 1993). In another article, Mem Fox (1993) expresses concern about the political message that *Wilfrid Gordon McDonald Partridge* sends about the elderly:

> There is cultural acceptance in *Wilfrid* that old people should be separated from their families and placed in homes where they can die together in the care of paid personnel. . . . In Singapore, *Wilfrid* contributes to an understanding of our peculiar custom of abandoning the elderly in our society. Singaporeans find it shocking. . . ." (p. 656)

Author Videos

Meeting an author on videotape is a powerful culmination to an author study. In terms of researching an author, though, videos often present only a brief glimpse and tend to place the accent on the author as writer. For example, the Mem Fox video by Trumpet Club (1992) begins with Mem Fox in an Australian zoo, moves to her home, and then to her writing studio, where she talks about her writing habits and writing process as well as the genesis of her books. While the video does a delightful job of capturing the wonderful and wild Mem Fox, it only skims the surface. Videos cannot replace written autobiographical material. Available also are audiotapes of speeches that authors give at national conventions such as the National Council of Teachers of English (NCTE) and the International Reading Association (IRA). Figure 5-5 presents a list of author videos.

Hunting down biographical references can be time-consuming. Although it is enlightening to access as much reference material as possible, it is not necessary to track every resource in order to implement an author study. If you have an autobiography, you have enough to support an author study. If an autobiography doesn't exist, a combination of the author's video/audiotape and the material in the reference books mentioned previously should suffice. Of course, as you revisit this author in subsequent years, you can expand your reference file.

ALEXANDER, LLOYD
A visit with Lloyd Alexander. New York: Penguin.

AVI
Avi. Nashua, NH: Delta Education.

BABBITT, NATALIE
Natalie Babbitt. Nashua, NH: Delta Education.
Good conversations! A talk with Natalie Babbitt. Tim Podell Productions.

BROWN, MARC
Meet Marc Brown. Hightstown, NJ: American School Publishers.

BUNTING, EVE
A visit with Eve Bunting. Boston: Houghton Mifflin.

CARLE, ERIC
Eric Carle: Picture writer. New York: Philomel.

CHERRY, LYNNE
Get to know Lynne Cherry. New York: Harcourt Brace.

COONEY, BARBARA
A visit with Barbara Cooney. New York: Penguin.

DE PAOLA, TOMIE
A visit with Tomie de Paola. New York: Putnam.

EHLERT, LOIS
Hands. New York: Harcourt Brace.
Get to know Lois Ehlert. New York: Harcourt Brace.

FOX, MEM
Trumpet video visits Mem Fox. Weston, CT: Weston Woods.

FOX, PAULA
Paula Fox. Nashua, NH: Delta Education.

GEORGE, JEAN CRAIGHEAD
A visit with Jean Craighead George. New York: Penguin.

KEATS, EZRA JACK
Ezra Jack Keats. Weston, CT: Weston Woods.

KELLOGG, STEVEN
How a picture book is made. Weston, CT: Weston Woods.
Trumpet video visits Steven Kellogg. Weston, CT: Weston Woods.

L'ENGLE, MADELEINE
Madeleine L'Engle. Nashua, NH: Delta Education.

LOWRY, LOIS
A visit with Lois Lowry. Boston: Houghton Mifflin.

MACAULAY, DAVID
David Macaulay in his studio. Boston: Houghton Mifflin.

MARSHALL, JAMES
James Marshall in his studio. Boston: Houghton Mifflin.

MARTIN, BILL
A visit with Bill Martin. New York: Holt.

McCLOSKEY, ROBERT
Robert McCloskey. Weston, CT: Weston Woods.

FIGURE 5-5   *Author (fiction) videos*

McDermott, Gerald
Get to know Gerald McDermott. New York: Harcourt Brace.

McKissack, Patricia
Good conversation: A talk with the McKissacks. Weston, CT: Weston Woods.

McPhail, David
In flight with David McPhail: A creative autobiography. Portsmouth, NH: Heinemann.

Milne, A. A.
Meet the author: A. A. Milne (and Pooh). Hightstown, NJ: American School Publishers.

Most, Bernard
Getting to know Bernard Most. New York: Harcourt Brace.

O'Dell, Scott
A visit with Scott O'Dell. Boston: Houghton Mifflin.

Paterson, Katherine
The author's eye: Katherine Paterson. Hightstown, NJ: American School Publishers.
Meet the Newbery author: Katherine Paterson. Hightstown, NJ: American School Publishers.

Peet, Bill
Bill Peet in his studio. Boston: Houghton Mifflin.

Pinkney, Jerry
A visit with Jerry Pinkney. New York: Penguin.
Meet the Caldecott Illustrator: Jerry Pinkney. Hightstown, NJ: American School Publishers.

Polacco, Patricia
Patricia Polacco: Dream keeper. Weston, CT: Weston Woods.

Potter, Beatrix
Beatrix Potter: Artist, storyteller and countrywoman. Weston, CT: Weston Woods.

Rylant, Cynthia
Meet the Newbery author: Cynthia Rylant. Hightstown, NJ: American School Publishers.
Meet the picture book author: Cynthia Rylant. Hightstown, NJ: American School Publishers.

Sendak, Maurice
Sendak. Weston, CT: Weston Woods.

Speare, Elizabeth George
A visit with Elizabeth George Speare. Boston: Houghton Mifflin.

Steig, William
Getting to know William Steig. Weston, CT: Weston Woods.

Tudor, Tasha
Take joy! The magical world of Tasha Tudor. Weston, CT: Weston Woods.
Take peace! A corgi cottage Christmas with Tasha Tudor. Weston, CT: Weston Woods.

Waber, Bernard
Bernard Waber in his studio. New York: Harcourt.

Wells, Rosemary
A visit with Rosemary Wells. Weston, CT: Weston Woods.

Yolen, Jane
Good conversation: A talk with Jane Yolen. Weston, CT: Weston Woods.

Figure 5-5 *(Continued)*

Organizing Learners: A Continuum of Literature-Based Perspectives

Central to the implementation of an author study are decisions about organizational aspects such as: Who chooses the author's book? Will these books be read aloud to the children or will they be read independently? How will the books be discussed— whole-class discussions? Literature circles? Independent response?

Hiebert and Colt's (1989) continuum of literature-based reading perspectives offers an organizing framework that is helpful in addressing these and other questions. These experts propose that most literature-based reading programs essentially fall at one of three points on the continuum: teacher-led instruction, teacher-student-led interaction, or independent application. They illustrate each point on the continuum by discussing older reading programs such as Great Books (teacher-led instruction) and Jeanette Veatch's Individualized Reading Program (independent application). A synopsis follows of each of these perspectives, with examples of more current literature-based programs and with implications for author studies.

Teacher-Led Instruction

Recall that, in Chapter 2, Mr. Underwood chose *Missing May* as the class book and involved the students in an analysis of the story's plot structure and of the story's primary and secondary themes. This is an example of teacher-led instruction, also known as the core-literature approach (Tompkins and McGee, 1993). In an author study grounded in this perspective, the teacher decides which book the students will read, whether the book will be read aloud or independently (or a combination thereof), how many chapters will be read during class or for homework, what instruction will be delivered, and so forth. Essentially, the teacher is in charge of the literary experience.

Many teachers design author studies from this perspective. They often begin with a read-aloud book and then move to a class set of another of the author's books, or vice versa. Generally, whole-class discussions of the author's works characterize this model as does whole-class instruction. The popularity of this model centers on the fact that, because students have read or heard the same books and have been introduced to the same instructional information, they share a communal experience as well as a bank of common knowledge that can be tapped in subsequent reading ventures. In addition, the teacher deals with only one book at a time. Potential drawbacks, though, include the selection of books by the teacher that are not of interest to some students, resulting in half-hearted participation, and the difficulty in running effective whole-class discussions.

Independent Application

In contrast to the teacher-led perspective, the independent application perspective rejects the centrality of the teacher in the literature program and insists that children will not become self-sustaining readers unless they are given daily opportunities to read literature of their own choice and at their own pace (Atwell, 1987). Teachers designing an author study from this perspective set up a display of an author's books and invite children to choose books of interest. Reading logs of book choices are kept by the students. Because whole-class discussions are impossible in this model, response primarily occurs in the form of dialogue journal entries—letters written to the teacher in which readers share their thoughts and feelings about books. These letters are read and responded to by the teacher. Minilessons—concentrated periods of instruction (five to fifteen minutes) that usually spring from the assessment of the children's needs and interests, but not from a common book experience—are conducted daily.

Author studies that adhere exclusively to this perspective rule out the possibility of a shared literary experience and make it more difficult to rally students around an author. In addition, teachers may feel overwhelmed by the sheer volume of books (chapter books in particular) they have to read in order to respond cogently to students' dialogue journals.

Teacher- and Student-Led Interaction

This perspective strikes a compromise between the two ends of the continuum. An example of this perspective is the literature-based program known as Literature Circles (Harste and Short, 1988; Routman, 1994). Believing that at least some choice is important, teachers implementing an author study from this perspective "sell" three or four books and then ask children to sign up for the book that appeals to them. Students, usually in groups of five or six, are assigned a certain number of pages to read by a certain date. They read the assigned pages independently, write responses, and meet with the teacher for discussion. Teachers espousing this model believe in the importance of social interaction—books need to be discussed with a community of readers, rather than just with the teacher in dialogue journals. They also believe that teacher participation in these discussions is important if children's understandings are to be extended. Direct instruction often takes place in these small-group meetings. As the groups finish, they sign up for another of the author's books and the cycle repeats itself. Challenges to this model include the degree of preparation it takes to be ready to discuss three books simultaneously in addition to teaching different minilessons per group. The continual juggling of literature groups demands strong organizational skills.

Rather than subscribing exclusively to any one of the above perspectives, many teachers strive to incorporate all three perspectives with the goal of affording: a) both student- and teacher-choice of literature, b) whole-group, small-group, and individualized grouping patterns, and c) social and independent response to literature. Whereas some teachers begin with literature circles or with independent choice, most start with a read-aloud or with a class set of the author's books in order to provide children with a communal experience that brings readers inside the aesthetic, critical, and biographical dimensions. With multiple opportunities for aesthetic response around this common book, children learn how to respond aesthetically to other books in the author study. With opportunities for instruction in a literary element such as theme or character development, children learn how to apply this knowledge to the author's other books. With opportunities to speculate on life-literature connections, children refine their biographical hunches as they journey through other books. Once this core book has been explored, children can continue to explore the author's other books in literature circles and during independent reading. Obviously, how we organize our author studies is tied to issues of time, age of learners, material availability, and so forth. When possible, it is advantageous to provide multiple literacy experiences during an author study.

Establishing a Tentative Timeline for the Author Study: Expect the Unexpected

I use the word *tentative* here intentionally. Becky Shepard, a second-grade teacher in Burlington, Massachusetts, launched the school year with a Marc Brown author study with the intention of completing it by the end of September. At the end of the month, the second graders refused to let go. They had heard about a Marc Brown Writing Contest on PBS and begged Becky to let them write stories so they could enter the contest. The Marc Brown author study was still going strong in December.

Joanne Lionetti (1992) describes an author study on Tomie de Paola that began "as a typical author study [that] grew into a project of such magnitude that it lasted a whole year" (p. 65). Enchanted with de Paola's *The Art Lesson*, the third graders begged for more books. Many of the read-alouds were followed by projects—making popcorn and growing unpopped kernels (*The Popcorn Book*); making quicksand (*The Quicksand Book*); and identifying clouds (*The Cloud Book*). In addition, the third graders completed task cards; for example, the third graders had to count the number of hearts in each book, make a graph, and glue it to their response logs. The culminating project was a class biography about Tomie de Paola that the third graders titled *The Art of the Heart Man*. When de Paola received a copy, he was so delighted with their efforts that he did a telephone interview with the third graders.

What began as an innocent read-aloud of Leo Lionni's *Frederick* torpedoed into a full-blown, yearlong rendezvous with the life and literature of Lionni—with Reeny, one of Vivian Paley's kindergartners, at the helm. (See Chapter 3 for a synopsis of Paley's (1997) *The Girl with the Brown Crayon*.) Once Paley realized the momentum that was building around Lionni, she asked herself, "Why not, in a manner of speaking, invite Mr. Lionni (excuse me, Leo Lionni) to spend the year in our classroom? He's right here, inside these books on the table. We can ask him anything we wish and, if we become persuasive enough, he cannot withhold answers" (p. 17).

But then she hears:

> "Hey, not so fast! What about us?" shout the hundreds of other books surrounding me. "You can't just go off with one author and forget the rest of us!" As if I could ever ignore these old favorites, so rich in language and lore. But surely there is merit in concentrating on a single author, if for no other reason than to discover what happens. The shelves of books glare at me, in the manner of Cornelius's [*Cornelius*] associates, scorning my radical notion. Even the librarian seems disapproving. But no, she simply wants to close. (p. 17)

Stymied, Paley talked to her co-teacher, Nisha, who grew up on the Hindu epic *Ramayana* from her earliest years, about the efficacy of this Lionni journey. Nisha counseled:

> You have to understand, Vivian, we heard stories from the great epic *every day*; this is why they had such an effect on our thinking. I'm certain the reason Leo Lionni seems abstract to some . . . is that we did not spend enough time with him. One or two books, isolated, are understood only superficially. But all of his books . . . now that would be something. (p. 20)

Paley and Nisha, with Reeny and her peers, plunged headlong into a year of glorious revelation and affirmation.

These teachers are telling us that, when we invite children to collaborate on an author study, we have to expect that it will take on a life of its own—a life buoyed by the children's unbridled enthusiasm and seriousness of purpose. This was certainly my experience with the Mem Fox author study (as well as the others profiled in this book).

As to the question that opened this section, there are no fixed answers. The Mem Fox author study took root in a mere two-week period; what I would have given for a two-month stretch! The life of an author study depends on many factors: the author chosen, the interest and investment of the children, and the curricular priorities that must be met. If I had to suggest a minimum number of weeks for a picture-book author study, I would say three weeks. (See Chapter 6 for a timeline on chapter books.) However, when we can push against the boundaries of time, the rewards, as we have seen, are bountiful.

Journeying Without a Detailed Road Map

The author studies conducted by Becky Shepard, Joanne Lionetti, and Vivian Paley, as well as those profiled in this book, sprouted wings because children were invited to guide the journey. None of these teachers began with a preplanned author unit. Rather, they trusted the constructive ability of the young mind to offer ideas worthy of pursuit. These teachers watched and listened each day, and went home each night to chart the next day's course of events—events that would bring to fruition the children's viable ideas. Central to execution of these ideas was responsive instruction, both direct and indirect. What to teach was determined, in large part, by the children's authentic ideas.

Author-Study Culmination

A culminating project is an essential feature of an author study because it provides a sense of direction and purpose, and because it holds the author study together. The best projects are usually those that the children have generated. Of course, as with every aspect of an author study, we need to judge the feasibility and educative value of their ideas. Examples of some of the culminating projects described in this book include: a videotape sent to Mem Fox that included biographical hunches and a Readers' Theatre performance; the creation of the class book *The Magic School Bus Goes to the Vernal Pool*, which was sent to Joanna Cole; and an interview with Carolyn Coman, conducted by the sixth graders.

One grand—but expensive—culmination is the author visit. For readers to meet the person who has moved or delighted them in some way through his or her literature heightens the literary experience tenfold. Avi, for example, often presents his life and his work in the form of a slide show. He shows pictures of his home, his family, his hobbies. He shares writing samples from his school days, talks about the humiliation he suffered because of his dysgraphia, and offers encouraging words to children who struggle in school. He talks about how he finds ideas and how he goes about the task of writing. A session with Avi is a very personal encounter for readers.

Successful author visits require careful planning (Buzzeo, 1998). The author's publishing company or agent should be contacted, usually a year in advance. A few months prior to the visit, the publishing company or agent should be recontacted with requests for photographs, autobiographical material, curricular suggestions, and promotional materials (e.g., bookmarks or posters). As the visit approaches, the children should be immersed in an author study that probes aesthetic, critical, and biographical dimensions; at the least, children should be listening to and/or reading as many of the author's books as possible. Children should be invited to respond to the author's works via art, music, drama, and/or written responses. Art and other written displays can be used to decorate the site of the author visit. Children may want to organize a brief performance to welcome the author. Fliers should be sent home informing parents about the upcoming festivities and encouraging them to participate in author activities at home. A few days before the visit, it is helpful for children to brainstorm appropriate questions and comments. A must-read before any author visit is Daniel Pinkwater's (1993) humorous but pointed *Author's Day*.

Concluding Comments

Unlike prescribed curricula, author studies turn on the creative and intellectual energy of collaborative partners: teachers and students. Although author studies are anchored in the dynamic interaction of this partnership, they require considerable knowledge on the part of teachers. They require knowledge about authors and their works, about the efficacy of literature-based programs, and about the fundamental literacy and literary principles that underpin author studies and about the research that marks children's literary understandings (Chapter 3). Only with this knowledge can the journey into an author's life and literature be sustained.

6

Chapter-Book Author Study: Featured Author: Avi

Charlotte Huck and colleagues (1987) write that "the province of literature is the human condition: life with all its feelings, thoughts and insights" (p. 4). Avi has a gift for bringing us inside the human condition and for allowing children to teach us life's enduring lessons. In *The Barn* we find ourselves reveling in the resilience and fortitude of a nine-year-old boy who pushes against the boundaries of hope to pursue his father's dream. In *The Fighting Ground*, we despair as Jonathan's thirst for manhood is quenched on the blood of the battlefield as he learns firsthand about man's inhumanity to man. In *To Tell the Truth*, a Newbery Honor book, we squirm uncomfortably as half truths mushroom out of control, and we are reminded of our own human frailties. In *The True Confessions of Charlotte Doyle*, another Newbery Honor book, we navigate the waters of good and evil with Charlotte, one of Avi's most powerful protagonists, and learn what it takes to fight injustice. In these books as well as in his other award-winning books, Avi accords children the highest level of human dignity, of intelligent thought, and of personal empowerment. It is little wonder that children and adults alike find his books intellectually and morally compelling.

Avi's journey to critical acclaim, however, was filled with bumps and bruises. At a conference in 1995, Avi spoke candidly and poignantly about his school history:

> . . . in 1951, I graduated from the eighth grade. I had not the slightest interest in writing. I was a voracious reader though. I was read to constantly as a kid, and taken to the library every Friday. Books were enormously important. At this time, I thought I wanted to be a scientist because I had won a science medal, and so I entered a major science high school in New York City. At the end of the first marking period, freshman year, I failed every class I had taken, and my parents yanked me out of that school. They didn't even ask. They put me into a very small private school in Manhattan that had a great emphasis on reading and writing.
>
> At the end of my third year, the English teacher called my folks and told them that I was the worst student he had ever had. He said that unless I had tutoring or went to summer school, they would not permit me to stay. Now I need to mention

that I am disgraphic. My parents knew it from a very early time in my schooling but chose not to tell me for reasons I truly don't know. Maybe it was the practice. Maybe they were embarrassed. When I found out about this, my mother already had died. When I asked my father about it, he said that was my mother's decision. It made for a lot of bad and bitter feelings.

It's important for you to understand that writing was highly valued by my family. My parents had wanted to be writers. My aunt was a newspaper reporter. My grandmother was a playwright; my great grandparents were writers. I grew up in a family of writers, and now my parents were being told that I couldn't write. It was an insult to my culture and to my family. So my parents asked a friend of the family to tutor me that summer. She was a wonderful teacher who taught me more than the basics of writing. She did something that nobody had ever done before. She asked to see my writing. Now, just the thought of showing her my writing was awful. I couldn't bear any more criticism but I was given no choice. When I went to meet with her, she didn't talk about my terrible spelling or my bad grammar. To my amazement, all she did in that first session was talk about the ideas in the stories and plays I had written. And then she said the words that changed my life. She said, "You know, you're very interesting. If you wrote better, people would know that." For a twelve-year-old-looking sixteen-year-old, the thought that people would think I was interesting because I wrote something, was a revelation—it turned my life around.

When I tell this story to the kids, they really don't believe that I was a bad writer. So I bring along some of my high school papers to show them how much of a struggle writing was, and still is, for me. I show the kids a piece that I wrote to get some extra credit, and I read my English teacher's comments:

> You are not a good enough student to take on this sort of work. From now on, write two page stories that are correctly spelled and punctuated, that show effective sentence construction and possess interesting word choice. A half page of good work is better than twenty pages of sloppy work.

There absolutely is nothing wrong with what he is saying but there is a good deal wrong with how he is saying it.

What is really interesting is that in my senior year I kept a diary, the only year I kept a diary. In March of 1955, I wrote, "I can't wait anymore. I'm going to be a writer." The diary has three interests: reading, writing, and girls. What I find fascinating is that there is almost no reference to this man, my English teacher. He is doing all this heavy criticism and I am paying no attention. It is so heavy that I've obliterated it. And I am totally consumed with reading and writing.

How, then, did I become a writer? That diary that I kept contains a list of books that I was reading—three or four books a week. I even put one of my own books—a short story—on the list. Next to this entry, I write, "That's nice to put down." I really believe I became a writer through my reading of masters such as Dickens, Hemingway and others.

When I get to college, I have been so traumatized by this English teacher that I take only one semester of English. I have a bachelor's degree and a couple of masters degrees but I have never taken another English class again. I just won't do it. I don't take writing classes either. But I am writing all the time in college. I start off by writing plays. How clever of me to have done that because if I used bad grammar, I could say, "Well, that's how people talk." This shrewd move represents one of the totally unconscious ways that I taught myself to write. When I was a junior in college at the University of Wisconsin, there was a play writing contest and I submitted my play. People wrote anonymous comments about the plays. I didn't win, of course, and one of the comments was:

> This writer should be encouraged. Clearly, he is a foreign-born, non-English speaking person, struggling to write in English and he should be encouraged.

However, the following year I did win that play writing contest and that was my first taste of communicating effectively.

It was not until I had kids of my own that I started to write for children. I wrote an animal story for my son, Shawn. The first book I published came out in 1970; it was a collection of very short stories—stories that I told to Shawn. Most of the copies are still in my basement—not too successful but I was enormously pleased. From that time on, I only wrote children's books. Thirty-four books have been published, more than 100 editions, in this country and elsewhere, and I am very proud of them. It's wonderful to do something well, when you are told you can't do it at all.

Thus, it was a fusion of factors—Avi's tenacity, a book filled homelife, and the instruction of one teacher and of several master writers—that enabled Avi to defy the odds, and eventually to earn critical acclaim:

> *The Fighting Ground* (1984): Avi has written a taut, fast paced novel that builds to a shattering climax. His protagonist's painful, inner struggle to understand the intense and conflicting emotions brought on by a war that spares no one is central to this finely crafted novel. (Traxel, 1985)

> *The True Confessions of Charlotte Doyle* (1990): "Not every thirteen-year-old girl is accused of murder, brought to trial, and found guilty." This direct opening line powerfully launches a novel of extraordinary achievement and resonance. . . . Expertly crafted and consistently involving, it is sure to excite, enthrall, and challenge readers. (Mercier, 1991)

To study Avi's works is to study the complex moral issues that penetrate the substance of our lives. It is to study his triumph of personal fortitude and his vindication of a history of school failure. It is to study the art of storymaking—memorable stories with "spirited plots, believable characters, vivid atmosphere, accurate historical detail, and considerable irony and wit" (Senick, 1991). And finally it is to study the tenuous connections between Avi's life and literature.

This chapter profiles excerpts of an author study on Avi's works implemented with Maura Albert and her fifth graders. It is grounded in the principles of author study as multiple response that were explored in Chapter 3. It begins with a brief overview of the design features of chapter-book author studies. It then presents the classroom context in which the author study on Avi took place, and highlights the aesthetic, critical, and biographical events that were implemented with the fifth graders.

Designing and Implementing a Chapter-Book Author Study

The design and implementation of a chapter-book author study parallels, in significant ways, that of the picture-book author study (Chapter 5). These parallels include:

1. *Decisions about author selection.* Avi (1982) reminds us of the power of aesthetic evocation when he writes, "Give them a world they can understand and they will read you. Give them a world that expands, or better, defines their unspoken, often hidden perceptions and extraordinary sensibilities, and they will embrace you" (p. 28). Authors who touch the sensibilities of young readers through the telling of a well-crafted tale and who offer a glimpse of how their works connect to their lives are worthy of sustained study. The decision about which author to study can be made by the students themselves, in collaboration with the teacher, or by the teacher. If the results of an author-interest survey reveal the popularity of one author whose works evoke multiple responses and are of high literary quality, it is judicious to follow the students' lead. However, because students' affinity for authors can be as wide-ranging as that of adults, it also is appropriate for the teacher to work with students to select an author. Students can be asked to vote for one of three acclaimed authors. It is also entirely appropriate for a teacher to do the choosing—to bring his or her love of a particular author to students or to choose a particular author whose works dovetail with a curriculum area such as social studies or science. Such is the case of the author study profiled in this chapter. Maura Albert, the classroom teacher, chose Avi for her author study because *The Fighting Ground* illuminated the fifth graders' study of the American Revolution, a curricular requirement.

   Of course, the issue of book availability also enters the selection equation. If survey results show a strong interest in Katherine Paterson, but no class sets or multiple sets of any of her books are available, a challenge arises. Yes, the author study on Paterson can be launched with a read-aloud, but at some point children need access to her works, which means the teacher must raid school and local libraries to gather sets of some of her books as well as individual copies of other books.

2. *Decisions about ways in which children will experience the author's literature.* Will a whole-class core book be used to launch the author study, or will children select one of three books to read and discuss the book in small groups? Will children have opportunities to self-

select and to read independently some of the author's other works? Offering as many of these experiences as possible heightens the literary experience.

3. *A commitment to the guiding principles of author study as multiple response.* These principles are presented in Chapter 3.

One major difference, however, between chapter-book author studies and picture-book author studies is the time factor—at both the preparation and implementation stages. At the preparation stage, what is an afternoon of delightful adventure with the picture books of authors such as Mem Fox or Eve Bunting turns into many afternoons of equally delightful engagement with the works of prolific authors such as Avi or Lois Lowry. Ideally, to really know an author's works, we need to adhere to Avi's advice about reading all of an author's works in chronological order to examine recurring themes and the evolution of the writer's craft. However, reading an author's entire body of work may be a formidable task. (Avi, for example, has written more than forty books.) Prior to beginning the of the Avi author study, I had read seven of his award-winning books. Because much of Avi's literature is not autobiographical in nature—with the exception of minor links such as settings, characters modeled after family members and friends, and a few endearing childhood experiences—I decided to pursue the three books that Avi considers to be loosely autobiographical (*S.O.R. Losers*, *"Who Was That Masked Man, Anyway?"* and *Wolf Rider*). In addition, because the Avi author study was tied to the American Revolution, I read all of his historical fiction that I hadn't read before, in the event that the author study might move in this direction. In total, I read fifteen books prior to the author study.

At the implementation stage is the question of how many chapter books are needed to make an author study viable. Some educators suggest that one core chapter book and one or more additional books, read independently or with the teacher, constitute an author study (Tompkins and Hoskisson, 1995). Others suggest three or four chapter books (Roberts and Nicoll, 1988). Obviously, the answer is linked to the time frame available, to the length and density of the novels, to student interest, and to other curricular demands. Although some chapter books can be read and discussed in two weeks, others take significantly longer. In the Avi author study that follows, Maura's fifth graders spent over a month on *The Fighting Ground* alone because of its integration with an American Revolution unit. While *The Fighting Ground* served as a core book, the fifth graders also were reading other Avi books independently and writing personal reflections. In addition, because eight of the fifth graders had read *Poppy*, a literature circle was convened to provide opportunities to respond aesthetically and critically to this and other Avi books. In general, I recommend a minimum of four chapter books—one core chapter book read by everyone, one read aloud by the teacher, and at least two other books read independently or as part of a literature circle.

Classroom Context

Literacy is woven into the fabric of Maura Albert's classroom—from the start of the day to the final bell. Each morning opens with two "news broadcasters," with microphones and newspapers in hand, reporting on current events. Different students then take turns reading a favorite poem, sharing a book review of a recently finished novel, and telling or reading a few favorite jokes. An integral part of the literacy curriculum is a program called *The Kids on the Block*, which is designed to promote understanding of disabilities. Eight life-size puppets, each with a different disability such as blindness or dyslexia, are introduced to the class over time. For example, the fifth graders met the puppet Ellen Jane Peterson, who has Down syndrome, by listening to an audiotape in which she explains her disability. Then a group of students, sensitized to the challenges of this disability, practiced and eventually performed a series of Readers' Theatre scripts in which Ellen Jane encounters prejudice and works to put stereotypes to rest. These puppets literally become members of the class. The fifth graders bring them to class meetings and sometimes answer questions in the persona of their puppet; they reenact skits during free time. The fifth graders also visit with real individuals who have various physical and mental challenges. This year, two of the fifth graders wrote an article about one of these visits that was published in the local newspaper. This program and many other activities such as a Reading Marathon—the fifth graders bring sleeping bags to school and read for four consecutive, uninterrupted hours—keep literacy at the forefront.

Maura's literacy program is exclusively literature-based. The fifth graders choose their own books, read a minimum of fifty pages a week, and complete book cards that contain the main idea of the story and a personal response. These cards are shared during morning meeting and then tacked to the Book Review bulletin board. Independent reading occurs in the reading corner, complete with two couches and throw pillows. In addition to independent reading, students read core books throughout the year. Some of these core books become part of an author study. For example, the fifth graders read Mildred Taylor's *The Friendship* (1987), *The Gold Cadillac* (1987), and *Mississippi Bridge* (1990) and were encouraged to read other books by Taylor during independent reading. They listened to an audiotape in which Mildred Taylor talks about her life and her literature.

The Avi Author Study

During the second half of the school year, Maura's fifth graders study the Revolutionary War; Avi's *The Fighting Ground* anchors this study. A synopsis of *The Fighting Ground* is presented in Figure 6-1. However, because *The Fighting Ground* assumes a good deal of background knowledge on the part of the reader, the unit begins with a brief introduction to the Revolutionary War—why the war started, who the Tories were, and so forth. This introduction includes analysis of the famous painting of Paul Revere and the Boston Massacre. As the fifth graders inquire about the columns of

134

Longing for the glory of battle and the fame of victory, Jonathan, a thirteen-year-old boy, disobeys his father's order and joins a small band of militia men whose mission is to defeat the Hessians, mercenaries hired by the British. Leading the motley band is the Corporal, a man with little respect for life, who lies to his men about the arrival of auxiliary forces. They are outnumbered by the Hessians, and the skirmish ends in mayhem with the Americans retreating and Jonathan captured. Struggling with feelings of terror and cowardice, Jonathan makes no attempt to escape. Following the bellow of a cow, the Hessians come upon an empty house. Jonathan, unable to speak German, motions to the soldiers that the cow needs milking. With a wink from the young Hessian soldier, Jonathan enters the shed to retrieve a bucket. To his shock, he finds a young boy. Unsure about whether to tell the soldier, Jonathan leaves the boy, milks the cow, and returns to the house. The soldier gives him some milk and bread. Jonathan begins to wonder if the Hessians are his friend or his enemy. Under the pretext of milking the cow again, he enters the shed and, deciding that he must trust the soldiers, brings the boy back to the house. The boy leads Jonathan and the soldiers to the field where the boy's parents, shot to death, lie. Jonathan, distraught that the Hessians probably killed the parents, finds the courage to insist that they help him bury the bodies. They do so grudgingly. Angered by this butchery, Jonathan decides to kill one of the sleeping Hessians. With gun pointed, he tries but cannot pull the trigger. Feelings of failure crush him. He decides to escape with the boy and to find the Corporal so he can do what Jonathan could not do. Exhausted and dejected, he finds his troop and relates what transpired, only to learn that it was the Corporal who killed the boy's French Papist parents, alleged allies of the Tories. The Corporal insists that Jonathan lead them back to the house. Sickened by the horror of it all, he refuses, but is given no choice. When they arrive, the Corporal orders Jonathan to open the door, and to signal if the Hessians are sleeping. Jonathan, however, enters the house and tries to warn the Hessians of the ambush. The Americans fire at the house, calling for the Hessians to surrender, knowing that none speak English. The Hessians, using Jonathan as a shield, step outside. Jonathan frees himself, and the Hessians are murdered. In a moment of outrage, Jonathan smashes his gun and walks home alone. His father thanks God for his son's return.

FIGURE 6-1 *Synopsis of Avi's* The Fighting Ground

smoke surrounding the soldiers, Maura asks them to offer hypotheses. However, it is not until they meet Jonathan, loading and firing his gun in *The Fighting Ground*, that their hypotheses are confirmed or rejected.

As with other novels read during the school year, Maura asks the fifth graders to begin *The Fighting Ground* by surveying the book. They study the title page, note the copyright and dedication, read the back cover, and thumb through the book, noting chapter titles and illustrations. As they survey, they record their observations and predictions about the story. Figure 6-2 presents an example of Lyra's survey; note the

The Fighting ground Survey

1. By Avi, an exellent writer
2. Takes place in Revolution
3. About a boy who fights
4. very "realistic, a stunner
5. what it's like to be in a war (is what you expierience
6. recieved a Scott O'dell) award for Historical fiction
7. Copyright 1984
8. Jonathan (the main character) finds the real war is inside himself
9. In 1778-New Jersey
10. has a glossary for the German language.

FIGURE 6-2 *Lyra's survey of* The Fighting Ground

astuteness of this avid reader's eighth item on the survey. With regard to the survey, Maura notes:

> It's important for kids to think about the book's setting—time and place—before reading. Often I find, for example, that they'll say, "Hey, the artist didn't get the picture right." With the front cover of *The Fighting Ground*, they noted that the artist made Jonathan look eighteen instead of thirteen. As one of the fifth graders asked, "Don't artists have to read the book?" In addition they come up with intriguing predictions about the story. I think these predictions sharpen their attentiveness to the book.

Because the opening of the *Fighting Ground* contains many new terms and concepts not previously introduced, such as German-speaking Hessians, mercenaries, traitors, and French Papists, Maura reads aloud the first twenty-five or thirty pages over a few days as her students follow along. They discuss these new concepts and connect them to previously learned Revolutionary War concepts. With this careful jump-start, the fifth graders are ready to read independently the rest of the book.

Because the Avi author study took two months to complete, it is not possible to replay daily sessions here. Rather, we turn now to specific sessions that illustrate the three dimensions of author study as multiple response—aesthetic, critical, and biographical.

Aesthetic Response to The Fighting Ground

The fifth graders read independently a certain number of assigned pages per week and write a one- or two-sentence summary statement as well as a personal reflection in their response journal. In general, the fifth graders choose one of three questions to guide their personal reflections:

1. What did you wonder about as you read the story?
2. What were your thoughts and feelings as you read the story?
3. Is there a part of the story that reminds you of something that happened in your own life?

These questions are crafted to evoke aesthetic response to the story. Not surprisingly though, the fifth graders, like most readers, shuttle back and forth across the aesthetic-efferent continuum. Figure 6-3 attempts to illustrate the range of their aesthetic and critical response. The top section of Figure 6-3 identifies two categories of aesthetic response: Personal Connections and Identification with a Character. Personal Connections are responses that spiral out of the book and into the readers' lives. The second category, Identification with a Character, occurs when readers assume the identity of a character, assess the wisdom of the character's decisions, and then extrapolate about what they would do in the same situation. Both categories of response move

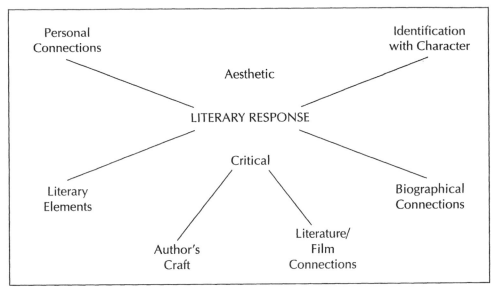

FIGURE 6-3   *Range of the fifth graders' responses*

the reader beyond the text and into the domain of self-reflection. Excerpts from the fifth graders' response journals, presented in Figure 6-4, illuminate each of these categories. (Note: The bottom half of Figure 6-3, which captures the range of readers' critical response, is explained in the next section.)

When asked specifically for personal revelations, the fifth graders write convincingly about parallels between their lives and Jonathan's, as Jennifer's response reveals (Figure 6-5). Others tell tales of disobeying and lying, and their consequences; tales of being reunited with loved ones; and tales of having expectations about events that end in disappointment. Many of the fifth graders acknowledge the moral power of literature:

- "What I learned was not to trust the friend that told because she would probably do it again. It was the exact opposite of what Jonathan learned. He learned to trust his father, because most of the time he was right."
- "I learned to trust whom you should."
- "Don't let your so-called friends use you like the Hessians used Jonathan."
- "I learned that being brave is not always doing what people say is right, but doing something because you believe it is right."

Critical Response to The Fighting Ground

The lower section of Figure 6-3 captures the range of the fifth graders' critical response to *The Fighting Ground*. These responses differ from the aesthetic responses at the top of

Personal Connections

"I know the feeling that Jonathan (J) felt when he was marching with the men. Last year, on the way to my first performance of the *Little Mermaid,* I was so nervous and so excited. I felt like if I said something I would throw-up."

"I know the feeling when everyone is telling you to do something. When I heard that, I began to think of when I played in a soccer game and everyone said to block the goal. I was so scared. I did not block it and the other team won."

"Now J understands war. He used to think it was fun and games. He used to think he would always win. It's like when I play 'Oregon Trail II' (computer game), I just click on the animal in front of me and BANG. It's dead. None of this is true in real life. I wouldn't want to kill any animals. J now truly understands war."

Identification with Character

"If I were J, I would eat, rest, and give the boy some food, blankets, and something to drink. Then when I went out in the morning to 'milk the cow,' I would grab the boy and run. The soldiers left him alone sometimes, so he would have time to run and the boy so small and would be easy to carry."

"If I were J, I would have thrown up burying the boy's parents."

"If I was J, I would refuse to stay with the Corporal and the men who are going back to capture the Hessians. I wouldn't want to see any more killing."

FIGURE 6-4   *Excerpts of fifth graders' journals: Aesthetic responses to* The Fighting Ground

Figure 6-3 in that they are text-bound—rather than spiraling out of the text, readers remain anchored in the text. Four categories of critical response along with supporting evidence from the fifth graders' journals are presented in Figure 6-6 on page 142:

1. *Analysis of literary elements:* When readers of any age are asked what they think about a particular book, they first offer a global, evaluative response ("It was great," "It was boring."). When asked for elaboration, they often critique the literary elements of the story. They tell you the degree to which the plot was engaging and fast paced. They note how well the characters were developed, interpreting their actions and analyzing their motives. They offer their analyses of the story's major and minor themes. As Figure 6-6 reveals, the fifth graders assume the role of story critic with ease.

2. *Critique of author's craft:* Children often are forthright in their assessment of how well the author has crafted the literary elements that undergird the story.

NAME: Jennifer Keating

Think about something that happened in the *Fighting Ground* that reminds of something that has happened in your life. Write what happened, how you felt about it, and perhaps, like Jonathan, something you learned.

When Jonathan disobeyed his father by going to war reminded me of when I was in 1st grade, and in time out. I remembered that I had to return something to my friend Jackie. That was when I made the wrong decision. I had decided to go to her house and return it. So I quietly snuck out of the house. After returning it to her I stayed and played on the computor with her and her baby-sitter for about 20 min. Then I remembered that I was supposed to be in time out. I tried to sneak back into my house without getting caught but my mother was panicking because she didn't know where I was. Then she saw me and I had to stay in time-out double time (which meant a lot when I we seven.)

Jennifer Keating
(Jennifer E Keating)

FIGURE 6-5 *Jennifer's aesthetic response to* The Fighting Ground

3. *Biographical hunches:* When readers are moved or jolted by a certain story event, they ask, "I wonder if this really happened to the author?" and hypothesize biographical connections.

4. *Literature/Film connections:* Literary acumen triggers an awareness of intertextual influences. When readers detect similarities between plot structures or theme explorations, they think, "This reminds me of that other book I read or of that film I saw."

Many of the fifth graders' critical responses are invitations to further exploration. Obviously, though, we have to be selective about which dimension(s) of their response will be examined in greater depth, attending to factors such as the extent of their intrigue, what has and hasn't been covered in the literacy curriculum, and the potency of the critical element in the works.

The pursuit of character development in the Avi author study emerged from the fifth graders' persistent comments about Avi's characters in their response journals (see Biz's example in Figure 6-7), and from a powerful class discussion that Maura led. As you read the following excerpt, note the skill with which Maura guides their thinking:

MAURA: How is Jonathan changing?

KRISTEN: After he tried but couldn't kill the Hessians—he just couldn't do it— he threw himself on the ground and looked up at the sky and realized how stupid war was. He's getting more responsible and mature.

MAURA: What makes you think he's getting more responsible and mature?

JEN: Because he's been taken prisoner and he's starting to realize what war is really like.

MAURA: What's he doing that shows he's becoming more responsible?

JEN: One thing he did was he didn't shoot the Hessian soldiers. He took the little boy instead.

MAURA: Why didn't he shoot the soldiers?

SAM: Because one big bang would wake up the Hessians and then Jonathan would be dead. So instead of letting off a big bang, he should have stabbed them with the bayonets on the guns.

CLASS: Ewww! Gross! Then they'd all be dead.

MAURA: How many people think that if Jonathan had a way to kill the Hessians, he would have? (About a quarter of the hands go up.) How many think he would not have killed them? (About half raise hands.) Why not?

TOM: Well, I think he didn't shoot them because he was too scared. He's just a lousy soldier. Plus he knew he couldn't kill them all because the others would wake up as soon as he shot one.

BARRY: He could have loaded all the guns first.

MAURA: We know how long it takes to load a gun so it might be a little tough.

Analysis of Literary Elements

Character Analysis:

"When Jonathan (J) is being pulled by the rope, I think the pain in his heart is either heartburn or emotional. He thought the soldier was being nice, then he just yanks him along."

"I wonder why the Corporal doesn't just have everyone [his militia men] go into the Hessian's hideout. Are they all afraid so they have a 13 year old boy do it for them?"

"I feel bad for the boy because he has to be with the Corporal who killed his parents, and chased his brother away. I think the Corporal likes killing too much."

Plot Analysis:

"I think the part where the soldiers are scared of a cow is dumb. I can recognize the sound anywhere. Either the Hessians have their dairy products imported or may be they don't live in a rural area. Maybe cows there make different moos."

"I'm happy they are finally at the fighting ground and this chapter will not only be the soldiers walking."

"When J is marching and listening to the drum, it made me feel like something bad or exciting is going to happen like in a movie you can tell by the music, you can feel the drum.

Theme Analysis:

"When the lady was at the well, I began to think of all the unfairness between men and women back then. Of course, when the lady heard the word enemy she ran inside all scare. I bet if a man was out there he'd be acting all tough and everything."

"I think J had a few good reasons not to shoot the Hessian. 1. He knew it was pointless to take a man's life. 2. He would probably have a guilty conscience for the rest of his life."

Critique of Author's Craft

"I like the way Avi puts in detail but sometimes it's gross like finding the boy's dead parents. I don't think Avi puts it in to be gross, but to be a better writer and to make you feel like you are in the story."

"I can't believe how many times Avi has the corporal says, 'Damn.' He must have a really bad temper. It is getting kind of annoying."

Biographical Hunches

"I wonder if Avi was in a war or something. He might be because he is kind of old. He knows a lot about guns and soldiers."

"When the Corporal congratulates J on how he did, I found some kindness in the Corporal's heart which is kind of strange. I wonder if the corporal has some other hidden feelings like sadness. Maybe Avi had a rough childhood and when he wrote this part, he was remembering one of his parents so he thinks of how a child should be treated."

Literature/Film Connections

"This part reminds me of the movie *Titanic*. All the adults just leave their kids to fight there way to a life boat."

"I felt sad when he passes his dead friend's house. It reminded me of the story *Dicey's Song* when she lives in her dead mother's home. I am in suspense now!"

"When J didn't turn back at the beginning of the story, it reminded me of a time in *Shabanu* when the father has to sell Guluband to keep his pride just like J."

FIGURE 6-6   *Excerpts of fifth graders' journals: Critical responses to* The Fighting Ground

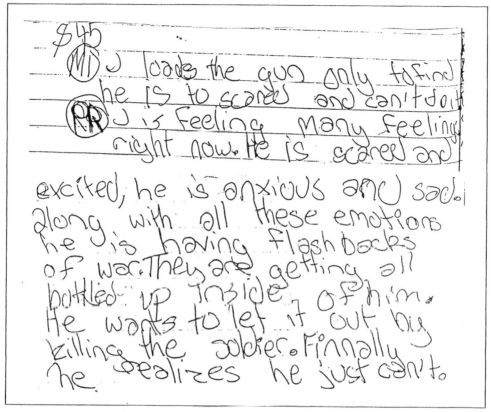

Figure 6-7 *Biz's critical response to* The Fighting Ground

LYRA: He was too chicken to do what he was supposed to do and he didn't want to because he was too sad and he thought that they were his friends.

MAURA: You've given me two reasons. Was he chicken or did he think of the Hessians as friends?

LYRA: He thought the enemy was his friend.

MAURA: What do think about that?

LYRA: I think it was stupid. I think they [the Hessians] tried to make him think that he was their friend.

MAURA: So you think they planned that. Someone else?

ADAM: I think he did the right thing—grabbing the boy and running but he should have done it sooner.

BIZ: I think he might have done the right thing because the Hessians could have shot him anytime like when they caught him but they didn't.

MAURA: Why didn't they shoot him?

BIZ: There's two reasons. He's a child and he could be bait for them.

MAURA: Ah, so they may have a good reason and a not-so-good reason.

JESSICA: But Avi doesn't say that the Hessians were using him for bait. I don't think they are. I think they don't want to hurt him because he's just a kid.

JEN: I think he shouldn't have shot them [the Hessians] anyway. It was a good choice not to shoot them because he might not be alive if they didn't take him hostage.

MAURA: What would have happened to him?

JEN: He could have died from not enough food. He didn't have any water. They fed him and stuff.

MAURA: So in a funny way, the Hessians helped him.

JEN: They basically saved his life and that's why he didn't shoot them. He probably would have felt too guilty.

TED: I think he was scared not because he was chicken but because he would have a guilty conscience about killing. It just wasn't right to take their lives.

MAURA: How many agree with Ted and others that even if he could think of ways to kill the soldiers, he wouldn't have used any of these ways because he felt it was wrong to kill. (Most hands go up.)

As this conversation reveals, the fifth graders were taken with Jonathan as a character. They struggled to sort out the internal conflict that paralyzes Jonathan throughout much of the story—his duty as a soldier versus his duty as a human being. Because of their intrigue with Jonathan, and because the literary element of character development had not yet been explored, I designed and implemented a series of minilessons to deepen their understanding of this literary element. Descriptions of these minilessons follow.

Minilesson One: Coming to Know the Characters: Author Techniques

I present a large spider map with Jonathan's name in the middle and ask the students to write their thoughts about him on their individual spider maps. As they share ideas, I record them on the large map: disobedient and dishonest, caring, brave, coward, crazy to go to war, immature, bad soldier . . .

I ask them to give evidence that Jonathan was disobedient and/or dishonest in story. Jen replies, "In the beginning when his mother and father told him not to go beyond the tavern, he did." I record this information in the top left box on another chart (a blank version of Figure 6-8). Kyle adds, "There's another place too at the end when he disobeys the Corporal at the Hessians' hideout." He then qualifies his answer, "But in some ways he was helping someone even though he was disobedient to the Corporal." I acknowledge this critical observation about two different kinds of disobedience and note the moral decision making connected with this second incidence of disobedience. I then ask for additional evidence about disobedience and dishonesty. John replies: "He lied because he told his father's friend that he was allowed to go to war." Using the actual dialogue that verifies John's statement, I tape this response to the second box (Figure 6-8). I ask if Jonathan lied to anyone else. Biz

Disobedience/Dishonesty	
Author's Technique	Evidence
Actions	Disobeyed his parents about going to war
	Disobeyed the Corporal when he didn't follow orders at the Hessian hideout
Words	FATHER'S FRIEND: Your father know? Give permission?
	JONATHAN: Yes, sir . . .
	FATHER'S FRIEND: You sure he sent you?
Others' Comments	TAVERN KEEPER: Ah you. Your father came a-looking for you. Had permission, did you? You're a sly boots, you are.

FIGURE 6-8   *Three techniques authors use to develop characters*

notes, "He also lied to the tavern keeper that he had his father's permission to go to war." Again, I attach the actual dialogue to the chart.

At this point, I explain that we have generated two important ways that we come to know characters—by their actions and by their words. I ask them to examine each of the two completed boxes and to label them accordingly. They do this with ease. I note that there also is a third way that readers come to know characters. I write the words "Others' Comments" in the bottom right-hand box of the chart (Figure 6-8). I then present two excerpts from *The Fighting Ground* and ask which is evidence for the category "Others' Comments":

1. Tavern keeper: What's your father to say?
   Jonathan: Told me to come.
   Tavern keeper: Did he?

2. Tavern keeper: Ah you. Your father came a-looking for you. Had permission, did you? You're a sly boots, you are.

After some discussion about who's doing the commenting, the class agrees that the second scene involves comments of another character.

As we review the three techniques that authors use to bring their characters to life, I ask if Avi is the only author to use them. They respond that all writers use these techniques, making reference to Mildred Taylor.

Minilesson Two: Experimenting with Character Techniques

Returning to the spider map in the previous lesson, I circle two other attributes they ascribed to Jonathan: caring and cowardly. I then hand out a puzzle worksheet (a blank version of Figure 6-9) and explain that they will work with partners to complete it. On the left side are the character techniques: "Actions," "Words," and "Others' Comments." At the top of the worksheet are the two attributes, "Caring" and "Felt Like a Coward." (I shifted from their term, *cowardly*, to "felt like a coward" to make the distinction at a later point about the difference between being a coward and not doing the right thing, and feeling like a coward but doing what is right.) Under each of the attributes are three blank boxes. I explain that each team will receive an envelope that contains five events or excerpts from *The Fighting Ground*, and that its job is to decide where these cards go in accordance with the attributes and techniques. I point out that, on each card, there are two events or excerpts; I encourage them to add another piece of evidence. I also remind them that they have six boxes but only five cards. The completed puzzle sheet is presented in Figure 6-9.

The students easily sort the "Caring" versus "Cowardly" cards and correctly categorize the "action" and "word" cards for each attribute. In addition, they are eager to share additional pieces of supporting evidence. For example, for the "Caring/Actions" category, they suggested examples such as:

- "At first, he didn't want to tell the Hessians about the little boy because he didn't know what they would do to the boy."
- "He tried to save the Hessians."
- "He buried the boy's parents."

With regard to the final quote, Michael comments, "But it says that on the 'Words' card." This insight provides an opportunity to note the interplay among the techniques.

The one category that causes some confusion is "Others' Comments." About a third of the class put the card with the excerpt "'Don't worry,' said one of the men. 'You're here. Don't you worry'" under the "Caring" column. These students viewed the man and the Corporal as caring in these episodes. I clarify the statement for them.

As the session ends, I note that we have studied only three of the techniques that authors use to bring characters to life, and mention other techniques such as character appearance and character's thoughts.

Minilesson Three: Round and Flat Characters in The Fighting Ground

I place a blank character map on the overhead with "The Boy" written in the center and ask students to brainstorm attributes about this character. They reply that he speaks French, is young, and is an orphan. I note the factual nature of their observations and ask if we can generate a list of adjectives for the boy, similar to the list we did for Jonathan. The only characteristic they offer is scared. I ask what would happen if we tried to complete our "Actions"/"Words"/"Others' Comments" chart. "We really couldn't do it because we really don't know much about the boy other than he's scared," replies Biz.

I introduce the terms *round character* and *flat character* without defining them. I

	Caring	*Felt Like a Coward*
Actions	1. J comforted the baby by giving him some milk, setting up his bed, and patting his head. 2. While it would have been much easier to escape on his own, J takes the baby with him. 3.	1. After J ran into the woods to escape the Hessians, he collapsed and started to cry. (p. 54) 2. After the soldiers fell asleep, he got his gun and tried to shoot the old soldier. But his fingers would not move. 3.
Words	1. "Anyway, I buried them," said J. "Thought it was right." (p. 117) 2. "We went farther after that," he continued, "till we found the house. It was a cow needing to be milked . . . I milked her." (p. 115). 3.	1. While hiding in the woods, J noticed blood on his shoe. "Oh, God, O God, O God," he whispered. He had failed in all he meant to do. (p. 55) 2. "I tried to kill them," he said, his voice, faltering, "I really did. But I couldn't . . . I just . . . couldn't." (p. 119) 3.
Others' Comments		1. "Don't worry," said one of the men. You're here. Don't you worry." (p. 118) 2. "How old are you?" asked the Corporal. "Thirteen." "Listen to me," he said. J looked up into the man's face. He saw sadness there. "You did very well," said the Corporal. 3.

FIGURE 6-9   *Puzzle activity on author techniques*

explain that most books have these two types of characters and ask if they can guess which term applies to the boy. They immediately reply, "Flat." Lyra explains, "Well, the boy is flat because Avi makes him speak French so we don't know what he's saying or thinking." Sara adds, "And he doesn't have hardly any actions." I concur and note that flat characters are not well-developed—thus the term *flat*. I ask why Avi would put a flat character like the boy in his story. Philip replies, "Because Jonathan would have been able to take his gun and run but he couldn't because of the boy." I follow Philip's lead and explain that flat characters are essential to most stories because they interact with and reveal things about the lead characters.

With the term *flat* assigned to the boy, I ask what makes Jonathan round. They note how much more they know about Jonathan as compared to the boy. Then Ed observes, "There is another flat character—the young soldier. We know he was a little kinder than the other soldiers but that's about it." Vanessa adds, "And the Frenchman too." They have the distinction.

Minilesson Four: Round and Flat Characters on Television

To reinforce the concepts of round and flat characters, I explain that books are not the only place where we find such characters. I present a blank version of the worksheet in Figure 6-10 with the show "Home Improvement" labeled on the TV screen. Before I ask my next question, Ted shouts, "Tim is the round character." I ask for evidence. Their comments range from "His wife thinks he's hopeless" to "He's always goofing around like the time he shaves a balloon on his show." I ask if they could come up with evidence for all three author techniques. They agree they could if they watched one of the shows. Again without prompting, Michael exclaims, "Oh I know a flat character. You know that guy you never see his mouth."

"Mr. Wilson," others shout. Again, I ask them to substantiate; they do so without hesitation.

"What about Al? Isn't he flat?" asks Jessica.

Steve replies, "I don't think so because he always expresses himself and he puts Tim down."

As others enter the debate, Vanessa suggests, "He's not as round as Tim but he's not as flat as Mr. Wilson either."

"Yeah, he's in the middle. Let's make him an oval!" exclaims Tom. The others delight in his suggestion. After convincing arguments about his "oval" status, I add an oval and Al to the overhead.

They then plunge into their TV worksheets. I delight in their enthusiasm, but as

FIGURE 6-10   *Jen's assignment of round, flat, and oval TV characters*

they share their ideas (Figure 6-10), I recognize a huge flaw in the activity. As they are blurting out shows such as "Xena: Warrior Princess," "South Park," "Buffy: The Vampire Slayer," I realize that I haven't heard of, never mind watched, any of these shows. Unable to confirm or reject their choices for round and flat characters, I end up emceeing the activity: "Raise your hand if you agree that Tommy Pickles is a round character in 'Rugrats.'"

Minilesson: Avi Meets Aristotle

I ask the group to recall the discussion we had with Mrs. Albert about how Jonathan changes over the course of the story. I direct them to three posters, presented in Figure 6-11, and place three scrambled title strips—"False Courage," "True Courage," and "Feeling Cowardly"—above the posters. Without further explanation, I ask groups to match titles to posters. Before discussing their choices, I hang a picture of Aristotle next to the title strips and explain that this famous, ancient philosopher wrote about courage and cowardice. I ask what a philosopher is. Michael replies, "Well my friend's father is a philosopher and he just sits and thinks and writes about life, at least that's what my friend says. Kinda strange." I explain that the word *philosophy* is composed of two root words: *philo* meaning love,

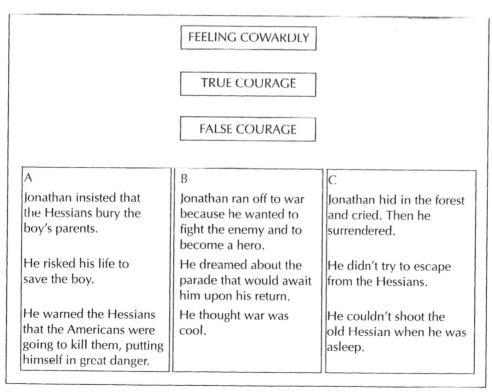

A	B	C
Jonathan insisted that the Hessians bury the boy's parents.	Jonathan ran off to war because he wanted to fight the enemy and to become a hero.	Jonathan hid in the forest and cried. Then he surrendered.
He risked his life to save the boy.	He dreamed about the parade that would await him upon his return.	He didn't try to escape from the Hessians.
He warned the Hessians that the Americans were going to kill them, putting himself in great danger.	He thought war was cool.	He couldn't shoot the old Hessian when he was asleep.

FIGURE 6-11   *Students match titles to episodes in* The Fighting Ground

and *sophos* meaning wisdom. Given that definition, I ask again what a philosopher is. Lyra replies, "Someone who loves wisdom?" I continue that philosophers are scholars who try to answer questions such as "What's the purpose of life?" and "What is a good life?" I explain that philosophers read and think deeply about the great works of ancient philosophers like Aristotle and then try to fashion their own answers to these important questions.

We begin with poster A. Biz matches the title *"True Courage"* to the poster, explaining, "Jonathan knew that the baby's parents had to be buried because it would be terrible to just leave them there so he got the Hessians to help him even though they could have killed him or hurt him because he was their prisoner of war." I ask if the group thought that Jonathan was nervous or frightened while he was insisting that the Hessians bury the parents. They agree that he was. I share Aristotle's conviction about true courage (Figure 6-12); we discuss Aristotle in relation to Biz's example and to the third example on poster A. I add, though, that a truly courageous person is not just one who risks his life as Jonathan did. I explain that quiet acts of courage fill our daily lives when we do the right thing for the right reason. I then share, "When I was about nine years old, I dropped my parent's wedding picture and broke the glass. When my mother found it, she blamed my sister. At first, I didn't say anything because I was afraid of getting punished. But then I felt guilty, and confessed. My mother scolded me and told me I had to do extra jobs around the house to earn money to replace the picture frame. I wasn't happy about being punished but I felt better about doing the right thing." My story prompts similar tales of their quiet courage that range from being truthful about starting a fight to stealing money and confessing to the crime. I note also that, according to Aristotle, bravery is not about doing the right thing because you expect a reward or you want fame. Instead, bravery is doing the right thing simply because you know it's right.

We move to poster B; the group agrees that it should be titled *"False Courage."* As Philip remarks, "It's false courage because Jonathan wanted to be a famous sol-

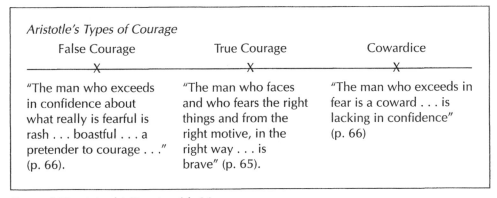

Aristotle's Types of Courage		
False Courage	True Courage	Cowardice
X	X	X
"The man who exceeds in confidence about what really is fearful is rash . . . boastful . . . a pretender to courage . . ." (p. 66).	"The man who faces and who fears the right things and from the right motive, in the right way . . . is brave" (p. 65).	"The man who exceeds in fear is a coward . . . is lacking in confidence" (p. 66)

FIGURE 6-12 *Aristotle's Doctrine of the Mean*

dier but he didn't even know anything about war." I explain that Philip's idea that "he didn't even know anything" is what Aristotle calls ignorance. Aristotle believes that you can only be brave if you know the risks involved. If you are ignorant of the risks and you jump into a situation just because you think others will think you're great or tough, you are not brave at all— rather, you are foolish. John says, "One time me and my friends were playing dares and they dared me to pull the fire alarm but I didn't and they called me a chicken but I didn't care because I didn't want to get in trouble."

I probe further, asking: "What other reason would there be for not pulling a fire alarm?"

Lyra responds, "Because everyone thinks there might be a fire. You shouldn't scare everyone like that."

Discussion of the final poster centers on the interplay of fear and courage. I ask why Jonathan felt cowardly when he tried but couldn't kill the old, sleeping Hessian.

"Because soldiers are supposed to be brave enough to kill the enemy and Jonathan wasn't," replies Kristin.

"Was it simply a matter of not having the courage to shoot or was something else holding him back?" I ask.

"He knew it was the right thing to do so he didn't do it [shooting the Hessian], even if it made him feel like a coward," notes Tom.

I review Aristotle's courage continuum (Figure 6-12). I then ask the students to sequence the posters in Figure 6-11 in accordance with Avi's storyline. They note that, at the beginning of the story, Jonathan exhibits false courage, then experiences cowardly feelings for much of the story while continuing to do brave acts, and finally exhibits true bravery without guilt or shame. I ask why Avi would have Jonathan go through these changes. "So it makes Jonathan real to us. If Avi had Jonathan be brave and tough throughout the story, he wouldn't seem real," comments Jen.

I reply, "And vice versa. If Jonathan remained cowardly throughout the story, we'd lose interest in him. To make Jonathan believable, Avi had him experience the same range of emotions that we would experience if we were in the same situation. When characters go through believable changes, we call them dynamic characters. Jonathan, then, is a round, dynamic character."

Biz asks, "What would the Corporal be? He doesn't really change. He wanted to kill the Hessians at the beginning and end of the story."

I introduce the final character term, *static*. They are quick to attach the "Static" label to other nonchanging characters in *The Fighting Ground*, such as the Frenchman.

Literature Circle: Poppy

Because eight of the fifth graders had read *Poppy* independently, I convene a literature circle to revisit Aristotle's courage-cowardice continuum. I divide the students into two groups and hand each group three posters: the first is labeled "False

Courage," the second "Feeling Cowardly," and the third "True Courage." I ask them to write episodes in which Poppy exemplifies each stance.

Tom asks, "Does it have to be Poppy because Ragweed is a great example of false courage?"

I ask Tom to explain. "Well, at the beginning of the story Ragweed is so crazy because he goes out in the open to get some nuts and he makes fun of Poppy for hiding in the log. He says he's not going to let any old owl scare him. But his false courage gets him eaten by Mr. Ocax."

I reply, "Ragweed is a perfect example of false courage. He thinks he is fearless, and goes to great lengths to boast about his bravery and to belittle Poppy in the process. But he pays the ultimate price for his recklessness."

In response to Tom's question, I ask them to focus only on Poppy. "But," observes Philip, "I don't think there is a false courage situation for Poppy." I explain that I found one instance and encourage them to try to find this episode. When we reconvene, each group successfully identifies episodes for feeling cowardly and for true courage (Figure 6-13). Only one group arrives at the false-courage episode: "When Mr. Ocax told Poppy she was awesome, she came out of the cornfield and almost got eaten." We talk about how Poppy, feeling cocky about outsmarting the owl, decides to taunt Mr. Ocax about being a coward. Wooed by Mr. Ocax's praise of her intelligence, she drops her guard and becomes reckless.

Reminding them about how Avi moved Jonathan from false bravery to true bravery, I ask if the same sequence is apparent in *Poppy*. They respond that Poppy starts off feeling cowardly, and then moves to true courage when she decides she must risk her life to find a new home for her family. We talk about how Poppy faces her fear and takes no unnecessary risks while on her mission. However, with her mission accomplished, Poppy becomes boastful just as Ragweed did at the beginning of the story, but her near-death experience with Mr. Ocax restores her humility. We discuss the differing courage sequences that Avi employed across the *Fighting Ground* and *Poppy*, and agree that both sequences result in believable, engaging characters.

"What matters," says Lyra, "is that we feel for the characters and the changes they go through."

Autobiographical/Biographical Response

Lesson One: Hunches About Avi

During the reading of *The Fighting Ground*, Kyle asked if we could play "Jeopardy!" with the book. I suggested that instead of the book, we try a modified version of "Jeopardy!" to explore what they already knew about Avi's life. While I had reservations about turning Avi's life into a game, I decided to use it as a prelude to the important part of the session—their hunches about Avi as a person and writer. Obviously, this game format would only work if they has some knowledge about Avi. After *The Fighting Ground* was read, Maura had shared the contents of a brochure

FIGURE 6-13   *Biz's team's evidence of Poppy's true courage*

that Avi distributes to audiences. In the brochure, Avi includes answers to the most frequently asked questions about himself as a writer and a person. Therefore, the fifth graders already had some autobiographical information.

I open the lesson by presenting a large chart to which twenty-five index cards are attached. The cards are arranged in two columns of ten (cards labeled A–J) and one column of five in the following fashion:

Avi as a Child (100 points)	Avi as a Writer (200 points)	Avi's Careers (300 points)
A	A	A
B	B	B
C	C	C

Each card has one statement about Avi; game participants must decide if the statement is true or false. Figure 6-14 presents the game items and answers.

I also explain, though, that the game is incomplete—missing are the 400- and 500-point questions—and that their job is to create these items by generating hunches about Avi as a person. To illustrate, I present a chart with a section labeled "Hunches" and one labeled "Possible Evidence." On the hunch side, I write: "Avi is a history buff." Before I can ask for evidence, the fifth graders call out three books: *The True Confessions of Charlotte Doyle*, *The Man Who Was Poe* and *The Fighting Ground*. I ask for evidence specific to each book. I add another hunch to the chart: "Avi is athletic." Silence follows this item until Sarah says, "Not in *S.O.R. Losers*—all the kids are clods and can't even play soccer." I ask for further evidence. Ted replies, "He doesn't really put sports into his books so I don't think he's too athletic." We talk about the thinness of our data on this hunch. I stress that our hunches, even those supported by Avi's books, are still only hunches that will need verification from autobiographical sources.

I then pass out the hunch/evidence worksheet and ask partners to propose other hunches about Avi along with possible evidence. I explain that because these items will be used in our "Jeopardy!" game, groups are not to share their ideas with other teams. As Figure 6-15 reveals, they are brimming with ideas.

"Jeopardy!" begins with much excitement. Players correctly answer eight of the ten childhood questions (Figure 6-14, column A); missing only Avi's reading habits and his favorite subject. The history answer surprises them because "he uses a lot of history in his books." They answer correctly eight of the ten questions about Avi as a writer (Figure 6-14, column B). When I ask how they knew that Avi rarely writes about things that have happened to him, Biz replies, to my amazement, "In *Something Upstairs*, Avi told Kenny in the interview at the beginning of the book that he hardly ever writes about things that happened to him." For the item "Avi loves words," the team guessed false because, "If he flunked reading and writing, how could he love words?" Michael counters, however, "But how can he be a writer if he doesn't love

Avi as a Child	Avi as a Writer	Avi's Careers
Avi's parents read to him when he was young. T	Avi learned to write by reading voraciously. T	Avi began his career as a playwright. T
Avid got good grades in school. F	Writing is still a struggle for Avi. T	Avi is artistic and has illustrated books. T
Avi loved to play sports. F	Avi rarely has to revise his drafts. F	Avi is an experienced sailor. F
Avi was shy as a child. T	Avi includes messages in his books that he wants readers to think about. T	Avi was a farmer before becoming a writer. F
Avi was very popular in school; he had lots of friends. F	Avi mainly writes about things that happened to him. F	Avi worked as a librarian for 20 years. T
Avi almost flunked out of high school. T	Avi has a hard time coming up with ideas for his next book. F	
Avi was a poor writer when he was in school because he had a disability called dysgraphia. T	Avi loves words. He cares about choosing the right word, and about creating the right imagery. T	
Avid read three or four books a week. T	Avi likes to write books that have a lot of suspense. T	
Avi's favorite subject was history. T	Avi has never won an award for his writing but his works are very popular. F	
Avi got his name from his twin sister. T	Avi writes only about strong male lead characters. F	

FIGURE 6-14   *True/false items about Avi's life*

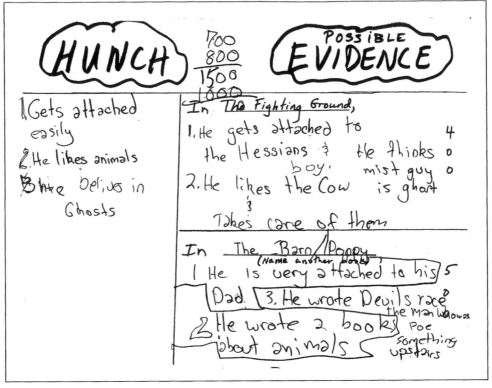

FIGURE 6-15   *Lyra's team's Hunch/Evidence activity sheet*

words?" The third set of questions (Figure 6-14, column C) prove to be difficult, with only two correct answers. For example, they guess that Avi was a farmer because of *The Barn*. They guess that he was an experienced sailor, citing *True Confessions*, *Windcatcher*, and *Beyond the Western Sea*. Puzzled, Kyle asks, "But how can he write those books?" When I turn the question back to them, Brad suggests that, "Maybe he talked to sailors and read some books about sailing." I confirm that Avi does extensive research for most of his books.

The hunch aspect of the game results in interesting life-literature connections. Each team reads its hunch about Avi (see Figure 6-16), and other teams offer possible evidence from *The Fighting Ground* and from other books. If they connect their hunch to *The Fighting Ground*, their team earns 400 points; if they support this hunch with evidence from another Avi book, they earn an additional 500 points. As the session ends, I explain that I will cull their hunches and possible evidence for the next lesson and will share excerpts from Avi's autobiographical and biographical information so that we can confirm or reject their hunches. I remind the class that our hunches are based on a limited number of books; if we had time to read more books, our hunches would be stronger.

Hunches About Avi	Possible Evidence	Biographical Data
Avi is close to his dad.	In *The Fighting Ground*, his dad is so happy to see him at the end. In *The Barn*, Ben's father was proud of him and Ben built the barn for his dad.	"Even though Avi's family did things together, he often felt isolated from his family members—especially his parents. John Wortis (Avi's father) did not show affection readily, and he was particularly distant with Avi" (Markham, 1996, p. 39). Avi often felt ignored by his parents (Markham, 1996). "Avi uses the father in *Poppy* to poke fun at some of his father's traits" (Markham, 1996, p. 95).
Maybe his mother died or left the family when he was a kid	In *The Fighting Ground*, the mother is hardly mentioned and the boy's mother died. In *The Man Who Was Poe*, the mother was missing. In *The Barn*, the mother is dead.	Avi's mother did not die or get divorced when Avi was young. Avi doesn't talk about his relationship with his mother, other than his anger about her decision not to tell him about his dysgraphia (1995). "It was my twin sister who gave me the name Avi when we were infants. Since my family tried to discourage me from becoming a writer, I decided not to put their name on my books" (Avi, 1996).
He gets attached easily.	In *The Fighting Ground*, he gets attached to the Hessians and the boy. In *The Barn*, he is so attached to his Dad that he builds the barn to save him.	"I've led a very ordinary life in most respects. I think my adolescence was unhappy in the way that most adolescents' lives are unhappy. It has given me great empathy for the outsider" (Collier et al., 1993, p. 2505).

FIGURE 6-16   *Fifth graders' hunches about Avi: Confirmed or rejected*

Hunches About Avi	Possible Evidence	Biographical Data
He believes in ghosts.	In *The Fighting Ground*, he thinks the mist guy is a ghost. He wrote about ghosts in *Devil's Race, The Man Who Was Poe,* and *Something Upstairs.*	In the introduction of *Something Upstairs*, Avi explains that he listened to Kenny's story about a slave ghost and decided to write the story. He ends the introduction: "This is it. His story. My writing. I think it's true" (1998, p. 5).
He thinks young people are *interesting*.	In *The Fighting Ground*, he writes about Jonathan (J) the most. In *Something Upstairs*, he writes mostly about Kenny. And kids are main characters in *The Barn* and *Charlotte Doyle*.	"On the one hand, our culture likes to give a lot of lip service to support our kids, but on the other hand, I don't think the culture as a whole likes kids. . . . Children's literature is about the place and the role of the child in society. . . ." (Collier et al., 1993, p. 2505). "To Avi, all stories are maps—maps for life's journey. . . . Avi's desire to make story maps comes from his respect for young people. He has said most young people are as emotionally complex as adults. . . . He's also convinced that today's young people are aware of the harsh realities of life" (Markham, 1996, p. 89).
He saw a lot of violence when he was little.	In *The Fighting Ground*, there is war and people are killed. In *Poppy*, Mr. Ocax does cruel things. Poppy conquers her fears by killing Mr. Ocax. In *Charlotte Doyle*, the Captain does horrible things like murdering his men.	Avid does not mention experiencing violence personally, but because Word War II was raging while he was in elementary school, he listened with his family to the daily news reports and heard about the battles and casualities. Because it was feared that Germany might bomb New York, the city where Avi lived, he had to wear a metal identification tag around his neck so his

FIGURE 6-16   (*Continued*)

Hunches About Avi	Possible Evidence	Biographical Data
		parents would be able to find him. Avi also loved reading comic books, but his mother wouldn't let him read them in the house because she thought they were too violent. He listened to radio programs such as "Captain Midnight"; the Captain battled evil around the world.
He gets bored easily.	All of his books are different. He gets bored of one idea for a book so he writes about a different kind.	"People constantly ask, 'How come you keep changing your style?' I think that's a misquestion. Put it this way, 'What makes you so fascinated with technique?' and that's the answer. You know that there are a lot of ways to tell a story. To me that's just fun" (Collier et al 1993, p. 2505).
		"If you do anything all the time, it's nice to get away from it now and again. My hobby is photography" (1996, Internet).
He likes animals.	In *The Fighting Ground*, he likes the cows and takes care of them. He wrote two books with animals—*The Barn* and *Poppy*.	He loved to read animal stories best. One of his favorite books was *The Wind in the Willows* (Markham, 1996).
He stands up for what is right.	In *The Fighting Ground*, J disobeys the Corporal's order to spy on the Hessians because killing them is wrong. In *True Confessions*, Charlotte turns against the Captain because he was so cruel to his men.	Avi's parents were crusaders for social causes such as feminism, racism, the right of workers to unionize. "Although Avi often felt alone and isolated from his family, today he realizes what an important effect this had on his interests and his values, for much of his writing is dedicated to exposing injustices, especially suffering by young people" (Markham, 1996, p. 44).

FIGURE 6-16 (*Continued*)

Lesson Two: Avi Hunches: Confirmed or Rejected

I present Figure 6-16 on the overhead projector with the biographical data column covered. I read their first hunch about Avi's father, and possible evidence. Before uncovering the final column, I ask the class how much we know about Jonathan's relationship with his father aside from the reunion at the end of the story. They admit we know little. I then ask about Poppy's relationship with Lungwort, her father. Ted notes, "He doesn't care when Poppy's crying about Ragweed's death. He just says, 'Well, he deserved it.' And then he makes her go with him to Mr. Ocax's."

Kyle says, "And when she marches with Lungwort, he is yelling at her to keep the flag up. He should have carried the flag himself."

Ted adds, "When Poppy returns home, Lungwort takes credit for sending her."

We talk about Lungwort's attitude of self-importance, and his bossy nature. As we discuss other episodes, we agree that Lungwort appeared to care more about his pride than his daughter. I then ask them to think about Charlotte's relationship with her father in *The True Confession of Charlotte Doyle*. Jen replies, "He was really mean to her when she got home. He accused her of being a liar and burned her journal."

I then ask how confident they are now about this hunch. Kyle suggests that maybe Avi is not very close to his father. I uncover the verification column and talk about Avi's strained relationship with his father (Figure 6-16). I note that because teams generated this hunch on limited book data, it is not surprising that it wasn't verified. The point is made again that the more books we read by one author, the stronger our hunches, but even then, we can be wrong.

We move through the remaining hunches in a similar fashion. The students are surprised that some of their hunches are rejected, but are pleased overall that a number of their ideas are confirmed.

Lesson Three: Avi as a Young Writer

I ask the class to recall what they already know about Avi's early writing. They reiterate that he was a poor writer, but a great reader. I then place a play that Avi wrote in fifth grade on the overhead projector (Figure 6-17). Without prompting, students comment: "What a mess!" "He had terrible spelling, didn't he?" "No wonder he flunked school." I share excerpts from Avi's speech, presented at the beginning of this chapter, about the criticism and humiliation he endured from his teachers because of his difficulty with written language. We also talk about how most of us would have been crushed by this criticism and would never have dreamed about becoming a writer. I ask, "How do you think Avi was able to ignore the negative feedback?" Michael replies, "He decided that he wanted to be a writer and no one was going to stop him. Just like me, I'm going to play for the Red Sox and no one will stop me." I note that, indeed, Avi attributes his staying power to stubbornness. I add, though, that strong convictions and stubbornness are not enough—a great deal of self-discipline, hard work, and talent also are critical.

I ask the class to read Avi's play orally with me, acknowledging that some words are not legible. Ted remarks, "Now I really know Avi had dysgraphia. I have

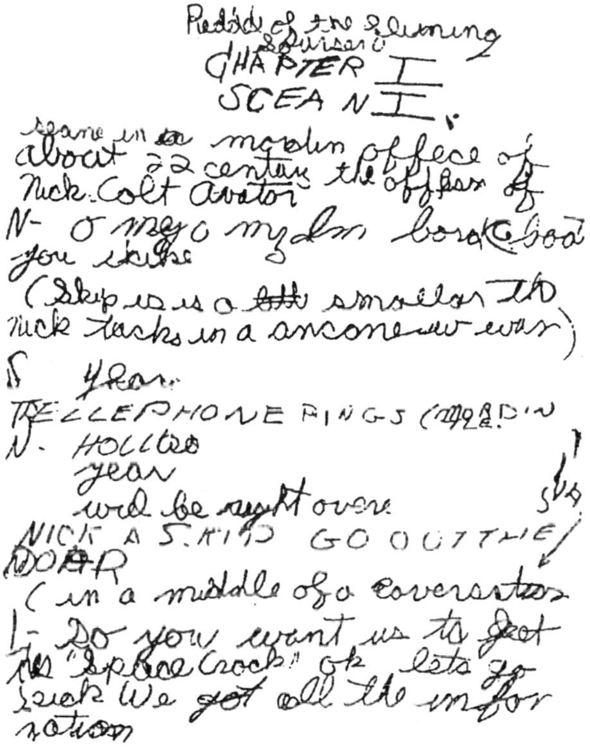

RIDDLE OF THE FLYING SAUCER

Chapter 1
Scene I

Scene in modern office of about the 22nd century; the office of Nick Colt, Aviator

NICK: Oh my, oh my, I'm bored. How about you, Skippy?

(Skip is a smaller th---- Nick talks in a ----(intercom?) even.)

SKIP: Yeah.

TELEPHONE RINGS (MODERN TELEPHONE).

NICK: Hello.

　　　Yeah.

　　　We'll be right over.

Nick and Skip go out the door —SLAM—

(in the middle of a conversation).

Scene II

NICK: So you want us to get this "Space Crook?" OK. Let's go.

SKIP: We got all the information.

FIGURE 6-17 *Avi's play, written at age nine or ten*

Scene III
JET ROCKET GOING THROUGH SPACE

Scene IV
IN JET

NICK: *Having fun!*
SKIP: *You bet, cleaning this gun of yours (sarcastically).*

Scene V
IN SPACE CROOK'S PLANE

SPACE CROOK: *I've got those police all baffled. They'll never get me. Ha, ha! And I got the nearest hideout, don't I, boy.*
(Murmurs from the other men.)

Scene VI
IN NICK'S PLANE

FIGURE 6-17 *(Continued)*

dysgraphia and he's worse than me. My spelling is better too." Maura then asks Ted about the first piece that he wrote at the beginning of the school year. Ted replies, "A play about a pencil coming to life. And one thing is that Avi has good ideas for that play but he needs more details." I then read the excerpt from Avi's speech in which he talks about his cleverness in beginning his writing career as a playwright. The fifth graders, then, rally around Ted with comments such as, "You'll be famous some day if you keep writing plays like Avi." Ted, a bit embarrassed but enjoying the attention, replies, "No way! Writing is too hard."

I return to Ted's earlier point about Avi's ideas. We talk about the importance of distinguishing Avi as a thinker and playwright, and Avi as a speller and scribe. I ask, "What separates talented writers from mediocre writers—intelligent ideas or perfect spelling?" They quickly acknowledge the importance of ideas, although Kristin wonders why Avi didn't use Spellcheck!

Avi's Autobiographical Works

Ideally, any author study on Avi should include the four works that he considers to be loosely autobiographical. While some of the fifth graders read independently some of these books, most did not possess the shared knowledge needed to analyze Avi's life-literature links. I regret that time did not permit exploration of these important books:

"Who Was That Masked Man, Anyway?"

Avi considers this to be his most autobiographical book. Life-literature connections include:

- Avi grew up in Brooklyn during World War II; Frankie, the lead character, lives in Brooklyn during World War II.

- Avi loved listening to radio shows such as *The Lone Ranger*; *Captain Midnight*; and *The Green Hornet*; Frankie is obsessed with the same shows.

- Avi used his vivid imagination to create plays based on these radio shows (see Figure 6-17); Frankie, as master spy Chet Barker, takes his fantasies one step further—he lives the life of master spy whose mission is to stamp out evils he concocts.

- During the War, Avi's family took in boarders to help with the housing shortage. One border was Millicent Selsam, author of many children's science books, and her husband; another was a medical student who kept a human skeleton in his room. Frankie's family also takes in a medical student who keeps a skeleton in his closet and who becomes "Chet Barker's" first target of evil.

- Avi played these imaginative games with his cousin and best friend, Michael Saltz; Michael is transformed to Mario, Frankie's sidekick, in the story.

163

- Avi's brother's best friend, Mario, and Avi made telephones using string and tin cans and talked to each other across the alley that separated their houses; Frankie and Mario also create and use telephones.

However, unlike Frankie, who is boisterous and fearless, Avi was shy and reserved as a child. Frankie repeatedly disobeys and lies to this parents and others; Avi acknowledges no such misbehavior on his part. Frankie's older brother, Tom, is a war hero; Avi's older brother, Henry, was not old enough to be in World War II. Thus Avi, like most writers, weaves some life events into a few of his stories, but much of his work remains fictive.

S.O.R. Losers

When Avi was in high school, he was required to play a sport. Although a sports fan, he had no interest in playing a sport. However, he not only had to join a soccer team but had to coach the team—with dismal results. His team lost every game they played. In S.O.R. Losers, Edmund Sitrow (Avi's last name spelled backwards), a seventh grader, is forced to join a new soccer team composed of other nonathletic but academically talented kids. The team is coached by a history teacher who has never played or coached soccer. The team goes down in the school's annuls as the worst team ever. In S.O.R. Losers, Avi challenges our obsession with and glorification of sports, and asks readers to rethink their priorities.

Wolf Rider: Tale of Terror

According to biographer Markham (1996), when Avi was in high school:

> He received a random and anonymous phone call from someone claiming to have killed a woman. Avi kept the caller talking for forty-five minutes while the police tried unsuccessfully to trace the call. The police told Avi to forget about the incident. He had done all he could. Naturally, Avi couldn't forget it. He found the woman's name in the phone book and called to warn her. She was a police officer, and Avi's anonymous caller had described her accurately. Avi felt this woman had reason to be concerned, but he had been told by the police not to get involved. Later, he told a reporter that he felt he should call the woman again to express his concern. The reporter warned him, 'Don't do it. The police will think that you were the caller, that it was a hoax.' Avi took his advice, but the whole incident haunted him, and he wrote Wolf Rider to try to put the incident behind him. (p. 94)

Avi uses this chilling life event to play out the reporter's prediction. Andy alerts the would-be victim, Nina, who interprets Andy's phone calls as harassment and calls the police. The police blame Andy's deviant behavior as a response to his mother's recent death. Andy's father doesn't believe Andy and insists that he cease all pursuit of the matter. Andy persists until he finds himself face-to-face with the psychotic caller, and the "Tale of Terror" begins. Underpinning the story is the strained father-son relationship that never fully resolves itself.

The Barn

When asked, "Why is *The Barn* your favorite book?" Avi (1995) replied, "Emotionally, it is as close to me as you can get. It's not literally about me, but the emotions there are my emotions. That book is about me, in one way or another." *The Barn*, set in Oregon in the mid-1800s, is about a nine-year-old boy who is called home from school because of his father's illness. Ben is shocked to find that his father can no longer move, feed himself, or speak. While his older brother and sister tend to the farm, Ben cares for his father, feeding and cleaning him, reading to him. Refusing to accept the inevitable, Ben convinces himself and his siblings that their father can communicate by blinking his eyes. When Ben asks his father if he wants them to build the barn he dreamed about before his illness, his father blinks. The siblings work feverishly to complete the barn even as their father's health deteriorates. Ben is sure, however, that the barn will restore his father's will to live. The night the barn is completed, Ben's father dies without acknowledging their accomplishment. Wracked with guilt that he built the barn, not as a gift to his father but as a gift to himself—a way of earning his father's respect—Ben crumbles. His brother consoles him, "Look Ben . . . if it weren't for him getting sick, you'd never have talked us into building that barn. You kept saying *he* wanted it. Don't you see, it was *his* gift to you."

Concluding Comments

I left this author study on Avi with a renewed appreciation for the acute sensibilities and constructive powers of the young mind. I also left it with the same sense of frustration that I have left other chapter-book author studies—too few books read and savored. The luxury of doing a yearlong chapter-book author study has such appeal. However, given the choice of no Avi author study or an Avi author study with time constraints, I'd eagerly opt for the latter.

Avi is a particularly intriguing author for an author study, not only because of his genius as a writer, but also because of the nonbiographical nature of most of his works. Avi chooses not to tie his literature to life events, although, like any writer, he cannot escape revealing what he holds dear. For two decades now, on the advice of writing experts such as Donald Graves (1994) and Lucy Calkins (1991), we have been telling children that writers anchor their stories in their life experiences and that they should do the same. Avi offers a decidedly different perspective on the art of story writing. The fact that Avi wrote *The True Confessions of Charlotte Doyle* without any firsthand knowledge of ships or sailing, relying exclusively on extensive research, sends an important message to young writers: Nonfiction can anchor fiction. In talking about *The Barn*, Avi (1995) notes:

I was taking a picture of a barn in northern California and a woman came out from an adjacent house and said, "There's a story connected to this barn. A man started to build it. He got sick and his sons finished it for him." Out of that conversation came the idea for *The Barn*. . . . Once I have an idea for a historical book such as *The Barn*, I retire to my library and start reading. Because I knew nothing about barn-building, I had to do a lot of research and to study photographs to answer questions such as, "What did people do in Oregon in 1855?" "How did they dress?" The library is a writer's best friend.

Avi reminds us that children deserve to know that story can transcend personal experience and take root in the wonderment of the world around them.

Author Response:
Avi on Author Studies

CAROL: Did you have a favorite author when you were growing up?

AVI: The answer is both yes and no. My favorite authors kept changing, which is what I hope is true for kids. I can remember picture books when I was very young and I can remember the first chapter books. There were many authors, but truly not one. I can remember reading *The Poky Little Puppy, Otto the Giant Dog, And to Think That I Saw It on Mulberry Street,* and *Ferdinand the Bull.*

CAROL: Do you have a favorite author today?

AVI: No. Too many good writers to pick just one.

CAROL: What would you like to see teachers do with your books?

AVI: Enjoy them; share them with kids. Teachers and parents need to focus on the sheer pleasure of reading. I tell teachers that the most important thing they can do is to read long books, which they enjoy, to kids every day, for at least a half hour. I also advise them to take a course in acting and voice diction so that they become better readers. It's very easy to learn to read well once you know how.

CAROL: Do you think it is a good idea for children to study the works of one author?

AVI: Well, it depends on what grade level you're talking about. I've taught college courses that focus on exactly this idea. When you read an author's work, you begin to see similarities in themes, continuity of thought, and even variation. I think an author study is a fine thing to do but not too early because I love the notion that kids are given a variety of authors. People always speak of the variety of my writing and maybe that works for kids in an author study but there are some wonderful writers who essentially write a somewhat similar kind of book. I would think that might be boring for a child.

CAROL: Teachers are pursuing author studies with young readers. For example, Marc Brown is a very popular author study in first and second grade. Do you think this kind of author study is appropriate on occasion?

AVI: Absolutely. Kids often gravitate to the books by one author because they feel comfortable with this author, or they like the kind of humor, style, etc. That can be very productive—and even fun. But you have to grasp why kids like to read these books. The *Arthur* books are series books and I think that kids have an affinity for series books because they allow them to visit time and again with a family or a group of familiar friends. There's a comfort factor in the predictability of characterization for young readers. One of the reasons readers love the *Nancy Drew* books is because she had a same circle of friends. I think both kids and adults enjoy that familiarity. Series books do more to help kids become readers and writers than any other kinds of books because they identify them as uniquely their own books.

CAROL: One of my friends began the school year with Marc Brown, thinking the author study would last a couple of weeks, but the kids just would not let go. In October, they saw a PBS writing contest and begged Becky to let them write their Arthur stories so they could enter the contest. By December, they were still pursuing Arthur books. Of course, Becky did a lot of other literature along with the Arthur books, but the staying power of Marc Brown was incredible.

AVI: I think adults also read this way. I don't know if you're familiar with a mystery writer by the name of Tony Hillerman. He has a particular slant when he writes; his detective has a singular way of thinking. I enjoy reading them because I'm interested in that way of thinking. Similarly, people read Sherlock Holmes, surely not for its originality, but for the enjoyment of the deductive process.

CAROL: Let me sketch the historical timeline with respect to the literary movements of the past because these perspectives are directly influencing the way teachers approach author studies. In the 1800s, literary biography was prominent; literature was viewed through the lens of the life and times of the author. Readers looked for and found Dickens in *David Copperfield* and in *Little Dorrit* because so much of his work was autobiographical. Many teachers approach author studies from this biographical perspective. They begin with a video in which the author talks about his or her life and then ask the children to search for these life events in their works. With your books, for example, teachers might tell children that you grew up in Brooklyn, loved radio shows, and had boarders in your house during the war. Then they'd have the children read *"Who Was That Masked Man, Anyway?"* and draw parallels. How do you feel about author studies that examine your literature primarily through the lens of your life?

AVI: I think that this focus is part of the cult of celebrity that we now live in and I think it's unfortunate. It's not that I think it's wrong to make some of these connections. But it saddens me to think that the kids feel so removed from literature that they need to make some kind of personalized contact with the author to sense that this writer is real. It's not that it's wrong; I just wish it weren't true, but if it helps, fine.

CAROL: At one of the teacher conferences I attended, you said that *The Barn* is very close to you emotionally. You didn't say why but if teachers had that information, should they try to help readers figure out your emotional life while reading *The Barn*?

AVI: The connection is very simple. I didn't get along well with my father and so I wrote a story about a kid who connects to his father in a positive way. *The Barn* is satisfying to me in two ways, first because metaphorically I was making this connection through the book, and secondly, because I think the book is extremely well written.

CAROL: It's my favorite of all your books.

AVI: As a work, there's not a word wasted; the totality of the writing experience was complete for me. I've written nothing else like it—I would like to, but I just haven't. Emotionally it was very difficult to write, short as it is, and very satisfying in that sense that it all fit together.

CAROL: Dickens talks about having to walk the streets of London at night to separate himself from his characters and about weeping uncontrollably when he had to kill Little Nel.

AVI: I've had experiences like that. Bach, the great composer, said something to the effect, "If the composer is not moved, the audience will not be moved."

CAROL: Why are so few of your works autobiographical?

AVI: Emotionally, I think they are all autobiographical.

CAROL: But we can't tap that emotion easily because you don't share the life events that underpin the emotions; we can only access the surface details of your life: you grew up in Brooklyn, you were a lousy soccer player, and so forth.

AVI: To tell you the truth I don't think I've had a very interesting life in terms of the incidents. You have a writer like Gary Paulsen who has done many things in his life. I have not had an adventurous life. I like to think I've had an interesting life, but there's nothing terribly special about it. My life is not one that is full of incidents, it just isn't.

CAROL: Another aspect of the autobiographical dimension is learning about the author's writing history and habits. You are very candid about your difficulty in school with writing and the humiliation you endured. Is this useful information to share with children?

AVI: I know it's useful because teachers tell me so. It's the converse of the cult of the personality, if you will. If you're going to hold me up as a model, it's important to hold up my writing struggles. Kids believe that I'm a successful writer today because I was successful in school and that's not true at all. Kids, in general, don't have a belief in their ability "to become." They think the good athlete is just a good athlete; he doesn't become one. They tend to shy away from what they are not capable of doing. There's so much emphasis on achievement in our culture rather than on the process of becoming. As a culture, we don't have much patience.

CAROL: During your author study, I shared examples of your early writing with the fifth graders and talked about your difficulty with written language. When I explained how your writing career began with playwriting because you didn't have to worry as much about grammar, one of the fifth graders who also has dysgraphia exclaimed that the first writing that he did at the beginning of the school year was a play for the same reason. There was such a level of enlightenment for him in listening to your story and a glimmer of hope that he too could write, although he felt that writing was too hard to pursue as a career.

AVI: One of the contradictions in the way that teachers teach is that they tell kids that they can write and that it's not that hard. But it is very, very hard.

CAROL: What cautions would you have for teachers who perceive author study as literary biography?

AVI: I think it can potentially confuse kids because kids don't think their lives are interesting. If you are constantly saying that this is a work that derives from someone's life, they look at their lives and think, "Well, my life is boring. What am I going to write about?" Most twelve-year-olds haven't had adventurous lives, so why focus on that for the basis of writing? Rather the focus needs to be on their emotionality. They don't doubt their own level of emotionality, and, to the extent that you can legitimize what they feel, that's the basis for their writing. A good example of this is in a wonderful essay written by Eudora Welty in which she expresses the capacity for living in a small community yet being enriched by an enormous degree of observation and internal development. That's really what it's all about.

CAROL: Let's move to the next literary movement called the New Criticism that emerged at the turn of this century. New Critics such as T. S. Eliot deplored this autobiographical obsession and insisted that literature is an art to be analyzed for its inherent richness and complexity. Some teachers approach author studies from this critical angle, asking readers to analyze the characters, themes, literary devices of an author's work while paying no attention to the author's life or intentions. For example, as part of your author study with the fifth graders, we focused on characterization because they were very taken with Jonathan and his personal struggle. We looked particularly at the issue of courage. I introduced them to Aristotle's doctrine of the mean, exploring the categories of false courage, true courage, and cowardice. They immediately made connections, recognizing Jonathan's false courage at the beginning of the story and so on. What do you think about this kind of critical response?

AVI: Well, bear in mind that what I try to do is to write good stories. I'm not thinking very consciously about any of this stuff. I don't think there's anything wrong with this kind of critical response as long as you don't think you're going to develop lifelong readers solely with this kind of analysis. You have to teach children to read on their own and allow them to make those private, personal connections. Now, doing this kind of analysis can be important in teaching kids to be observant and to diminish some of their self-centeredness. They need to be taught a methodology for looking at a bigger world than just themselves. To do this, critical analysis has to go beyond fiction, which occupies too much of a focus in schools anyway. Why not teach kids to be critical about newspapers? Why not teach them to be critical of the text on television or advertising? There's an excessive focus on fiction and, curiously enough, it is not the kind of literature, in the broader sense of the word, that kids are most in contact with. Think of what you could do in terms of having kids do a literary analysis of the sitcoms they watch. Bring in ten "Seinfeld" shows and say to the kids, "Let's watch these and talk about the similarities." That's the stuff of critical analysis. Instead of only bringing in people like me to classrooms, I urge teachers to contact their local newspaper and bring in the reporters, the editorial writers, the advertisers. Obviously, I'm not opposed to classroom visits because I do it all the time, but fiction is not the be-all and end-all of writing. It's a big mistake to think that it is.

CAROL: Shifting back to the historical timeline, it's clear to me that you align yourself with the current literary movement of reader response. You believe that critical response cannot come before the reader lives the book, before the evocation of personal connections. In your author study, for example, I asked the students to write about something that happened in *The Fighting Ground* that reminded them of something that happened in their own lives and to talk about what happened, how they felt. The responses were poignant—times when they disobeyed and suffered the consequences; times when they thought they could trust someone but they couldn't.

AVI: I agree 100 percent with this kind of focus. But I'll give you an example where that doesn't happen. In secondary schools and sometimes even starting in sixth and seventh grade, there is such pressure on the part of parents and teachers to have children read adult books, the classics.

Basically, they take from the child the capacity to judge the literature because it is outside the range of their own experiences.

CAROL: I can't tell you how many fifth and sixth graders are reading John Grisham's books.

AVI: Yes, they do, and they read King's books too. That's why I wrote *Beyond the Western Sea*. The kids were telling me that they were reading these enormous books, often to the surprise of their teachers. I thought, clearly, the length of a book is not a barrier to their reading, so why not write something for them at that length. If it's good enough, they'll read it. I've met fourth graders who tell me that *Beyond the Western Sea is* their favorite book.

CAROL: It reminds me of the conversations I have with third graders about their best piece of writing. When asked why it is their best piece, they tell me, "Because it's six pages long and has chapter headings." Quantity matters to them. But, returning to this perspective of reader response, let me ask you what you think a teacher should do when a child, who has been touched deeply by a piece of literature, shares a very personal, private matter. For example, the opening scene of Carolyn Coman's book on child abuse, *What Jamie Saw*, may evoke a similar sharing on the part of the child. In addition to reporting this to the legal authorities, what should the teacher do about this very personal response?

AVI: In my view, anything that happens in a classroom that enables a young person to reach out and make contact with an adult about experiences is positive. When you get into areas of abuse and other taboo subjects, it gets complicated. At the end of one of my school visits, a girl came up to me and thrust a letter in my hand, which is not unusual. I put it in my briefcase and read it on the way home. It said something to the effect, "Today, I had a good day in school. I made a new friend who is Avi. But when I get home, I will be miserable because my stepmother will hit me." When I got home, I called my host and shared the letter along with as much as I could remember about the girl because the letter was not signed. The host recognized this as a cry for help. I was the vehicle but I have no idea whether they tracked her down. Conversely, I was talking to a teacher recently who said she won't read any ghost stories anymore because the religious right objects to so-called "demonic" tales. In my view, that's nonsense. But here is a teacher deliberately avoiding what I would say is the most innocent kind of literature. In many ways, these issues go beyond the literature per se because they have to do with cultural norms, the values in the schools, and attitudes of teachers.

CAROL: Let's bring our conversation full circle. In the book, I propose the idea of author study as multiple response. My experience with author studies has taught me that children respond in a variety of ways to an author's books. I believe our job as teachers is to acknowledge this range of response, promoting aesthetic engagement before the critical or biographical. Do you think that teachers should include all three aspects, with the aesthetic response leading the way?

AVI: Sure, although I'm not a believer in the absolute in educational theory. What works with children is important. If the autobiographical approach gets kids engaged in books at some point in an author study, go for it. But, above all else, I think it is crucial to emphasize the pleasure principle in reading. That's what's going to hook the kids. It should be fun for them.

7

Nonfiction Author Study:
Featured Author: Joanna Cole

When I was ten years old, I watched a television documentary on the excavation of Pompeii and decided that I was going to become an archeologist. I would unearth the artifacts of past civilizations and offer startling revelations. I trotted off to the library and took out two archeology books. However, as I tried to access these limp, lifeless texts, published in the 1950s, my newfound passion quickly dwindled. Although I'm quite sure that archeology was a passing fancy, I wonder what would have happened if I had ventured upon the treasures that grace classroom libraries today: *Pompeii* (Connolly, 1990), *Into the Mummy's Tomb* (Reeves, 1992), *The Roman News* (Langley and DeSouza, 1996), or *Buried in Ice: The Mystery of the Lost Arctic Expedition* (Beattie and Geiger, 1992).

The embrace of nonfiction literature by teachers is a recent phenomenon. Up until the 1990s, nonfiction literature was shunned in many classrooms for a number of reasons. First, the emergent literacy research highlighted the centrality of story in the child's literacy development. Children who are enveloped in books from the earliest years have stronger vocabularies (Snow, 1983), more advanced language development (Chomsky, 1972), and greater success in learning to read in school (Durkin, 1966; Snow, 1983). As a result of this research, literature-based programs that were launched in the 1980s focused almost exclusively on fiction.

Second, researchers note that elementary children have more difficulty comprehending and writing nonfiction than they do fiction (Britton, Martin, McLeod, and Rosen, 1975; Chall and Jacobs, 1983; Alverman and Boothby, 1982). Survey results corroborate this finding. Children report that they prefer to read and to write fiction over nonfiction by a three-to-one margin (Langer, 1986). Some researchers attribute this difficulty with expository text to cognitive limitations—to children's inability to handle the complexity of informational books (Britton et al., 1975; Moffett, 1968). Other researchers, however, believe that these findings are an indictment of our instructional practices rather than a window on children's cognitive abilities (Durkin, 1978–1979; Armbruster et al., 1991). If we don't read nonfiction to children and we don't show them how expository texts work, how can we expect them to be successful nonfiction readers and writers? Preliminary research substanti-ates that direct instruction in exposition strengthens comprehension and composi-tion (Berkowitz, 1986; McGee, 1982). As for the findings about children's attitudes about nonfiction, recent research, which takes into consideration the context of the classroom, is encouraging. When young children are given the freedom to choose their own writing topics, they write cards, signs, shopping lists, directions, and "all-about" books (Bissex, 1980; Schickedanz, 1990; Sowers, 1985). In addition, in a classroom where both fiction and nonfiction were given equal billing, kindergart-ners said that they preferred the informational texts that were read to them over the fictional texts (Pappas, 1991). Indeed, the expository challenge may reflect, in part, our failure to bring nonfiction into the classroom rather than any failure on the child's part.

Third, the archeology books that sunk my fleeting dream with their forbidding presentation of facts, poor organization, and lack of illustrations tended to be stan-dard fare prior to 1980. It is not surprising that little, if any, attention was given to nonfiction literature either by teachers or children. As Milton Meltzer admitted in 1976, only a few nonfiction works had literary merit and that "a number should never have been published" (p. 22). This is not to suggest no quality nonfiction was published prior to 1980. Indeed, writers such as Jean Fritz, Joanna Cole, Milton Meltzer, and David Macaulay paved the way for the revolution that would move nonfiction into the literary limelight during the 1980s.

Last, transcending all these factors, is belief that narrative is "the primary act of the mind. . . . For we dream in narrative, daydream in narrative, remember, antici-pate, hope, despair, doubt, believe, doubt, plan, revise, criticize, construct, gossip, learn, hate and love by story" (Hardy, 1978, pp. 12–13). In essence:

> stories have a role in education that goes far beyond their contribution to the acqui-sition of literacy. Constructing stories in the mind . . . is one of the fundamental means of making meaning; as such, it is an activity that pervades all aspects of learn-ing. . . . (Wells, 1986, p. 194)

A striking manifestation of our affaire de coeur with fiction is found in the annuls of the literary associations that award the prestigious Newbery and Caldecott Medals for outstanding children's literature. Between 1922 and 1976, only five works of non-fiction received the Newbery Medal, four of which were biographies (Meltzer, 1976). Between 1938 and 1976, only two nonfiction books won the Caldecott Medal. Why? According to Milton Meltzer (1976), "The books we write are still, in many places, by many people, dismissed as 'fact' books."

What turned the tide? Essentially, the publication of beautifully crafted nonfic-tion works such as *Lincoln: A Photobiography* (Freedman, 1987), and *Volcano: The Eruption and Healing of Mt. St. Helens* (Lauber, 1986) as well as enormously popular series such as the *Eyewitness* books and the *Magic School Bus* books. These and other books published during the 1980s appealed not only to children's cognitive imaginations but also to their aesthetic sensibilities. These books made us think and feel just as deeply as some of our favorite fiction books did.

Significant also were reports about the poor performance of American children on the National Assessment of Educational Progress (NAEP) as well as on international assessments in subjects such as literacy, history, and science (Anderson, Hiebert, Scott, and Wilkinson, 1986; Finn and Ravitch, 1988). Concerns that future generations would not be prepared to face the challenges of a technologically advanced society nor to assume the responsibilities of a democracy prompted many educators to call for greater inclusion of expository texts in the curriculum (Finn and Ravitch, 1988; Daniels, 1990).

In addition, renewed calls for thematic curriculum—curriculum rooted in deep multidisciplinary understandings of a vital theme or topic—have resulted in the adoption of authentic literature and cross-curricular projects. For example, students who study Pompeii study Roman life in the first century A.D. with its great wealth, poverty, and slavery. They study the city's tragic burial by the volcanic eruption of Mount Vesuvius, and they study its subsequent excavation in the 1800s. To study Pompeii, then, is to study history, geography, economics, science, archeology, math, and mythology. Intrinsic to this thematic study is literature—historical fiction such as *The Secrets of Vesuvius* (Bisel, 1990) and nonfiction such as *Pompeii* (Connolly, 1990) and the letters Pliny the Younger sent to historian Tacitus in which Pliny gives his eyewitness account of the volcanic eruption.

The convergence of these various events has resulted in the endorsement of nonfiction literature by classroom teachers. As nonfiction literature has emerged from the literary shadows of fiction, so too have its authors. Interest in the nonfiction author studies has begun to percolate in recent years (Duthie, 1996; Keck, 1992).

In addition to celebrating the place of nonfiction in the classroom, this chapter makes the case for studying nonfiction writers with the same zeal and rigor as for studying fiction writers. This chapter showcases the wildly popular work of Joanna Cole, whose *Magic School Bus* books took elementary classrooms by storm in the late 1980s and have been delighting young readers ever since. The decision to study Joanna Cole came from the third graders in Alice Earle's classroom. (These third graders succeeded the third graders who studied Mem Fox.) A description of Alice's literacy program is presented in Chapter 3.

In creating the author study on Joanna Cole, I essentially moved through the same decision-making process as I did when creating the Mem Fox author study. Because this process is described in detail in Chapter 5, I will only highlight some of the particulars of the Joanna Cole author study in the section that follows.

Designing the Joanna Cole Author Study

Choosing an Author

The selection of an author—fiction or nonfiction—for an author study rests on the quality and age-appropriateness of an author's works, on the availability of autobiographical and/or biographical material, and on the interests of the children and of the teacher.

In order to gauge which, if any, nonfiction writers appealed to these third graders, I administered the questionnaire in Figure 7-1. To my surprise, only six children (four boys and two girls) reported not having a favorite nonfiction author. Their reasons ranged from " . . . I don't read that many nonfiction books" to " . . . I like fiction books more than nonfiction." Interestingly, two boys, both of whom are avid nonfiction readers, had no favorites. In conversations, it became clear that they select their nonfiction by topic (e.g., dinosaurs, sharks) without any awareness of author.

Thirteen out of nineteen students recorded a favorite nonfiction author. Single votes were cast for Angela Sheeman, Jackie Budd, and two votes for Bill Nye, "The Science Guy." The remaining nine children (six girls and three boys) chose Joanna Cole. Before reading their responses, I suspected that the zany, fun-filled storyline of the *Magic School Bus* books accounted for their attraction to Cole's work. I was delighted to find that their reasons spanned the fact–fiction continuum. Their fascination with the science content is evident in their responses:

- "It teachis me alot about eath."
- "They have adventures they go on and how Carlos says funny jokes."
- "They are nice to read because they help me and my sister learn about all sorts of things like under the ocean."
- "They have good facts . . . and because they have very funny caricters."
- "They tell allot and thier non-fiction and the bus is cool and give allot of facts."

Of course, what the third graders took as "fact" from Cole's works is uncertain. Zarnowski (1995), in her critique of informational storybooks—books such as the *Magic School Bus* which weave fact into a fictional storyline—argues that young readers are unable to sort fact from fiction and are distracted by irrelevant information. Preliminary research, though, shows that third graders retained significantly more scientific information from a informational storybook than from an information book on the same topic (Leal 1993; 1995). Leal concludes that informational storybooks, such as the *Magic School Bus*, engage student interest and permit a deeper level of processing of factual information.

Measuring Up: Criteria for Quality Nonfiction

As noted in Chapter 5, the children's choice of an author is not the only criterion for author selection. Because our time with children is precious, we must assess whether the author's body of work meets the standards of quality nonfiction and whether autobiographical and/or biographical materials are available. As I read all of Cole's *Magic School Bus* books and many of her other nonfiction works, I weighed them

Name *Abby Clare elizebeth grosslein*

1. Do you have a favorite nonfiction author?   (Yes)   No

2. If you have a nonfiction favorite author, write his or her name on the line.

 Joanna Cole

3. If you don't have a favorite nonfiction author, tell me why.

_____

_____

_____

_____

4. What are some of the nonfiction books you have read that were written by your favorite nonfiction author.

 Magic school bus inside the body Hungry Hungry Sharks, At the Water Works, M.S.B. Earth In Hurricane M.S.B in Dino time.

5. If you were to tell your favorite nonfiction author why you like his or her books, what would you write? Write a letter to your favorite nonfiction author and tell him or her two reasons why you like his or her books:

Dear *Joanna,*

I like your books because

1. *They are nonfiction and nonfiction books teach you things.*

2. *They're also funny and exiting.*

_____

FIGURE 7-1 *Abby's nonfiction author survey*

178

against the primary criteria that literature experts such as Huck et al. (1987) and Cullinan et al.(1994) suggest. Figure 7-2 presents a synopsis of these criteria.

Cole's books fare very well during this criteria check:

Accuracy From the start of her career as a science writer, Cole has taken seriously her responsibility to provide accurate, current information. Her first book, *Cockroaches*, published in 1971, was reviewed and critiqued by an entomologist. With the exception of a few of her easy-to-read books such as *My New Kitten*, she has faithfully

---

Criteria for Quality Nonfiction

Accuracy

The content of nonfiction literature must be accurate and up-to-date. Accuracy hinges on the author's expertise. If the author's credentials do not suggest expertise, documentation must be provided to show that the work has been reviewed by an expert.

Writing Style

In the words of Russell Freedman (1992), award-winning nonfiction author, "Certainly the basic purpose of nonfiction is to inform, to instruct and hopefully to enlighten. But that's not enough. An effective nonfiction book must animate its subject, infuse it with life. It must create a vivid and believable world that the reader will enter willingly and leave only with reluctance. A good nonfiction book should be a pleasure to read. It should be just as compelling as a good story. The task of nonfiction is to find the story—the narrative line— that exists in nearly every subject" (p. 3). Eloquent, vivid language, passionate intrigue about the topic, and attentiveness to the reader are the staples of nonfiction writing.

Organization

To facilitate comprehension, authors often fold facts into one of five organizational structures: description; compare/contrast; sequence; cause and effect; problem/solution (Meyer, 1975). A book about alligators and crocodiles requires a compare-and-contrast organizational framework; a book about the birth and development of a chick demands a sequence structure. Obviously some topics necessitate multiple text structures. In addition, readability is often enhanced with inclusion of headings and subheadings as well as with access aids such as tables of contents, indexes, glossaries, and bibliographies.

Visual Displays

Photographs, illustrations, diagrams, maps, and tables work hand in hand with the author's words to stimulate curiosity and to ignite the imagination. The author's ability to harmonize images and words, along with the quality and quantity of these visuals, affect the totality of the work.

FIGURE 7-2 *Criteria for quality nonfiction (Adapted from Huck, Helper, and Hickman [1987])*

enlisted the service of experts. All of the *Magic School Bus* books have been authenticated by discipline-appropriate scientists.

With respect to Zarnowski's (1995) concern about the fact/fiction issue in informational storybooks, Joanna Cole tackles the issue head-on. In each of her *Magic School Bus* books, she uses the last two pages to alert readers to the interplay of fact and fiction. For example, in *The Magic School Bus Inside the Human Body*, readers encounter a "true-or-false test" and an answer page with the goal of bringing to a conscious level the fact/fantasy dichotomy:

1. A school bus can enter someone's body and kids can go   True or false?
on a tour.

6. White blood cells actually chase and destroy disease   True or false?
germs.

Writing Style   The *Magic School Bus* books are a testimony to Joanna Cole's love affair with language. These books are filled not only with puns, jokes, and humorous one-liners, but also with engaging similes and metaphors that bring complex science concepts into memorable grasp. The successful interplay of the fictional storyline and the nonfiction content support young readers' entrée into the world of nonfiction. Cole's sensitivity to the reader scaffolds her other nonfiction works as well. In *Plants in Winter* (1973), Cole uses a conversation between a child and a botanical expert to explain what happens to plants during the winter. The child's unfettered curiosity drives this book forward. After the expert explains why trees must lose their leaves in winter to survive, the child asks, "What about pine trees? . . . Why don't they shed their leaves in the fall, too?" (unpaged). The continuing dialogue, the use of the first-person narration, and the child's insights carry the reader through complex ideas. When Cole is not using first- or second-person narration or a conversational tone, she weaves intriguing pieces of historical fact into her content presentation to engage readers. For example, in *Fleas*, readers learn that until the invention of the vacuum cleaner, people throughout history—including kings and queens—suffered the perpetual annoyance of human fleas.

Organization   In each of her *Magic School Bus* books, Cole uses the antics of a frazzled science teacher and her students to scaffold the continual flow of science information. The storyline weaves in broad science concepts and content; the science reports written by Ms. Frizzle's "kids" extend these concepts with intriguing detail. In addition, because the science reports are organized in accordance with text structures such as compare/contrast, sequence, and description, they are powerful teaching tools. Cole's other nonfiction works also sport an array of organizational structures—structures that flow naturally from the content to be covered. For example, the sequence text structure undergirds books such as *A Chick Hatches, My New Kitten, A Calf Is Born,* and *How You Were Born*. On the other hand, a description text structure holds together the content of books such as *A Bird's Body* and *A Snakes' Body*, although other text structures such as comparison and sequence are embedded periodically. Anchoring this range of text structure is Cole's gift for clarity—her ability to translate complex ideas for children by using clear, understandable language.

Visual Displays   While many authors in the 1970s were inattentive to the impor-tance of visual information for young readers, Cole understood the impact that visual displays have in piquing curiosity and in fostering further inquiry. Her corpus of work stands as a historical record of the visual transformation that has occurred over the last three decades in nonfiction: from black-and-white photography in *A Calf Is Born* to the engaging color photography in *My New Kitten*; from single-color illustrations in *Cockroaches* to beautiful paintings in *Large as Life: Nighttime Animals Life Size*. Coles gives careful attention to the art medium that works best with the content—photographs for *My New Kitten*, illustrations for the *Magic School Bus* books. *Cuts, Breaks, Bruises, and Burns* wisely includes gray and red illustrations rather than vivid photographs to engage readers.

Accessing Autobiographical/Biographical Data

To bring any author study to fruition, children need access to autobiographical and/or biographical information. Cole's autobiography, *On the Bus with Joanna Cole*, opens with a poignant portrayal of her father, whose dyslexia robbed him of the joys of reading but whose storytelling and rhetorical skill enlivened every family meal. Joanna credits her argumentative streak and her work ethic to her father. She then moves readers from her earliest years as an avid bug watcher to her junior-high en-counter with an inspiring science teacher, Ms. Bair (the inspiration for Ms. Frizzle), to her careers as a teacher, librarian, and book editor. Cole talks extensively about her work as a science writer and about the origin and evolution of the *Magic School Bus* series. Supporting this delightful autobiography is the *Meet the Author* videotape of Joanna Cole as well as Cole's Web site (Figure 7-17). In addition, Cole is featured in *Meet the Authors and Illustrators* (Kovacs and Preller, 1991) as well as in the refer-ence journals, *Something About the Author* (Gale, 1995) and *Children's Literature Re-view* (Hedblad and Telgen, 1996).

With full confidence that Joanna Cole's works will both inform and delight, I propose the idea of the author study to the third graders and receive resounding affirmation.

Aligning Theory and Practice

In Chapter 3, the case was made for viewing author study as a co-constructive cur-riculum venture—one in which the children and the teacher collaborate to gener-ate and to pursue a course of study. Such collaboration obviates the preplanned "unit" and finds its compass in a set of operating principles that define the essentials of the learning-teaching dynamic. The set of principles that guided my creation of the Joanna Cole author study is the same set that guided the other author studies in this book:

181

Principle One: Readers respond in multiple ways to an author's works.

Principle Two: Aesthetic engagement must precede critical and biographical response.

Principle Three: Critical response deepens and extends the literary experience.

Principle Four: Biographical response heightens and intensifies the literary experience.

Principle Five: Children are drawn to meaningful endeavors and learn best through interaction with more knowledgeable others.

While the first, fourth, and fifth principles need little additional explanation, the second and third principles warrant further discussion in light of the emphasis on nonfiction literature.

Can Nonfiction Evoke Aesthetic Sensibilities?

At one point in his life, Milton Meltzer, acclaimed nonfiction writer, was "deeply troubled by the course [his] life was taking," and sought refuge in Henry David Thoreau's *Walden*, where he encountered this passage:

> Who knows what beautiful and winged life, whose egg has been buried for ages under many concentric layers of woodedness in the dead dry life of society, deposited at first in the laburnum of the green and living tree, which has gradually been converted into the semblance of a well-seasoned tomb—heard perchance gnawing out now for years by an astonished family of man, as they sit around the festive board—may unexpectedly come forth from amidst society's most trivial and handselled furniture, to enjoy its summer life at last! (Meltzer, 1988, p. 82)

Meltzer (1988) writes:

> As I finished reading [Thoreau's] lines, I began to sob. The image of the bug emerging into life after all those years in its wooden tomb touched something deep in me. The tears poured out in relief. Feelings that had been frozen so long, melted in a rush. My wife, who had come running at the sound of crying, looked at me in amazement, then put her arms around me. I felt like one reborn. (p. 82)

While I read Thoreau's piece with a sense of wonderment, even disbelief, Meltzer lived the piece—deeply and cathartically. *Both are aesthetic responses*, with Meltzer's response landing at the farthest point of the aesthetic end of the transactional continuum (see Chapter 2). The notion that nonfiction is read efferently while fiction is read aesthetically is completely misguided and misses the crux of reader response theory. As Rosenblatt (1991c) writes:

> Instead of thinking of the text as either literary or informational, efferent or aesthetic, we should think of it as written for a particular *predominant* attitude or stance, efferent or aesthetic, on the part of the reader. (p. 445)

Any text—fiction or nonfiction—can be read aesthetically or efferently, depending on the purpose of the reader. Most reading includes both stances.

Are children capable of responding aesthetically to nonfiction literature? Any teacher who has launched a literature-based animal study of any kind knows the levels of exhilaration and wonderment that children bring to such study. In fact, any mention of animals will activate these levels. For example, in preparation for a presentation that I was doing on the limitations of standardized testing, I asked a group of third graders to read one test paragraph on cats and to answer four comprehension questions so that I could tap their problem-solving strategies. The task was clearly efferent—read and take away public meaning. As we were about to talk about their answers, Kyle remarked, "My cat is just like that. He's always licking himself and me too."

Caitlyn added, "My friend has a cat and it licks her hair [the friend's] like it's brushing it."

"No way," said Ted. "My cat never licked my hair."

"I used to have two cats but they died. I really miss them," Jason shared.

Their cat talk extended far beyond the confines of the test passage. After all, as Russell Freedman reminds us, nonfiction is story at its core. These children had their stories to tell. Of course, tests are not the place for this aesthetic stance. Children need to be taught that if they are to be successful test-takers, they must remain dispassionate and analytical.

What Are the Critical Dimensions of Nonfiction? What Should We Be Teaching?

Once aesthetic response has been honored, "conscious contemplation" (Peterson and Eeds, 1990, p. 12) about the intricacies of exposition is essential if we want to move children ahead as readers and writers. Although it is beyond the scope of this chapter to survey all the possibilities, a sampling of three possible minilessons that examine critical aspects of nonfiction follow.

1. *When is a fact a fact?* When Russell Freedman was drafting his Newbery Medal book, *Lincoln: A Photobiography*, he included a harrowing detail that captured the extent of Lincoln's grief at the death of his eleven-year-old son: "Lincoln twice had his son's body exhumed, so he could gaze upon his face again" (1992, p. 8). However, because Freedman could find only one reference to this haunting image, he edited it out of the final draft. Unfortunately, not all nonfiction writers are as fastidious as Freedman about what constitutes "truth." As Freedman notes, "Facts can't always be trusted" (1992, p. 2). Indeed, contradictory information fills many nonfiction books as the third graders in the Cole author study discovered. Cole's book, *Sharks*, prompted additional questions about sharks and led us to other sources where we encountered a host of disparate "facts." One book claimed, "They [sharks] can hear a wounded fish thrashing in the water from as much as 3,000 feet away" (Simon, 1995, unpaged). Another reported, "It can hear a wounded animal struggling for as far away as a football field" (Markle, 1996, p. 17).

"How might we explain this?" I ask the third graders. They are quick to reply:

- "One author made a big mistake."
- "Maybe one book is old and now we know more."
- "Maybe one's telling about the hammerhead and the other one is talking about the great white."

All are viable explanations. When I ask how we can resolve this discrepancy, they suggest we call a shark expert. I show Markle's acknowledgment page, on which she thanks seven scientists for their expertise and note that Simon appears not to have consulted experts. Children need to understand that we have a responsibility as writers to report accurate information. They also need to understand that, especially in the world of science, what is fact today may be fiction tomorrow. (Patricia Lauber's [1989] *The News About Dinosaurs* is a superb resource with which to make this point.)

2. *Swimming Noses?* What image surfaces as you read "Sharks are like 'swimming noses' . . ." (Simon, 1995, unpaged)? Perhaps a great white shark torpedoing through the water in pursuit of a wounded prey? Or perhaps the whale shark standing on its tail, bobbing up and down? Whatever the image, Seymour Simon's simile alerts the reader to the shark's most defining feature, its sharpest sense. Simon uses similes and metaphors to make the unfamiliar familiar. These literary devices, so often associated with fiction, play a vitally important role in nonfiction in that they allow readers to compare one known concrete object with a more abstract unknown entity. The strength of the imagery in Joanna Cole's simile "Your stomach is like a built-in food processor" in the *Magic School Bus Inside the Human Body* (1989, unpaged) delights readers intellectually and affectively and makes the new information memorable. Instruction in these cognitive scaffolds enhances understanding and recall, and invites experimentation in young writers' nonfiction.

3. *Structure Please?* As noted earlier in this chapter, young children are immersed in fictional stories to a much greater degree than they are nonfiction books. Parents and teachers choose storybooks over informational books during storytime (Sulzby and Teale, 1987; Putnam, 1991). Unlike the story grammar elements that children intuit from their extensive exposure to narrative, children in general have not had enough exposure to expository text to absorb prominent nonfiction text structures (description, cause and effect, comparison . . .) underlying exposition. Their inability to recognize the particular organizational structure of an expository piece impacts negatively on their comprehension of that text (McGee, 1982; Taylor and Samuels, 1983) and on their expository writ-

ing (NAEP, 1991). Fortunately, when children receive instruction in these text structures, comprehension and writing improve (McGee, 1982; Taylor and Beach, 1984). In the Joanna Cole author study that follows, minilessons on three text structures are implemented.

Implementing the Joanna Cole Author Study

As already mentioned, I surveyed the third graders and discovered that almost half of them had chosen Joanna Cole as their favorite nonfiction author. The lag time between asking them to complete the survey and sharing the results was about a week because I needed this time to walk through the steps described previously to establish that a Joanna Cole study would not only delight these third graders but also move them forward as readers and writers.

Before school starts, I hang a bar graph of the results of the nonfiction author survey. As some of the third graders arrive, they inspect the graph. Before long the buzz about Joanna Cole permeates the room. By the time I assemble the third graders to read the graph, they are eager to share the Joanna Cole books they have read and the *Magic School Bus* programs they have watched on TV. When I ask if they would be interested in studying the works of Joanna Cole, they cheer. I explain that what we will doing is called an author study, and that I have invited two experts from fourth grade to explain what they did last year during a Mem Fox author study.

Day One: What Is an Author Study, Anyway?

A hush falls over the third graders as the fourth graders, Kevin and Alexis, arrive with their kangaroo report. I introduce our guest speakers, explaining that they were third graders in Ms. Earle's classroom last year and that they participated in a Mem Fox author study. Kevin explains that an author study is "When you read all the books of Mem Fox and talk about them and do projects about them and learn stuff about Mem Fox like she loves Australian animals, especially kangaroos." He then talks about how he loved being Hattie in the Readers' Theatre of *Hattie and the Fox* performed for the kindergartners, and about being a pirate in the role play of *Tough Boris*. He shares that his favorite Mem Fox book was *Koala Lou* "because it reminds me of me and my mother." As Alexis takes the floor, I expect her to talk about the video we made for Mem Fox because she was master of ceremonies. However, she shares that her favorite part of the Mem Fox author study was working with her team to research kangaroos and to write their kangaroo report (Figure 4-10 in Chapter 4). Alexis unravels this gigantic report and explains that they did a lot of research before writing their book. They read books, checked the Internet, and printed out sections from the Encarta program. Alexis and Kevin take turns reading the part of the flap book that they wrote, and explain that because they wanted "to make it real interesting" and "to give a lot of information," they added "a tail" to the book. The "tail" primarily contains pictures and printouts from the Encarta program. Our guest speakers then entertain questions from the audience: "Why did you pick the kangaroo?" "How long did it take to do the report?" "Is your report on the grey or the red kangaroo?" The specificity of some of the third graders' questions catch the fourth graders by surprise but, for the most part, they hold their own. We thank our guest speakers and promise to invite them back to see the projects we might pursue.

After our guests depart, I share my excitement about the Joanna Cole author study. Predictably and without any prompting, Brandon asks if we can make a videotape for Cole. Eddie adds that we can get on a bus and wave to her. Abby suggests "an e-mail on the Internet." Kelly comments that we could tell her we love her books, and "Could she send us books?" After I explain the financial impossibility of Kelly's suggestion, Cayton suggests that we write a book for Joanna Cole. Abbie piggybacks, "A *Magic School Bus* book about our school." Continued brainstorming leads to the idea of a book about a field trip. When I ask about field trips that they have taken this school year, Eddie exclaims, "The vernal pool!" I suggest that because there are no published books about vernal pools, we might donate a copy of our book to the Audubon Society so that other children who visit the vernal pool can learn about its important place in our ecosystem. As we break for snack, the third graders are still brainstorming ideas such as a videotape of the vernal pool to go with the book "in case Joanna Cole doesn't really understand what it is." We are off and running.

Day Two: Introducing Joanna Cole's Books

The third graders gather on the rug as I place a pile of Joanna Cole books on my lap. I hold up each book and ask them to raise their hands if they have read it. I show *A Bird's Body*; no hands go up. I stand the book on the floor in front of me. Many hands shoot up as I show *The Magic School Bus in the Time of the Dinosaurs*, and two hands for *My New Kitten*. I place the books beside each other. After an almost unanimous show of hands for *The Magic School Bus Inside the Human Body*, as if anticipating my next question, Cayton calls out, "Put it behind the other *Magic School Bus* book." They do a superb job categorizing the remaining books, placing *A Dog's Body* behind *A Bird's Body* because "They are about animal's bodies" and *A Chick Hatches* behind *A New Kitten* because "It's a new chick that has just hatched like a new kitten that's born." As I finish the pile, they alert me to the fact that I am missing some *Magic School Bus* books. I encourage them to bring in their Joanna Cole books so that we can expand our display.

Cayton announces that he saw Joanna Cole on a talk show. Anticipating autobiographical talk, I move to the chart pad. Cayton explains that Joanna Cole loves science and loves to read about "regular science stuff." He adds, though, that he was disappointed because she didn't talk about her *Magic School Bus* books. I ask Cayton to let me know if he recalls any other information to add to our hunch chart. Samantha notes that sometimes on the flap of a book you can find out more about an author. I suggest that, as we read more of Cole's books, we'll be able to make other guesses and then to check them against her autobiography, *On the Bus with Joanna Cole*. Biographical response has been launched.

In order to gauge the extent of their experience with the *Magic School Bus* books, I ask the students to fill out a survey on the books they have read. No sooner have I shared the first set of directions than Eddie asks a question I should have anticipated: "Where do you put a check if you've seen it on TV?" I modify the directions, asking them to put a check next to each book read and to write "TV" next to the check if they also have watched it. Survey results indicated that every child had read at least one *Magic School Bus* book, with a median of 2.5 books. Three children had read six or more books. The most popular book was *The Magic School Bus in a Hurricane*, followed by *In the Time of the Dinosaurs*. Fourteen out of the nineteen children had watched one or more of the television versions.

Day Three: Readers' Theatre and Aesthetic Response

The third graders are taken with the huge neon yellow bus (8' x 8') that I hung on the wall outside the room before school. I show a picture of Joanna Cole that I have enlarged, but before I can explain my intent, Stephanie says, "We can put it on the bus—put Joanna Cole in the driver's seat."

"Can we take pictures of us and put them on the bus?" asks Nicole.

Abby wants to know if we are still going to make our own *Magic School Bus* book, because, if so, she will ask her mom (who is an editor) to do some of the pictures for the book on her computer. Collaborative curriculum is in the making.

I place the first page of a Readers' Theatre script I have created for *The Magic School Bus Inside a Beehive* (Figure 7-3) on the overhead projector and ask what we're going to do today. Nicole replies, "We're gonna read the characters' parts and do a play." I explain the difference between Readers' Theatre and a play, and discuss the role of the narrator. I ask the class to figure out how I got the characters' names that are listed on the script. John replies, "From the kids in Ms. Frizzle's class." For our Readers' Theatre, Mrs. Earle will be Ms. Frizzle and I will narrate. I then ask each child to pick a character name tag from a brown bag. I pass out the scripts and ask them to circle their character, to read their lines silently, and to ask for help on any words they don't know. Alice and I move around the room to assist.

Because our script begins on the sixth page of the story, I read the first five pages, including dialogue bubbles but omitting the reports. I transition to the script and the children follow suit. They are absorbed in their performance reading; they laugh at the funny quips of Arnold and other characters. Some read with engaging expression.

The script ends as the bear, who is raiding the hive, is attacked by bees. I say, "Raise your hand if you have encountered a bee or a beehive on a summer day." Hands go up, along with spontaneous chatter. I ask them to write about one of their encounters.

They can't wait to read their bee stories. Cayton, the bee warrior of the group,

---

The Magic School Bus Inside a Beehive by Joanna Cole

Characters

Ms. Frizzle, Phoebe, John, Carmen, Keesha, Arnold, Ralphie, Alex, Amanda, Dorothy, Florrie, Tim, Michael, Rachel, Carlos, Wanda, Shirley, Molly, Gregory, Jane, Narrator

Scene Two: The Magic School Bus is shrinking!

NARRATOR: But just as she opened a jar of honey, her elbow knocked a strange little lever. The honey jar fell, and we heard a weird buzzing sound.

MS. FRIZZLE: Oops!

NARRATOR: It was the bus. It was vibrating and getting smaller. So was everything in it—including us!

FLORRIE: We're shaking!

RALPHIE: We're shrinking!

ARNOLD: I hate when this happens!

NARRATOR: Before we knew it, the bus looked like a little beehive and we looked like real bees! We really did!

MS. FRIZZLE: All out, class. Be a bee everyone!

WANDA: Stop poking me with your antenna!

TIM: Stop stepping on my wing!

NARRATOR: One by one, we stepped out the door and looked over at the nearest hive. At the entrance, worker bees were standing guard.

MS. FRIZZLE: Guard bees usually keep out bees from other hives.

DOROTHY: According to my research, guard bees will bite and sting strange bees.

PHOEBE: Do we qualify as "strange bees"?

SHIRLEY: No doubt about it!

FIGURE 7-3 *Readers' Theatre script*

shares the lesson he learned about beehives. (See Figure 7-4.) Questions follow about where the hive was and how many bees chased him. Allyson then reads her piece about how her dad got stung in the eye by a bee and had to go to the hospital; her peers gasp and ask questions. At one point, the third graders are comparing their mothers' home remedies for bee stings—baking soda, creams, cold water, and so forth. Cayton comments that we should ask Mr. Oles, the fifth-grade teacher and vice principal, what to do because he is a beekeeper! The others pipe in at the mention of Mr. Oles's name because he shared his beekeeping hobby last year. Their response is so enthusiastic that I promise to ask Mr. Oles if he would consider doing a "Part Two" guest spot for us.

Later that day, I read the seventeen bee responses. Eleven writers included an aesthetic rendering, explaining how it felt to get stung, offering advice to others about bees, illustrating that the literature of fact evokes the same range of response as

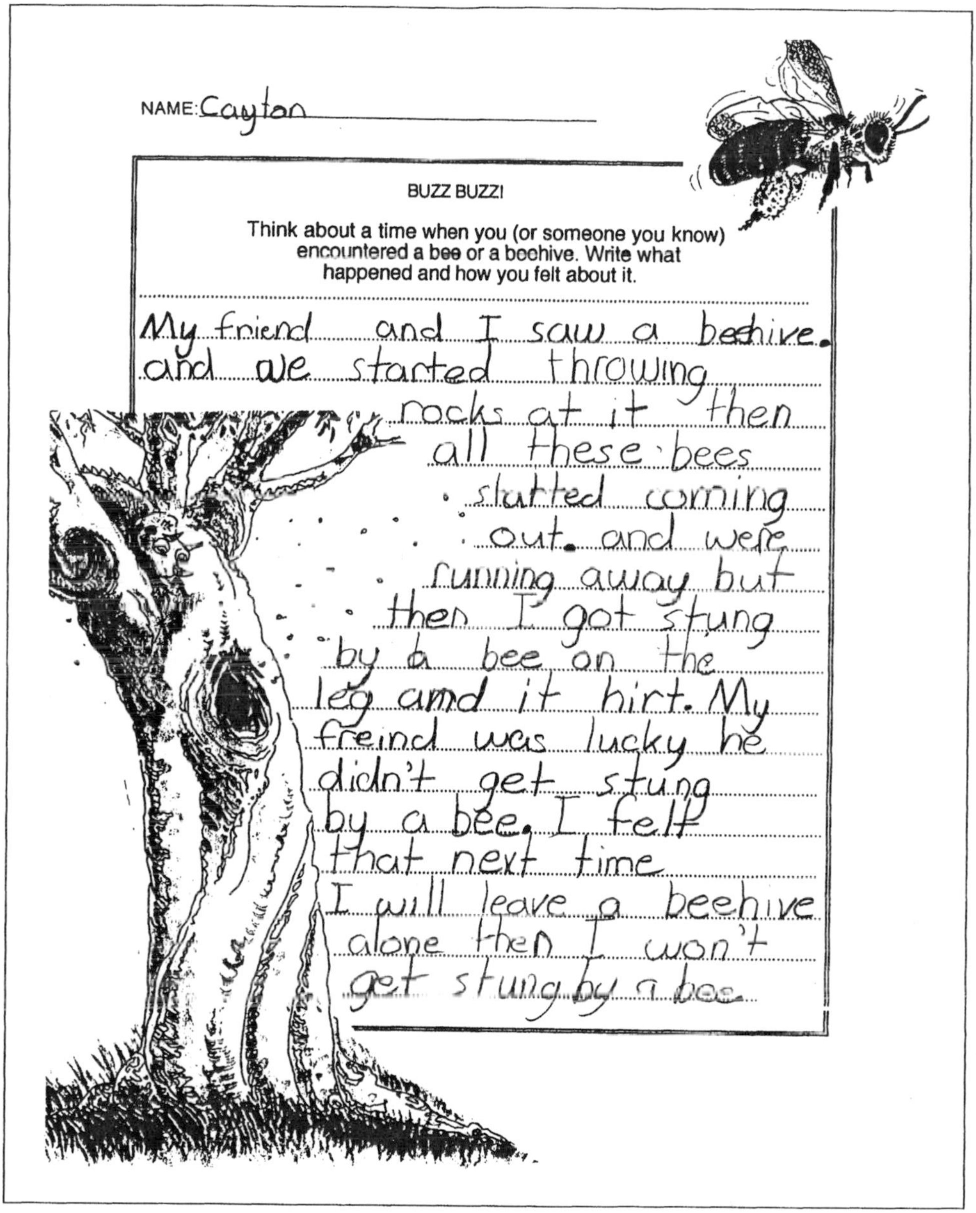

NAME: Cayton

BUZZ BUZZ!

Think about a time when you (or someone you know)
encountered a bee or a beehive. Write what
happened and how you felt about it.

My friend and I saw a beehive.
and we started throwing
rocks at it then
all these bees
slatted coming
out and were
running away but
then I got stung
by a bee on the
leg amd it hirt. My
freind was lucky he
didn't get stung
by a bee. I felt
that next time
I will leave a beehive
alone then I won't
get stung by a bee.

FIGURE 7-4   *Cayton's personal response to* The Magic School Bus Inside a Beehive

fiction. Six writers adopted a more critical stance, telling only the details of their bee encounter.

Day Four: *Critical Review and Response to* Inside a Beehive

I suggest that one way to help the rest of the school know that we are studying Cole's works is to hang reviews of her books around our neon bus. Because the third graders are experienced at rating and responding to the books, they need little direction. I suggest that if they choose to read a Cole book during reading workshop, they can complete a book review. By the end of the day, two reviews (Figure 7-5) join the big bus on the corridor wall.

Samantha asks if I will read Joanna Cole's autobiography. I explain that although I don't have the autobiography with me, I would be interested in their hunches about Joanna Cole. Bobby laughs, "I think she has a pet lizard called Lizzie just like Ms. Frizzle in the book." I record his response on a hunch chart.

Sam adds, "I think she is a teacher because she knows a lot about field trips, even if they're crazy field trips."

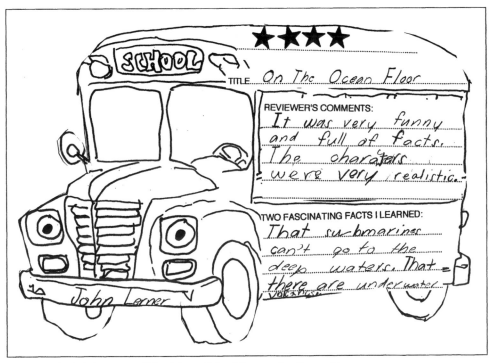

FIGURE 7-5 *John's review of* The Magic School Bus on the Ocean Floor

190

"I think she's a bus driver—she loves driving that bus," says Maggie.

I explain that as we read more of her books, other ideas about Cole as a person and as a writer will surface. I then hold up Cole's very first book—called *Cockroaches*—to a chorus of "yucks," and ask why they think she picked this topic for her first book. Kelly suggests, "Maybe she has cockroaches in her house and she wanted to find out how to kill them."

Cayton counters, "We know she likes science and cockroaches are science."

I add that I hope Joanna talks about her first book in her autobiography so that we can check our hunches.

Returning to yesterday's Readers' Theatre, I finish reading *Inside a Beehive* and ask for their response to the book. Samantha comments, "I like how Joanna Cole makes each kid in the story have a different personality—like Arnold is always afraid on the field trips and some of the kids think it's fun."

"She writes her books not like other nonfiction books, but they're like temptation. They're like 'oooooh.' Like when it's recess and I'm reading, I say, 'I can't put this down,'" Kelly exclaims.

Nicole continues with critical response, "I think her books are funny because when they go to school, it starts out like a regular day but then they go on the field trip and they get stuck, and Arnold says, 'I knew I should have stayed home today.'" She then asks, "When we write our book on the vernal pool, can we do story bubbles too?"

Although it is clear that the fictional thread of the *Magic School Bus* books preoccupies these third graders, they also are enamored with their nonfiction discoveries. As Cayton puts it, "She writes a lot about science and you learn a lot that you didn't know before." His comment triggers a string of factual responses.

"I like how the guard bees were checking them [the characters] to see if they could go in and they were scared because they were taking a risk," says Brandon.

"I like the part about the dance when the bees dance around to tell the other bees where the flowers are," remarks Eddie.

To capture the momentum of their nonfiction roll, I move the third graders back to their tables and ask them to write down as many facts as they can remember about bees on a bee map. I explain that I will read all their facts and will choose one fact that no one else has mentioned and edit it. Tomorrow, writers will copy their edited fact onto a bee cell that will be pasted onto a comb I have created. Our "honeycomb" (Figure 7-6) will go on the wall with our neon bus for readers to enjoy. The class takes up this challenge with intense interest. The third graders average seven facts, with four recording over ten facts and two recording as few as four facts. A few third graders include facts that were not in Cole's book, such as "Some bee's have no stingers." Misunderstandings also are evident ("The queen bee has no stinger").

We end the session with a fact whip: We "whip" around the room with each child reading one bee fact without comment from others, unless erroneous information is given.

FIGURE 7-6   *Honeycomb (on left) of third graders' bee facts*

Day Five: Sequence Reports in Inside a Beehive and Bee Dances

Three more book reviews arrive this morning. To capitalize on peer influence, I ask volunteers to read their reviews. I then ask reviewers to edit their pieces, to cut out their buses, and to leave them on my desk for a final edit.

In addition, I share my delight that many are reading Joanna Cole's books—books other than the *Magic School Bus* books—and are writing reports in their writer's notebooks during writing workshop. With Bobby's permission, I place his piece on the overhead projector (Figure 7-7) and ask him to read it aloud. Kelly exclaims that she too wrote about fleas, one of Cole's books. Nicole wants to share her piece on kittens, another Cole topic.

I then show the "honeycomb" of bee facts (Figure 7-6), and read Eddie's fact about bees doing dances that communicate to other bees where the flowers are. I ask, "Did we learn what kinds of dances bees do when we read the story?"

"No," they reply.

I ask, "Where do you think we might find the details about the dances in *Inside a Beehive?*

"In the kids' reports," replies Meghan.

I place a copy of "Phil's" [a character in the *Magic School Bus* book] report called "The Round Dance" on the overhead projector. I ask the class to pay close attention to "Phil's" report because, later in the session, Mrs. Earle is going to become a bee and do the round dance for us. They laugh with delight.

We chorally read "Phil's" report. I ask someone to tell Mrs. Earle the steps of the round dance. Bobby begins, "First, you go around in a circle, then . . ." I ask what would have happened if "Phil" wrote the steps in a mixed-up order. The third graders are quick to explain that the reader would get confused—"Mrs. Earle wouldn't know

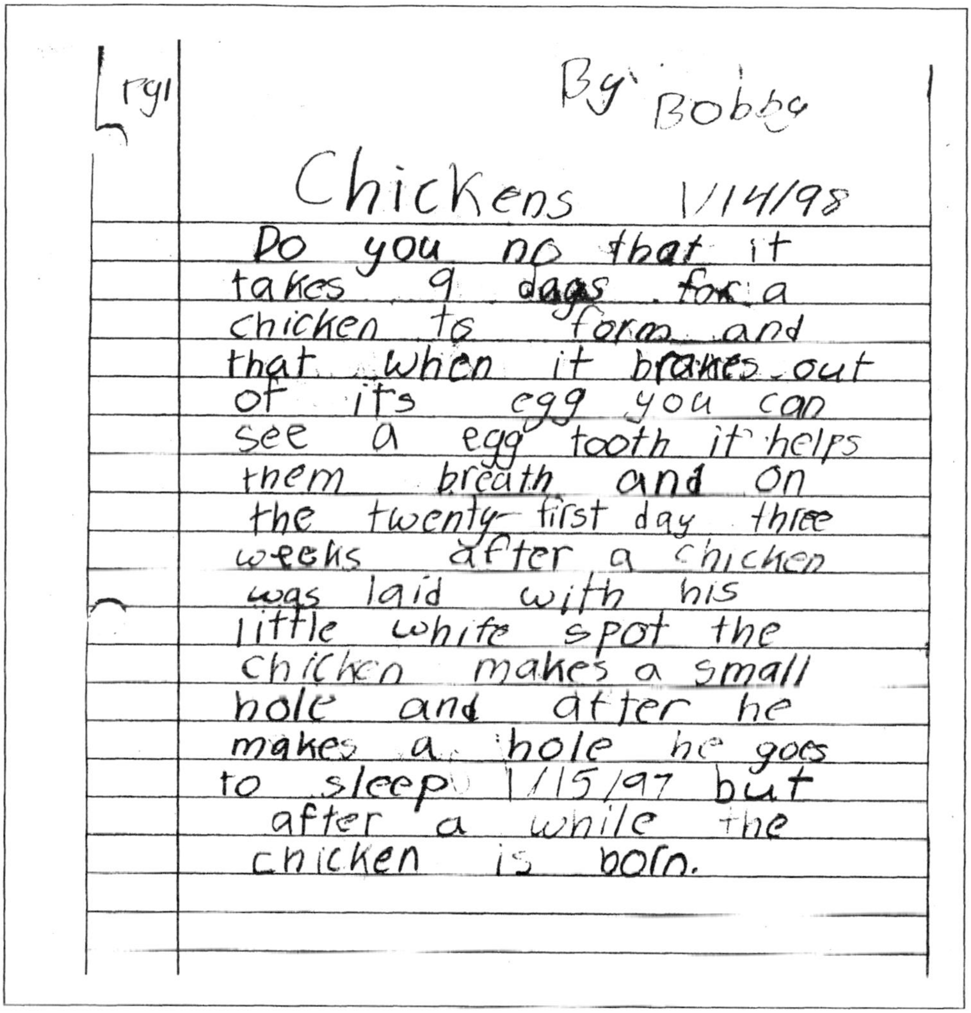

L ryl

By Bobby

Chickens   1/14/98

Do you no that it takes 9 days for a chicken to form and that when it brakes out of its egg you can see a egg tooth it helps them breath and on the twenty first day three weeks after a chicken was laid with his little white spot the chicken makes a small hole and after he makes a hole he goes to sleep 1/15/97 but after a while the chicken is born.

FIGURE 7-7   *Bobby's nonfiction piece on chickens*

what to do first." I then explain that "Phil" has written a special kind of nonfiction report called a sequence report. We talk about the term *sequence*, and Jim makes the immediate connection, "The bee has to do things in the right order or the other bees won't get it." I emphasize that when authors write a sequence report, they must put the facts in the right order. I also note the key words, *first, then, next*, and *finally*, that nonfiction writers often use to signal sequence. We can find only one key word in "Phil's" report, but Cayton adds that he could have used the word *first* at the beginning of the second sentence. We then read "Carmen's" [another *Magic School Bus* character] report about the waggle dance, focusing on the sequence of steps.

We move to the rug to give Bee Earle plenty of room to dance. As she dons her bee hat, I ask the third-grade "bees" to study Bee Earle's moves and to figure out where the flowers are. Using cue cards, Bee Earle buzzes her way through the round dance and the children quickly guess that the flowers are nearby. Brandon demonstrates the circular pattern that the bees would make to find the flower. Bee Earle then does three waggle dances and the children, with some coaxing, figure out whether the bees would fly toward the sun or the left or right of the sun to locate distant flowers.

Day Six: What Other Kinds of Reports Do Ms. Frizzle's Kids Write?

I direct the children's attention to the match-up activity I have written on the board.

Kinds of Reports	Definitions
Description	The writer explains things about a topic in order. Key words include *first, then, finally* . . .
Sequence	The writer explains how two or more things about a topic are alike or different. Key words include *like, same, unlike, different, differ* . . .
Comparison	The writer explains the details about a topic but can explain them in the order he or she wishes. A key phrase is *for example* . . .

I ask if they recall the kind of report "Phil" wrote about the round dance. They reply, "Sequence." I read each of the definitions and ask which one describes a sequence report. They choose the first definition, so I draw a line between the two items. I explain that I have added two new kinds of reports called description and comparison to the list. As I read the second definition, I ask the students to try to figure out what kind of report each definition describes. Nicole replies, "Comparison because when you tell how two or more things are alike, you, like, compare them—compare-ion." By default, they identify the definition of description structure.

I place the following *Inside a Beehive* report by "Arnold" [another Magic School Bus character] on the overhead projector:

A QUEEN BEE CAN STING MANY TIMES
Unlike worker bees, which can sting only
once, the queen bee can pull her stinger
our of the victim and sting again. (unpaged)

We read the report chorally and I ask the class to decide whether "Arnold" wrote a comparison report or a description report. I remind them to think about our key words. Jim responds that it is a comparison report because "Arnold" is comparing the worker bee and the queen. When I ask how many agree, about half of the students raise their hands. Abby wonders why it isn't description. We talk about the fact that indeed there is description ("bees have stingers . . .") in "Arnold's" report. I explain that all nonfiction reports have description but that some reports convey the description in special ways such as sequence and comparison. I emphasize how key words can help us make the distinction. The class has no trouble finding the key word in "Arnold's" report. As I expected, these concepts are challenging and will need repeated discussion and many examples.

We try one more example on the overhead:

WHAT ARE SOCIAL INSECTS?
Social insects live and work together in a community.
Some social insects: Ants nest in the ground. Paper
wasps make a nest out of wood pulp. Bumble bees
nest in grass-lined holes in the ground. Termites
nest in wood. (unpaged)

I ask if "Wanda's" [another *Magic School Bus* character] report is sequence or description. John replies, "It's description because she could do the animals in any order." I reread the report as John suggested, and ask if anyone is confused by a different order. They are not. But Eddie thinks it might be comparison too because "Bumblebees and ants have nests in the ground." I explain that "Wanda" could turn this into a comparison report by telling us how ant and bumblebee nests are alike (if they are alike).

I close the session by saying, "Joanna Cole isn't the only writer who uses description, comparison, and sequence reports. I was very impressed to find that some of you have been writing these special kinds of reports in your writer's notebooks, even though you didn't know you were writing them. I am going to ask permission to place some of your reports on the overhead during our next session so we can examine them." They are very curious as to who these writers are.

Then Bobby asks, "Are we going to write reports in our vernal pool book?"

"Yes, indeed," I reply.

Day Seven: Ms. Frizzle's Kids Aren't the Only Ones Who Write Reports

I place Alexa's (an accomplished equestrian) report on pony games, presented in Figure 7-8, on the overhead. The third graders are ever so attentive as Alexa reads her piece. I ask, "What kind of report has Alexa written?" Eddie replies, "Sequence because you can't switch it around or you'll be wrong."

I play out his explanation and then write the term *sequence* on Alexa's piece. We repeat this procedure with Brandon's description paragraph on dinosaurs and with John's comparison paragraph on penguins and birds, which is presented in Figure 7-9.

To reinforce these text structure concepts, and to make the point that Joanna Cole uses these structures in books other than the *Magic School Bus*, I introduce *Hungry, Hungry Sharks*. As I read this "easy-to-read" book, aesthetic response takes hold; they interject comments, tell stories of shark sightings, and add information not mentioned by Cole. Having enjoyed the book, I place one page of *Hungry, Hungry Sharks* on the overhead projector and ask the third graders to identify the text structure. They do this with ease. I then hand each table an

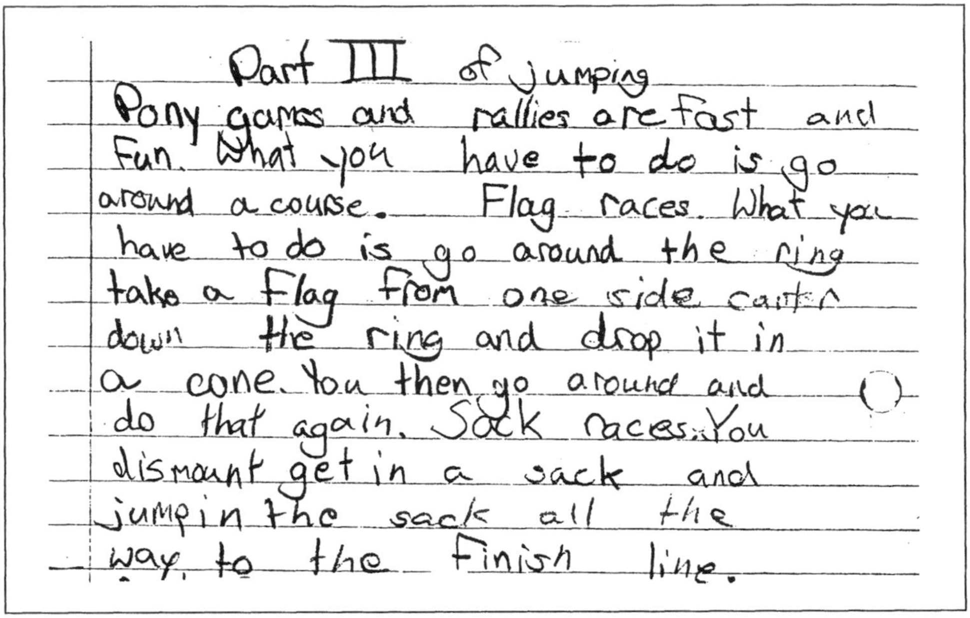

> Part III of jumping
> Pony games and rallies are fast and
> fun. What you have to do is go
> around a course. Flag races. What you
> have to do is go around the ring
> take a flag from one side canter
> down the ring and drop it in
> a cone. You then go around and
> do that again. Sack races. You
> dismount get in a sack and
> jump in the sack all the
> way to the finish line.

FIGURE 7-8   *Alexa's nonfiction piece on pony races*

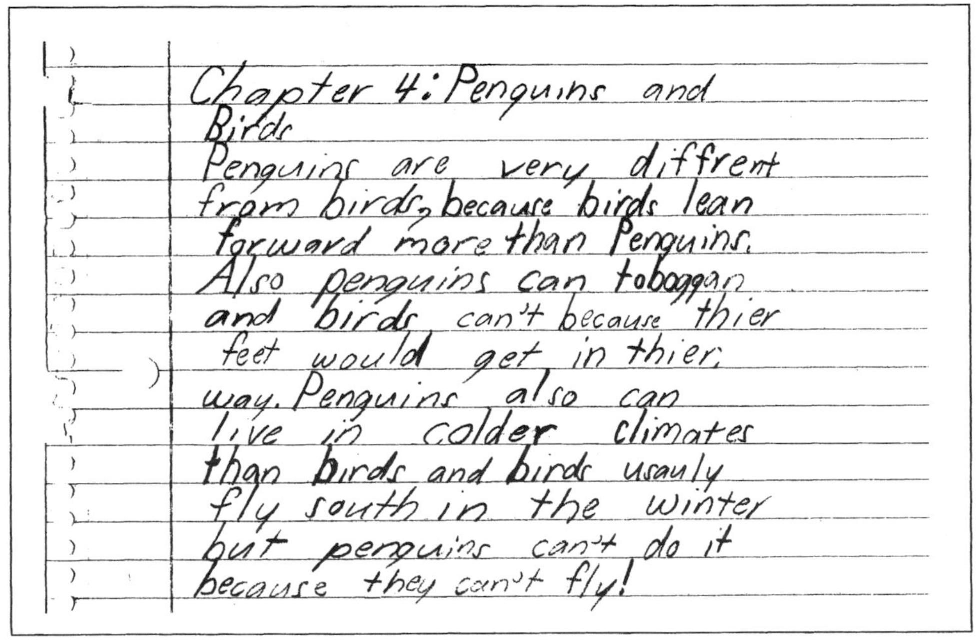

> Chapter 4: Penguins and
> Birds
> Penguins are very diffrent
> from birds because birds lean
> forward more than Penguins.
> Also penguins can tobaggan
> and birds can't because thier
> feet would get in thier
> way. Penguins also can
> live in colder climates
> than birds and birds usauly
> fly south in the winter
> but penguins can't do it
> because they can't fly!

FIGURE 7-9   *John's nonfiction piece on penguins*

overhead of a different page from the book and a marker. I ask each group to read its overhead, to label the kind of report structure used, and to share results. They do well with the comparison and sequence paragraphs, even when key words are not used. The description paragraphs, however, continue to challenge them as they try to argue a sequence or comparison angle.

We end the day with the creation of literature circles. I explain that during free time they can sign up for one of the four *Magic School Bus* books that are listed on the charts. I explain that, over the next few days, they will have a chance to read and to talk about one of Joanna Cole's *Magic School Bus* books in small groups.

Day Eight: Hunches About Joanna Cole

In preparation for our upcoming session on Cole's autobiography, I reread their hunch chart and ask if they have any new hunches. As hands go up, I pass out "Joanna Cole maps" and ask them to jot down their new hunches. An example of Bobby's map is presented in Figure 7-10. I explain that, when they are finished, I will pool their ideas onto one large map.

Maps completed, students begin reading their self-selected literature circle books (*Magic School Bus* books) during reading workshop. I am delighted when some of the third graders, of their own volition, arrive at my desk to show me a "comparison" or "sequence" report. As they are finishing reading, I ask them to write their personal response to the book in their dialogue journals—letters in which they share their thoughts and feelings. Because they have been writing these entries during reading workshop since September, they write with confidence.

I close the session with the announcement that Mr. Oles will make a return appearance to talk about bees and beekeeping. Because they learned many things last year, I ask each table to brainstorm some questions that they would like to ask Mr. Oles. They come up with an impressive range of questions, such as "What do bees and beekeepers do in the winter?" After we talk about why we don't want to send all twenty or so questions, I ask them to decide on their best question per table and to circle it. Later that day, we send a letter to Mr. Oles with our six questions and our gratitude.

Day Nine: How Did You Become a Beekeeper, Mr. Oles?

Ken Oles arrives with his beehive, his beekeeper suit, his honey-excavating equipment, and a television monitor. The room buzzes with excitement. While Mr. Oles is setting up, I display our "honeycomb" of bee facts and ask the third graders to share their bee knowledge with Mr. Oles. Mr. Oles qualifies some information—"A bear can get stung in the face but it doesn't seem to bother it"—and expands on other information—"The reason that the queen bee can sting again and again is that her stinger is very thin, like a needle. It doesn't have the barbs like the worker bee's stinger." Mr. Oles hangs our chart-size letter and explains that he enjoyed it so much

FIGURE 7-10   *Bobby's Joanna Cole hunch map*

that he plans to bring it to his next beekeeper meeting. He begins with our first question, "How did you become a beekeeper?"

> I never really thought about beekeeping until a few years ago. I've always loved gardening and one day I was reading an article about honeybees and their importance in the garden. Then I read and I read about honeybees for about five or six years. I decided that someday I would raise honeybees. I went to bee school and then got my first hive. . . . Oh, boy, did I make a lot of mistakes my first year. . . .

The children are fascinated and ask many questions. Mr. Oles then dons his beekeeping suit and demonstrates how he removes the honey from the combs. He passes around two empty combs so we can touch and smell the sweet wax. He then shows a homemade video of the entire honeymaking process—we want to reach out and scoop up the honey.

We extend a hearty round of applause to Mr. Oles. After he departs, we share our thoughts about the presentation. Bobby says he wouldn't be a beekeeper because he's allergic to pollen and doesn't want to get stung. Jim wonders why the bees don't suffocate when Mr. Oles smokes the hive. We hypothesize that because the hive is arranged in three boxes, perhaps the bees only smell the smoke but don't actually inhale it. I promise to check our hypothesis with Mr. Oles. Abby wonders if there are female beekeepers; the class is certain that there are.

Day Ten: *The* Magic School Bus *Books Go to the Literature Circle*

Kelly has written two things she learned about bees and beekeeping from Mr. Oles on our "honeycomb" cells and asks if she can paste them on our poster. I delight at her suggestion and offer the opportunity to others. Because our "honeycomb" will be read by others outside the class, I ask that they draft, reread, revise, and edit their work before I do a final edit. Over the next few days, many cells are added to the poster.

We then move to our literature circles. I call my first circle to the table and ask who would like to read his or her letter. Alexa reads her entry:

> Dear Dr. Jenkins,
> I read the whole book (cover to cover) and enjoyed it. I have the book at home but I've only browsed through it. But you want to know what I think is gross? I think fish sticks and P.B. and Banana sandwiches are gross! But other than that the book was good. I think you know what book I'm reading. I will give you a hint: It has to do with the Magic School Bus in the human body. Alexa

Stephanie agrees that peanut butter and banana sandwiches are gross. Brandon adds that even grosser are the fish sticks floating in Arnold's stomach. When Nicole asks what he is talking about, Brandon directs us to the picture of the Magic School Bus sloshing around in Arnold's stomach. Sure enough, there are fish sticks bobbing around the bus. Cayton then reads the dialogue bubble, "Your stomach is like a built-in food processor" and remarks, "I love that. Now I know what it's like to live in my stomach—gross." Without taking a breath, Cayton then shares his favorite part of the book: "I liked the part about the white blood cells the best because they are eating diseases and germs." Cayton tries to demonstrate how the white cells envelope a diseased cell but decides it is easier to lead us through the diagram in the book. He then explains, "I like when they do that because then I don't have to be sick. I'm so lucky because if nobody had white blood cells they would die."

I tell the circle that I, too, wrote a journal entry about the white blood cells because one of my friends has leukemia, or cancer of the blood. I read part of my entry: "Something went wrong in his blood and his white cells started multiplying much faster than his red cells. He was very sick for a while. Luckily, he had a bone marrow transplant and is feeling better now." Students want to know how old he is, how he got leukemia, and if it is contagious. Nicole asks why Joanna Cole didn't do a report about leukemia. We talk about the decisions a writer has to make about the most important things to put in a book that is only thirty-six pages long.

Nicole redirects us to her favorite part of the book—the taste bud report. She asks if we can have a "taste contest." Because there is much enthusiasm for this idea, I ask them to write an entry in their reading journal, explaining an experiment that we could do with the food they volunteer to bring to class tomorrow.

I then call my second literature circle to the table. Their responses to Cole's *The Magic School Bus Lost in the Solar System* shuttle back and forth across the domains of the personal and factual. The conversation darts from one topic to the next with much enthusiasm and with little, if any, discussion. This roaming around is a natural response to a new book—one that is to be expected. It is the same kind of talk that we often have with peers when we chat about a book or a movie. Our job as teachers is to find the point of intrigue in the conversation and to invite readers to write about this one substantive point for a subsequent meeting. It is then that the conversation deepens. The point of intrigue emerges when Bobby offers to recite the planets in order. When his peers express their amazement, he shares the mneumonic device his father taught him (Mary's Violet Eyes Make John Stay Up At Night Pacing). When asked about a project that they might pursue, John suggests that they make a model of the solar system. Each member agrees to choose a planet, to make a model of it, and to write a brief report.

Day Eleven: Literature Circle Projects

The third graders rush through the classroom door to show me the food they brought in for their taste experiments and the planets/asteroid belt they made for the solar system model. So as not to distract the rest of the class, I ask the *Inside the Human Body* circle to take their chairs, reading journals, and project materials into the corridor and to read their suggested experiment. Alexa reads:

> We take samples of the food and take notes. As we eat we then compare notes. The foods are a lemon for bitter, cookies for sweet, sour lollipops for sour and saltines for salty.

Stephanie then shares her idea: "We blindfold ourselves, taste each food and guess sour, salty, sweet, and bitter. Cayton suggests we do what the *Magic School Bus* recommends: "If you want to taste sour, you put it in the middle of your tongue. If you want to taste sweet, put it where the book says."

I ask what kind of text structure a scientist uses when he or she writes an experiment. After some discussion, they arrive at the sequence structure. With guidance, we merge ideas and create a sequence of steps that we each will follow. We agree to place each piece of food on the four target places of our tongues and to record the place where the food tastes the sweetest, sourest, and so on. We then compare our answers and check them against the book. Execution of the experiment is a sight to behold. And the test results? There was little agreement among the tasters and even less with Joanna Cole. As we bring the activity to a close, Stephanie asks if we can put experiments in our vernal pool book because they are so much fun. I explain that if we can design some experiments for the vernal pool, we certainly can include them.

Our taste testers return to their tables to start a new Joanna Cole book while the solar system group convenes to share their research on their self-assigned planets and to assemble their model of the solar system. During this same time block, Mrs. Earle meets with her two groups.

Day Twelve: On the Bus with Joanna Cole

Joanna Cole day has arrived. Having compiled their hunches about Joanna Cole, presented in Figure 7-11, I ask students to respond. Some hunches receive a resounding "Yes" or laughter as they are read. Other items, such as "She never finished a book she wrote," need clarification. John explains, "Maybe she started a report about cockroaches when she was in third grade but never finished it and so when she grew up she decided to finish it." Some hunches are challenged. For example, some students contest the hunch that Joanna Cole is not a good artist. Meghan suggests that

---

Joanna Cole as a Child:
- Liked school and got good grades
- Was a hard worker
- Had lots of hobbies
- Was a writer when she was a kid
- Never finished a book she wrote and so she decided to finish it when she grew up
- Wanted to grow up to be a writer
- Liked science
- Rode the bus to school

Joanna Cole as a Writer:
- Reads a lot of books to get ideas
- Likes doing reports on science like hurricanes and bees
- Uses real people for her characters

Joanna Cole as a Person
- Is very funny
- Is Ms. Frizzle
- Is a science teacher
- Is a bus driver
- Is not a good artist
- Likes comics
- Has a real lizard for a pet named Lizzie

FIGURE 7-11   *Third graders' hunches about Joanna Cole*

if Cole was a good artist, she would have illustrated her own books. I suggest they listen carefully as I read Cole's autobiography to confirm or reject hunches.

I do not read the autobiography cover-to-cover; rather, I read excerpts that tie to the third graders' hunches. I read about the young Joanna Cole and how she loved science, writing reports, and watching insects. I read that:

- She never thought about being a writer when she grew up because she didn't know that a house painter's daughter could be a writer.
- Her favorite science teacher, Miss Bair, was the inspiration for Ms. Frizzle.
- She thinks she is most like Arnold, who loves to read about science but who is not crazy about going on science expeditions.
- She has had a number of careers: teacher, librarian, and editor of children's books.
- She doesn't think she is funny in person but how she enjoys writing the funny lines for the characters, and slipping jokes, puns, and riddles into her stories.

Throughout the reading, the third graders interject comments. For example, Abby says, "Hey, my mother is an editor. She corrects all the spelling in people's books."

Samantha comments, "Oh, I know that experiment about the vacuum cleaner and ping pong balls (an experiment Joanna did in Miss Bair's classroom). My brother did that. He had vacuum cleaner parts all over the house!"

After I finish reading the excerpts, I reread each hunch and ask the class to respond chorally, "true" or "false." A number of items yield both responses and necessitate discussion. For example, some thought Joanna Cole didn't have hobbies; others argued that she did.

"She liked watching bugs," said Kelly.

"Indeed, bug watching is a hobby," I note.

"She liked writing. She's like me. Writing is one of my hobbies too," adds Eddie. We decide that the hobby hunch gets a true vote. Some hunches, such as "She rode a bus to school" and "She likes comics," aren't addressed in the autobiography. I am about to score those items with a question mark when Abby says, "Wait. She never rode the bus to school. I read that on the book jacket of *Inside the Human Body* I think." I ask her to check while we move ahead. She returns to the circle with a smile and reads that neither Joanna Cole nor Bruce Degen, the illustrator, rode the bus to school.

We tally twelve correct hunches, four incorrect hunches, and four still-to-be-verified hunches. Students revel in the degree to which their predictions are affirmed. We conclude that Joanna Cole, like other writers, reveals facets of her life in her writing. We also conclude, though, that a writer's book is not necessarily a mirror of his or her life. Writers pluck ideas for their books from their own lives, from their dreams, from other people's lives, and from current or historical events. For example, Joanna Cole got the idea for her cockroach book from an article her dad read—not from direct experiences with cockroaches.

Third Graders Write and Illustrate *The Magic School Bus Goes to the Vernal Pool*

Recall that the idea to write our own *Magic School Bus* book emerged on the first day of the author study and fueled much of our subsequent discussion. For example, on day three, Abby wanted to know if her mother, who is an editor, could do the pictures for our vernal pool book. On day four, Nicole asked if they could write the dialogue bubbles. On day six, Bobby inquired if they would be writing reports for the book. On day twelve, Stephanie asked if they could put experiments in the book. The success of the book project, however, hinged on the groundwork that was laid during the twelve sessions presented here. For example, to write successful nonfiction reports, the third graders needed not only to read Joanna Cole's reports, but also to analyze the three report structures prominent in her work as well as other criteria. To create a successful storyline, they needed to understand the interplay of fact and fiction.

The actual writing of *The Magic School Bus Goes to the Vernal Pool* consumed two and a half weeks of daily reading and writing. While space does not permit a day-by-day description of lesson events, highlights of this book-writing venture follow.

KWL Chart on the Vernal Pool

Joanna Cole (1996) writes in her autobiography, "In every *Magic School Bus* book, the science is the skeleton of the book. It forms a frame on which the fiction part of the book hangs" (p. 29). The science of the vernal pool, then, had to be our starting point. Because the study of the vernal pool crossed the school year, the third graders had some nascent knowledge about this transitory wetland. They had visited the vernal pool in autumn to find nothing but a large puddle. They took observation notes on the vernal pool habitat and listened to a wildlife expert talk about plant, animal, and insect life. In early winter, they revisited the vernal pool only to find a blanket of snow. They drew diagrams of animal tracks in the snow and hypothesized about the creatures who populated the habitat in winter. They returned again in spring to find a sprawling pool (100' x 150') teaming with life. This time, with the guidance of the wildlife expert, they scooped water out of the pool, poured it into ice trays, and used magnifying glasses to search for tiny vernal pool creatures such as fairy shrimp and flatworms (Figure 7-12). As part of this curricular study, they also had listened to nonfiction read-alouds about vernal pool creatures such as frogs, salamanders, and dragonflies.

Thus, when I present the KWL chart (a three-columned chart labeled What I *Know*; What I *Want* to Know; What I *Learned*) and ask the class "What do you know about the vernal pool?" they rattle off information about the wetland: "In spring, it's wet and in winter it's dry." "There are lots of leaves at the bottom." They offer facts about vernal pool species: "There are lots of burrows that animals make." "Salamanders hide under rocks." About plant life, they advise: "Watch out for poison ivy!" When I move to the next column, "What do want to know about the vernal pool

FIGURE 7-12   *Third graders examine vernal pool life*

and its creatures?" their questions come easily. "Why do mosquitoes sting people?" "Why couldn't we find any salamanders at the vernal pool?" Their questions set the stage for the scientific curiosity that will underpin many of their nonfiction reports.

Vernal Pool Story Skeleton

Having activated their rudimentary knowledge, the third graders offer ideas about their *The Magic School Bus Goes to the Vernal Pool* storyline. Tapping their sense of the story grammar elements, I ask how every *Magic School Bus* book begins. They reply, "The kids are doing science projects."

"Then what happens?" I asked.

"Ms. Frizzle tells the kids that they are going on a field trip," they answer.

The third graders have no difficulty generating Cole's generic storyline. With the reminder that Joanna Cole weaves general science content into her storyline, I ask how our book might open. John suggests that, like Ms. Frizzle's "kids," we could be doing vernal pool projects, "like making clay models of the animals." I record this idea on a chart, draw a downward arrow, and ask what might happen next. Kelly replies that Mrs. Earle says, "Let's go on a field trip to the vernal pool." I write this idea under the arrow.

I then explain that we are creating a story skeleton. We talk about what a skeleton is and draw parallels to the story skeleton. I then explain that this is exactly what Joanna Cole does when she starts a *Magic School Bus* book. She sends a two-page outline to her editor for feedback and she worries about the details later (1996, p. 15).

At this point, I ask them to complete individual story skeletons with ideas about where the story might go. I urge them to write down the next big event, to draw an arrow and then to write the next big event. I remind them not to worry about the details. I then explain that I will take their individual story skeletons and merge all the ideas into one skeleton.

Later that day, as I read their skeletons (see example in Figure 7-13), I am impressed by their ideas. Because children have an affinity for writing stories in which they catapult characters from one event to another in the "and then . . . and then . . . and then" framework, this task comes easily. While reading the skeletons, I tally their ideas. For example, almost half of the class turns the bus into a salamander; a few turn it into a turtle or a frog. I merge their ideas into a class skeleton. For example, I turn the bus into a salamander that joins the salamander migration to the vernal pool. I purposely include an erroneous event in the skeleton: A huge frog swallows the salamander bus and then burps it out. I do so because I want the class to understand that the storyline, while having fictional characters and events, must be grounded in scientific fact.

When I share the class story skeleton, I explain the popularity of the salamander bus idea. I also share that, because I didn't know much about salamanders, I had to read about some salamander books to figure out that the salamander bus would join a salamander migration. I stress the importance of scientific accuracy in the storyline. When I get to the frog-burping episode, I ask if anyone knows whether frogs burp. No one does. I note that when our research teams are created, we will need the frog "experts" to investigate this burping event. If their research shows that frogs don't burp, we'll have to revise our storyline. I explain that this holds true for all the science events in our storyline because, as Joanna Cole writes, "At the same time that I am fleshing out the plot and giving the characters things to say, I am still reading, reading, reading about my subject. I want the science to be rock solid" (p. 15).

The third graders are pleased with the story skeleton. Their feedback ranges from "Well, if the frog doesn't burp, maybe when he ribbits, he can push out the bus," to "It's not called a herd of dragonflies, I think it's a swarm." I explain that many of our uncertainties will be resolved when our research teams collect their evidence.

Notetaking the Joanna Cole Way

Teams of three or four researchers are formed as the third graders choose the vernal pool topic that interests them (the vernal pool, frogs, salamanders, turtles, mosquitoes, or dragonflies). We begin by reviewing what they know about notetaking. Fortunately, notetaking was introduced at the mid-point of the year and practiced on occasion. I probe their understanding by asking questions such as:

1. Do you need to write whole sentences when you take notes?
2. Should you copy the exact words of the author whom you are reading?

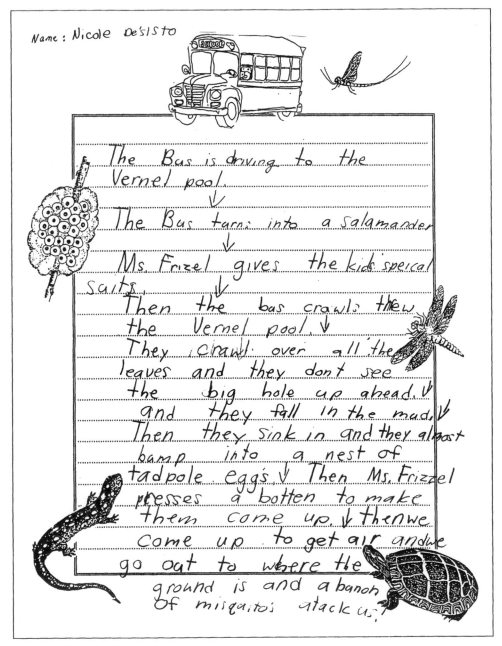

Name: Nicole De'SISto

The Bus is driving to the Vernel pool.

The Bus turns into a salamander

Ms. Frizel gives the kids speical saits.

Then the bas crawls thew the Vernel pool.
They crawl over all the leaves and they dont see the big hole up ahead.
and they fall in the mud.
Then they sink in and they almost bamp into a nest of tadpole eggs Then Ms. Frizzel presses a botten to make them come up thenwe come up to get air andwe go oat to where the ground is and a banoh of misqaitos atack us!

FIGURE 7-13   Nicole's story skeleton

3. Should you read only one book on your topic?

4. If you find the same fact about frogs in another book, do you need to record it again?

5. What do you do if you find conflicting facts?

6. How do you organize your notes?

The researchers then are given the option of taking notes the way they have learned or of doing it the Joanna Cole way. In her autobiography, Cole explains that she doesn't take traditional notes when researching. Rather, she writes key information on sticky notes and then attaches them to dummy pages. The third graders, intrigued by this idea, are eager to adopt Cole's strategy.

I work with individual teams to establish what might be addressed in their reports and to help them locate resources. However, I decide not just to turn the books over to them (mainly because of the time factor). Rather, I facilitate their fact finding by reading the books ahead of time and by attaching Post-its with pages marked that address major research categories (e.g., why mosquitoes bite; pp. 23–24). This enables the researchers to move right into the content. Because they only have a limited amount of reading to do, they record their notes on Post-its fairly quickly and then move on to another book. They use a different color Post-it for each book. An example is presented in Figure 7-14.

Although nearly all of the third graders write complete sentences rather than phrases, surprisingly few copy the text verbatim. They also do a fine job at *not* recording the same facts from different sources. However, none of the students seem to notice the few conflicting pieces of information in their material. When the third graders have exhausted their available resources, I ask them to think about the kind of report they will be writing and to put their Post-its in the order that they will use them in their first draft. Because their first instinct is to sequence the facts from one book and then sequence the facts from another book, I model the process, emphasizing the integration of information across different colored Post-its.

Writing the Vernal Pool Reports

With Post-its arranged, the third graders are ready to begin their first drafts. We review the three types of reports that nonfiction writers use by having three children come to the front of the room to hold charts that contain the definitions of the three report structures (description, sequence, and comparison); the actual report terms are covered up. I read each definition and ask the class to pinpoint the kind of report. I then hold up various report titles (e.g., "How the Frog Grows from an Egg to an Adult") and ask volunteers to decide what kind of report it is and to stand beside the person with the corresponding definition. The third graders match these items quickly. We review the key words that the nonfiction writer should include in each type of report.

We then examine some of Ms. Frizzle's "kids'" reports in various *Magic School Bus*

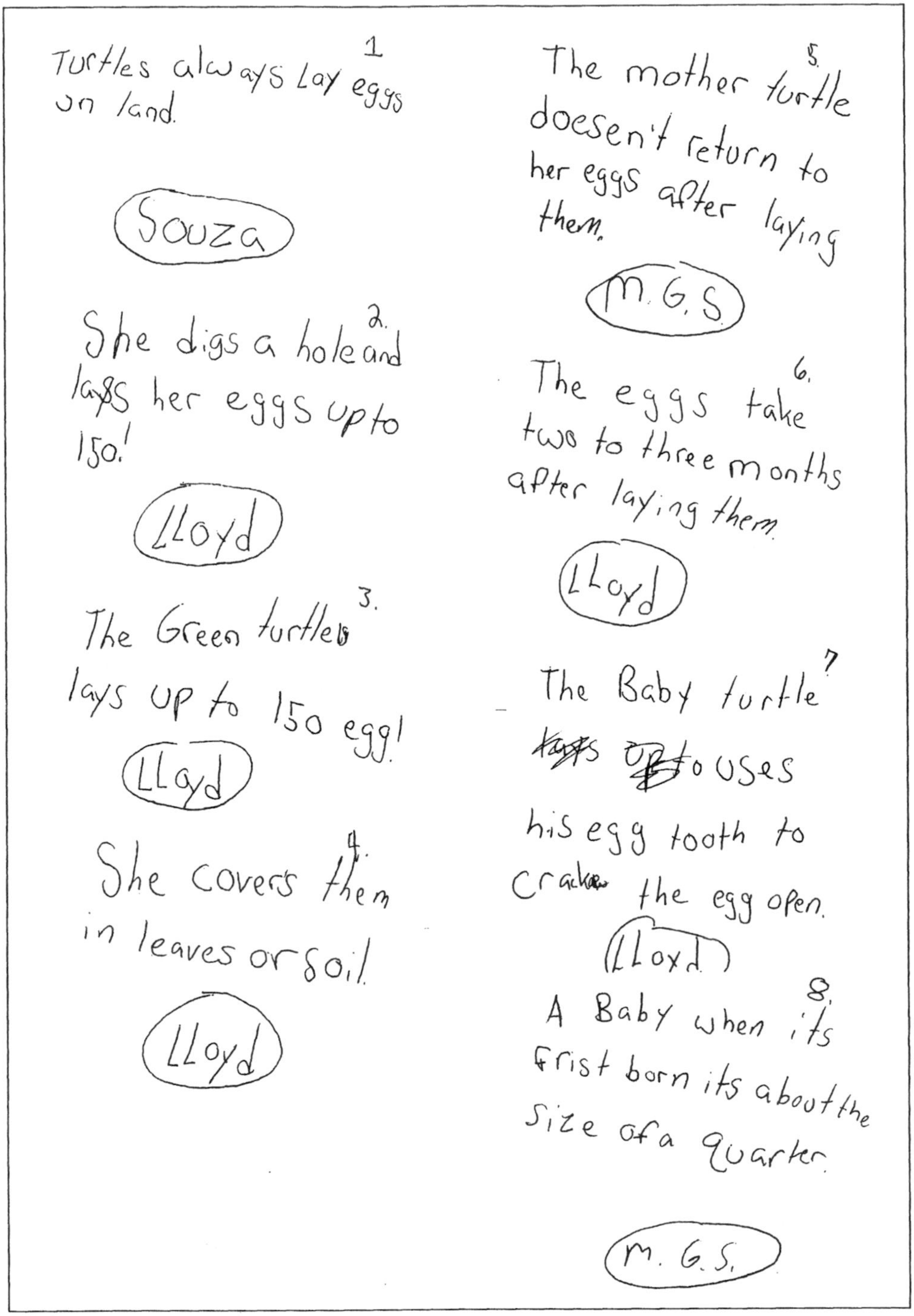

Turtles always Lay eggs
on land.

1

(Souza)

She digs a hole and
lays her eggs up to
150!

2.

(Lloyd)

The Green turtles
lays up to 150 egg!

3.

(Lloyd)

She covers them
in leaves or soil

4.

(Lloyd)

The mother turtle
doesen't return to
her eggs after laying
them.

5.

(M.G.S)

The eggs take
two to three months
after laying them

6.

(Lloyd)

The Baby turtle
lays up to uses
his egg tooth to
crack the egg open.

7

(Lloyd)

A Baby when it's
frist born its about the
size of a quarter.

8.

(M.G.S.)

FIGURE 7-14   *Kelly's research notes on Post-it Notes*

books to reinforce concepts covered. Interestingly, John points out that "Molly's" sequence report, "HOW ROCK LAYERS ARE FORMED" in *Inside the Earth* is missing key words. As we look at another report, we notice the omission again. We talk about the fact that a writer can leave these terms out and not confuse the reader, but that inclusion of the sequence terms ensures that the reader will pay attention to order. I smile as Nicole suggests that "maybe Joanna Cole left them out because the 'kids' write the reports and they probably don't know the key words." The following day we examine another Cole sequence report—"HOW A DEAD DINOSAUR COULD BECOME A FOSSIL"—and find the items in the sequence numbered. Another structural possibility presents itself.

Because text structure is only one criterion of a good report, I have the class generate other criteria. "You can make the title kind of funny so kids will look at it more," notes Abby. We talk about how Cole uses humor to entertain readers and to keep them engaged. Meghan reiterates a point that we have stressed throughout, "You have to use true facts." When I ask about copying another author's words, Cayton replies, "You can't. You can't steal from someone else. You have to write the report in your words."

I pass out scrap paper for first drafts. I encourage third graders to consult Cole's reports for ideas as they begin to compose their vernal pool reports. Over the next day or two, as they finish first drafts, I ask them to reread their ideas and to make revisions with particular attention to our criteria for a good report. Their drafts are checked by a teacher and suggestions are made.

When most of the students are ready for their second draft, we examine additional Cole reports and make new observations. For example, Cole uses both questions and statements for report titles. I ask them to think about what they will use. We talk about Joanna Cole's extensive use of similes and why readers enjoy these comparison statements. Do they want to insert any similes in their second revisions? We note that many of Cole's reports include illustrations. Do they want to add pictures? The third graders begin draft two. When second drafts have been self-edited and then teacher-edited, the third graders are given white paper and black felt-tip pens and are asked to write their final drafts in their best penmanship. Kelly's second draft is presented in Figure 7-15.

When second drafts have been self-edited and teacher-edited, the third graders are given white paper and black felt-tip pens, and asked to write their final drafts in their best penmanship.

Finalizing the Storyline

Primed with vernal pool knowledge, the third graders critique the original story skeleton. I reread the opening segment of the story skeleton—"The kids are doing science projects on the vernal pool like making clay models of the animals"—and ask for their thoughts. Ted replies, "It's kind of boring because it's kinda copying what's in the other *Magic School Bus* books." When I ask for clarification, he notes, "At the beginning of the *Dinosaur* book, the kids have clay models of the dinosaurs and I

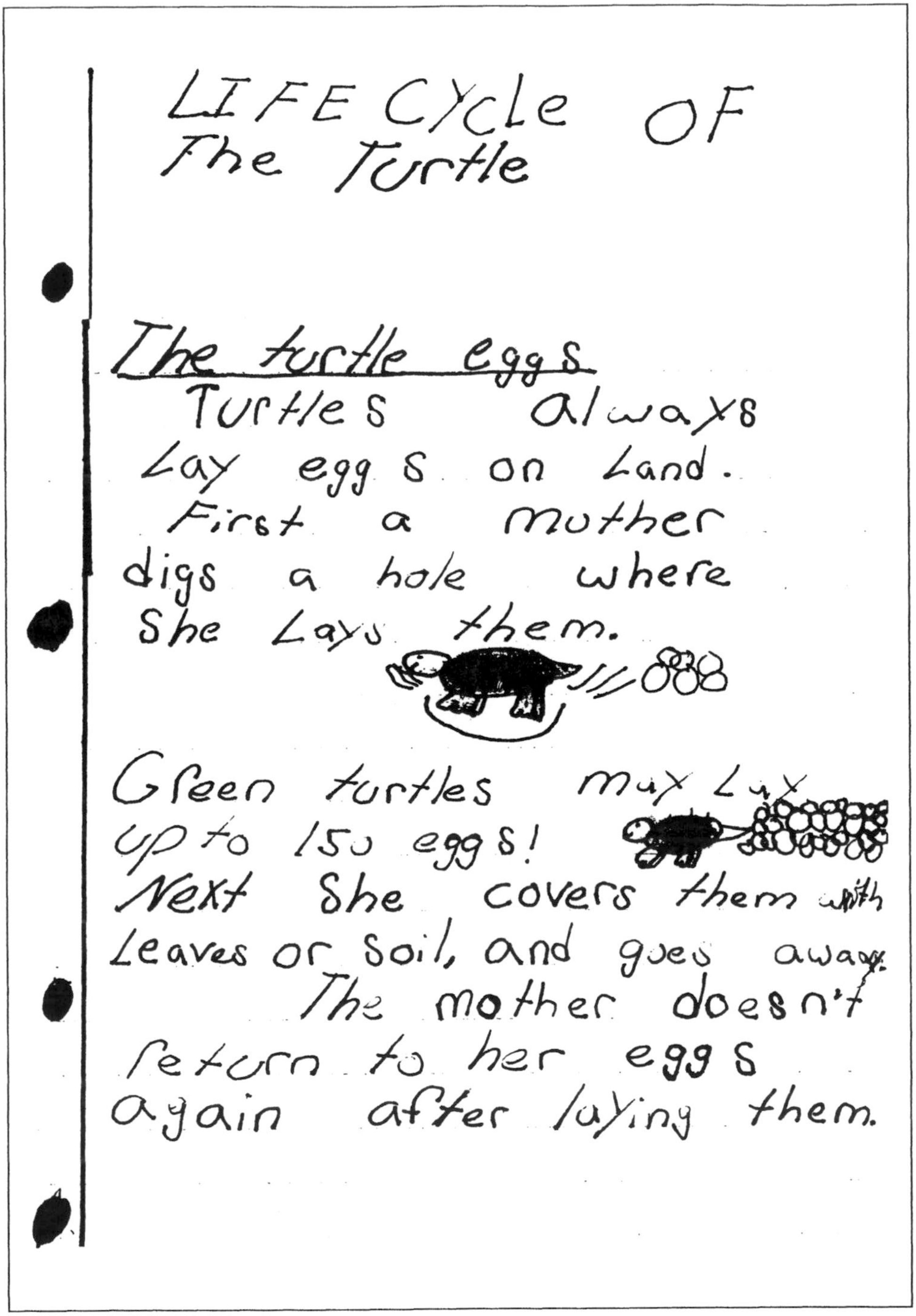

LIFE CYCLE OF
The Turtle

The turtle eggs

Turtles always Lay eggs on Land. First a mother digs a hole where She Lays them.

Green turtles may Lay up to 150 eggs! Next She covers them with Leaves or Soil, and goes away. The mother doesn't return to her eggs again after laying them.

FIGURE 7-15   *Kelly's final draft*

think in other books too." Abby adds that the *Beehive* book starts with models of insects. The class agrees that we need our own original beginning.

"Maybe the kids could be doing what we did—using magnifying glasses to look for things in the vernal pool water that we put in ice cube trays," says Stephanie.

"You know how Ms. Frizzle has Lizzie her pet reptile. Well, Mrs. Earle could come into class with her salamander pet, Iggeboo, and tell the class about salamanders," says Brandon.

"Mrs. Earle could bring in some boxes and have the kids guess what's in them like turtles and salamanders," offers Kelly.

They generate nine different possibilities for the opening. Because many ideas are wonderfully original, I ask for a vote on the best opening. After the vote and discussion, we decide to merge three ideas: the mystery boxes, Mrs. Earle's salamander, and a class mural.

We continue moving through the text in this fashion, with our "experts" challenging certain points. For example, Eddie says that we can't have the turtle swimming across the vernal pool because box turtles live at the edge of the vernal pool but don't swim in it. Bobby agrees with Eddie, but notes that other turtles, like the spotted turtle, do swim in the vernal pool. We agree to specify that the turtle in our story is a spotted turtle. When we arrive at the frog-burping episode, our frog "experts" comment that they found no information about frogs burping. With no scientific evidence, we agree that the frog-burping episode has to go. As we work to revise this episode, Eddie comes up with the idea of the snapping turtle chasing the salamander bus, which meets with enthusiastic support.

Artwork for **The Magic School Bus Goes to the Vernal Pool**

The third graders are concerned about how they, as story characters, will appear in the book. I suggest that they draw pictures of themselves. Eddie suggests that they bring in photographs and cut out themselves or their heads. Nicole exclaims, "No wait, we can bring in pictures and scan them into the computer! I have a scanner at my house we can use." We agree that Nicole's idea is intriguing if we can access the computer equipment. Fortunately, the school has a digital camera and scanning software. They are delighted when I explain that I will take pictures of each team. I meet with groups to have members decide what pose they will assume for the picture. Their first poses are wonderfully humorous but are often unrelated to the corresponding text. Once I help them understand the connection between the text and the photographs, they work out their scenes; then we take the photographs.

The creation of the dialogue bubbles generates much excitement. Of course, knowing that most of the third graders would want to be an "Arnold" clone, delivering his famous one-liners, I announce, to a chorus of groans, that the person with a June birthday will assume the role of "Arnold." We then talk about how Joanna Cole creates funny as well as informative dialogue bubbles for characters. They readily give examples of funny lines and mention that "Dorothy" knows everything about everything and isn't shy about telling what she knows. Given their knowledgeable responses, I turn them loose. However, when I read their lines after school, I note that about half of the class misunderstood the relationship between the scene and the content of their dialogue bubbles. Many just copied their lines from the storyline, even after we talked about what the reader would think about a repeated line. To illustrate, a page from *The Magic School Bus Goes to the Vernal Pool* is presented in Figure 7-16. Matt's dialogue bubble— "They're sucking my blood!"—extends the scene. Eddie's (Jeremy's), on the other hand, is a copy of his line from the story. As I reflect on their responses, I realize that I was sidetracked by their facile comments about the nature of dialogue bubbles and didn't check the extent of their understanding. They needed to spend more time examining how Joanna Cole creates these funny one-liners. I also realize that our storyline departs significantly from Joanna Cole's prototype in that her "kids" have no dialogue in the *Magic School Bus* books. All of their lines occur in the dialogue bubbles. The only person who speaks in the storyline is Ms. Frizzle. If I had analyzed the storyline more carefully at the outset of this project, I could have eliminated this confusion.

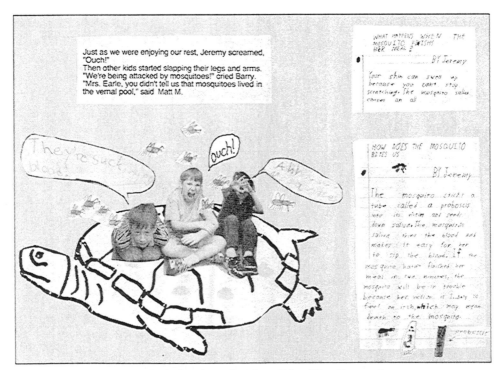

FIGURE 7-16   *A page from the third graders'* The Magic School Bus Goes to the Vernal Pool

Grand Finale: Videotape of The Magic School Bus Goes to the Vernal Pool

Recall that during our first session of the author study, Brandon suggested making a videotape for Joanna. We decided to videotape our book and send it to her. To prepare for the videotape, I distribute the script of the storyline. I ask the third graders to find their pen names and to highlight their lines. As we rehearse, we attend to the meaning clues contained in dialogue carriers such as "groaned the class" and "whispered Barry," and experiment with various ways to read corresponding lines. They are adept at this expressive reading. The third graders then practice reading their individual nonfiction reports to partners.

Our last task before videotaping is to decide to whom to dedicate our book. Suggestions are offered for Joanna Cole, Mrs. Earle, and myself. Then Kerry suggests that we dedicate it to Michael Altfillisch, Mrs. Earle's father, who had died during the school year. Students cast a unanimous vote for Alice's father. It was a touching and emotional moment for all.

With scripts and nonfiction reports in hand, the third graders assemble on the rug. *The Magic School Bus Goes to the Vernal Pool* is placed on a chart stand; in front of the chart is a chair. I explain the following procedures:

> We will read one page of the script at a time; the camera will be focused on the book during our script reading. At the end of each page, I will announce the author and the title of the nonfiction report that accompanies that page. The author will move to the chair in front of the camera and read his or her report.

In preparing for this finale, I worry that reading the entire book will be too demanding and that the third graders will not be able to attend for this stretch of time. However, the commitment to do a good job for Joanna Cole and the aura of the videotape hold them steadfast. It is an impressive performance, with few glitches. Upon completion, they beam. Alice and I congratulate them on a job well done.

Concluding Comments

This chapter began with disquieting research findings about children's difficulty in reading and writing nonfiction, and about their preference for fiction by a 3-to-1 margin. Some researchers attributed this difficulty to limited cognition without acknowledging that children had little, if any, exposure to nonfiction literature and that instruction in nonfiction reading and writing was rarely pursued. As later research has revealed, what we do as teachers makes all the difference. When children are immersed in quality nonfiction and are armed with instructional strategies, they become nonfiction readers and writers (Pappas, 1991; McGee, 1982).

However, there is still much we need to know in order to support and to extend children's forays into the world of nonfiction. For example, we know surprisingly little about how children read nonfiction texts (Helper, 1998). My informal observations of and conversations with the third graders suggest that they rarely read a standard nonfiction book cover to cover. Rather, they do a visual survey of a book,

ALIKI
<http://www.acs.ucalgary.ca/~dkbrown/k6/aliki.html>

ARNOSKY, JIM
<http://www.penguinputnam.com/catalog/yreader/authors/506_biography.html>

ASHABRANNER, BRENT
<http://www.childrensbookguild.org/Ashabranner.html>
The times of my life: A memoir. (1990). New York: Cobblehill

COLE, JOANNA
<http://www.evansday.com/cole.html>
On the bus with Joanna Cole. (1996). Portsmouth, NH: Heinemann
Joanna Cole (video). Nashua, NH: Delta Education.

EHLERT, LOIS
HANDS. New York: Harcourt.
Get to know Lois Ehlert (video). New York: Harcourt Brace.

FREEDMAN, RUSSELL
<http://www.indiana.edu/~eric_rec/ieo/bibs/freedman.html>
A visit with Russell Freedman (video). Boston: Houghton Mifflin.
Meet the Newbery Author: Russell Freedman (video). New York: SRA/McGraw Hill.

FRITZ, JEAN
<http://www.penguinputnam.com/catalog/yreader/authors/309_biography.html>
Good conversation: A talk with Jean Fritz (video). Weston, CT: Weston Woods.

GIBBONS, GAIL
<http://www.iren.net/cfpl/youth/author.html>

GIBLIN, JAMES CROSS
<http://www.meet.edu/broadcast/programs/98055.shtml>

LASKY, KATHRYN
<http://www.xensei.com/users/newfilm/homelsk.htm>

LAUBER, KATHRYN
<http://www.indiana.edu/~eric_rec/ieo/bibs/lauber.html>

MACAULAY, DAVID
<http://www.hmco.com/hmco/trade/newmedia/catalog/AboutAuthor 1-56458-901-3.html>
David Macauley (video). Nashua, NH: Delta Education.

MARKEL, SANDRA
<http://www.mindspring.com/~cquest>

MELTZER, MILTON
Starting from home: A writer's beginnings. (1988). New York: Viking Press.

PRINGLE, LAWRENCE
<http://www.a-two-z.com/monarch.html>
Nature! Wild and wonderful. (1997). Katonah, NY: Richard C. Owen.

SIMON, SEYMOUR
<http://www.pipeline.com/~simonsi> *or*
<http://www.ipl.org/youth/AskAuthor/simon.html>

STANLEY, DIANE
<http://www.penguinputnam.com/catalog/yreader/authors/469_biography.html>

FIGURE 7-17   *Web sites of acclaimed nonfiction authors*

studying the pictures and reading the captions. If a particular picture/caption ignites their imagination, they read the adjacent text. Their nonfiction reading appears to be a process of shuttling back and forth across the text—a process driven by the visual data—without returning to read the text from start to finish. If these informal observations are verified, we need to ask questions such as: Does this visual-governing strategy provide an effective entrée into nonfiction? What is the impact of this strategy on the breadth and depth of children's understanding of the material? Answers to these and other questions are needed if we are to move children ahead as nonfiction readers.

One observation that I can make with confidence is that the Joanna Cole author study sparked an insatiable appetite for nonfiction reading and writing on the part of the third graders. Long after the Joanna Cole author study ended, the third graders continued to choose to read and write nonfiction. Make no mistake though—their pursuit of nonfiction was inextricably linked to peer and teacher influence.

Author studies of nonfiction writers are as powerful and as engaging as those of fiction writers. They evoke that same range of aesthetic and critical response as well as curiosity about the person behind the books. Children deserve to meet acclaimed nonfiction writers (Figure 7-17) and to savor their works.

Author Response:
Joanna Cole on Author Studies

Dear Carol,

I decided to write my response in the form of a letter to you, because I feel that we really know each other after all that e-mailing!

What was my response to reading your chapter about the author study of me? My very first reaction was to walk on air. It is one thing to see a nice review of my book. It's quite another to read that kids *cheered* when asked if they'd like to study my work.

Of course I had other responses to the study as well: I was gratified that nonfiction is being taken seriously nowadays and delighted with the children's reactions and their creation of their own *Magic School Bus* book.

It's been almost thirty years now since I wrote my first science book for children. In that time, I've read a lot of nonfiction—I may read as many as a hundred books preparing to write one of my books, and I subscribe to about six science journals. That keeps me busy professionally, and for pleasure I read both fiction and nonfiction. At any moment, I am usually in the middle of reading a science book. For instance, right now I am halfway through *Eve Spoke*, by Philip Lieberman, a book about the evolution of human language. Since evolution is one of my special interests and language is a major part of my job, I bring an almost voracious curiosity to this book and read it as eagerly as I would any mystery novel.

Because nonfiction has been my pleasure reading since childhood, it's never surprising when I hear someone say that many kids like it. What *is* surprising is when adults seem puzzled by this, or when they say children are "bored by science." Science is about how the world works, and surely finding out about that is one of children's main development tasks—which means they love to do it. Some adults, reviewers included, make so much of the fictional aspects of the *Magic School Bus* books that I'm glad you told us that the third graders in the study didn't read them for the humor alone. They were also engaged by the content.

You thoughtfully sent a list of questions I might want to answer in this piece, although you stressed that I didn't *have* to use them. That's good, because I don't know the answers to most of them. I never consciously ask myself questions like "What do I want kids to get out of my books?" or "Should children be encouraged to do author studies?" or "Do I think teachers should help children analyze books?" This is probably why I am not a teacher! As selfish as it may sound, I write my books for my own reasons. I started the *Magic School Bus* series because I couldn't resist the fun and challenge of trying to make a combination book that would succeed equally in the fiction and nonfiction departments.

Of course, that is not to say that I don't consider my audience. I think most people who write and publish children's books have an intuitive sense of what kids will like and understand. A great deal of my writing involves translating complex information into simple prose that, I hope, will appeal to kids. Here's an example of an everyday task I face in writing the *Magic School Bus* "reports." For *The Magic School Bus Explores the Five Senses* (to be published in spring 1999), I wrote a report for Keesha entitled "Even the Tiniest Animals Have Senses." Now if I were writing for adults I might write something like, "One-celled animals like paramecia have rudimentary senses and can detect gradients of pleasure and noxious chemicals." For children I translated that to, "One-celled animals have simple senses. They can tell when their surroundings are too hot, too cold, or too poisonous." It may seem that the second passage, because it's easier to *read* than the first, must be easier to *write* as well. Nothing could be farther from the truth. The first sentence comes tripping off the tongue if you have spent upward of three decades reading science texts! The second requires finding just the right simple words, keeping it short, and within these confines being true to the meaning of the original. Now *that's* work. (Someday, I might make a list of all the pitfalls that lie in wait for an author of easy science books.)

I was interested in your discussion of the three types of reports—sequence, description, and comparison. It was an eye-opener to me mostly because I didn't know I wrote in these different styles. I'm so involved trying to make my reports understandable and meaningful that I honestly couldn't tell you what forms I use. I suppose such analysis helps students learn to think and it helps with their writing, but I don't know.

I loved school as a child and never thought of how it could be improved, but I admit that your chapter has shown me how. I feel a little envious of the third graders' high-quality school experiences: the fun of acting in the Readers' Theater activity; the chance to do an ongoing, in-depth study of vernal pools, including field trips, reading, and lab work; the visit from Mr. Oles, the principal/beekeeper; and the bee dances of Mrs. Earle. An aside about the last one: I usually dislike activities in which people get up and make formations with their bodies to illustrate a concept, because the exercises often seem only tenuously related to the subject and performed mainly with the hope that they will "make learning fun." Even that goal seemed questionable when I took part in one of these pantomimes. I loved Mrs. Earle's bee dances because they actually did help make clear the abstract concepts. They also seemed to be genuinely fun—and funny, too.

I was especially impressed with how much you encouraged the children to relate their *feelings* to what they were learning. I can't remember a single instance of that in my schooling. Yet how essential it is! When I write for children I always think of how the material may affect them emotionally. This is especially important for books like *How You Were Born*, which addresses science and feelings directly, but even a subject that is not obviously psychological touches our emotions. My own fascination with evolution surely has its roots in basic human questions like "Who am I?" and "Why am I the way I am?" I'm working on a book now that affects my feelings everyday. It's currently titled *Ms. Frizzle's Adventures in Ancient Egypt*, and I have become very fond of the Ancient Egyptians. I take real pleasure in finding out that they wrote each other notes on chips of pottery; that women had more rights in Egypt than in other ancient cultures; that artisans working on tomb paintings once went on strike; and all sorts of other "facts" that make these ancient people human to me.

Speaking of facts, I loved the children's discussion of accuracy in books. It's terrific that they realize that facts may change. That's why the material in the *Magic School Bus* series is constantly being updated as the books go back for new printings. I'm pretty passionate about accuracy in my work. However, I think that if the readers misapprehend anything about nonfiction writing, it's the value of having "correct facts." Concern for accuracy is certainly important: it shows respect for the material and for the scientists' work, and it's important for understanding concepts. But it's not an end in itself. I prefer to think that my books are about ideas rather than facts.

I was pleased to read your comments on the visual aspects of my work. Not everyone would think of this, because I do not illustrate. However, I have always thought of myself as a picture-book writer, which to me means being careful that there's a good marriage between text and illustrations. That's why I usually write in dummy form: to make sure there is an appropriate amount of text on a page, and to see that each chunk of text lends itself to a picture that will increase interest and comprehension. Not being an artist, however, means that I own a great deal (I should say an incalculable amount) to the talented illustrators who have worked on my books—Bruce Degen most of all.

One truly cannot talk about the *Magic School Bus* series without talking about Bruce. He is the reason the books look the way they do. (While Ms. Frizzle's personality was inspired by my junior high science teacher, her looks come from Bruce's high school geometry teacher.) His art gives the books a gusty vitality and enhances comprehension by its superior draftsmanship. He often adds funny jokes to the book, and he puts charming touches in his pictures that I never thought of. One reason it's possible for me to do the books is because of him. I have the utmost confidence that whatever I write about—be it a visit to Ms. Frizzle's taste buds or a trip down the Nile—Bruce will make it happen in an accurate and witty fashion.

While reading a previous chapter of this book in manuscript, I was deeply touched by your quote from Charles Dickens telling how difficult writing was for him. As a writer who must struggle, I've always idealized other authors who I thought wrote easily. I think it was George Orwell who said that Dickens's imagination was like a weed, and I had believed that Dickens, of all authors, wrote with ease and speed. I was greatly reassured to find out that he struggled too.

Knowing how important an insight like that can be to me, who's been writing for so many years, I was glad to learn that some of the third graders got that kind of reassurance from my autobiography. I hope it will be helpful to the writers among them as they grow up.

With thanks for including me,

Joanna

8

The Endless Possibilities of Author Studies

Eighteenth-century English essayist William Hazlitt (1982) wrote:

> Books wind into the heart. . . . We read them when young, we remember them when old. We read there of what has happened to ourselves. . . . We owe everything to their authors. . . . Even here, on Salisbury Plain, with a few old authors, I can manage to get through the summer or winter months, without ever knowing what it is to feel *ennui*. They sit with me at breakfast; they walk out with me before dinner—and at night, by the blazing hearth, discourse the silent hours away. (unpaged)

This chapter presents three additional authors with whom we can sit, walk, and "discourse the silent hours away": Patricia Polacco, Mildred Taylor, and Kathryn Lasky. Each of these authors has won critical acclaim and numerous literary awards—Polacco for her picture books about intergenerational bonds, Taylor for her novels about social injustice and racial pride, and Lasky for her photographic essays about nature's wonders. This chapter profiles each of these artists, exploring both autobiographical connections and critical dimensions of their work.

What of the aesthetic dimensions of these works? Throughout this book, I have emphasized the primacy of aesthetic response over critical and autobiographical response. As readers, we deserve to talk first about the emotional impact of a piece of literature because:

> We all have, in our experience, memories of certain books which changed us in some way by disturbing us or by a glorious affirmation of some emotion we knew but could never shape in words, or by some revelation of human nature. Virginia Woolf calls such times "moments of being," and James Joyce titles them "epiphanies." (Sayers, 1965, p. 16)

These epiphanies, though, are highly personal. What triggers a deep response in one reader may leave another unmoved. Each semester, I read the book *Faithful Elephants* (Tsuchiya, 1988) to my preservice teachers. It is a true story about the Japanese government's decision to kill all zoo animals during World War II to prevent their escape in the event of a bombing. Each semester, at least one student talks about the agony he or she feels for the zookeepers because he or she, too, has had to put a beloved pet to sleep. Another expresses distress about the killing of innocent life and his or her involvement with associations that work to protect endangered species. My response, one that no student has ever shared, is tied to that moment when the elephants are on the verge of death from starvation and one of the zookeepers, violating the government mandate, rushes in with food for the last remaining elephant. Tormented by the sight of Tonky's lifeless body, the zookeeper cannot bear to watch, and leaves him to die alone. Through my tears, I explain that I cannot bear the thought that he left him because I cannot bear the thought that my sister, Maureen, died alone. What I would have given to be at her side during her final hours. These emotions are so deep-seated that, even though Maureen died in 1983, I relive this terrible pain each time I read this book.

For this reason, sections on aesthetic response are not included in the author studies of Polacco, Taylor or Lasky. However, aesthetic response must be the starting point of every book encounter—fiction or nonfiction. With each book, readers first must be encouraged to share the ways in which the literature has touched them, has connected to their lives. After these discussions, critical and autobiographical responses can be tapped.

Patricia Polacco

Polacco's works are rich in themes of family, particularly grandparent-child bonds, of ethnic heritage, of social tolerance, and of magical moments. Because Polacco reveals these themes both explicitly and implicitly, she invites critical exploration. Many of Polacco's stories are about her babushka (Ukrainian grandmother). These stories offer explicit themes about right and wrong because storytelling in her grandmother's era was inherently moral. Stories were told to children not only to entertain but also to instill virtue. Polacco's courage to respect this tradition is laudable because most authors today steer clear of explicitly moral stories, believing that such tales are pedantic or preachy.

> A good story is alive, ever changing and growing as it meets each listener or reader
> in a spirited and unique encounter, while the moralistic tale is not only dead on arrival, it's already been embalmed. (Paterson, 1997, p. 7)

Paterson (1997) argues that stories such as *The Little Engine That Could* should not be read to children because "there's such a great difference between a moralistic tale and a genuine story that even a four-year-old can detect it" (p. 7). Yet, no research is available to show that young children find such tales preachy. Indeed, Polacco's work stands in testimony to the fact that stories can be alive—emotionally engaging, beautifully written—and also can impart wisdom about right and wrong.

Of course, not all of Polacco's stories contain explicit messages. Once she moves away from tales passed down by or about her grandmother, Polacco tends to allow her themes to unfold implicitly. This contrast, then, lends itself to critical analysis by young readers. We turn now to the works of this versatile writer.

Critical Response: Explicit Themes

The Bee Tree

When Mary Ellen complains, "I'm tired of reading to Grampa . . . I'd rather be outdoors running and playing," Grampa whisks her off on a bee tree adventure through the Michigan countryside. Grampa captures a few bees in a jar and then sets one bee free at a time. As Grampa and Mary Ellen pursue the bees, they are joined along the way by neighbors. When they arrive at the bee tree, Grampa smokes the tree, reaches in, and pulls out pieces of dripping honeycomb. As neighbors enjoy honey-covered biscuits and tea, Grampa takes Mary Ellen aside, spoons honey on the cover of one of her books, and asks her to taste the honey just as his father, and his father before him, asked him to do. Grampa then explains:

> "There is such sweetness inside of that book too!" he said thoughtfully. Such things
> . . . adventure, knowledge and wisdom. But these thing do not come easily. You have
> to pursue them. Just like when we ran after the bees to find their tree, so you must
> also chase these things through the pages of a book! (Polacco, 1993a, unpaged)

From that day on, Mary Ellen savors the honey of her books.

Babushka's Doll

When Babushka is washing clothes, young Natasha wants to be pushed on the swing. When Babushka is hanging clothes, Natasha demands a ride in the goat cart. When she is feeding the goats and Natasha whines that she wants to eat, Babushka explains, "Don't be selfish, darling. These poor creatures need to be fed. They cannot fix their own lunch." When they sit down to eat lunch, Natasha notices a doll on a shelf. Babushka tells Natasha that she can play with the doll while she is shopping. When Babuska leaves, the bratty doll comes to life and demands that Natasha do one thing after another When her grandmother arrives home, an exhausted Natasha sobs:

> Your little doll came to life and she was very naughty. All she wanted me to do was
> work. She never let me rest. She made me iron her dress and I don't even know how.
> I'm just a little girl. (Polacco, 1990a, unpaged)

Once she has learned her lesson, Natasha turns "out to be quite nice after all."

Babushka Baba Yaga

Baba Yaga (a Russian witch) longs to be a grandmother, but she is feared by the villagers, who tell tales about how Baba Yaga casts evil spells, steals children in the dead of night, and then eats them. Driven by loneliness, she borrows clothing to cover her long, pointy ears and enters the village. Welcomed by the village babushkas, she becomes a babushka for a young child, Victor. Baba Yaga loves Victor with all her heart. One day, though, the other babushkas gather in the village to tell tales of the evil Baba Yaga to the children. Baba Yaga, fearing her identity will be revealed, returns to the forest. One day, as Victor is at the edge of the woods, a pack of wolves surrounds him as the babushkas look on helplessly. Baba Yaga appears, scares off the wolves, and then embraces Victor, who knows it is his Babushka. Seeing her gentleness, the babushkas welcome her back. In the midst of the celebration, one of the babushkas holds Baba Yaga's hand and says:

> Those who judge one another on what they hear or see, and not what they know of them in their hearts, are fools indeed! (Polacco, 1993b, unpaged)

Thunder Cake

As thunder roars, a little girl (Patricia Polacco) cowers under her bed until her Grandma announces that this is the perfect weather for Thunder Cake. When they go outside, Grandma asks Patricia to begin counting as soon as she sees a bolt of lightning and then to stop when she hears the thunder, so she will know how far away the thunder is. With ten miles between them and the thunder, they scurry to find the ingredients such as eggs from Nellie Peck Hen, and milk from old Kick Cow. They rush to the kitchen, mix the ingredients, and pop the Thunder Cake into the oven just as the thunder roars overhead. While they wait for it to bake Grandma says:

> Why you aren't afraid of thunder. You're too brave . . . you got eggs from mean old Nellie Peck Hen . . . you climbed the trellis in the barnyard. From where I sit, only a very brave person could have done all them things! (Polacco, 1990b, unpaged)

And Patricia "never feared the voice of thunder again."

Critical Response: Implicit Themes

Intercultural Friendships

Pink and Say   Pinkus (Pink) Aylee, "with skin the color of mahogany," finds Seldon (Say) Russell Curtis, a fellow Union soldier, lying in a pool of blood on a Georgian battlefield. Both are fifteen years old. Worried that marauders will find Say, Pink carries the white boy through fields and across streams for miles to the slave quarters of his mother, Moe Moe Bay. Moe Moe, with loving tenderness, nurses Say back to life. When Say is conscious, Pink explains that he was separated from his unit and that when Say heals, they will return to fight the Confederates. Later, Say confesses to Moe Moe that he was shot while deserting his unit and that he is too cowardly to return to battle. Moe Moe comforts him, explaining that fear goes hand in hand with courage. Out of gratitude for Pink's humanity and friendship, Say decides to return to battle with Pink. As the boys are preparing to depart, marauders sweep in. Moe Moe hides the boys in a root cellar and then tries to ward off the invaders. The boys hear a gunshot and find Moe Moe dead; grief overtakes them. It is the senseless death of Moe Moe Bay that shocks Say into realizing the terrible injustice that plagues his homeland and that has taken the life of this brave, loving woman. Say now is ready to return to battle, not only to express his gratitude, but also to fight at Pink's side for the cause of freedom. As they depart, it is Say who now carries Pink, sick with fever, through the fields. However, the Confederates find and send them to a notorious prison camp. The boys embrace for the last time; Pink is hanged that day. While the themes of social injustice and of the tragedy of war undergird *Pink and Say* (1994a), it is the friendship between these two boys from separate worlds that strikes a fierce emotional chord. While Polacco makes no explicit statement about their friendship, it is etched repeatedly in Polacco's powerful illustrations—the shoulder-to-shoulder embraces, the clasped hands that the soldiers try to pry apart.

Mrs. Katz and Tush   Larnel's mother stops by every day to comfort Mrs. Katz, an elderly, recently widowed Polish immigrant who now will have to spend Passover and Hanukkah alone. Touched both by his mother's humanity and by Mrs. Katz's sorrow, Larnel arrives the following day with Tush, a scrawny, tailless kitten. Mrs. Katz agrees to take Tush if Larnel promises to help her care for it. And so begins a friendship between an African American boy and a Polish Jew. They exchange stories of discrimination, dance a Polish dance, and visit the cemetery. When Tush escapes out the window, Larnel and other neighbors search for and find her. With the family reunited, Larnel asks if he can celebrate Passover with Mrs. Katz. Overjoyed, Mrs. Katz prepares the seder; Larnel learns much about Passover. The following day, Tush gives birth to a litter of kittens, and Mrs. Katz becomes a bubee (grandmother). *Mrs. Katz and Tush* (1992a) sprang from Patricia's deep sadness over the clash of Hasidic Jews and African Americans after a nationally publicized tragedy in New York a few years ago. Having grown to love the richness of her multicultural community of Oakland, California, Polacco aches to think that cultural differences pull people apart rather than together. She wrote *Mrs. Katz and Tush* to affirm intercultural friendship and to draw historical parallels between the African American and Jewish struggle for justice (Gilles, 1998).

Intergenerational Love and Ethnic Pride

As is evident from the stories summarized to this point, the bond between grandparent and child resonates in Polacco's work. This intergenerational love is intimately tied to ethnic pride and the importance of one's heritage. As will be revealed in the next section, both of these deep and abiding themes find roots in Polacco's life.

Autobiographical Connections

Polacco: Life-Literature Connections

Like Cynthia Rylant, Mem Fox, and many others, Patricia Polacco's work is highly autobiographical. She credits her gift for storytelling to her Ukrainian grandparents, especially her grandmother: "My fondest memories are of sitting around a stove or open fire, eating apples and popping popcorn while listening to the old ones tell glorious stories about the past" (1990, book jacket). Polacco's stories about the special relationship between grandparent and child are her own stories. In her most autobiographical work, *The Keeping Quilt*, Polacco (1988) introduces her Great-Gramma Anna, who immigrated with her parents in the late 1800s. They arrived on Ellis Island in thick coats and boots, carrying two burlap bags of clothes. Anna wore a blue linen dress and red babushka (also a scarf)—prized possessions that reminded her of her Ukrainian homeland and the family whom she was never to see again. Soon, though, Anna outgrew her clothing. To stay her sadness, her mother suggested that they use her dress and babushka, along with some of the clothes from the burlap bags—Uncle Vladimir's shirt, Aunt Havalah's nightdress—to make a quilt so that "the family back home in Russia dance around us at night" (Polacco, 1988, unpaged). Anna used this keeping quilt as a huppa (canopy) at her wedding, as a tablecloth for holidays, and as a blanket to welcome her daughter, Carle, into the world. Carle and her husband married under the huppa, moved to Michigan, and wrapped Mary Ellen—Patricia's mother—in the quilt. Mary Ellen also married under the huppa, snuggled newborn Patricia in the quilt, and celebrated her first birthday with the quilt tablecloth. When Patricia was a little girl, her Babushka would come to her bed and point to the yellow horse on the quilt and ask, "Whose dress made this horse?" Patricia would rattle off names of relatives whom she never knew but carried in her heart. When she grew up, Patricia also married under the huppa and wrapped her daughter, Traci Denise, in the quilt. Patricia continues to use the quilt tablecloth for the Sabbath, Passover, and other special occasions and awaits the day when she will pass it with love to Traci Denise (Polacco, 1996a).

Just as the quilt preserves Polacco's Jewish Ukrainian heritage, so too do her books. *Rechenka's Eggs*, a tale about a babushka who paints exquisite *Pysanky* eggs (Ukrainian Easter eggs), has its roots in the egg-painting art that Patricia learned from her grandmother, an art she continues to pursue (1994). In *Uncle Vova's Tree*, Polacco (1989) recreates the Russian Orthodox Epiphany festivities such as decorating the tree with candles, bells, and Pysanky eggs, and taking the sleigh ride. *Thunder Cake*, in her own words, "is the story of how my grandma—my Babuska—helped me overcome my fear of thunder" (1990, unpaged).

Ukrainian storytelling is filled with magical moments. *Meteor!* (1987), Polacco's first book, is based on an actual meteor that crashed into the yard of her Ukrainian grandparents. Townspeople came from far and wide to touch the rock that had "flown across the galaxy," certain that the rock would endow them with special powers or feelings. When Polacco's grandmother died, the meteor was used as the family headstone. "In our family we believe that if you touch it and make wishes on it, the wishes come true. I take a piece of that meteor to schools with me and invite kids to wish on it" (1994, p. 22). This belief in life's magical moments fills many of Polacco's books: *Uncle Vova's Tree*, *Appelemando's Dream*, *Babushka's Doll*, and *Rechenka's Eggs*. In her own words, "People on both sides of my family saw perfectly ordinary events as miraculous and without this appreciation of even the smallest, tenderest little thing, you're doomed" (1996b, p. 178).

Polacco was five years old when her beloved Babuska died; the family left the

Michigan farm and moved to Oakland, California. There, she became best friends with Stewart and Winston Washington, African American brothers who lived next door. It is her special bond with Stewart and Winston, and with their Gramma, Eula May Walker, that is recalled in *Chicken Sunday*. Patricia, "adopted" by Miss Eula, often went to church with the family and returned home for "Chicken Sunday"—fried chicken, collard greens, corn, and fried spoonbread. Filled with love for their Gramma, the trio decided to earn money to buy the Easter bonnet that Miss Eula wanted but couldn't afford. Their efforts became complicated when they were unjustly blamed for throwing eggs at the door of Mr. Kodinski, a holocaust survivor who owned the hat store. When the trio explained their innocence, Miss Eula believed them but she explained that they must do something to change Mr. Kodinski's perception of them. They decided to create a basket of *Pysanky* eggs. Mr. Kodinski, heartened by the reminder of his homeland and convinced of their goodness, gave them the Easter hat for Miss Eula. Polacco ends the story this way:

> Winston, Stewart, and I are grown now. Our old neighborhood has changed some, yet it's still familiar, too. The freeway rumbles over the spot where Mr. Kodinski's shop once stood. I think of him often and his glorious hats. We lost Miss Eula some time back, but every year we take some chicken soup up to Mountain View Cemetery and do just as she asked. Sometimes, when we are especially quiet inside, we can hear singing. A voice that sounds like slow thunder and sweet rain. (unpaged)

Stewart Washington, who still lives next door, continues to be Patricia's best friend.

> We celebrate all of each other's holidays, all of each other's meaningful events. . . . For instance, Stewart would celebrate Hanukkah with me. We would light the menorah and in my fractured Hebrew, I would take him through the festival of lights. . . . He, in turn, would invite me to celebrate Christmas with his family. I remember the first Christmas I had with them. . . . They had big bulbs on the trees that you don't see anymore. One of them arched and flamed and caught on fire at the base of the tree. Uncle Bike . . . grabbed the tree, and out the front door it went in a pyrotechnic art. . . . As we danced around this burning tree, I thought, . . . "Jews just light a menorah, Baptists light a whole tree." (Polacco, 1996a)

It was also from Stewart and his family that Patricia learned:

> About the poison of racism . . . I saw these decent wonderful people dealing with something I had never in my life thought that any person should have to deal with. They lived in a country where it was a sin to be the color they were. I wish I could tell you things are better, I thought they were but these days I don't know. So that is where that writing comes from. (Polacco, 1993)

Polacco's parents divorced when she was only three years old, and although she lived with her mother, her bonds with her father remained strong. Patricia and her older brother, Richard, returned to Michigan every summer to spend time with their father and paternal grandmother. About these summers, Patricia writes, "My summers with my dad are golden memories" (1994, p. 10). Her father, William Barber, filled these summers with stories, laughter, dreams, and much love. *My Ol' Man*, Patricia's (1995) loving tribute to her father, recaptures the magic of one of these Michigan summers. The inside covers of the book are filled with pictures of Patricia, Richie, and Dad. As the story opens, Patricia tells us that her dad, a traveling salesman, was "a flimflam man. He worked his words the way other artists work in oil or clay. Steaming all over the state in his big old cruiser, with his radio on tuned to WJIM, he was dream saver, a wish keeper" (unpaged). Patricia and Richie would stand on the porch each evening, awaiting the tales that he would spin about his day. On one such evening, he drove them to Potter's Pond to see the wonder he had come upon earlier in the day. When Richie saw that Dad's surprise was a "dumb ol' rock," he was deflated, and disbelieved his father's tale about the rock's magical powers. But knowing that Richie needed some magic in his life to help him cope with his parents' divorce, Patricia urged him to touch the rock. When he did, he whispered, "It is magic." They left the rock and waited for its powers to take effect. But the magic didn't happen—Dad lost his job and had to sell his car. Patricia begged Dad to return to the rock; again they felt its magic. Shortly thereafter, the magic worked— Dad was offered a job at WJIM because the station manager enjoyed a piece he had submitted about the rock, and the hope and dreams that it symbolized. No doubt, the recurring themes of magic, dreams, and hope that fill many of Patricia's books also find roots in her father's joie de vivre. As her dad put it, "We may be boot-poor, but we're rich in dreams."

It is, in fact, her father's Irish heritage that is retold in *Pink and Say*. Sheldon Russell Curtis, nicknamed Say, was Patricia's great-great-grandfather. He told his daughter, Rosa, the tragic tale of Pinkus, who in turn told it to her daughter, who told it to Patricia's father, who told it to Patricia. During the story, Pink explains that his slave owner illegally had taught him to read because the owner liked listening to poetry. Feeling embarrassed about his illiteracy, and wanting to impress Pink, Say tells Pink that he has touched the hand of Abraham Lincoln. He then says, "Touch my hand, Pink. Now you can say you touched the hand that shook the hand of Abraham Lincoln" (unpaged). After Patricia's father tells her this family story, he takes her hand and says, "This is the hand, that has touched the hand, that has touched the hand, that shook the hand of Abraham Lincoln" (1994a, unpaged).

Polacco (1994b) offers a similar tribute to her brother, Richie, in *My Rotten Redheaded Older Brother*; again the inside covers of this book are lined with actual photographs of the twosome. As the story title suggests, sibling rivalry was alive and well in the Barber family. Whatever Patricia could do, Richie could do better. He could pick more blueberries, eat more rhubarb, spit the farthest . . . all with the incessant taunt: "I'm four years older than you. . . . Always have been and always will be." All that changed when Patricia outlasted Richie on the merry-go-round. But her glory was fleeting, as dizziness caused her to tumble to the ground unconscious. Richie carried her home and ran for the doctor. When Patricia awakened, Richie announced that she finally did something special. When she thanked him, he replied, "What's a big brother for, anyway." And "it was from that exact moment that our relationship changed somehow" (unpaged).

Polacco as Writer

That Patricia Polacco draws deeply from the well of her life experiences has been amply illustrated. Polacco begins each writing day in her rocking chair—she has at least one rocker in every room—and waits for her imagination to take flight. She explains that she "sits down and listens to the voice. This is the same voice that dancers listen to, musicians listen to, filmmakers, authors, teachers, librarians . . . [this voice] connects us all in our humanity, no matter what, whether boys or girls, poor or rich, no matter where we come from or what culture or religion we are" (1996c). This voice guides her storytelling. Polacco spends so much time thinking through her storylines and imagining her illustrations that when she sits down to write and to draw, the story just spills onto the paper.

This gift, however, is not one that Polacco ever dreamed of possessing because, as a child, the joys of reading and writing eluded her. As Polacco explains:

> In my family, when a child is about to read, you are surrounded by family members and a book is put in your hand, a dollop of honey is put on the book and the child is asked to taste the honey. They ask, "What does this taste like?" And the child usually says, "This is sweet." And then the family responds, "Yes! And so is knowledge. Knowledge is like the bee that made the honey—you have to chase it through the pages of a book." The book, *The Bee Tree*, was about this. But this was a promise that never came for me because something you may not know about me is that I am severely learning disabled. I did not read well until I was fourteen years old. I have dyslexia and dysnumeria. So can you imagine how it felt to be in class watching other children read easily? For me, this was hell on Earth, especially if I had to read out loud in front of other people. Gales of laughter in the room. Children started calling me 'dummy'. . . . This broke my heart. I tell people that "Sticks and stones will break my bones, but names will never hurt me" is one of the most monstrous lies ever told. Names hurt even now. (Polacco, 1993)

It wasn't until she was fourteen that the teacher whom she immortalizes in *Thank You, Mr. Falker* recognized her struggle and paid to have her tutored:

> And I remember the day the penny dropped. I can't even tell you how but suddenly one day the words made sense. And I remember running all the way home . . . charging up the front steps . . . into the kitchen . . . grabbing the honey and grabbing a book from the bookshelf and pouring honey on the cover and knowing at last this promise belonged to me. (Polacco, 1993)

While reading came within grasp, writing, especially spelling and sentence construction, continued to challenge her. As one of her English teachers wrote on a paper, "Miss Barber, you still can't spell worth a tinker's damn, but you do tell a good story" (Polacco, 1993). She admits that she continues to struggle with the mechanical aspects of language: "the process that editors go through with me is pretty arduous, because I habitually reverse letters. . . . Sometimes the corrections take longer than actually writing the story" (Maughan, 1993, p. 179).

Polacco as Artist

"All my life, art has been a natural thing for me to do. Drawing is what validated me" (1996b, p. 177). Polacco means validated in the deepest sense of the word. When her school peers made fun of her reading problems, she had only to take pen to paper to redeem herself in their eyes, although feelings of failure continued. Determined to succeed, she eventually went on to earn a Ph.D. in art history, concentrating on Russian and Greek iconographic history. Before becoming a children's author at the age of forty-one, she restored religious icons for museums. Many of these wondrous icons are sprinkled throughout her Babuska books. In review after review, Polacco's artistry wins critical and enthusiastic acclaim:

> Polacco extends her stories through her illustrations, adding texture and detail with pencil, watercolor, gouache. Her characters tend to move with the same sort of invigorating energy that charges Polacco's own life. Children are appropriately captured, laughing, running, and playing pranks. Facial expressions speak volumes, from wide-eyed surprise to kindly, crinkly-eyed smiles. Older characters lend a wise and graceful presence to the stories. Polacco's unusually intense palette drenches her scenes with color, all the more striking when set against white backgrounds. Actual photographs of family or friends, or reproductions of Russian icons, sometimes find their way into the background of an illustration. In some cases, sturdy furnishing and old world costumes help give a sense of time and place. (Maughan, 1993, p.185)

Mildred Taylor

Through four sequels—*The Song of the Trees; Roll of Thunder, Hear My Cry; Let the Circle Be Unbroken;* and *The Road to Memphis*— Mildred Taylor traces the saga of the Logan family's struggle to survive the racial oppression that festered in rural Mississippi during the Great Depression. In each work, Taylor simultaneously sinks readers into the deep abyss of racial hatred and discrimination, and then lifts them above this abyss with the power of family strength and racial pride, and with the resiliency of the human spirit.

The family saga is narrated by Cassie Logan, a young, spirited child who gradually comes to understand the insidiousness of racial hatred. The saga traces Cassie's transformation from an innocent child unable to comprehend social injustice to a racially aware and resolved teenager. Her transformation, of course, is intimately tied to the events that cascade around her—events she experiences directly and events to which she bears witness. It is these events, in conjunction with the wisdom and loving support of her parents, that teach Cassie about the harsh reality of racial hatred and discrimination, and about the importance of social resistance. We turn now to an exploration of this critical dimension of Taylor's works—the interplay of character and theme across the sequels.

Critical Response: Interplay of Theme and Character Across Sequels

Song of the Trees (1975)

Each morning, Cassie awakens to the "song" of the trees. She loves the forest that is part of the land that has been owned by the Logan family for generations—a rare feat for a black family. One day, when playing with her brothers, Cassie notices that many trees are marked with a big white X. Alarmed, the children race home only to find Mr. Anderson, a white lumberman, pressuring Big Ma to sell him the trees. When Big Ma hesitates, Mr. Anderson threatens that David Logan, Cassie's father, could have an accident. Even as Mary, Cassie's mother, pleads with Big Ma not to sell, the deal is made. When David returns home in the middle of the night, he plants sticks of dynamite throughout the forest. The next day, he confronts Anderson and threatens to blow up the forest if Anderson doesn't get off his property.

Racial Bigotry   In *Song of the Trees*, Cassie has her first encounter with racial bigotry, although she doesn't recognize it as such. When Big Ma is coerced into accepting Mr. Anderson's offer, Cassie shouts, "No, Big Ma! You can't let him cut our trees. . . . I won't let him cut them. I won't let him! The trees are my friends and ain't no mean ole white man gonna touch my trees" (1975, p. 27). As her mother tries to calm her down, she says, "Now hush. I've told you how dangerous . . ." (1975, p. 28), but then stops in midsentence to hug her. Although Cassie has been told about this dangerous tension between the races, she hasn't internalized it. Cassie's outbursts, both verbal and physical, against Anderson suggest that she doesn't understand that her actions could bring harm to herself and to her family. She doesn't understand that Anderson's invasion of another family's property symbolizes the racial arrogance that characterizes black-white relationships in the South. Cassie's anger is about the loss of her trees, not about racism.

Social Resistance   In *Roll of Thunder, Hear My Cry* and *Let the Circle Be Unbroken*, David, Cassie's father, is a wise, principled but cautious man who weighs carefully the import of racial injustice and the risks involved in any action he may take. He knows when to stand firm for what he believes and when to accept realities that are beyond his control. When he acts on principle, though, he does so in nonconfrontational ways—that is, unless his family or his land is threatened. In *Song of the Trees*, David is fierce in his resolve to protect his land, no matter what the cost. He vows to destroy his own land before allowing Anderson to take as much as one twig. When Anderson calls David's bluff, David replies, "One thing you can't seem to understand, Anderson, is that a black man's always going to be ready to die. And it don't make me any difference if I die today or tomorrow. Just as long as I die right" (1975, pp. 43–44). When Anderson insists on taking the trees that have already been cut, and David refuses, Anderson alludes to an "accident" that might befall David. David replies, "That may be. But it won't matter none. Cause I'll always have my self-respect" (1975, p. 46). It is this enormous well of racial pride that David and Mary endow to each of their children.

Enduring Family Love and Pride   As Mary and Cassie survey the damage to their beloved trees, they cry in each other's arms. Upon their return, Little Man, Cassie's youngest brother, insists on seeing the forest too. When Little Man disobeys his mother's orders and takes off for the forest, Cassie and Christopher-John, fearful of what might happen, accompany him. When Anderson attempts to harm Little Man, Cassie charges, "You ain't got no right to push Little Man. Why don't you push on somebody your own size—like me, you ole—" (1975, p. 36). As Anderson prepares to take a belt to Little Man, Cassie and Christopher-John physically lash out at Anderson. The bond among the Logans runs deep.

Throughout the saga, readers continue to witness example after example of the closeness, protectiveness and racial pride of this family. Even in the midst of their racist society, Mary and David are able to instill in their children a sense of self-dignity, in part through stories of family history. Cassie and her brothers hear the story of their great-grandfather who was born a slave but who ran away from the plantation three times. They hear the story of their grandfather who worked as a carpenter to save enough money to buy two hundred acres of land from a northern land owner—the land that the family now protects with fierce determination. Cassie's immersion in this family pride reveals itself time and again.

Roll of Thunder, Hear My Cry (1976)

On the first day of school, Cassie, now a fourth grader, and her three brothers trudge along the dusty Mississippi road. Stacey's friend, T. J., joins them, asking if they have heard about the three neighbors who were set on fire by the night men (KKK) for allegedly flirting with a white woman. As T. J. is talking, Stacey hears the school bus coming and orders everyone to scramble up the steep bank out of the path of the bus. Little Man, who hates being dirty, hesitates. Within seconds, the bus speeds past, enveloping them in a cloud of dust. The white children with "faces pressed against the bus windows" on their way to their white school laugh at the sight. Acts of racial bigotry and discrimination then escalate until events spin out of control as T. J falls prey to the evil of the Simms brothers, two white boys, who murder a store owner and who frame T. J. for the crime.

Racial Bigotry   At the beginning of the story, Cassie experiences racist acts firsthand but does not recognize them as such:

- Cassie's fourth-grade teacher, Miss Crocker, announces that the class is to receive new books this year. When six-year-old Little Man realizes his "new" book is tattered and torn, he asks for another. Outraged, Miss Crocker berates Little Man, who, in turn, flings the book to the floor. As Miss Crocker prepares to whip Cassie's brother, Cassie comes to his defense, explaining his anger at reading the word *nigra* on the inside book label. Miss Crocker retorts, "That's what you are" (1976, p. 26). Cassie refuses to take her book; both she and Little Man are flogged.

- Cassie accidentally bumps into Lillian Jean Simms. Lillian Jean chides her and asks for an apology. Reluctantly, Cassie apologizes. Lillian Jean orders her to step off the sidewalk: "If you can't watch where you going, get in the road. Maybe that way you won't be bumping into decent white folks with your little nasty self" (1976, p. 114). Indignant, Cassie refuses, and Lillian Jean attempts to push her off the sidewalk. Lillian's father then grabs Cassie by the arm, pushes her onto the street, and insists on an apology. Frightened but determined, Cassie retorts that she's already apologized. When Mr. Simms lunges at Cassie, she jumps up and escapes his near-attack.

It becomes clear in talks with her parents about her encounter with Lillian Jean that Cassie doesn't understand that the Simms's actions are racially motivated. Cassie thinks that Lillian Jean and her father are just being mean to her. When Mary explains that Mr. Simms believes that his daughter is better than Cassie, Cassie asks, "Just 'cause she's his daughter?" Mary replies, "No baby, because she's white." When Cassie fires back, "Ah shoot! White ain't notin'!" Mary explains, "It is something, Cassie. . . . So now, even though seventy years have passed since slavery, most white people still think of us as they did then—that we're not as good as they are—and people like Mr. Simms hold on to that belief harder than some other folks. . . . For him to believe that he is better than we are makes him think he's important, simply because he's white" (1976, pp. 128–129). This realization hits Cassie hard.

Racial Discrimination   Cassie begins to understand that racial hatred begets racial discrimination as she witnesses or learns about a number of discriminatory events:

- Mary Logan is fired from her teaching job, ostensibly because she has been teaching lessons on slavery that weren't in the county's textbook. In fact, she is fired for organizing a boycott of Mr. Wallace's store so that the sharecroppers wouldn't have to endure the continual barrage of racial slurs and price-gauging.

- When the Wallaces douse kerosene on Mr. Berry and his two nephews, and set them on fire, no charges are ever filed—not even when the Wallaces brag about their deed, claiming that they'd do it again, "if some other uppity nigger gets out of line" (1976, p. 40). Mr. Berry and one of the nephews die.

- As rumors run rampant that T. J. has murdered a storekeeper—a murder actually committed by the white Simms brother—a mob of white men take matters into their hands, first beating up T. J. and his family, and then calling for a lynching.

Cassie, terrified for T. J. and terrified that Stacey will be implicated, witnesses this last event (which occurs at the end of the book) in silence, understanding that any outburst on her part could endanger many lives. She now understands that whites are above the law and that blacks, because of the color of their skin, are denied civil and human rights.

Social Resistance   At the beginning of the story, Cassie, unable to comprehend racism, physically fights for her self-worth:

- To avenge the humiliation endured at the hands of Lillian Jean, Cassie fools Lillian Jean into thinking that Cassie has realized the errors of her ways and that she has resigned herself to her subservient place in life. To show good faith, Cassie carries Miss Lillian's books to school for one month, listening at first to Lillian's idle chatter and eventually to her "secrets." Secure in their "friendship," Cassie then lures Lillian into the forest where she knocks her to the ground and demands an apology. Lillian's response, "Ain't gonna 'pologize to no nigger," provokes Cassie to pull out her hair. Lillian apologizes but once she is freed, she threatens to tell her father. When Cassie vows to reveal all her secrets to her friends, Lillian never bothers Cassie again.

- Angered again by the bus driver, who, during a downpour, swerves the bus so close to the side of the road that Cassie and her brother fall into a muddy gully and angered by the vicious laughter of the white children, Stacey plans their revenge. Leaving school during lunch, the Logan children dig a deep, rainfilled gully and watch with glee as the bus almost overturns when it hits the gully.

In time, though, Cassie learns the treachery of direct confrontation, and begins to appreciate the indirect but powerful acts of resistance undertaken by her parents:

- When Cassie's teacher, Miss Crocker, confronts Mary about the audacity of Cassie and Little Man to reject their "new" books, Mary studies the cover page that upset her children. Without saying a word, she glues a blank piece of paper over the cover page of each book. Shocked, Miss Crocker warns Mary that disciplinary actions could be taken by the superintendent, and comments, "Well I think you're just spoiling these children, Mary. They've got to learn how things are sometime" (1976, p. 30). Mary replies, "Maybe so but that doesn't mean they have to accept them . . . and maybe we don't either" (1976, p. 35). Cassie overhears this conversation and absorbs her mother's quiet resolve.

- Enraged by the burning of Mr. Berry and his nephews and by news of another mob lynching, Cassie's parents attempt to organize a boycott of Mr. Wallace's store. The sharecroppers, while hating the Wallaces, explain that, with no cash, they are tied to the credit he extends to them. When Mr. Jamison, a white lawyer, reviled by the rampant racism, offers to back the workers' credit, the boycott takes hold. The Logan's efforts, however, soon meet with threats of harm and expulsion for the sharecroppers by their plantation owners. When Mr. Jamison acknowledges that "The sad thing is, in the end, you can't beat him [Granger, the largest plantation owner] or the Wallaces" (p. 164), David, in the presence of his children, replies, "Still, I want these children to know we tried, and what we can't do now, maybe one day we will" (1976, p. 165).

- The strength of David's conviction manifests itself again when he engages in yet another act of resistance—one that puts his family in financial jeopardy. As the mob gathers to lynch T. J., David realizes that the only way to stop the momentum is to set fire to his land, which abuts Granger's plantation. Alarmed by the threat to his property, Granger orders the mob to leave T. J. and to fight the fire. After the fire has been doused, Mr. Jamison stops to tell David that he is taking T. J.'s folks into town to be near T. J., who has been taken to jail. When David offers to accompany him, Mr. Jamison advises against it: "It's better, I think, that you stay clear of this whole thing now, David, and don't give anybody cause to think about you at all . . . or somebody might just get wondering about that fire" (1976, p. 273). It is then that Cassie understands intuitively the sacrifice that her father has made to save T. J. from the mob.

Family as Moral Center   David and Mary believe that if their children are to grow up to be decent human beings, they must be taught right from wrong. While they don't spare the rod, they place much greater emphasis on example and explanation:

- When Stacey is caught by Mary (his teacher) with cheat notes, he refuses to confess that the notes are T. J.'s. With no recourse, Mary whips him publicly and fails him on the exam. Mary sends a clear message that cheating will not to tolerated in her classroom—son or no son.

- After the burning of the Berry men, David orders the children not to go to Wallace's store. Angered at T. J. for the cheating episode, Stacey disobeys his father's order and goes to the Wallaces' to confront T. J.; Cassie, Christopher-John and Little Man follow behind, fearful that something will happen to Stacey. When Stacey confesses the event, his mother scolds them severely. Instead of whipping them, though, she takes them to visit Mr. Berry, whose burns are so extensive that he has no nose or hair and cannot speak. His charred, mutilated body shocks the children. On the ride home, Mary explains that the Wallaces set Mr. Berry and his nephews on fire and, for that reason, they must never go to that store again.

- When Cassie continues to resent Lillian Jean, David reminds her of the Bible's teaching about forgiveness but adds, "But the way I see it, the Bible didn't mean for you to be no fool. Now one day, maybe I can forgive John Anderson for what he done to these trees, but I ain't gonna forget it. I figure forgiving is not letting something nag at you—rotting you out. Now if I hadn't done what I done [threaten to blow up the forest if Anderson didn't leave his land], then I couldn't've forgiven myself, and that's the truth" (1976, p.175). He then explains that the incident with Lillian Simms and her father was wrong but that the risk of confronting Mr. Simms was much greater. "If I'd gone after Charlie

Simms and given him a good thrashing like I felt like doing, the hurt to all of us would've been a whole lot more than the hurt you received, so I let it be. . . . But there are other things, Cassie, that if I'd let be, they'd eat away at me and destroy me in the end. And it's the same with you, baby. There are things you can't back down on, things you gotta take a stand on. But it's up you to decide what them things are. You have to demand respect in this world, ain't nobody just gonna hand it to you. How you carry yourself, what you stand for—that's how you gain respect. But little one, ain't nobody's respect worth more than your own. You understand that?" (1976, pp. 175–176)

Let the Circle Be Unbroken (1981)

Let the Circle Be Unbroken begins with the trial of T. J. Despite ample evidence that the Simms brothers are responsible for the store owner's murder, T. J. is found guilty by an all-white jury and hanged. News of a government-sponsored plan to reduce the cotton crop and to reimburse farmers ends in a sham as plantation owners abscond with the government checks. This, along with the fact that the Logans lost part of their cotton crop to the fire, and that David can now only find part-time work on the railroad, puts the farm in great jeopardy. The Logans reluctantly decide to join a union of white and black workers to seek restitution. Plantation owners, threatened by the union, escalate their acts of racial violence by throwing penniless sharecroppers off their lands, by shooting David during a night ride, and by burning the union meeting place. In the midst of this turmoil, Stacey, now fourteen, runs off to the wretched cane plantations to earn eight dollars a week for the family. David and Mary, after frantic journeys to the cane plantations, finally find Stacey, beaten and penniless, in a jail for a crime he didn't commit. When the culprit is caught, Stacey is released and the family joyously returns home.

Roll of Thunder, Hear My Cry is Cassie's story. It is her rite of passage into the thunder of racism. As racial assaults hit hard, she is bruised, but not broken. In *Let the Circle Be Unbroken*, while acts of injustice continue to swirl around Cassie and her family—although few are targeted at Cassie it is the momentum of social resistance, buoyed by family strength and determination, that carries this sequel. Innocence lost, Cassie is now ready to be inducted into her family's heritage of passive resistance, however dim the hope of social change, so that the circle will remain unbroken.

Racial Hatred Cassie continues to bear witness to acts of racial prejudice:

- When Mr. Jamison alleges the involvement of the Simms brothers in the murder, R.W. Simms screams, "What kind of country is this when a white man's got to defend hisself 'gainst a nigger? Huh? . . . . I done said the truth, and if a white man can't believe that over what that lyin' nigger said, then he jus' might as well be a nigger his own self" (p. 80).
- When Suzella arrives to spend the summer with the Logans, she enchants young men with her beauty. Suzella, daughter of Mary's nephew, Bud, and his

white wife, has creamy white skin and auburn hair. Talk of the town, even Stuart Walker, son of a plantation owner, flirts with her, not knowing about her black father. Wanting to be considered white, Suzella does not reveal her heritage. When Stuart learns the truth, he plans his revenge. As Bud is driving his daughter and the Logan children home, Stuart and his hoodlum buddies order Bud out of the car, accuse him of sleeping with a white woman, and force him to strip in front of the children.

Whereas the young Cassie would have lashed out at these offensive acts, regardless of the harm that might come her way, the socially conscious Cassie does not.

Racial Discrimination   The ever-widening scope of discrimination envelops Cassie and her family:

- When the government passed a crop-reduction plan to regulate the price of cotton, farmers and sharecroppers were ordered to plow under half of their crop, for which they were to be reimbursed. However, Granger, the plantation owner who is determined to reclaim the Logans' land, illegally claims that he holds the first mortgage on the Logan land and receives the government money.
- Intent upon earning eight dollars a week to help pay for taxes, Stacey disobeys his parents and runs off to a cane plantation in Louisiana with a friend. There, they endure terrible hardships. They slave from sunrise to sundown with the cane leaves cutting their hands. They live in a rat-infested shack with no beds, tables, or chairs. They must buy everything—blankets, clothes, even the machete to cut the cane; costs are deducted from their pay. Once they learn that the plantation has no intention of paying them for their three months of hard labor, Stacey and Moe escape.

Social Resistance   Cassie understands the full force of passive resistance:

- Fired from her teaching job, Mary Logan, at the request of her children's friends, begins an after-school program to tutor them. Mary believes that only education holds a ray of hope for these children, if they are to escape the servitude of the sharecropping life.
- Inspired by the fact that her father voted during the days of Reconstruction, Mrs. Lee Annie, a friend of the Logans, decides she, too, will vote. The fact that her father was almost beaten to death by the night men to set an example for others and that life for blacks had changed little since that time seems not to intimidate Lee Annie. While friends, fearing for her life, try to dissuade her, Lee Annie is determined: "Mary, child, all my life when I wanted to do something and the white folks didn't like it, I didn't do it. . . .

But now I's sixty-four years old and I's figure I's deserving of doing something I wants to do, white folks like it or not. And this old body wants to vote and like I done said, I gots my mind made up. I's gon' vote too" (pp. 195–196). Knowing the risks involved, Mary agrees to tutor Lee Annie on the constitution so that she can pass the test. On the day of the test, Mary and other neighbors accompany Lee Annie to the registrar's office. After weighing the risks, Mary decides to bring Cassie to witness this historical moment. Not only does the registrar claim that Lee Annie failed the test, but her plantation owner holds her up to public ridicule: "No natural mental ability to understand [the constitution] and she goes and does a thing like that! . . . You thought of what will happen to our great state if people like this try to perform tasks that they ain't even got the God-given make-up for?" (p. 372)

Family as Moral Center   Mary and David continue to teach their children about the harsh reality of racism, about what it takes to survive in a white world, and about morality. Mary, noting the fear that has taken hold of Christopher-John—fear that T. J. will not come home from jail and fear that what happened to T. J. will happen to him—helps Christopher-John understand that T. J. brought this tragedy on himself. She makes it clear that T. J. was wrong to take part in the robbery, and that he was wrong to involve himself with the racist Wallaces. She explains, "We teach you what we do to keep you safe. The way things are down here, what happened to T. J. was bound to come. I don't like it and your papa doesn't like it, and most decent folks don't like it, but right now all we can do is try to keep it from happening again" (p. 33).

The Road to Memphis (1990)

Two years have passed since T. J.'s hanging. Cassie, now seventeen, attends school in Jackson; Stacey works full-time in Jackson in a factory. Out from under the protective cloak of their parents, Cassie and Stacey face the barbs of racism on their own. Stacey, exasperated by the segregation laws governing buses, buys a 1937 Ford from Mr. Jamison. After a visit at home, Stacey, Cassie, and his three friends, Clarence, Little Willie, and Moe, begin the trek back to Jackson. However, their lives are turned upside down when Moe retaliates against the white Aames brothers for humiliating Cassie. Badly injuring the brothers, Moe must escape from Mississippi or face a mob lynching. Stacey knows that he must get Moe to Memphis and on a train to Chicago. The road to Memphis, however, is fraught with one racial incident after another, and with personal tragedy as Clarence succumbs to a brain tumor. Through it all, the friends remain loyal to each other and steadfast in their determination to save Moe, undeterred by personal risks.

The years of social-consciousness-raising and of moral guidance that David and Mary Logan imparted to their children come to full fruition in *The Road to Memphis*. Stacey, in fact, has become his father—wise, measured, and fiercely protective. Cassie, while still defiant at times, matures markedly, knowing when to exhibit restraint in the face of racial taunts and when to stand her ground. It is this underlying defiance that assures readers that Cassie will not only survive in this hateful society, but will work to bring it down.

Racial Hatred   The acts of racial bigotry by white teenagers turn vile:

- Cassie, Stacey, and friends join Harris, a gentle, overweight teenager on a coon hunt. When Harris's hunting dog begins barking, Cassie and Harris follow the barking with hopes of cornering a coon. As they approach the dog, they encounter the white Aames brothers, who earlier that day had harassed Harris about going on a coon hunt. The brothers force Harris to be "the coon," and set their dogs on him. Terrified, Harris runs and manages to climb a tree, only to have the limb break and to land in the midst of the vicious dogs. He barely escapes with his life.

- Having accompanied pregnant Sissy home, Cassie walks back to the church. A truck pulls up beside her; the Aames brothers harass her. Statler, who has a reputation for raping black girls, offers her a ride, saying, "got something here you might like." When Cassie retorts, "You've got nothing I want," Statler, moving in closer, grins, "Yeah . . . but you've got something I want." As Cassie is about to run, her father appears and defuses the situation.

Racial Discrimination   Legislated injustice continues to deny basic human rights to Cassie and the others:

- On the way to Memphis, Stacey stops at a gas station. When Cassie asks the attendant about the restroom, he points to the bushes. Spying the "White Ladies Only" sign, Cassie decides to defy the law. Just as she is about to enter the restroom, a white woman screams for the attendant. Outraged that Cassie would put "her black butt where white ladies got to sit" (p. 179), the attendant threatens to call the police. As Cassie runs for the car, she falls, spilling her purse, which contains the car keys and money. When she tries to gather the contents, the attendant stomps on the purse and kicks her. Wounded physically and emotionally, Cassie grabs the keys and runs for the car.

- Clarence, maddened by the pain of a thundering headache, races through the woods, falls, and is knocked unconscious. Stacey drives him to the only hospital in the area and begs a doctor to help him. The doctor turns them away from the white hospital, sneering: "Y'all niggers know y'all got no business here" (p. 206).

Social Resistance   Although acts of resistance continue on many levels, the saga ends with the hope that the Cassies of the world will use the system against itself to achieve racial justice.

- On their return to Jackson, Stacey, Moe, Clarence, and Cassie stop in town so that Stacey can make a payment to Mr. Jamison on the car loan. Noticing that the left tire is low, Stacey asks the others to take it to the gas station. As Moe is about the take off the tire with a crowbar, Statler Aames and his brother begin to taunt Moe: "Papa always told me it bring good luck to rub a nigger's head" (p. 117). Statler knocks off Moe's hat and orders him to pick it up. As Moe complies, the other brothers hit him on the head. When Statler spews sexual innuendoes about Cassie, Moe slams each of the brothers with the crowbar. Knowing the terrible jeopardy he has placed himself in, Moe is desperate to escape. Jeremy, a cousin of the Aames brothers who hates the racist attitudes of his family, risks his own life by sheltering Moe in the bed of his truck.

- Having internalized her mother's conviction that education may be the only way to turn the tide on racism, Cassie pursues her education with vigor, intent upon becoming a lawyer. As Cassie explains to Solomon Bradley, a black lawyer and newspaper owner, "I've been thinking about how white folks are always falling behind on the law. Maybe, if colored folks knew this law as well as they did, we could do something about it. . . . If we know the law like they do, we can use it like they do" (pp. 244–245).

Additional Possibilities for Critical Response

As with all superb writers, Taylor affords readers multiple invitations for critical response to her works. Such invitations might include the following.

Historical Fiction

Taylor's work has been acclaimed for its historical accuracy. Such accuracy intensifies the reading experience. To know that the life of the sharecroppers who worked on plantations seventy years after the Emancipation Proclamation was a life of servitude, that efforts to boycott racist businesses and to organize unions were crushed repeatedly, that "night men" waged a war of terror while the courts looked the other way, is to be revolted by the inhumanity of generations past. To know that racial prejudice and discrimination and KKK activity continue today is to indict our own generation. Readers need to understand not only this shameful period in American history, but also the continuing reverberations of racism in today's society.

Lyrical Prose

Taylor's exquisite use of language gives readers ample opportunities to analyze and to appreciate the splendor of her radiant imagery and striking similes:

> Before us the narrow, sun-splotched road wound like a lazy red serpent dividing the high forest bank of quiet, old trees . . . from the cotton fields. . . . (1976, p. 6)

> The moon slid from its dark covers, cloaking the earth in a shadowy white light, and I could see Mr. Morrison clearly, moving quietly, like a jungle cat, from the side of the house. . . . (1976, p. 6)

Sequel as Craft

Sequels require writers to weave characters and past events into present texts. This reweaving, however, must be done in a way that doesn't belabor what is already known, while simultaneously attending to the needs of readers who haven't read the presequels. Taylor successfully accomplishes this feat. For example, in *Roll of Thunder, Hear My Cry*, Cassie is indignant that Mr. Granger, a plantation owner, harasses her grandmother, Big Ma, about selling the family's land to him. Big Ma leads Cassie into the forest, where they come up to the trees that Mr. Anderson illegally felled a year ago. Big Ma surveys the devastation and comments that she is glad her husband isn't there to witness it. Cassie then briefly retells readers the story of *The Song of the Trees*. Big Ma talks about how Cassie's grandfather bought the land that the Logan family has vowed to keep at all costs. The story of the trees is again retold to Cassie's cousin, Suzella, who is visiting from New York in *Let the Circle be Unbroken*. Why the repeated tellings? Because Taylor wants readers to understand that the land, including these ancient trees, symbolizes the emancipation of the Logan family from the grip of white land owners.

Autobiographical Information

Taylor: Life–Literature Connections

Upon receipt of the coveted Newbery Award, Mildred Taylor (1988) wrote:

> The award was presented to me, but I never considered the award mine. I considered it my father's, for without my father's words and his teachings, without all the stories he told me, without his determination that I know the South as well as the North, *Roll of Thunder, Hear My Cry* would never have happened. (p. 268)

Taylor dedicates both *Roll of Thunder, Hear My Cry* and *Let the Circle Be Unbroken* to her father, Wilbert Lee Taylor: "To the memory of my beloved father who lived many adventures of the boy Stacey and who was in essence the man David."

Mildred Taylor was born in Mississippi in 1943, but only lived there for three months. Her father's decision to leave the South came on the heels of his involvement in a racial incident while working as a trucker. Sickened by the disease of racism, he vowed that his daughters would not live the segregated life that he had lived. He left Jackson on a segregated train, found a factory job in Toledo, Ohio, and moved the family.

While Taylor grew up in the North, she spent many summers in the South because her father wanted her to appreciate her heritage, to understand the poison of racism, and to embrace the freedom of the North. (In *Let the Circle Be Unbroken*, Mary's cousin, Bud, sends his daughter, Suzella to live with the Logans so that she, too, could experience the strength and fortitude of her black family.) It was on these pilgrimages to the land of her ancestors that Taylor learned firsthand about segregation, as she encountered the sign "White Only, Colored Not Allowed" on motels, restaurants, and restrooms. This segregation meant that the family had to drive from Toledo to Jackson, stopping at night to sleep on the side of the road. Time and again, though, her father was stopped and harassed by police who were suspect of a black person driving a new gold Cadillac. Whenever possible, Mr. Taylor brought along extra drivers so they could drive nonstop. Of these trips, Taylor recalls, "One summer I suddenly felt a climbing nausea as we crossed the Ohio River into Kentucky" (Collier and Nakamura, 1993, p. 2273). In her book *The Gold Cadillac*, Taylor (1987) chronicles the fear that gripped the family on these journeys south.

However, once they reached the home of her grandparents—built by her great-grandfather at the turn of the century—Taylor was drawn into the circle of family, a circle that opened her to "a sense of history and filled me with pride" (1988, p. 270). There, Taylor lived in the house in which her father grew up, a house with no electricity, running water, or telephones. It was in this house that Taylor was enchanted by story-filled gatherings of aunts, uncles, cousins, and neighbors.

Roll of Thunder, Hear My Cry has its emotional core in a story that Taylor's father and uncle told her after the publication of *The Song of the Trees*:

> They began telling another story about a boy, a black boy, who had taken up with two white boys. They told how the three had broken into a store, how the storekeeper had been killed, and the black boy accused. They told how a lynch mob had come for the boy and the white boys had been part of the mob. (1988, p. 284)

Taylor notes, "In writing *Roll of Thunder, Hear My Cry* as in writing *The Song of the Trees*, I drew upon people and places I had known all my life. The characterization of the Logan family I drew from my own family" (p. 284). David Logan personified her father, a man "highly principled . . . [of] strong moral fiber . . . and an unyielding faith in himself and his abilities, and who, knowing himself to be inferior to no one, tempered my learning with his wisdom" (p. 224). Just as David Logan taught Cassie that bigotry could not be fought with anger alone, so Wilbert Taylor taught his daughters. Cassie Logan, proud, indomitable, and protective drew her spirit from Taylor's sister, Wilma. Mary Logan was modeled after Taylor's grandmother, "an outspoken teacher." Cassie's brothers, Christopher-John and Little Man are based on two of Taylor's uncles.

Like her characters, "the land, the house, the school, the history are all drawn from that community of lives as I remember them back then and as I remember the stories told" (1988, p. 284). The "rusty Mississippi dust" roads that Cassie walked in *Roll of Thunder, Hear My Cry* are the roads that Taylor, as a child, walked to visit relatives. Cassie's segregated school is the school that Taylor's father attended. Cassie's house is the house that was built by Taylor's great-grandfather, which still stands and continues to be owned by the Taylor family. Taylor's great-grandfather was born into slavery, his father a white plantation owner, his mother a slave. After a dispute with his father, he took off to Mississippi and bought land in the late 1800s (Taylor, 1988). His story is retold by Big Ma to Cassie in *Roll of Thunder, Hear My Cry*.

Like the South, life in the North carries both warm and painful memories. The home that Taylor's parents bought within a year of arriving in Ohio was soon filled with aunts, uncles, and cousins who also were escaping the indignities of the South. Taylor loved growing up in the midst of this extended family, in the midst of the stories about generations past. Even as these family members rented or bought homes, the bonds of family remained. Her warmest memories are those of revivals, prayer meetings, and picnics (Cullinan and Galda, 1994). While life in the North afforded freedom and job opportunities, it was not prejudice-free. When Taylor couldn't understand why so many homes on her avenue—"grand" homes with rolling lawns and cascading Dutch elms—had "For Sale" signs on their lawns, she asked her father. He explained that as black families began to move into the neighborhood, white families, fearful of black people and of property devaluation, moved out. Here, Taylor's first layer of innocence was stripped away, much like Cassie's innocence when she learns the reason for Lillian Jean's cruelty.

Another layer was stripped away when Taylor could not fathom why the inside cover of her school textbooks listed not only previous students' names but also their race. Sensing an injustice, Taylor crossed off the race entries (Cullinan et al., 1994). This hurtful event is replayed in *Roll of Thunder, Hear My Cry*.

Yet another layer of innocence was peeled away during a family journey across the country as some motels and restaurants refused to serve them. Although the sign "White Only, Colored Not Allowed" was not in sight, the prejudice and discrimination were. Thus, the indignation, anger, and disillusionment that Cassie carries across the sequels is rooted not only in Taylor's father's stories, but also in her own stories.

But just as Cassie transcends the sting of racism with the wise counsel and loving support of her parents, so too did Taylor. Cassie's black pride is Taylor's pride—a pride instilled by her family and fortified by her two-year experience as a Peace Corps volunteer in Ethiopia. "I loved Ethiopia . . . I felt good about myself there. I admired their ancient history. I admired their pride in themselves. . . . I was not looking forward to returning to the second-class citizenship as a black person in the United States . . . to the rioting . . . in the cities [Detroit and Toledo] I knew so well" (1988, p. 280). Within a year upon her return to the United States, Taylor enrolled in a graduate journalism program. There, she became a member of the Black Student Alliance (BSA). The social activism of the BSA resulted in increased enrollment of black students at the university and in a black studies program. Now Taylor understood what her father meant when he taught her that "anger in itself was futile, that to fight discrimination I needed a stronger weapon . . . that I must gain the skill to destroy such bigotry" (1977, p. 401). This bank of knowledge and experiences in social resistance comes to full fruition in *Roll of Thunder, Hear My Cry*; *Let the Circle Be Unbroken*; and *The Road to Memphis*.

Taylor as Writer

When Taylor started high school, she knew that she wanted to a writer—a writer who would challenge:

> the lackluster history of Black people painted in those books [history textbooks], a history of a docile, subservient people happy with their fate who did little or nothing to shatter the chains that bound them. . . . There was obviously a terrible contradiction between what the books said and what I learned from my family and at no time did I feel that contradiction more strongly than when I had to sit in class which, without me, would have been all white and relive that prideless history year after year." (1977, p. 403)

Taylor vowed that she would rewrite this history by sharing her own family history, which included proud and heroic men and women who resisted the suffocating oppression, and who found fortitude in the bonds of family love. Taylor endows Mary Logan with this same conviction; rather than perpetuate the untruths in the history books, Mary rewrites black history by telling her students the truth about slavery.

Taylor began her career by writing stories for adults. Discouraged by rejections from publishers, she applied for and was offered a job as a television journalist at CBS. However, she turned down the offer because she wanted to be a writer. As fate would have it, she learned, last minute, about a contest sponsored by the Council on Interracial Books for Children. With only four days to meet the deadline, she wrote *The Song of the Trees* over a weekend:

> This story is based on a true story, one that actually happened in my family. As a small child, I often listened to my father recount his adventures growing up in rural Mississippi. His vivid description of the giant trees, the coming of the lumberman, and the events that followed made me feel I too was present. I hope my readers will be as moved by the story as I was. (1975, Author's note)

This first book about the Logan family won the contest; Taylor's career as a children's writer was launched. *Roll of Thunder, Hear My Cry* went on to win the Newbery Award. Sadly, Taylor's father died six months before its publication. As Taylor writes, "The stories as only he could tell them died with him. But his voice of joy and laughter, his enduring strength, his principles and constant wisdom remain a part of all those who knew and loved him. They remain also within the pages of this book, its guiding spirit and total power" (1976, Author's note). Taylor also admits that "when her father died, much of my will to write died as well" (1988, p. 285):

> In the last few years there have been times when I could not face going back into what I term "the void" and bringing the world of my childhood back into existence. There have been times when I could not face the racism or the violence of that world in which so many people who contributed so much to my growth, both as a person and as a writer, are now gone. There have been times when I felt as if I no longer had the power to write stories and the history as they were meant to be written, times when I wanted to give up writing altogether. Yet, I continue to write, partly because the stories and the history are part of my father's and my family's legacy, a legacy which had enriched me all my life. I continue to write because I feel the need to share that legacy. I continue to write because it is my hope that through my books that legacy will also help to enrich the lives of others. I continue to write, because in doing so, I can perhaps pass on a legacy of my own. (1988, pp. 286–287)

Kathryn Lasky

Kathryn Lasky was one of the early pioneers of the nonfiction genre called the photographic essay. In the early 1980s, few writers were interested in the melding of text and photograph in a way that not only illuminated the subject matter but also evoked an emotional response. For Lasky, nonfiction is best brought to life when the subject matter—whether it be dinosaur fossils, the art of weaving, or the lemurs of Madagascar—is presented in such a way that the reader becomes emotionally tied to the topic.

In her Newbery Honor book, *Sugaring Time,* Lasky (1983) and her photographer husband, Christopher Knight, introduce readers to the Lacey family, Vermont farmers who carry on the tradition of maple-syrup making. We journey with them as they break a snow path to the sugarbush, tap the trees, bucket and process the sap, and enjoy the fruits of their labor. Through Knight's photographs, we read the expression of anxiety in young Jeremy's face as he totters on the uneven brush with a maple-filled bucket in his hand; we feel the warm embrace that Jeremy's grandmother extends at the end of his long day. Thus, we imbue not only the details of this craft, but also the anticipation, diligence, and warmth of this family affair. *Sugaring Time,* along with Lasky's more recent works, offer young writers the opportunity to probe the essence of the photographic essay.

The Intrigue of the Photographic Essay

According to Charlotte Huck and colleagues (1987):

> Many informational picture books display photographs in a significant way, but only some of these can be called a photographic essay. Although the books by Selsam about plant growth (*Cotton,* for example) depend on Wexler's photographs for clarification and support of the text on every page, they are not photographic essays. The essay relies on the camera in different ways: to particularize general information, to document emotion, to assure the reader of truth in an essentially journalistic way. (pp. 606–607)

As the following works reveal, Lasky and Knight have mastered the art of the photographic essay.

Dinosaur Dig (1990)

This essay opens with a photograph of Kathryn Lasky and her two children, Max and Meribah, lying on a bed, pouring over *Dinosaurs Walked Here,* one of many books they read in preparation for a trip to the Montana Badlands to dig for dinosaur fossils. The family then departs for the blazing heat and blasting winds of the harsh prairie. As the buttes—the round, jagged rock hills that jut high on the barren wasteland—bulge on the horizon, they know they have reached the "graveyard of the dinosaurs." The Knights and five other families who have come to dig are met by Keith Rigby, a paleontologist, and Bob Sloan, a geologist. Upon arrival at the excavation site, Keith announces, "Get ready to sniff the dirt. . . . I want your noses this far off the ground." Lasky elaborates, "To sniff dirt, they must get down on hands and knees and crawl over the sandy terrain with their noses to the ground" (unpaged). Keith teaches the diggers how to distinguish rocks from fossils. Soon the novice excavators spot a jutting bone and Keith confirms that it is a dinosaur rib.

The diggers learn to gently scrape away the earth, to make a plaster cast, and to extract the ancient bone.

Dinosaur Dig is a splendid example of a photographic essay, easily meeting Huck et al.'s (1987) criteria. One essential feature of quality nonfiction is the unity of text and visual graphics; each dimension working in unison, clarifying, extending, and enlightening. In the photographic essay, however, the human element of science also is brought into play. In *Dinosaur Dig*, this human element operates at two levels. First, through Knight's lens, we see not only the buttes of the Badlands and their entombed creatures, but also the scientists and novice diggers engaged in their delicate artistry. While Lasky's description of "sniffing the dirt" enables us to visualize this process, Knight's photograph of Keith, a rather robust scientist, crawling with his nose three inches from the ground heightens our engagement. Secondly, we travel with the Knights and their children, hoping that they'll find their treasures and survive the sandstorms and temperatures in excess of 105 degrees. Knight's photographs of his family packing for the trip, descending the treacherous buttes, and digging the fossils bring us not only inside the excavation process but also inside their personal lives. We come to know the author as a real person with a genuine wonderment about the world around her.

As Lasky and young Meribah struggle to descend one of the steep buttes—"dark gray siltstone that has swelled and folded into deep wrinkles that look exactly like the hide of an elephant's back"—the siltstone crumbles under their feet, making it treacherous to walk and causing Meribah to cry. Knowing that because rattlesnakes slither up and down the buttes, forcing the climbers to talk nonstop to ward off any of these intruders, adds the tension. Knight's photographs of their steep descent and Meribah's tears "document emotion" (Huck et al., 1987).

If the Knight family embarked on this dinosaur dig armed with knowledge about fossils and digs but without the expertise and experience of the paleontologist and geologist, the accuracy of *Dinosaur Dig* would be highly suspect. Authenticity is essential to all genres of nonfiction, including the photographic essay. Authenticity, in this case, demands a mastery of paleontology that can only be achieved through a lifetime of field work and sustained study. One of the hallmarks of Lasky's and Knight's work is their devotion to accuracy.

The Most Beautiful Roof in the World (1997)

In this photographic essay, there are no photographs of the Knight family climbing into the canopy of the rain forest or slinking along the wobbly suspended walkway that hangs ninety-five feet above a river. Unlike dinosaur digs, excursions to the canopy require climbing skills and extensive knowledge of plant and animal life because, "there is much to conquer: gravity, stinging ants, rotten trunks and thorns" (unpaged); not to mention the vipers, tarantulas, and bats. Thus, this photographic essay is anchored in the work of Meg Lowman, a rainforest scientist, who studies insect life in the canopy, a world that has been inaccessible to scientists until very recently. From the outset, Lasky works to establish an emotional connection between

Meg and her readers. We learn that even in her earliest years, Meg was an avid collector of bugs, butterflies, and bird's nests. We learn that two of her heroes were Rachel Carson and Harriet Tubman, the latter whom Meg calls "a pioneer field naturalist" (unpaged). Tubman guided slaves to freedom by knowing that moss grows on the north side of trees, that only certain kinds of berries are edible, and that the sulfur and slime in muddy swamps destroys a hunting dog's sense of smell. Knight's photographs of Meg's ascent to the canopy top solidifies our attachment. The complex ascent give us pause, especially as she balances a ladder on top of the suspended walkway and climbs 115 feet above ground to the life that is teaming at the top of the canopy—macaws, spider monkeys, salamanders, insects, and tadpoles swimming in the gullies of bromeliad plants. Knight's photographs in collaboration with the text also particularize the scientific dimension of the scientist's work as we watch Meg observe insects and record their leaf-eating activity, design experiments to discover what stimulates leaf growth, collect and analyze samples, and record hypotheses about her data. This photographic essay has allowed us to venture into one of earth's "last frontiers" (unpaged).

Shadows in the Dawn: The Lemurs of Madagascar (1998)

Within the first two paragraphs of this exquisitely written and photographed essay, Lasky summons a deep affective response:

> At the edge of the long winding river, in the first milky light of dawn, their silhouettes appear, moving slowly under the tamarind tress. They are thin and ragged, exhausted and wary. Some have bald patches or torn ears, a slash wound on a hind leg or a missing tail top. For lemurs the dry season is a terrible time. Food and water are scarce. Fights break out between troops. Weak members are often forced out of a troop and left to die alone. (p. 7)

Unlike *The Most Beautiful Roof in the World*, where our first encounter is with the scientist who guides our journey, *Shadows of the Dawn* places the lemurs on center stage; it is essentially their story. It is not until we have experienced nature's threats to the lemurs, learned why Madagascar is the only place they can be found, and understood that Madagascar is being swept into the sea that we meet primatologist Alison Jolly. Although some primates have been studied extensively, little was known about the lemurs until Alison began her work thirty years ago. What little research had been done suggested, for example, that, like chimpanzees and gorillas, male lemurs were dominant. "Alison believed that too—until she met Aunt Agatha" (p. 28). As Alison watched Aunt Agatha sock a top-ranking male in the nose and steal his ripe tamarind, she expected the male to retaliate, but instead he scampered away. Alison documented this phenomenon time and again, rewriting the textbook on the social order of lemurs. Because primatologists need to track the movement and behavior of their subjects, they must assign the primates names, usually based on physical features, for easy identification. As Alison introduces members of various troops, the story again becomes theirs. There is the story of Fish and Fan, mother and daughter, who send Jessica into exile through starvation to usurp the female throne. There is the story of Annie Oakley, who charges at Kid, causing her baby to fall to the ground and die within a few hours. "Kid grieves for hours. She makes a strange crying sound; she holds and noses her baby's body" (p. 56). Knight's photograph of this tragic moment pierces the heart.

These are only four of the photographic essays with which Lasky and Knight have graced readers; others include *Think Like an Eagle* (1992b), *Monarchs* (1993), and *The Weaver's Gift* (1981). Within this cache, Lasky offers contrasting "story" leads, affording excellent opportunities for critical analysis. For example, *Sugaring Time* and *Think Like an Eagle* mirror *The Most Beautiful Roof in the World* in that these stories begin with the experts and are told almost exclusively through their eyes. *Monarchs*, like *Shadows in the Dawn*, begins with the species. It is only after readers witness the metamorphosis from egg to butterfly that readers meet Clara, an avid butterfly watcher, who shares her wonderment with children. Readers later meet the experts who lead the children on a monarch expedition in Mexico. These contrasting leads invite questions such as: Which type of lead do readers find most appealing and why? How does Lasky decide when to let the expert lead the narration and when to let subjects tell the story? *The Most Beautiful Roof in the World* would have been a very different story if spider monkeys had chaperoned us through the canopy.

Comparing the Photographic Essay and the Illustrated Informational Book

As is true of much learning, we often cement our understanding of a concept by understanding what it is *not*. To fully internalize the genre of the photographic essay, it is worthwhile for readers to compare and contrast it with the more standard fare of nonfiction, the illustrated informational book. As has been established, the photographic essay is Lasky's trademark. In surveying Lasky's work, only one book, *Surtsey: The Newest Place on Earth* (1992a), aligns itself more closely with traditional nonfiction than with the photographic essay, inviting a comparative analysis. Perhaps the most telling sign that *Surtsey* is not a photographic essay is the inclusion of a table of contents and an index—reference aids are not found in any of Lasky's photographic essays. Lasky begins *Surtsey* with a retelling of how crew members of an Icelandic boat witnessed a volcanic eruption. While Lasky's skillful retelling dramatizes the threat of this fiery explosion to the crew, readers do not meet any crew members. Furthermore, once their tale is recounted, they disappear from the story. Lasky then details the science of the volcanic eruption—why it erupted, the stages of the eruption, and how the island was formed. However, there is no volcanologist to narrate this majestic turbulence. Much of the content stands on its own, with the exception of a brief mention of the scientists (nameless) who come to study the newborn island. Because the volcano erupted in 1963, half of the photographs included in the book were taken by two Icelandic photographers during and after the eruption. Although many of these spectacular visuals support the content in a general way, they often do not detail specific content. For example, on the page where Lasky describes two solidified forms of lava, *hellu* lava and *apal* lava, the accompanying photographs are shots of lava flows, not the solidified forms. Because Lasky and Knight were not there at the time of the eruption, they had to weave in the photographs that were available. It is not until we encounter Knight's photographs toward the end of the book that greater unity is achieved between the picture and the word.

Thus, we connect to *Surtsey* in an emotionally different way than we do to Lasky's photographic essays. The emotional draw is the awe we experience as we learn that Surtsey is formed in twenty-four hours and that, as the seed-carrying birds alight the island, the promise of new life resurrects. But the human connections to this content are less pronounced. Lasky, acutely aware of the need to engage readers emotionally, recognized that *Surtsey* needed more than the science content to hold her readers. Her solution—a brilliant juxtaposition of the Nordic creation myth *The Edda* and the volcanic birth of Surtsey (named after Surtur, "who had come with fire to fight the serpent [volcano]" p. 23). Lasky prefaces each chapter of the book with an excerpt from the epic myth that synchronizes beautifully with the story of the volcano. This melding of folklore and science affirms the imaginative powers of the human mind in its quest to probe the forces of nature, to explain the unexplainable. Lasky acknowledges that she needed the myth as much as her readers to understand the power of geologic events:

> In my book *Surtsey: The Newest Place on Earth* . . . I had to read and pour over reams of material about plate tectonics, the structure of the earth—the crust, the mantle, the core, seismography, and a host of related geophysical questions. Oddly enough, none of this really sank into my brain in a way that was retrievable or accessible until I started rereading some of the Norse creation myths and sagas. When I could picture the mid Atlantic ridge as the tail of the Midgard serpent, a true thug of the Edda, a Norse creation saga, I finally could construct a picture in my mind of the lava squeezing through the ridge where the plates meet during volcanic eruptions. These images, stimulated by reading "fantasy" from legends and sagas written over one thousand years ago, were the shaft's light, not at the end but throughout a long murky tunnel of scientific inquiry and research. (1993a, p. 238)

Simile and Symmetry

The distinction between the photographic essay and the illustrated informational book is only one of the gems that can be mined in Lasky's literature of fact. For example, it is impossible not to be enchanted with the poetry of her prose, with her vibrant imagery:

> The buttes herd against the sky like massive creatures grazing silently on an endless plain. (1990, unpaged)

> The leading edges of such lava flows are called paws or snouts. Often times these paws looked more like giant lobster claws pinching the island in a red-hot grip. (1992a, p. 29)

It is the symmetry of Lasky's language that heightens our imagery. For example, the words *herd*, *grazing*, and *plain* in the first quote personify the buttes, entombing creatures of the past, suggesting a life force where there is no longer life. While a time-less tranquillity engulfs the buttes, a fierce mauling assaults the island, as suggested by the words *claws*, *pinching*, and *grip* in the second quote. Lasky explains the symmetry this way:

> To write a nonfiction book you have to have a thorough understanding of the subject matter. . . . Then once I had limited the inquiry and had begun to learn all I could, the big challenge for me is coming up with suitable imagery that can then translate all the scientific gobbledygook into word images that are truthful yet evocative; that can immediately help the reader grasp a difficult concept. . . . A word now about the use of metaphor in nonfiction writing, which is quite different from its use in fiction. For *Surtsey* I had to look for special kinds of images, metaphors, analogies and similes that had a dynamism that matched the tectonic ac-tivity of the geological phenomena. There has to be a kind of internal logic to the metaphors that is consistent with the physics of volcanoes and plate tectonics. And yet it must do what a metaphor does best—give a vivid picture in short hand. For ex-ample, in describing the flow of lava in the formation of Surtsey Island . . . I studied hundreds of photographs of lava flowing from active volcanoes and saw a film of a volcano erupting. Finally some fresh, "hot" images began to seep into my mind's eye. I came up with basically human metaphors comparing the lava to dancers and body-builders. . . . This kind of metaphor was dynamic not static. It was energetic and matched the physics of the event. . . . The challenge of good nonfiction is providing a steady stream of lively, yet accurate images that can help a mind grasp truths. My mission as a nonfiction writer is to provide plausible metaphor that can serve sci-ence. (1993, pp. 238–239)

Autobiographical Information

Lasky: Life–Literature Connections

In the following interview, Kathryn Lasky talks about the autobiographical dimen-sion of her nonfiction work.

> CAROL: In *The Most Beautiful Roof in the World*, you introduced readers to Meg Lowman, rainforest scientist, who as a child was an avid collector of rocks, insects, birds' nests, and so forth. Were you a Meg Lowman when you were young?
>
> KATHRYN: No, I was an outdoorsy kid but not in that way—no rock collec-tions, no interest in science. In fact, I was terrible in science. I went to this crazy, old, all-girls' school where the teachers thought that science was for boys so they scaled back whatever science courses they gave us. Of course, science was the textbook, no hands-on at all. Not surprisingly, I didn't like nonfiction as a kid—the nonfiction books were really dry and boring.
>
> CAROL: What influence, if any, did your parents have in your fascination with science?

KATHRYN: None. They weren't into science at all. They loved literature, and shared that love with us, but no science.

CAROL: So, what pulled you in?

KATHRYN: I got into science when I was forty years old [laughing]. It was through my own kids that I caught the science bug. My son, Max, was seven years old when I turned forty and he had a really quick mind for science (although he's an English major now [laughing]). We live here in Cambridge right behind the Peabody Museum, which was one of our favorite places to go. I loved it; I still love it because it's the way a museum is supposed to be—a place that's really creepy and dusty where they chop off your hands if you touch anything. It's not like the Children's Museum with all its hands-on focus, but it didn't matter because we loved the creepy, mysterious Peabody with its big old bones and weird professors wandering around. The Peabody is where we got into dinosaurs. And that was the beginning for me. I began writing what I call my "bone trilogy": *Traces of Life*, *Dinosaur Dig*, and the novel, *The Bone Wars*. These books grew out of our time at the Peabody with one book leading to the next. I saw this fabulous exhibit about origins of humankind and became so interested that I started reading about evolution. I audited Stephen Jay Gould's course on evolution at Harvard University and then moved onto David Pilbeam's course. These were basically the first science courses that I ever took—at the age of forty.

CAROL: This background knowledge gave you the courage to write?

KATHRYN: I know I'm never going to be a scientist but I realized that I have legitimate questions and that there are a lot of people like me who have the same science questions. When I realized that there is a narrative in science that is just as compelling as fiction, I knew I could begin to explore these questions. And I really got into it.

CAROL: Did *Dinosaur Dig* spin out of your son's interest in dinosaurs?

KATHRYN: No. I first wrote *Traces of Life: Origins of Humankind*. It took me six years to write mainly because I like doing research more than writing so I'd put off facing the blank page. I think this is true for many writers. Anyway, as I was researching the book at various university libraries, I discovered this fascinating story about Cope and Marsh, who were the two great paleontologists of the nineteenth century. Have you read *Bone Wars*?

CAROL: Unfortunately, I haven't. I've concentrated on your nonfiction.

KATHRYN: Oh, it's my favorite book. Anyway, it's about these two renowned but self-centered paleontologists who were the first to dig up dinosaur bones in the West. But the competition between the men was fierce—spying on and stealing from each other, destroying fossils so the other would not be able to claim them. They were involved in their own "bone war." I found this such a fantastic story and couldn't believe that no one had written this piece of historical fiction, so I decided to do it because I like writing novels about the Old West. I began crafting *The Bone Wars* but got to a certain point in the novel when I realized that I'd never been on a dinosaur dig. Nor had I been to the site of one of the most dramatic conflicts in American history—the Battle of Little Bighorn. This battleground and the dig site were key to the book. I knew I couldn't write the scene without going to the battlefield. As luck would have it, a friend called who is a science journalist and who was researching with a paleontologist in Minnesota. When I told her about my book, she urged me to join the dig. Max and I decided to go; first we went to the battleground and then joined the dig. I learned everything I needed to know for my novel but I thought the dig was so fascinating that I decided to return the next year with Chris [her husband] and the kids to write the nonfiction version of the dig.

CAROL: What about your beautifully written *Shadows in the Dawn*? I think it is your best photographic essay to date. I occasionally read a piece of fiction that moves me so deeply that I can't shake it off for two or three days. This has never happened to me with a nonfiction book—until *Shadows*.

KATHRYN: That's another one that grew out of the bone trilogy. As I mentioned earlier, I took David Pilbeam's course on hominid evolution at Harvard University. Now, you can't do hominid evolution without studying primate evolution. The textbook that we read for that course was by Alison Jolly [the primatologist featured in *Shadows of the Dawn*] Who has ever heard of sitting down and reading a textbook from start to finish, but I did. Alison is a fantastic writer. And I will say as a kid, I was fascinated by Jane Goodall. She was beginning her research when I was in high school. Of course, my teachers never dealt with her work in school. I used to sit at home or in the library reading Jane Goodall's articles in *National Geographics*. I couldn't wait for the next installment. I was intrigued by this young English woman who skipped college and went off to Africa with her mother. At the time, I thought this was a dream job; however, it was as remote to me as becoming a movie star. So I became hooked on primatology in high school, but I never took a course in college because I didn't think I was good in science. But I read all the time; I followed Dian Fossey's work too. So I didn't come into David Pilbeam's primate evolution course totally cold; I came in as someone who had read popular literature. It was David who arranged for me to meet with Alison Jolly at Princeton. I just loved her. Of the galaxy of very famous women primatologists, Alison is the most erudite in that she has the deepest and most solid science background. I think it's a riot that as a graduate student, Alison started out in marine biology studying sponges—can you imagine? I loved the way she talks [in *Shadows of the Dawn*] about walking into that lab, falling in love with those cute primates, and turning her career completely around. With that one visit, she realized the incredible range of primates. She said it was like, "Dial me up a primate" [laughing] and headed out to Madagascar. Her book covers all kinds of primates but lemurs are her special love.

251

CAROL: Well, you captured her life and that of the lemurs in your emotionally gripping book.

KATHRYN: The lemurs are in a particularly dramatic situation because of the problems of Madagascar. So I knew with this story that I had all of the ingredients. Dian Fossey had a similar situation because the gorillas' land was being encroached upon. In essence, a habitat is being destroyed for both humans and the lemurs.

CAROL: Did *The Most Beautiful Roof in the World* also connect to this habitat issue?

KATHRYN: No. That book spun out of a family vacation to Galapagos Islands and our journey into the rainforest in Ecuador. I was enchanted. I have a terrible fear of heights, but somehow I managed to get myself up into a Kapok tree, and stayed up there—probably because I was too afraid to come down [laughing]. Once there though, I was mesmerized by the life around me. In talking with a guide, I learned that there is a specialized field of rainforest canopy research. Of course, my interest in doing the rainforest coincided with the flood of other rainforest books, all of which I hated because they were either very moralistic in terms of emphasizing only the destruction aspect or they tried to do the whole rainforest. The rainforest is so huge and complex that you can't do it all in one book successfully. When I realized that nobody had focused on just one layer, I decided to do the canopy because I think it is the most interesting layer. I was thrilled to find Meg Lowman, a canopy researcher and a young mother. So this book grew out of that vacation. Chris [Kathryn's husband] took photographs while we were in the rainforest for our personal family albums, some of which we eventually used in the book, but we had to return to photograph Meg as well as the abundant life in the canopy.

CAROL: What about the origin of *Monarchs*?

KATHRYN: I get a lot of my ideas from reading newspaper articles. I read an article in *The New York Times* about the migration of monarch butterflies, and thought, "This is astounding." So I decided to do the book based on that article.

CAROL: What influence does Chris have in your choice of topic, given his illustrious career as a *National Geographic* photographer?

KATHRYN: Usually, I'm the one who figures out the topic. I do the initial work and then try to sell it to Chris. My first sell is to Chris.

CAROL: Has Chris rejected any of your ideas?

KATHRYN: No, he's accepted every one of my ideas but I have rejected some of his. He came up with an idea of doing bears, but I don't want to get eaten by a bear so we don't pursue it [laughing].

CAROL: Does personal safety enter into your decision about what science topic you pursue?

KATHRYN: Yeah, it does [laughing]. I can't imagine I'd do anything on sharks.

CAROL: Your early books, like *The Weaver's Gift, The Dollmaker, Puppeteer, Sugaring Time*, capture time-honored crafts. Are you interested in crafts on a personal level?

KATHRYN: No, I just thought they were interesting human stories and process stories—the process these people go through to bring us their art. I was so fascinated with the totality of each process, for example, with the artistry entailed in going from sheep to blanket in *The Weaver's Gift*.

CAROL: Are you working on another nonfiction book now?

KATHRYN: Yes, we doing one on the sea turtles that get stranded on Cape Cod. We're focusing on the Kemp's Ridley turtles because they are an endangered species.

Lasky as Writer

Lasky recalls:

> One summer night in northern Indiana, where my family had a cottage, we were riding in my parents' Chevy convertible on the way back from the A&W root beer. As we drove along, my sister and I were sitting in the backseat, our heads flung back, looking into the sky. There were no stars that night, but there were clouds, thick and woolly. Suddenly an image struck me. "It's a sheepback sky," I said to no one in particular. Hearing me, my mother turned around and said, "Kathy, you should be a writer." At that point, I realized that with my mother's belief in me, half the battle was already won. I really could become a writer! (Harcourt Brace brochure)

Thus began Lasky's dream to become a writer. When, as an adult, she decided to venture into the world of nonfiction, she was jettisoned back to her middle school years:

> . . . in my desperation I began where I used to [begin] eons ago—then I was a seventh-grader on a Sunday night, with a report due Monday morning on the Pleistocene Age. My route of research went something like this: First I went to the dictionary and looked up a definition. Webster really had a knack for providing material for desperate seventh-graders. Then I would proceed to the *World Book Encyclopedia*. If I was feeling very scholarly, I would persevere and take on the Mount Everest of research—*Encyclopaedia Britannica*. . . . I would tremble at the thought of those thousands of tissue-thin pages and masses of fine print under my arm. . . . But more often than not, I would skip the *Britannica* and go on to my final step in the research process. Bursting into my sister's room, I would fling myself on her bed and in anguish cry, "Quick, I need a first sentence about the Pleistocene Age! (Lasky, 1985, p. 527)

Stirring inside her, though, was the conviction that nonfiction was more than a clump of facts, more than "a sort of soulless exploration of phenomena" (Lasky, 1985, p. 30). As she set out to write her first photographic essay, *The Weaver's Gift*, she knew that it had to do more than teach children about how wool is sheared, sorted, carded, spun, and woven into a child's blanket. She knew she had to infuse this work with life by placing the art in the hands of the artist, by telling the story of weaver Carolyn Fry.

As a writer of both fiction and nonfiction, Lasky explains, "People often ask me how and why I do both fiction and nonfiction. I am equally attracted to both kinds of writing because for me the most important thing is that a story be real. Even in my nonfiction books, telling a story is more important than reciting facts. Real stories can be either fiction or nonfiction" (Little, Brown and Company brochure). Nonfiction for Lasky is about "searching for the story among the truths, the facts, the lies and the realities" (Kovacs and Preller, 1993b, p.102).

Central to any story, of course, are the characters. For Lasky, these characters include dollmaker Carolee Bowling, who was "trembling and pale, as she made the mold of her doll's clay head. If the original were damaged, she would have to scrap two months worth of painstaking work" (1981, unpaged). They include a mother lemur that "has only one goal—to survive so her baby may survive" (1998, unpaged). It is life's moments of triumph and tragedy—and all that is in between—that is the magic of nonfiction.

Lasky is a fastidious writer. Acknowledging that "to write a nonfiction book, you have to have a thorough understanding of the subject matter" (1993, p. 238), she does extensive research—books, films, archives. However, what distinguishes all of her nonfiction is her obsession "to listen, smell and touch the place that I write about" (Kovacs and Preller, 1993, p. 102). It is this obsession that transported her to the Montana Badlands to touch the rib of ancient life, to the mountain of El Rosario, Mexico, to chase monarchs to their roosting trees, and to Belize to climb to the canopy of the rainforest—tutored every step of the way by world-renowned scientists. Lasky serves as a superb model for young writers because she lives her subject, merging all that she has read and heard with what she has witnessed and has felt.

Brimming with knowledge, insight, and emotion, Lasky creates outline after outline. At first, she records "one idea for each heading. It might be a little scrap of dialogue, or a place where the story is going to start, or what the situation is" (Kovacs and Preller, 1993, p. 103). Then she fills in the details of each section; however, she doesn't stop there: "I outlined the first few chapters. Then I kept outlining smaller and smaller pieces. My outlines would be quite unintelligible to anybody else but me" (Kovacs and Preller, 1993, p. 103).

Asked why she never revisits the same topic, Lasky writes: "I can't stand doing the same thing twice. I don't want to change just for the sake of change. But the whole point of being an artist is to be able to get up every morning and reinvent the world. It's a question of challenge" (Kovacs and Preller, 1993, p. 103).

Concluding Comments

Judith Keck (1992) writes:

> It is not the day-to-day worksheets and textbook chapters that make the school lives of children memorable, but the special projects that engage them both in and out of school. An in-depth author study can create a touchstone in the lives of students. . . . (p. 128)

In the opening chapter of this book, readers of all ages acknowledged the magnetic pull of certain authors in their lives. Summoned by these authors, readers returned time and again for inspiration, solace, wisdom, self-revelation, and, of course, for a good story. The author studies profiled in this book speak to the power of communal engagement with authors and their literature. Together, readers come to know what matters to these authors and, in the process, what matters to themselves. They come to know the life events that triggered and sustained the storytelling of many authors, heightening readers' attachment to these authors. They also come to know, though, that for some writers, it is not life episodes that anchor their literature, but rather the world around them.

Fiction and nonfiction author studies become memorable when children are encouraged to live the literature of an author and to share the ways in which this author has moved, instructed, and delighted them. They become memorable when children's insights about the critical or biographical dimensions (which often spring forth during aesthetic renderings) are pursued at the appropriate time. They become memorable when children and teachers collaborate on the course that author study will take. In essence, author studies that respect and encourage the multiplicity of reader response bring a life force into our classrooms that endures long after the study has ended.

Author Response:
Kathryn Lasky on Author Studies

CAROL: Did you have a favorite author when you were growing up?

KATHRYN: Well, I grew up in an era when there weren't authors like Lois Lowry. So I read *Nancy Drew* and the *Wizard of Oz* books. My sister and I just loved *The Little Colonel* series because we felt as if we were living on a plantation. Today, of course, these books would be banned as racist because the main character owned a slave. I also read some bad teenage literature; I remember one series about a girl who was always going to a country club and dressing up for proms. These books were the popular books of the fifties. Then I advanced to *Jane Eyre*. My parents read constantly, so it was very natural for me to be glued to a book. My favorite book when I was twelve years old was Leon Uris's *Exodus*. I loved that book.

CAROL: I too loved Leon Uris but I was in high school at the time. In fact, now that I think of it, he was my first favorite author. I devoured *Exodus*, *Mila 18*, and *Trinity*. I couldn't wait for the next book to be published.

KATHRYN: I also read *The Naked and the Dead* [laughing] when I was thirteen. And I loved war literature like *Battle Cry*. Remember, I was the immediate post-war generation. I wouldn't have read this stuff if someone like Lois Lowry had been around.

CAROL: What would you like to see teachers do with your books?

KATHRYN: That's a good question. I think teachers need to help children know how we know. For example, with the lemur book, I included some of the strategies that primatologists use when observing and recording behaviors of the lemurs. One of the things that struck me about Alison [the primatologist in *Shadows of the Dawn*] was her ability to stand back, look, and listen—a lost art form in our society. Kids are always asking me, "Well, how do you write dialogue that sounds so real?" I tell them I spend a lot of time listening to people. I love going to restaurants by myself and just listening. I think children need to learn to look and listen, and to write what they observe. If teachers are using the lemur book, they can take children to a zoo and have them look at and listen to primates; then they can ask them to create an observation sheet of behaviors they have noted. This is so much more meaningful than having children try to emulate real life in a phony way. For example, I hate it when teachers bury things in a sand box and have the children "excavate." The kids know this isn't a dinosaur dig; this isn't about bringing them back to the 65-million-year marker.

CAROL: Good science teachers place much emphasis on observing, hypothesizing, and reflecting.

KATHRYN: I just attended parent-teacher night to meet my daughter's teacher and to hear about the curriculum. I was impressed with her marine-biology teacher. He talked about the yearlong project they are going to do and about how he encourages an interdisciplinary focus. He talked about a student who was quite artistic and who had independently created a mural of different zones of the ocean as a result of what they were studying in class. I think that kind of interdisciplinary curriculum around nonfiction is neat.

CAROL: Many teachers work hard to achieve this integration. Let me tell you about the focus of the author study book that I'm writing.

KATHRYN: Did you know that Twayne Publishers has just done a biography on me [*Presenting Kathryn Lasky*] that will be coming out in November, 1998? There's a whole section of my nonfiction in this biography that might be of interest to teachers.

CAROL: Great news, because to do an effective author study, teachers need access to biographical data. In fact, some teachers begin an author study with the author's life and then have the children read to find life-literature parallels. I'm arguing in the book that while autobiography has a place in an author study, the starting point has to be the book and how it moves young readers.

KATHRYN: I would agree. I never read an introduction to a book before I read the book. If you take a classic by Jane Austen or by George Eliot, the first thing you encounter is that essay written by some great scholar. I don't like to read that introduction before the book because I think it will prejudice me, cause me to read the book in a different way.

CAROL: That's a marvelous example of what I'm talking about. I think that when teachers precede *Shadows in the Dawn* with your autobiographical information and have readers focus on parallels, they deny the reader the most fundamental element of literature—the chance to be moved by the tenderness of lemur mothers, and to be disturbed by the threat to this species. Now, if during their personal responses, comments about you as author are interjected, as I have found to be the case, the biographical focus can be pursued at an appropriate time.

KATHRYN: It certainly makes sense to let the literature stand on its own and see where the readers go with it.

CAROL: Returning to your nonfiction, I'm wondering if you think it's appropriate for children to examine some of the critical elements of your nonfiction books after they have been savored? For example, you use different leads in your photographic essays. In the rainforest book, readers meet Meg Lowman, the rainforest scientist, at the beginning of the book and learn about the canopy through her eyes. In the lemur book, readers don't meet Alison (the primatologist) until we've established a bond with the primates. What do you think about this?

KATHRYN: I think that's great because I think critical thinking about what makes this good literature, which is what you're saying when you're comparing one of my books to another and how I structured them, is a valuable activity.

CAROL: What do you think makes a successful photographic essay?

KATHRYN: I can always find an exception for every rule I make in terms of my own work, but I think that there has to be some sort of human element. Now, the exception here is what's the human element in a book like *Surtsey*. But I do think there has to be that human element in the photographic essay. I think there has to be a story—a narrative where, as readers, we have many of the same expectations as we have for fiction. We want a beginning, a middle, and an end with resolution. I don't think nonfiction is about answering questions, but rather about raising questions in the mind of the readers. There's a contradiction here, of course, in that is it possible to have a book with resolution that only raises questions? I think so. *Surtsey* is a good example because it leave readers with the questions: "But how long will Surtsey last? Will it be worn away by the sea?" In other words, I don't want to come off as having the last word. I want to come off as having the beginning word because it's the beginning of an intellectual quest. I never read nonfiction when I was a kid because the books were so boring. It was like reading textbooks. They didn't have the human element and I never had the idea that science was a quest. These books had stupid titles like "The Wonderful World of Asteroids." It was as though the authors felt that the subject was so boring that they had to put the word *wonderful* in the title to make you read the book. But these authors never connected to the reader. If "The Wonderful World of Asteroids" began with the notion that the same bits of carbon that are in an asteroid are the same bits of carbon that are in you and me, boy, would they have hooked me!

CAROL: So it's this personal connection for which you strive.

258

KATHRYN: Absolutely. The lemur story is a very dramatic story because it's about babies and mothers, about jealousy and envy, and about life and death. I love that chapter in the book called "Spite and Death" because it captures the soap opera I felt I was watching as the lemurs jostle for positions of power in the troop. I saw that baby lemur fall from the tree during an act of aggression by one female against the baby's mother. I watched as Fish and Fan wouldn't let the mother near the dead infant, out of pure spite. Every insult I ever endured on a playground as a child, every person that I ever thought was an evil person [laughing] came to mind as I sat there on that log, during the dwindling sunset, watching these creatures. Somehow, you have to communicate this to the kids and then you have to say, "This is what they call science" and leave the judgment call up to the kids. In my opinion, a lot of primatology isn't science. I do not believe that psychiatry is science. I don't think there's a shred of evidence for anything anyone does in a psychiatric office. I'm not condemning psychiatry and I'm not saying it's not worthwhile. And, of course, this said, the Christian Fundamentalists will challenge me by saying that if primatology isn't a science, then we have no proof that we evolved from apes.

CAROL: What's your response to their charge?

KATHRYN: Well, in some ways, primatology is a soft science but it's getting harder every day so I'd direct the Fundamentalists to the DNA research. One of the problems with the Fundamentalists is that they abuse science. They aren't willing to submit their data to scientific scrutiny, to let their data be tested. There is plenty of primatology that is testable, fossil evidence and so forth. So, in the end, we have to help children understand how to weigh evidence and how to value it.

CAROL: And that's what your books do brilliantly.

KATHRYN: You know, there's a parallel here with fiction, particularly fantasy. Take a book such as *Where the Wild Things Are*. Maurice Sendak is very clear in that book about what's real and what's fantasy. When that book came out, a lot of people criticized it, saying it was going to scare kids. That was the political correctness of that era. But I think that what is so great about Sendak is that he always makes the distinction between what's real and what's not real. There are very clear signposts—for example, how the illustrations are framed at both the beginning and the end—that every child understands. Nobody knows the difference between fantasy and reality better than a top-notch children's writer. I see an analogy with science in this—there's a fine line between what's real and what isn't; what's real changes all the time. For example, until Alison Jolly started doing intensive observation of lemur troops, it was believed that only the males were aggressive. When she really looked, she documented numerous instances of female aggression. What was thought to be science wasn't.

CAROL: What is the best part about being a science writer?

KATHRYN: For me, it's not the answers; it's the questions I raise. It's not the facts but it's the mystery among the facts.

References

Professional References

Allington, R. (1983). Fluency, the neglected reading goal. *The Reading Teacher, 30*, 556–561.

Alverman, D., & Boothby, P. (1982). Text differences: Children's perceptions at the transition stage in reading. *The Reading Teacher, 36*, 290–302.

Anderson, R., Hiebert, E., Scott, J., & Wilkinson, I. (1985). *Becoming a nation of readers: The report on the commission of reading*. Champaign, IL: The Center for the Study of Reading.

Angelou, M. (1969). *I know why the caged bird sings*. New York: Bantam Books.

Applebee, A. (1978). *The child's concept of story*. Chicago: University of Chicago Press.

Aristotle. (1980). *The Nicomachean Ethics*. (D. Ross, Trans.). New York: Oxford University Press.

Aristotle. (1991). *The art of rhetoric*. (H. C. Lawson-Tancred, Trans.). New York: Penguin.

Armbruster, B., Anderson, T., Armstrong, J., Wise, M., Janisch, C., & Meyer, L. (1990). Reading and questioning in the content areas. *Journal of Reading Behavior, 23* (1), 35–59.

Atwell, N. (1987). *In the middle: Writing, reading, and learning with adolescents*. Portsmouth, NH: Boynton/Cook.

Avi. (1982). Writing books for young people. *The Writer, 95* (3), 18–20.

Avi. (1992). *Boston Globe–Horn Book* award acceptance speech. *Horn Book, 26*, 24–27.

Avi. (1995). An evening with Avi. Presentation to the Greater Boston Council of the International Reading Association, Boston, MA.

Avi. (1996). Avi. Internet Public Library http://www.ipl.org.

Bakhtin, M. (1986). *Speech genres and other late essays*. Austin: University of Texas Press.

Beach, R. (1993). *A teacher's introduction to reader-response theories*. Urbana, IL: National Council of Teachers of English.

Bearse, C. I. (1992). The fairy tale connection in children's stories: Cinderella meets Sleeping Beauty. *The Reading Teacher, 45*, 688–695.

Bennett, W. (1993). *The book of virtues: A treasure of great moral stories*. New York: Simon & Schuster.

Berkowitz, S. (1986). Effects of instruction in text organization on sixth-grade students' memory for expository reading. *Reading Research Quarterly, 21* (1), 161–178.

Bissex, G. (1980). *GNYS AT WRK: A child learns to write and read.* Cambridge, MA: Harvard University Press.

Bleich, D. (1975). *Readings and feelings: An introduction to subjective criticism.* Urbana, IL: National Council of Teachers of English.

Bloom, A. (1986). *The republic of Plato.* (A. Bloom, Trans.). New York: HarperCollins.

Booklist. (1994). A review of *Tell me everything. Booklist, 90,* 1353.

Britton, J., Martin, T., McLeod, A., & Rosen, H. (1975). *The development of writing abilities (11–18).* London: Macmillan.

Bruce, B. (1978). What makes a good story? *Language Arts, 55* (4), 460–466.

Buzzeo, T. (1998). The finely tuned author visit. *Book Links, 7* (4), 10–15.

Cairney, T. (1990). Intertextuality: Infectious echoes from the past. *The Reading Teacher, 43,* 478–485.

Calkins, L. (1991). *Living between the lines.* Portsmouth, NH: Heinemann.

Cambourne, B. (1988). *The whole story: Natural learning and acquisition of literacy in the classroom.* New York: Ashton Scholastic.

Carlsen, G., & Sherrill, A. (1988). *Voices of readers: How we come to love books.* Urbana, IL: National Council of Teachers of English.

Chall, J., & Jacobs, V. (1983). Writing and reading in the elementary grades: Developmental trends among low SES children. *Language Arts, 60,* 617–626.

Charlton, J. (Ed.). (1997). *The writer's quotation book.* Boston: Faber & Faber.

Chomsky, C. (1972). Stages in language development and reading exposure. *Harvard Educational Review, 42,* 1–33.

Chukovsky, K. (1965). *From two to five.* Berkely: Univeristy of California Press.

Coles, R. (1986). *The moral life of children.* New York: The Atlantic Monthly Press.

Coles, R. (1989). *The call of stories.* Boston: Houghton Mifflin.

Collier, L., & Nakumura, J. (1993). *Major authors and illustrators for children and young adults.* Detroit: Gale Research Inc.

Cox, C., & Many, J. (1989). Reader stance toward a literary work: Applying the transactional theory to children's response. Paper presented at the Annual Meeting of the American Educational Research Association, San Francisco, CA.

Cox, C., & Zarillo, J. (1993). *Teaching reading with children's literature.* New York: Macmillan.

Cramer, E., & Castle, M. (1994). Developing lifelong readers. In E. Cramer and M. Castle (Eds.), *Fostering the love of reading: The affective domain.* Newark, DE: International Reading Association.

Cullinan, B., & Galda, L. (1994). *Literature and the child.* New York: Harcourt Brace.

Cullinan, B., Harwood, K., & Galda, L. (1983). The reader and the story: Comprehension and response. *Journal of Research and Development in Education, 16,* 29–37.

Cunningham, J. (1979). On automatic pilot for decoding. *The Reading Teacher, 32,* 420–424.

Daniels, H. (1990). Young writers and readers reach out: Developing sense of audience. In T. Shanahan (Ed.), *Reading and writing together: New perspectives for the classroom* (pp. 99–125). Norwood, MA: Christopher-Gordon.

Daiches, D. (1981). *Critical approaches to literature.* New York: Longman.

Delattre, E. (1988). *Education and the public trust.* Washington, DC: Ethics and Public Policy Center.

Dewey, J. (1909/1933). *How we think: A restatement of the relation of reflective thinking to the educative process.* Boston: D.C. Heath.

Durkin, D. (1966). *Children who read early.* New York: Teachers College Press.

Durkin, D. (1978–1979). What classroom observations reveal about reading comprehension. *Reading Research Quarterly, 15,* 481–533.

Duthie, C. (1996). *True stories: Nonfiction literacy in the primary classroom.* York, ME: Stenhouse.

Eagleton, T. (1983). *Literary theory: An introduction.* Oxford, England: Basil Blackwell.

Edelsky, C. (1994). Education for democracy. *Language Arts, 71* (4), 252–257.

Eeds, M. & Peterson, R. (1995). What teachers need to know about the literary craft. In N. Roser & M. Maartinez (Eds.), *Book talk and beyond: Children and teachers respond to literature* (pp. 10–23). Newark, DE: International Reading Association.

Eeds, M., & Wells, D. (1989). Grand conversations: An exploration of meaning construction in literature study groups. *Research in the Teaching of English, 23* (1), 4–29.

Ehrmann, J. (1970). *Structuralism.* Garden City, NY: Anchor-Doubleday.

Emery, D. (1996). Helping readers comprehend stories from the characters' perspectives. *The Reading Teacher, 49* (7), 534–541.

Finn, C., & Ravitch, D. (1988). No trivial pursuit. *Phi Delta Kappan, 69* (8), 559–564.

Fish, S. (1980). *Is there a text in this classroom? The authority of interpretive communities.* Cambridge, MA: Harvard University Press.

Fletcher, R. (1993). *What a writer needs.* Portsmouth, NH: Heinemann.

Fox, M. (1992). *Dear Mem Fox, I have read all your books even the pathetic ones.* New York: Harcourt Brace Jovanovich.

Fox, M. (1993a). Men who weep, boys who dance: The gender agenda between the lines in children's literature. *Language Arts, 70* (1), 84–88.

Fox, M. (1993b). Politics and literture: Chasing the "isms" from children's books. *The Reading Teacher, 46* (8), 654–658.

Freedman, R. (1992). Fact or fiction? In R. Bamford & J. Kristo (Eds.), *Making facts come alive: Choosing quality nonfiction literature K–8.* Norwood, MA: Christopher-Gordon.

Freire, P. (1970a). *Pedagogy of the oppressed.* New York: Continuum.

Freire, P. (1970b). Reading the world and reading the word: An interview with Paulo Freire. *Language Arts 62* (1), 15–21.

Frye, N. (1957). *Anatomy of criticism.* Princeton, NJ: Princeton University Press.

Galda, L. (1982). Assuming the spectator stance: An examination of the response to three young readers. *Research in the Teaching of English, 16,* 1–20.

Giacobbe, M. (1995). Using writing folders as a means of informing daily instruction. Paper presented at The 12th Annual Literacy Institute, Lesley College, Cambridge, MA.

Gilles, C. (1998). Talking about books: Patricia Polacco. *Language Arts, 75* (2), 151–157.

Giroux, H. (1983). *Theory and resistance in education*. South Hadley, MA: Bergin & Garvey.

Golden, J. (1984). Children's concept of story in reading and writing. *The Reading Teacher, 37,* 578–585.

Graves, D. (1989). Research currents: When children respond to fiction. *Language Arts, 66,* 776–783.

Graves, D. (1991). Trust the shadows. *The Reading Teacher, 45,* 18–25.

Graves, D. (1994). *A fresh look at writing*. Portsmouth, NH: Heinemann.

Guerin, W., Labor, E., Morgan, L., Reesman, J., & Willingham, J. (1992). *A handbook of critical approaches to literature*. New York: Oxford University Press.

Harcourt Brace Children's Books. (n. d.). *Kathryn Lasky*. San Diego, CA: Harcourt Brace.

Hardy, B. (1977). Narrative as a primary act of mind. In M. Meek, A. Warlow, & G. Barton (Eds.), *The cool web: The pattern of children's reading* (pp. 6–12). New York: Lothrop, Lee & Shepard.

Harste, J., & Short, K. (1988). *Creating classrooms for authors*. Portsmouth, NH: Heinemann.

Hazlitt, W. (1982). (quote). In *Books & readers*. La Jolla, CA: Green Tiger Press.

Hedblad, A., & Telgen, D. (Eds.). (1996). *Children's Literature Review*. New York: Gale Research Inc.

Helper, S. (1998). Nonfiction books for children: New directions, new challenges. In R. Bamford & J. Kristo (Eds.), *Making facts come alive: Choosing quality nonfiction literature K–8*. Norwood, MA: Christopher-Gordon.

Helper, S., & Hickman, J. (1982). "The book was okay. I love you."—Social aspects of response to literature. *Theory into Practice, 21,* 278–283.

Hibbert, C. (1969). Dickens' London. In E. F. Tomlin, *Charles Dickens 1812–1870* (pp. 73–99). New York: Simon & Schuster.

Hiebert, E., & Cole, J. (1989). Patterns of literature-based reading. *The Reading Teacher, 43,* 14–20.

Hirsch, E. (1967). *Validity in interpretation*. New Haven, CT: Yale University Press.

Horn Book. (1996). A review of *What Jamie Saw*. *Horn Book, 72,* 194.

Huck, C., Helper, S., & Hickman, J. (1987). *Children's literature in the elementary school*. New York: Holt, Rinehart and Winston.

Iser, W. (1978). *The act of reading: A theory of aesthetic response*. Baltimore: Johns Hopkins University Press.

Jenkins, C. (1996). *Inside the writing portfolio: What we need to know about to assess children's writing*. Portsmouth, NH: Heinemann.

Johnson, E. (1969). Dickens: The dark pilgrimage. In E. F. Tomlin, *Charles Dickens 1812–1870* (pp. 41–63). New York: Simon & Schuster.

Jose, P., & Brewer, W. (1984). Development of story liking: Character identification, suspense, and outcome resolution. *Developmental Psychology, 20,* 911–924.

Kagan, J. (1981). *The second year: The emergence of self-awareness*. Cambridge, MA: Harvard University Press.

Kaplan, F. (1988). *Dickens: A biography*. New York: William Morrow.

Keck, J. (1992). Using a nonfiction author study in the classroom. In E. Freeman & D. Person, *Using nonfiction trade books in the elementary classroom: From ants to zeppelins*. Urbana, IL: National Council of Teachers of English.

Keifer, B. (1986). The child and the picture book: Creating live circuits. *Children's Literature Association Quarterly, 11*, 63–68.

Keller, H. (1965). *The story of my life.* New York: Airmont.

Kilpatrick, W., Wolfe, S., & Wolfe, G. (1994). *Books that build character.* New York: Touchstone.

Kovacs, D., & Preller, J. (1991). *Meet the authors and illustrators.* New York: Scholastic.

Kovacs, D., & Preller, J. (1993). *Meet the authors and illustrators* (Vol. 2). New York: Scholastic.

Langer, J. (1986). *Children reading and writing: Structures and strategies.* Norwood, NJ: Ablex.

Lasky, K. (1985). Reflections on nonfiction. *The Horn Book Magazine, 59* (5), 527–532.

Lasky, K. (1993). Shuttling through realities: The warp and the weft of fantasy and nonfiction writing. *The New Advocate, 6* (4), 235–242.

Leal, D. (1993). Storybooks, information books and informational storybooks: An explication of the ambiguous grey genre. *The New Advocate, 6*, 61–70.

Leal, D. (1995). When it comes to informational storybooks, the end of the story has not yet been written: Response to Zarnowski's article. *The New Advocate, 8*, 197–201.

Lehr, S. (1988). The child's developing sense of theme as a response to literature. *Reading Research Quarterly, 23*, 337–357.

Lehr, S. (1991). *The child's developing sense of theme: Response to literature.* New York: Teachers College Press.

Levine, G. (1974). Politics and the form of disenchantment, *College English, 36*.

Levi-Strauss, C. (1968). *Structural anthropology.* (Trans. C. Jacobson). New York: Basic.

Lewis, C. S. (1955). *Surprised by joy.* New York: Harcourt Brace Jovanovich.

Lionetti, J. (1992). An author study: Tomie de Paola. In B. Cullinan (Ed.), *More children's literature in the reading program* (pp. 64–71). Newark, DE: International Reading Association.

Lukens, R. (1976). *A critical handbook of children's literature.* Glenview, IL: Scott Foresman.

Lukens, R. (1995). *A critical handbook of children's literature.* New York: HarperCollins.

Mackey, M. (1990). Filling the gaps: *The Baby-sitters Club*, the series book, and the learning reader. *Language Arts, 67* (5), 484–489.

Mandler, J., & Johnson, N. (1977). Remembrance of things parsed: Story structure and recall. *Cognitive Psychology, 9*, 111–151.

Many, J. (1991). The effects of stance and age level on children's literary responses. *Journal of Reading Behavior, 21*, 61–85.

Many, J., & Cox, C. (1992). *Reader stance and literary understanding: Exploring the theories, research, and practices.* Norwood, NJ: Ablex.

Markham, L. *Avi.* Santa Barbara, CA: The Learning Works.

Masonheimer, P., Drum, P., & Ehri, L. (1984). Does environmental print identification lead children into word reading? *Journal of Reading Behavior, 16*, 257–271.

Maughan, S. (1993). PW interview with Patricia Polacco. *Publishers Weekly, 240* (7), 179, 184–185.

McCord, D. (1986). *One at a time.* New York: Little, Brown.

McGee, L. (1982). The influence of metacognitive knowledge on expository text structure on discourse recall. In J. Niles & A. Harris (Eds.), *New inquiries in reading research and instruction*. Rochester, NY: National Reading Conference.

McGee, L. (1992). An exploration of meaning construction in first graders' grand conversations. In C. Kinzer & D. Leu (Eds.), *Literacy research, theory, and practice: Views from many perspectives*. Rochester, NY: National Reading Conference.

McKeough, A. (1984). Developmental stages in children's narrative composition. (ERIC ED 249 461).

Meltzer, M. (1976). Where do all the prizes go? The case for nonfiction. *The Horn Book Magazine, 52*, 17–23.

Meltzer, M. (1988). *Starting from home: A writer's beginnings*. New York: Viking Penguin.

Meltzer, M. (1994). *Milton Meltzer on writing, history, and social responsibility*. New York: Teachers College Press and Newark, DE: International Reading Association.

Mercier, C. (1991). Review of *The true confessions of Charlotte Doyle*. *The Five Owls, 5*, 56–57.

Meyer, B. (1975). *The organization of prose and its effects on memory*. Amsterdam: North Holland.

Murray, D. (1990). *Shoptalk*. Portsmouth, NH: Heinemann.

Paley, V. (1997). *The girl with the brown crayon*. Cambridge, MA: Harvard University Press.

Pappas, C. (1991). Fostering full access to literacy by including information books. *Language Arts, 68*, 449–462.

Paterson, K. (1990). Heart in hiding. In W. Zinsser (Ed.), *Worlds of childhood* (pp. 145–177). Boston: Houghton Mifflin.

Paterson, K. (1997). Family Values. *New Advocate, 10* (1), 5–14.

Peterson, R., & Eeds, M. (1990). Grand conversations: Literature groups in action. New York: Scholastic.

Polacco. P. (1993). *Many voices of family*. (Cassette Recording). Annual Convention of the International Reading Association, San Antonio, TX. Mableton, GA: Audio Master.

Polacco. P. (1994). *Firetalking*. Katonah, NY: Richard C. Owen.

Polacco. P. (1996a). Banquet speech at International Reading Association in New Orleans, LA.

(Cassette Recording). Mableton, GA: Audio Master.

Polacco. P. (1996b). The Keeping Quilt. In A. Hedblad & D. Telgen (Eds.), *Children's Literature Review*. New York: Gale Research Inc.

Polacco. P. (1996c). *Patricia Polacco: Dream Keeper*. Video. New York: Philomel.

Powell, J., Gillespie, C., Swearingen, R., & Clements, N. (1998). The history of gender roles in the Newbery Medal winners. *Journal of Children's Literature, 24* (1), 42–57.

Propp, V. (1968). *The morphology of the fairytale*. (L. Scott, Trans.) Austin: University of Texas (Original work published in 1928).

Publishers Weekly. (1993). A review of *Tell Me Everything*. *Publishers Weekly, 240*, 49.

Putnam, L. (1991). Dramatizing nonfiction with emerging readers. *Language Arts, 68*, 463–469.

Raphael, T., & Hiebert, E. (1996). *Creating an integrated approach to literacy instruction*. New York: Harcourt Brace.

Roberts, V., & Nicoll, V. (1988). Conducting an author study. In C. O'Sullivan (Ed.), *Australian literature in the primary classroom* (pp. 33–43). Rozelle, Australia: Primary English Teaching Association. (ERIC ED 297 372).

Rosenblatt, L. (1938). *Literature as exploration.* New York: Noble and Noble Publishers.

Rosenblatt, L. (1978). *The reader, the text, the poem: The transactional theory of the literary work.* Carbondale: Southern Illinois University Press.

Rosenblatt, L. (1985). The transactional theory of the literary work: Implications for research. In C. Cooper (Ed.), *Researching response to literature and the teaching of literature* (pp. 35–53). Norwood, NJ: Ablex.

Rosenblatt, L. (1988). Writing and reading: The transactional theory. *Reader, 20,* 7–31.

Rosenblatt, L. (1991a). The reading transaction: What for? In B. Power & R. Hubbard (Eds), *Literacy in process* (pp. 114–127). Portsmouth, NH: Heinemann.

Rosenblatt, L. (1991b). Literary theory. In J. Flood, J. Jensen, D. Lapp, & J. Squire (Eds), *Handbook on Teaching the English Language Arts* (pp. 57–62). New York: Macmillian.

Routman, R. (1994). Invitations: Changing as teachers and learners K–12. Portsmouth, NH: Heinemann.

Rumelhart, D. (1975). Notes on a schema for story. In D. Brown & A. Collins (Eds.), *Representation and understanding: Studies in cognitive science* (pp. 211 236). New York: Academic.

Ryan, K. (1997). The missing link's missing link. *Journal of Education,* Boston: Boston University.

Rylant, C. (1985). Thank you Miss Evans. *Language Arts, 62,* (5), 460–462.

Rylant, C. (1989). *But I'll be back again: An album.* New York: Orchard Books.

Rylant, C. (1990). The room in which Van Gogh lived. In N. Atwell (Ed.), *Workshop 2.* Portsmouth, NH: Heinemann.

Sabine, G., & Sabine, P. (1983). *Books that make a difference: What people told us.* Hamden, CT: Library Professional Publications.

Samuels, J. (Ed.). (1979). What the research has to say about reading instruction. Newark, DE: International Reading Association.

Sayers, F. (1965). *Summoned by books.* New York: Viking.

Schickedanz, J. (1990). *Adam's righting revolutions: One child's literacy development from infancy through grade one.* Portsmouth, NH: Heinemann.

School Library Journal. (1995). A review of *What Jamie Saw. School Library Journal, 41,* 128.

Senick, G., & Gunton, S. (Eds.). (1991). *Children's literature review* (Volume 24). Detroit: Gale Research Inc.

Shannon, P. (1990). *The struggle to continue: Progressive reading instruction in the United States.* Portsmouth, NH: Heinemann.

Shannon, P. (1993). Developing democratic voices. *The Reading Teacher, 47* (2), 86–94.

Shor, I. (1992). *Empowering education.* Chicago: University of Chicago Press.

Silber, J. (1998–1999). Philosophy educating humanity. *Bostonia, 4,* 25–29.

Smith, K. (1990). Entertaining a text: A reciprocal process. In K. Short & K. Pierce (Eds.), *Talking about books: Creating literate communities.* Portsmouth, NH: Heinemann.

Snow, C. (1983). Language and literacy: Relationships during the preschool years. *Harvard Educational Review, 4,* 165–189.

Snow, C., & Ninio, A. (1986). The contracts of literacy: What children learn from reading books. In W. Teale & E. Sulzby (Eds.), *Emergent literacy: Writing and reading.* Norwood, NJ: Ablex.

Sowers, S. (1985). The story and the all-about book. In J. Hansen, T. Newkirk, & D. Graves (Eds.), *Breaking ground: Teachers relate reading and writing in the elementary school* (pp. 73–82). Portsmouth NH: Heinemann.

Squire, J. (1964). *The responses of adolescents while reading four short stories.* Urbana, IL: National Council of Teachers of English.

Stein, N., & Glenn, C. (1979). An analysis of story comprehension in elementary school children. In R. Freedle (Ed.), *New Directions in discourse processsing* (pp. 53–129). Norwood, NJ: Ablex.

Sulzby, E., & Teale, W. (1987). Young children's storybook reading: Longitudinal study of parent-child interaction and children's independent functioning. Final report to the Spencer Foundation. Ann Arbor: The University of Michigan.

Taylor, B., & Beach, R. (1984). The effects of text structure instruction on middle-grade students' comprehension and production of expository text. *Reading Research Quarterly, 19,* 147–161.

Taylor, B., & Samuels, S. (1983). Children's use of text structure in the recall of expository material. *American Educational Research Journal, 20,* 517–528.

Taylor, M. (1988). Mildred Taylor. In A. Sarkissian (Ed.), *Something about the author: Autiobiography series* (pp. 401–409). Detroit: Gale Research Inc.

Taylor, M. (1977). Newbery Acceptance Speech.*The Horn Book Magazine, 53* (4), 401–409.

Tompkins, G., & McGee, L. (1993). *Teaching reading with literature.* New York: Macmillan.

Traxel, J. (1985). Review of *The fighting ground. The ALAN Review, 12,* 33.

Trumpet Club. (1992). Trumpet video visits Mem Fox. New York: Teachers College Writing Project, Columbia University.

Vendler, H. (1990, May 31). Feminism and literature. *The New York Review of Books,* 19–25.

Vygotsky, L. (1978). *Mind in society.* Cambridge, MA: Harvard University Press.

Wagenknecht, E. (1957). *The man Charles Dickens: A Victorian portrait.* Norman: University of Oklahoma Press.

Wason-Ellam, L. (1997). "If only I was like Barbie." *Language Arts, 74* (6), 430–437.

Wellek, R. (1982). *The attack on literature.* Chapel Hill: The University of North Carolina Press.

Wellek, R., & Warren, A. (1949). *Theory of literature.* New York: Harcourt Brace.

Wells, G. (1986). *The meaning makers: Children learning language and using language to learn.* Portsmouth, NH: Heinemann.

Whaley, J. (1984). Story grammar and reading instruction. *The Reading Teacher, 34,* 762–771.

Wilson, E. (1941). *The wound and the bow: Seven studies in literature.* Boston: Houghton Mifflin.

Woiwode, L. (1992). Television: The Cyclops that eats books. *Imprintis, 2* (1), 1.

Wollman-Bonilla, J. (1994). Why don't they "just speak"? Attempting literature discussion groups with more or less able readers. *Research in the Teaching of Reading, 28,* 231–258.

Woman on Words & Images. (1972). *Dick and Jane as victims: Sex stereotyping in children's readers*. Princeton, NJ: Woman on Words & Images.

Yolen, J. (1973). *Writing books for children*. Boston: The Writer, Inc.

Yolen, J. (1991). The route to story. *The New Advocate, 4,* 143–149.

Zarnowski, M. (1995). Learning history with informational storybooks: A social studies educator's perspective. *The New Advocate, 8,* 183–196.

Children's Literature References

Avi. (1984). *The fighting ground*. New York: HarperTrophy.

Avi. (1986). *S.O.R losers*. New York: Avon Books.

Avi. (1987). *Devil's race*. New York: Avon Books.

Avi. (1988). *Something upstairs*. New York: Avon Books.

Avi. (1989). *The man who was Poe*. New York: Avon Books.

Avi. (1990). *The true confessions of Charlotte Doyle*. New York: Orchard Books.

Avi. (1991). *Nothing but the truth*. New York: Avon Books.

Avi. (1991). *Windcatcher*. New York: Avon Books.

Avi. (1994). *The barn*. New York: Orchard Books.

Avi. (1995). *Poppy*. New York: Avon Books.

Avi. (1996). *Beyond the western sea*. New York: Orchard Books.

Beattie, O., & Geiger, J. (1992). *Buried in ice: The mystery of the lost Arctic expedition*. New York: Scholastic.

Bisel, S. (1990). *The secrets of Vesuvius: Exploring the mysteries of an ancient buried city*. New York: Scholastic.

Coerr, E. (1977). *Sadako and the thousand paper cranes*. New York: Putnam.

Cole, J. (1971). *Cockroaches*. New York: William Morrow.

Cole, J. (1973). *Plants in winter*. New York: Thomas Y. Crowell.

Cole, J. (1975). *A calf is born*. New York: William Morrow.

Cole, J. (1976). *A chick hatches*. New York: William Morrow.

Cole, J. (1981). *A snake's body*. New York: William Morrow.

Cole, J. (1982). *A cat's body*. New York: William Morrow.

Cole, J. (1983). *A bird's body*. New York: William Morrow.

Cole, J. (1984). *How you were born*. New York: William Morrow.

Cole, J. (1985). *Cuts, breaks, bruises and burns: How your body heals*. New York: Thomas Y. Crowell.

Cole, J. (1985). *Large as life: Nighttime animals, life size*. New York: Knopf.

Cole, J. (1986). *A dog's body*. New York: William Morrow.

Cole, J. (1986). *Hungry, hungry sharks*. New York: Random House.

Cole, J. (1986). *The magic school bus at the waterworks*. New York: Scholastic.

Cole, J. (1987). *The magic school bus inside the earth*. New York: Scholastic.

Cole, J. (1989). *The magic school bus inside the human body*. New York: Scholastic.

Cole, J. (1990). *The magic school bus lost in the solar system*. New York: Scholastic.

Cole, J. (1992). *The magic school bus on the ocean floor*. New York: Scholastic.

Cole, J. (1994). *The magic school bus in the time of the dinosaurs*. New York: Scholastic.

Cole, J. (1995). *The magic school bus inside a hurricane*. New York: Scholastic.

Cole, J. (1995). *My new kitten*. New York: Morrow Junior Books.

Cole, J. (1996). *Magic school bus inside a beehive*. New York: Scholastic.

Coman, C. (1993). *Tell me everything*. New York: Farrar, Straus and Giroux.

Coman, C. (1995). *What Jamie saw*. Arden, NC: Frint Street.

Connolly, P. (1990) *Pompeii*. New York: Oxford University Press.

Freedman, R. (1987). *Lincoln: A photobiography*. New York: Clarion.

Lasky, K. (1981). *The weaver's gift*. New York: Warne.

Lasky, K. (1983). *Sugaring time*. New York: Macmillian.

Lasky, K. (1990). *Dinosaur dig*. New York: Morrow Junior Books.

Lasky, K. (1992). *Surtsey: The newest place on Earth*. New York: Hyperion.

Lasky, K. (1992). *Think like an eagle*. New York: Little, Brown.

Lasky, K. (1993). *Monarchs*. New York: Harcourt Brace.

Lasky, K. (1997). *The most beautiful roof in the world. Exploring the rainforest canopy*. New York: Harcourt Brace.

Lasky, K. (1998). *Shadows in the dawn: The lemurs of Madagascar*. New York: Harcourt Brace.

Lauber, P. (1986). *Volcano: The eruption and healing of Mount St. Helens*. New York: Bradbury.

Lauber, P. (1989). *The news about dinosaurs*. New York: Macmillan.

Langley, A., & DeSouza, P. (1996). *The Roman news*. Cambridge, MA: Candlewick.

Markle, S. (1996). *Outside and inside sharks*. New York: Atheneum Books.

Numeroff, L. (1985). *If you give a mouse a cookie*. New York: Harper.

Parish, S. (1992). *ABC of Australian animals*. Australia: Steve Parish Publishing Pty Ltd.

Pinkwater, D. (1993). *Author's day*. New York: Macmillan.

Polacco, P. (1987). *Meteor*. New York: Dodd.

Polacco, P. (1988). *The keeping quilt*. New York: Simon & Schuster Books for Young Readers.

Polacco, P. (1988). *Rechenka's eggs*. New York: Philomel.

Polacco, P. (1989). *Uncle Vova's tree*. New York: Philomel.

Polacco, P. (1990). *Babushka's doll*. New York: Simon & Schuster Books for Young Readers.

Polacco, P. (1990). *Thunder cake*. New York: Philomel.

Polacco, P. (1991). *Appelemando's dreams*. New York: Philomel.

Polacco, P. (1991). *Some birthday.* New York: Simon & Schuster Books for Young Readers.

Polacco, P. (1992). *Chicken Sunday.* New York: Philomel.

Polacco, P. (1992). *Mrs. Katz and Tush.* New York: Philomel.

Polacco, P. (1993). *The bee tree.* New York: Philomel.

Polacco, P. (1993). *Babushka Baba Yaga.* New York: Bantam Books.

Polacco, P. (1994). *My rotten redheaded older brother.* New York: Simon & Schuster Books for Young Readers.

Polacco, P. (1994). *Pink and Say.* New York: Philomel.

Polacco, P. (1995). *My ol' man.* New York: Philomel.

Polacco, P. (1998). *Thank you Mr. Falkner.* New York: Philomel.

Reeves, N. (1992). *Into the mummy's tomb: The real-life discovery of Tutankhamen's treasures.* New York: Scholastic.

Resnick, J., & Davis, J. (1993). *Kolah the Koala.* Australia: True-To-Life Books.

Rylant, C. (1982). *When I was young in the mountains.* New York: Dutton.

Rylant, C. (1984). *Waiting to waltz: A childhood.* New York: Bradbury Press.

Rylant, C. (1985). *A blue-eyed daisy.* New York: Bradbury Press.

Rylant, C. (1985). *The relatives came.* New York: Bradbury Press.

Rylant, C. (1986). *A fine white dust.* New York: Bradbury Press.

Rylant, C. (1989). *A kindness.* New York: Orchard Books

Rylant, C. (1989). *But I'll be back again: An album.* New York: Orchard Books.

Rylant, C. (1992). *Missing May.* New York: Bradbury Press.

Simon, S. (1995). *Sharks.* New York: HarperCollins.

Taylor, M. (1975). *Song of the trees.* New York: Dial Books for Young Readers.

Taylor, M. (1976). *Roll of thunder, hear my cry.* New York: Bantam Books.

Taylor, M. (1981). *Let the circle be unbroken.* New York: Puffin Books.

Taylor, M. (1987). *The gold cadillac.* New York: Dial Books for Young Readers.

Taylor, M. (1990). *The road to Memphis.* New York: Puffin Books.

Tsuchiya, Y. (1988). *Faithful elephants.* Boston: Houghton Mifflin.

Index

Abandonment
in Cynthia Rylant's work, 28
ABC of Australian Animals (Parish),
91
Abstract symbolism, 59
Accuracy
of nonfiction literature, 179–80,
218
in work of Kathryn Lasky, 245
Actions
character development through,
145–46
Adventures of Huckleberry Finn, The
(Twain), 7
Aesthetic response, 94. *See also*
Reader response
activating (minilessons), 49–51
as element of multiple response,
43
factors affecting, 54–55
to *Fighting Ground, The* (Avi),
137–38, 140
identification with a character,
137–38, 139
to *Koala Lou* (Fox), 84–87
modeling, 49–50
multiple response during, 52–53
to nonfiction literature, 182–83
personal revelations, 137–38,
139
primacy of, 48–49, 54
questions encouraging, 48–49
research on evocation of,
53–55
for *What Jamie Saw* (Coman),
46
Aesthetic stance, 35–37
adoption of, 48
for nonfiction literature, 182–83
Agee, James, 10
Aggression
in children's literature, 63
Albert, Maura, 70, 131, 134, 137,
141, 149, 163
Altfillisch, Michael, 212
Amazing Grace, 61
Ambiguous endings, 53, 62
Amos and Boris (Steig), 60
Anatomy of Criticism (Frye), 31
Andrews, Julie, 13
Angelou, Maya, 2–3

Animal reports
for Mem Fox author study, 87,
91–94, 96–99, 109, 111,
185–86
Antagonist
conflict patterns, 60
Antihumanism, 40
Appelemando's Dream (Polacco),
225
Applebee, A., 45, 62, 65
Archetypal criticism, 31
Aristotle, 10, 11, 31, 43
doctrine of the mean, 149–51,
171
Arthur books (Brown), xi, 167,
168
Art Lesson, The (de Paola), 125
Artwork. *See also* Illustrations;
Visual display
for *Magic School Bus Goes to the
Vernal Pool* (student project),
211–212
by Patricia Polacco, 229
Assonance, 11
Audience
for *Magic School Bus* books,
217
Authentic curriculum, 79
Authentic literacy instruction,
78–79
Author interviews
Avi, 167–73
Joanna Cole, 216–19
Carolyn Coman, 71–73, 75–77,
81–82
Kathryn Lasky, 249–53, 256–60
Authors. *See also specific authors*
autobiographies of, 116–17
biographies of, 118
choosing for author studies,
112–14, 132, 176–77
delight from, 10–13
emotional response to, 2–3
favorite, 1–2, 14, 16
inspirations for ideas, 13–14
instruction by, 3–9
interest in, as people, 13–14
lack of favorites, 14
meaning intended by, 38–39
research by, 156
reverence for language by, 10–13

student hunches about, 91,
94–96, 152–60, 186–87, 190,
197, 198, 201–202
videotapes about, 120–22
Web sites, 115, 119
writing approaches of, 74–78
Author's craft
critique of, 139, 142
Author's Day (Pinkwater), 127
Author studies
activities, 19–20
author selection for, 112–14, 132,
176–77
Avi, 129–66
Avi's views on, 167–73
beliefs about, 26–27
chapter-books, 132–33
classroom context, 134
Joanna Cole, 176–213
Joanna Cole's views on, 216–19
Carolyn Coman, 44–48, 56
Carolyn Coman's views on,
81–82
communal, 16
culminating projects, 127
defining, 185–86
designing, 112–28
Mem Fox, 83–111
independent application,
123–24
Kathryn Lasky's views on,
256–60
picture books, 83–111
preparation for, 114–15, 133
purpose of, 14–22
reading author's works, 114–15
researching
biographical/autobiographical
links for, 115–22
student advice to teachers about,
22
student enjoyment of, 16–22
student-teacher collaboration in,
109, 124–25, 126–27, 128
teacher-led instruction, 123
time lines for, 125–26
value of, 14, 16, 19, xi–x
Author study perspectives, 23–42.
See also Aesthetic response;
Biographical response; Critical
response; Multiple response

272

aesthetic (reader) response,
 25–26, 34–39, 43
 critical response, 24–25, 26,
  30–34, 43
 historical roots of, 27–39
 literary biography, 23–24, 26,
  27–30, 43
 multiple response, 43–82, 133
Author-study questionnaires, 4, 5,
 15
Author surveys
 Mem Fox, 17–19
 nonfiction, 178
Author visits, 127
Author Web sites. *See* Web sites
Autobiographical information. *See
 also* Biographical response;
 Biographies
 assessing, 181
 Cynthia Rylant, 23–24, 69
 for fiction authors, 69, 116–17
 Mildred Taylor, 240–42
Autobiographical literature, 13–14
 Avi, 163–65
 biographical response to, 46
 Mem Fox, 110–111
 Patricia Polacco, 224–28
 responding to the past with, 106
 student enjoyment of, 16–22
Avi, 6, 8, 9, 12, 15, 68, 113, 114
 author visits by, 127
 dysgraphia, 130, 160, 163, 170
 early writing experiences,
  129–31, 154, 155, 157,
  160–63, 170
 parents, 157, 159, 160, 169
 school experiences, 129–31
 writing style, 159
Avi author study, 129–66
 aesthetic response, 137–38
 autobiographical works, 163–65
 biographical response, 152–65
 critical response, 138–52
 interview, 167–73
 nonbiographical works, 165–66
 overview, 134–37
 student hunches, 152–60

Babbitt, Natalie, 54, 68
Babushka Baba Yaga (Polacco),
 222–23
Babushka's Doll (Polacco), 222, 225
Babysitters Club series, 113
Bach, J. S., 169
Bakhtin, M., 74
Barber, William, 226–27
Barn, The (Avi), 129
 autobiographical nature of, 165,
  168–69
 biographical hunches bases on,
  156, 157, 158, 159
 research for, 165–66
Basal readers
 feminist criticism of, 40–41
Beat the Turtle Drum, 45

Bee Tree, The (Polacco), 222, 228
Beyond the Western Sea (Avi), 156
Bible, 32
Biographical hunches. *See* Hunches
Biographical response, 69–78, 82.
 See also Autobiographical
  literature; Life-literature
  connections
 aesthetic response and, 52–53
 children's use of, 70
 critical response and, 54
 to *Fighting Ground, The* (Avi),
  152–65
 to Mem Fox books, 105–106
 to *Koala Lou* (Fox), 95–96
 to *Possum Magic* (Fox), 90–91, 95
 researching, 115–22
 for *What Jamie Saw* (Coman), 46
Biographies. *See also*
 Autobiographical information
 assessing data, 181
 author studies as, 23–24, 26,
  27–30
 of fiction authors, 118
Bird's Body, A (Cole), 180, 186
Black Student Alliance (BSA), 242
Bleich, David, 35
Blue-Eyed Daisy, A (Rylant), 24, 25
Blume, Judy, 12, 54
Bone Wars, The (Lasky), 250–51
Book Links (Feldman), 115
Books
 categorization for author studies,
  186–87
 chapter books, 132–33, 165
 choosing for author studies,
  112–14, 132, 176–77
 formula, 113
 illustrated informational, 247–48
 informational storybooks, 177,
  180, 191
 photographic essays, 220,
  243–48, 258–59
 picture books, 220
 series, 112–13, 167–68
Books that Made a Difference
 (Sabine and Sabine), 7–8
Bowling, Carolee, 254
Brave Irene (Steig), 60
Bridges, Ruby, 7
Bridge to Terabithia (Paterson), 45,
 56, 62
Brown, Marc, 11, 125, 167, 168, xi
Bruce, B., 62
Budd, Jackie, 177
Buffalo Tree, The (Rapp), 73
Bunting, Eve, 11, 13, 114
But I'll Be Back Again (Rylant),
 23–24

Cadence, 51
Caldecott Medal, 175
Calf is Born, A (Cole), 180, 181
Calkins, Lucy, 165
Call of Stories, The (Coles), 1, 2

Cambourne, B., 78
Capitalism, 41
Carlsen, G., 114
Carrot Seed, The, 66
Carson, Rachel, 246
Categorization
 of books for author studies, 186
Celebrity
 author as, 168, 169
Chapter-book author studies
 guidelines, 132–33, 165
Character-against-character plots,
 60–61
Character-against-nature plots, 60
Character-against-society plots,
 61–62
Character analysis, 46
 in *Fighting Ground, The* (Avi),
  142
Character development, 59,
 62–65
 author techniques, 144–46
 in children's writing, 63
 in *Fighting Ground, The* (Avi),
  141, 143–44
 through description, 64
 through dialogue, 64
 through literature, 8–9
 through reactions, 64
Character maps, 146
Characters
 dynamic, 65, 151
 flat, 63–65, 146–49
 friend, 64
 generic, 64
 invented, 64
 multiple, 63
 reader concern about, 11–12
 reader identification with,
  137–38
 round, 63–65, 146–49
 static, 65, 151
Charlotte's Web (White), 34, 68
Chicken Sunday (Polacco), 226
Chick Hatches, A (Cole), 180
Child abuse
 response to, 172–73
 as theme, 44
Child-centered curriculum, 114
Children Literature Review, 181
Children of Christmas (Rylant), 68
Children's literature. *See* Literature
Christopher, Matt, 9
Chrysanthemum, 60
Chukovsky, K., 6
Classroom context
 for author studies, 134
Classroom practice
 belief-based, 23
 random, 23
Cleary, Beverly, 106
Client, The (Grisham), 6–7
"Close reading," 30
Cloud Book, The (de Paola), 125
Cockroaches (Cole), 179, 181, 191

Co-constructive curriculum, 181–82
Coerr, Eleanor, 35
Cognitive limitations theories, 45, 56
Cole, Brock, 73
Cole, Joanna, 175
  autobiographical/biographical data, 181
  biographical hunches about, 186–87, 190, 197, 198, 201–202
  popularity of, 176
  views on author studies, 216–19
Cole, Joanna, author study, 176–213
  categorizing books for, 186–87
  defining, 185–86
  experiments for, 199–200
  literature circles, 199–201
  reports for, 194–97
  speakers, 197–99
Coles, Robert, 1, 2, 3, 6, 8
Collaboration
  peer, 55
  student-teacher, 78–79, 109, 126–27, 128, 181–82
Colt, J., 123
Coman, Carolyn, 172
  interview, 70–77
  student hunches about, 70
  views on author studies, 81–82
  as a writer, 74–78
Coman, Carolyn, author study, 44
  aesthetic response, 48–55
  biographical response, 69–74
  character development, 62–65
  critical response, 55–69
  multiple responses, 44–48, 52–53
  plot, 60–62
  point of view, 67–69
  symbolism, 56–59
  teaching literary elements, 59
  theme, 65–67
Comic books, 113
Communal author studies, 16
Comparison reports, 194–95, 207, 217
Conflict patterns, 60–62
Connections through writing, 81–82
Core-literature approach, 123
Council on Interracial Books for Children, 243
Courage
  Aristotle's doctrine of the mean, 150–51, 171
  in *Fighting Ground, The* (Avi), 149–51
  in *Poppy* (Avi), 151–52
Cowardice
  in *Fighting Ground, The* (Avi), 149–51
  in *Poppy* (Avi), 152

Critical Handbook of Children's Literature, A (Lukens), 34
Critical response
  author studies as, 24–25, 26, 30–34
  Avi's views on, 170–71
  biographical response and, 54
  categories of, 139, 141
  character development, 62–67
  as element of multiple response, 43
  to *Fighting Ground, The* (Avi), 138–52
  importance of, 47–48
  to *Koala Lou* (Fox), 87–90
  as a learned response, 48
  personal engagement and, 52
  plot, 60–62
  point of view, 67–69
  value of, 55–59, 82
  to *What Jamie Saw* (Coman), 46
Cullinan, Bernice, 45, 55, 69, 179
Culminating projects, 126–27
Curriculum
  co-constructive, 181–82
  thematic (multidisciplinary), 176
Cuts, Breaks, Bruises, and Burns (Cole), 181

Dahl, Roald, 5
David Copperfield (Dickens), 27, 28, 29–30, 168
Davis, Jan, 97
Dear Mem Fox, I Have Read All Your Books Even the Pathetic Ones (Fox), 83, 115
Death
  responses to, 220–21
  as theme, 44
Death in the Family, A (Agee), 10
Deconstructionism, 33, 39–40
Degen, Bruce, 218
Delton, Judy, 12
"Demonic" tales, 173
Description
  character development through, 64
Description reports, 194–95, 207, 217
Devil's Arithmetic (Yolen), 65
Devil's Race (Avi), 158
Dewey, John, 23, 78
Dialogue
  character development through, 64
Dialogue bubbles
  for *Magic School Bus Goes to the Vernal Pool* (student project), 211–212
Dialogue journals, 39, 84, 125
Dickens, Charles, 27–29, 29–30, 168, 169, 218–19
Dinosaur Dig (Lasky), 244–45, 250

Direct teaching
  aesthetic response modeling and, 49
Discussion questions. *See* Questions
Doctrine of the mean (Aristotle), 149–51, 171
Dog's Body, A (Cole), 186
Dollmaker, The (Lasky), 253, 254
Drama. *See also* Readers' Theatre
  literature as, 102–105
Dynamic characters, 65, 151
Dysgraphia
  in Avi, 130, 155, 157, 160, 163, 170
Dyslexia
  in Patricia Polacco, 228
Dysnumeria
  in Patricia Polacco, 228

Earle, Alice, 84, 176, 187, 212, 217
Edelsky, Carole, 41
Eeds, M., 55, 56
Efferent stance, 35–37, 48, 94, 182
Eliot, T. S., 30, 170–71
Emotional response, 49–50. *See also* Aesthetic response
  by adults, 2–3
  by children, 3
Epilogue, 61
Ethnic pride
  in Polacco's work, 224
Eve Spoke (Lieberman), 216
Exodus (Uris), 256
Expectations
  about characters, 62
  aesthetic response and, 55
  ambiguous endings and, 62
Experiments
  for Joanna Cole author study, 199–200
Explicit theme, 66–67
Expository writing
  direct instruction in, 175
  reports, 192–97
  story skeletons (outlines) for, 204–205, 206
  structure of, 184–85
Eyewitness books, 175

Face Off (Christopher), 9
Fact whips, 191
Faithful Elephants (Tsuchiya), 61, 220–21
False courage
  in *Fighting Ground, The* (Avi), 149–51
  in *Poppy* (Avi), 151–52
Family themes
  in Patricia Polacco's work, 220, 221–24
  in Mildred Taylor's work, 231, 234–35, 237, 241–42
Fantasy, 259
Faulkner, William, 62

Favorite authors, 1–2, 14, 16
  Avi's views on, 167
  nonfiction, 177
  readers without favorite authors,
    14
Fear, 49
Feathers and Fools, 78
Feldman, Roxanne, 115
Feminist criticism, 40–41
Fighting Ground, The (Avi), 8, 9,
    129, 131, 132
  aesthetic response to, 137–38,
    140
  autobiographical/biographical
    response to, 152–65
  background knowledge for,
    134–37
  biographical hunches based on,
    154, 156, 157–59
  character development in, 141,
    143–44, 144–46
  critical response to, 138–52
  moral issues in, 138
  reader response to, 172
  round and flat characters in,
    146–48
  survey of, 135–37
  synopsis, 135
Figurative meaning, 57–58
Fine White Dust, A (Rylant), 25, 28,
    29, 34, 61
First person narration, 34, 67
Fish, Stanley, 35, 38
Fitzhugh, Louise, 54
Flashback, 61–62
Flat characters, 63–65, 146–49
Fleas (Cole), 180
Folktales
  Russian, 32
  structural similarities in, 32
  Ukrainian, 221, 224–25
Formal operations stage, 44
Formula books, 113
Fossey, Dian, 251, 252
Fox, Mem, 10, 16, 17–20, 21, 66,
    69, 80, 114, 115, 185
  class letter to, 85, 87
  journal articles about, 120
  videotape about, 120
Fox, Mem, author study, 83–111
  animal reports, 87, 91–94, 96–99,
    109, 111, 185–86
  assessment of, 109, 111
  autobiographical connections,
    110–111
  biographical response, 90–91,
    105–106
  class letters, 85, 87
  critical response, 87–90
  dramatization, 102–105
  hunch charts, 96
  hunches about, 91, 94–96
  preparation for, 126
  Readers' Theatre, 100–102
  student videotape, 107–109

teacher reading for, 114–15
  themes, 102–103, 105
Frederick (Lionni), 20, 125
Freedman, Russell, 179, 183
Freire, Paulo, 41
Friend characters, 64
Friendship, The (Taylor), 134
Fritz, Jean, 175
Fry, Carolyn, 253
Frye, Northrop, 31–32
Ftizgerald, F. Scott, 13
Functions
  narrative, 32

Galda, L., 45, 55, 69
Generic characters, 64
Ghost stories, 173
Girl with the Brown Crayon, The
    (Paley), 20, 22, 125
Giroux, Henry, 41
Giver, The (Lowry), 61
Goats (Brock), 73
Goebbels, Joseph, 3
Gold Cadillac, The (Taylor), 134,
    240
Goodall, Jane, 251
Goosebumps books, 112–13
Grammar, story, 32–34, 60–65
*Grand Conversations: Literature
    Groups in Action* (Peterson and
    Eeds), 55
Graves, Donald, 63, 165
Great Books, 123
Great Kapok Tree, The, 61
Grisham, John, 6–7, 172, 256
Guerin, Wilfred, 30–31

Happy endings, 62
Harriet the Spy (Fitzhugh), 54
Hatchet, 60
Hattie and the Fox (Fox), 110,
    185
  Readers' Theatre, 100–102, 106,
    107, 109
Hazlitt, William, 220
Headings, 97–98
Hellerman, Tony, 168
Hemingway, Ernest, 10
Henkes, Kevin, xi
Hermeneutics, 38
Hey, Al (Yorinks), 54
Hiebert, E., 55, 123
High mimetic mode, 31
Hinton, S. E., 13
Hirsch, E. D., 38
Historical fiction
  Mildred Taylor, 239
Hockey Machine (Christopher),
    9
Homer, 2, 10
Hopkins, Gerald Manley, 3
Horn Book, 115
How You Were Born (Cole), 180,
    218
Huck, Charlotte, 129, 179, 244

Humor, 12
  in *Magic School Bus* books
    (Cole), 180, 184, 202, 218
  in *Magic School Bus Goes to the
    Vernal Pool* (student project),
    209, 211–212
Hunch charts, 96
Hunches
  about Avi, 152–60
  about Joanna Cole, 186–87, 190,
    197, 198, 201–202
  about Carolyn Coman, 70
  about Mem Fox, 91, 94–96
  biographical, 141, 142
  forming, about authors, 91
Hunch/Evidence activity sheets,
    156
Hungry, Hungry Sharks (Cole), 195
Hurwitz, Joanna, 3
Hutchins, Pat, 54

Idea generation, 74, 76
Identification with characters
  in *Fighting Ground, The* (Avi),
    137–38, 139
If You Give a Mouse a Cookie
    (Numeroff), 41
I Know Why the Caged Bird Sings
    (Angelou), 2–3
Iliad, The (Homer), 2, 10
Illustrated informational books,
    247–48
Illustrations. *See also* Artwork;
    Visual displays
  by Patricia Polacco, 229
Imagery
  literary, 10
  in works of Kathryn Lasky,
    248–49
Implicit theme, 67
Independent application, 123–24
Indirect teaching, 49
Individualized Reading Program,
    123
Informational storybooks, 177
  fact and fiction in, 180, 216
  fact whips for, 191
Intercultural friendship
  in Patricia Polacco's work,
    223–24
Intergenerational themes
  in Patricia Polacco's work, 220,
    221–24
International Reading Association
    (IRA), 120
Inter-racial friendships
  in Patricia Polacco's work, 226
Intertextuality, 74, 78
Interviews. *See* Author interviews
Intuitions
  about symbolism, 56
Invented characters, 64
Invisibility
  as theme in *Possum Magic* (Fox),
    92–94

Ira Sleeps Over, 61
Irony, 31
Irving, John, 62
Iser, Wolfgang, 35
Island of the Blue Dolphins, 60

Jacob Have I Loved, 60
James, Henry, 27
James, William, 35
Jeopardy!
    exploring Avi's life with, 152–56
Jolly, Alison, 246, 251
Journal articles
    as source of author information,
    120
Journal of Children's Literature, 120
Julie and the Wolves, 60

Keck, Judith, 254–55
Keeping Quilt, The (Polacco), 225
Keller, Helen, 2
Kids on the Block, The, 134
Kindness, A (Rylant), 25
King, Stephen, 172, 256
Knight, Christopher, 244, 245, 246,
    248, 252
Koala Lou (Fox), 20, 83, 109,
    110–111, 185
    aesthetic response to, 84–87
    animal reports, 87, 91–94, 96–99,
    109, 111, 185–86
    biographical response to, 95–96
    critical response to, 87–90
KWL charts
    for writing nonfiction, 203–204

Language
    cadence of, 51
    deconstructionism and, 40
    reverence for, 10–13
Language Arts, 120
Large as Life: Animals Life Size
    (Cole), 181
Lasky, Kathryn, 220, 221, 243–60
    autobiographical information,
    249–53, 257–58
    illustrated informational books,
    247–48
    life-literature connections,
    249–53
    photographic essays, 243–48,
    258–59
    scientific background, 249–50
    views on author studies, 256–60
    writing process, 253–54
Lauber, Patricia, 184
Lawrence, D. H., 30, 42
Leal, D., 177
LeGuin, Ursula, 45
Lehr, Susan, 63, 65–66
Let the Circle Be Unbroken (Taylor),
    61, 229, 230, 235–237, 240,
    242
Let Us Now Praise Famous Men
    (Agee), 10

Levi-Strauss, C., 32
Lewis, C. S., 10, 68
Lieberman, Philip, 216
Life-literature connections. *See also*
    Biographical response
    in Avi's work, 131, 133
    in Kathryn Lasky's work, 249–53
    in Patricia Polacco's work,
    224–28
    in Mildred Taylor's work, 240–42
Limited omniscient perspective, 59,
    68
Lincoln, Abraham, 227
Lincoln: A Photobiography
    (Freedman), 183
Linguistic rules, 32–33
Lion, the Witch and the Wardrobe,
    The (Lewis), 68
Lionetti, Joanne, 125, 126
Lionni, Leo, 20, 22, 125–26
Listeners
    effect of author's works on, 43
    literary experience and, 43
Literacy instruction
    authentic, 78–79
    literature-based, 134, 174
    nonfiction literature and, 174
Literal meaning, 57–58
Literary biography, 42
    appeal of, 29
    author studies as, 23–24, 26,
    27–30
    Avi's views on, 168–70
    as element of multiple response,
    43
    limitations of, 29–30
Literary devices
    epilogue, 61
    flashback, 61–62
Literary elements, 11–13
    analysis of, 139, 142
    character development, 8–9, 59,
    62–67, 144–46
    critique of, 139, 142
    deciding when to teach, 59
    plot, 12, 46, 60–62, 142
    point of view, 59, 67–69
    symbolism, 31, 43, 56–59
    teacher knowledge and, 59–69
Literary experience, 43
Literary imagery, 10
Literary interpretation
    (hermeneutics), 38
Literary modes, 31
Literary movements, 26–27
    Avi's views on, 168–73
    New Criticism, 26–27, 30–32,
    33, 42, 170–71
    reader response theory, 27,
    35–39, 42
    Structuralism, 26–27, 32–34, 42
Literature
    Bible as source of, 32
    as drama, 102–105
    grammar (rules) of, 32–34, 60–65

quality of, aesthetic response
    and, 54
teaching power of, 6–9
Literature as Exploration
    (Rosenblatt), 35
Literature-based perspectives
    continuum of, 123–25
    independent application, 123–24
    student-teacher collaboration,
    124–25
    teacher-led instruction, 123
Literature circles, 25, 199–201
Literature/film connections, 141
    in *Fighting Ground, The* (Avi),
    142
Literature logs, 39
Little Dorrit (Dickens), 27, 168
Little Red Hen, The, 78
"Lived through" experience, 37
Lolah: The Koala (Resnick and
    Davis), 96–98
Lowman, Meg, 245–46, 252, 258
Low mimetic mode, 31
Lowry, Lois, 3, 49, 61, 64, 66, 67,
    68, 256
Lukens, Rebecca, 34, 55, 63, 69
Lyrical prose
    of Mildred Taylor, 239

Macaulay, David, 175
MacDonald, Ross, 13
Magic
    in Patricia Polacco's work, 225,
    227
Magic School Bus books (Cole)
    appeal of, 175–76, 191
    fact and fiction in, 180, 216
    humor in, 184, 202, 218
    as informational storybooks,
    177
    measuring quality of, 177–81
    organization of, 180–81
    Readers' Theater, 187, 188, 191
    science as basis for, 203
    sequence reports, 192–95, 207,
    209
    television versions, 185, 187
    visual displays in, 181, 211–212,
    218
    writing style, 180
Magic School Bus Goes to the Vernal
    Pool (student project), 186,
    203–213
    artwork for, 211–212
    KWL charts for, 203–204
    opening, 211
    storyline, 209–211
    story skeleton, 204–205, 206
    videotape of, 212
    writing, 207–211
Magic School Bus Inside a Beehive
    (Cole), 187–90
    critical response to, 190–91
    personal responses to, 187–90
    sequence reports, 192–95, 207

Magic School Bus Inside the Human Body (Cole), 184, 200
  fact and fiction in, 180
Magic School Bus In the Time of the Dinosaurs (Cole), 186, 187
Magic School Bus Lost in the Solar System (Cole), 200
Magic School Bus on the Ocean Floor (Cole), 190
Major Authors and Illustrators for Children and Young Adults, 115
Man Who Was Poe, The (Avi), 154, 157, 158
Markham, L., 164
Marxist criticism, 41–42
Matching game
  teaching symbolism with, 57
May, Kay, 100
McGee, L., 55
McHugh, Vincent, 62
Meaning
  deconstructionism and, 40
  figurative, 57–58
  literal, 57–58
  private, 35
  public, 35
  reader response theory and, 35, 38
Meet the Author videotapes
  Joanna Cole, 181
Meltzer, Milton, 175, 182
Memories
  as theme in *Wilfrid Gordon McDonald Partridge* (Fox), 99, 102–103
Message tree, 88
Metaphors, 180, 184
Meteor! (Polacco), 225
Microsoft *Encarta*, 106
Minilessons, 125
  activating aesthetic response, 49–51
  on symbolism, 57–59
Mirette on the High Wire, 61
Missing May (Rylant), 24–25, 28, 33–34, 61, 123
  point of view in, 68–69
Mississippi Bridge (Taylor), 134
Modes, 31
Monarchs (Lasky), 247, 252
Moral issues
  in Avi's works, 131, 138
  in Patricia Polacco's works, 221
  in Mildred Taylor's work, 234–35, 237
  teaching through literature, 6–9, 221
Moral Life of Children, The (Coles), 8
Moral relativism, 8
Most Beautiful Roof in the World, The (Lasky), 245–46, 247, 249, 252
Ms. Frizzle's Adventures in Ancient Egypt (Cole), 218

Mrs. Katz and Tush (Polacco), 224
Mufaro's Beautiful Daughters, 60
Multidisciplinary curriculum, 176
Multiple response, 43–82
  aesthetic response and, 52–53
  in author studies, 43–82, 133
  Avi's views on, 173
  to *What Jamie Saw* (Coman), 44–48
My New Kitten (Cole), 179, 180, 181
My Ol' Man (Polacco), 226–27
My Rotten Red-headed Older Brother (Polacco), 227
Myth, 31
Myth criticism, 31

Nancy Drew books, 167–68
Narrative functions, 32
National Assessment of Educational Progress (NAEP), 176
National Council of Teachers of English (NCTE), 120
Naylor, Phyllis Reynold, 8
New Advocate, The, 120
Newbery Medal, 175
New Blue Shoes, 66
New Criticism, 26–27, 30–32, 33, 42
  Avi's views on, 170–71
News About Dinosaurs, The (Lauber), 184
Newspapers, critical analysis of, 171
Night Noises (Fox), 10–11, 69, 83, 84, 109, 111
Nihilism, 40
Nonfiction author surveys, 178
Nonfiction literature, 174–219
  accuracy of, 183–84, 218
  aesthetic response to, 182–83
  assessment criteria for, 177–81
  author study design, 176–85
  author study implementation, 185–213
  author Web sites, 214
  Joanna Cole interview, 216–19
  critical dimensions of, 183–85
  guidelines, 213–15
  humor in, 180, 184
  Kathryn Lasky interviews, 249–53, 256–60
  literary merit of, 175
  recent interest in, 174–76
  structure of, 184–85
  student attitudes toward, 174–75
Note taking, 205–207, 208
Number the Stars (Lowry), 8, 49, 61, 62, 66, 67
  character development in, 64–65
Nye, Bill, 177

Oates, Joyce Carol, 14
Objective point of view, 68–69
O'Connor, Flannery, 38–39

O'Dell, Scot, 3
Odyssey, The (Homer), 10
Old Curiosity Shop (Dickens), 28
Oles, Ken, 197
Oliver Twist (Dickens), 27
Omniscient point of view, 68
  limited, 59, 68
Onomatopoetic words, 11
On the Bus with Joanna Cole (Cole), 181, 187
Open-ended questions, 54–55
Organization of nonfiction literature, 179, 180–81
Orwell, George, 218–19
Others' words
  character development through, 145–46
Outlines
  for expository writing, 204–205
  Kathryn Lasky, 254
"Oval" characters, 148

Pain and the Great One, The (Blume), 54
Paley, Vivian, 20, 22, 125–26
Paola, Tomie de, 125
Parental love
  as theme in *Koala Lou* (Fox), 85, 88–90
Parish, Steve, 91
Passion in writing, 83
Paterson, Katherine, 3, 11, 45, 132, 221
Paterson (Williams), 2
Paulsen, Gary, 169
Peace Corps
  Mildred Taylor's experience in, 242
Peck, Robert Newton, 13
Peer collaboration, 55
Personal engagement
  critical response and, 52
Personal meaning, 39
Personal response. *See also* Aesthetic response
  defined, 45
  to *Koala Lou* (Fox), 84–87
  to *Magic School Bus Inside a Beehive*, 187–90
  to *What Jamie Saw* (Coman), 46
Personal revelations. *See also* Aesthetic response
  in *Fighting Ground, The* (Avi), 137–38, 139
Peterson, R., 55, 56
Philosophers, 149–50
Photographic essays, 220
  effectiveness of, 258–59
  illustrated informational books vs., 247–48
  Kathryn Lasky, 243–48
Photographs
  in Kathryn Lasky's work, 243–44, 252
  for *Magic School Bus Goes to the*

Photographs (*Continued*)
  Vernal Pool (student project),
    211–212
Picture books, 83–111, 220
Pilbeam, David, 251
Pink and Say (Polacco), 223–24,
    227
Pinkwater, Daniel, 127
Plagiarizing, 209
Plants in Winter (Cole), 180
Plato, 6
Pliny the Younger, 176
Plot, 12, 60–62
  analysis, in *Fighting Ground, The*
    (Avi), 142
  character-against-character,
    60–61
  character-against-nature, 60
  character-against-society, 61–62
  critique of, 46
  retrieval, for *What Jamie Saw*
    (Coman), 46
Poetics (Aristotle), 31
Point of view, 67–69
  first person, 67
  limited omniscient, 59, 68
  objective, 68–69
  omniscient, 68
Polacco, Patricia, 220, 221–29
  as an artist, 229
  autobiographical connections,
    224–28
  explicit themes, 222–23
  family (intergenerational)
    themes, 220, 221–24
  implicit themes, 223–24
  as a writer, 228
Popcorn Book, The (de Paola), 125
Poppy (Avi), 9, 151–52
  biographical hunches based on,
    158, 159, 160
Possum Magic (Fox), 83, 92–94,
    110
  biographical response to, 90–91,
    95
Post-It notes
  for note-taking, 207
Poststructuralism, 33. *See also*
    Deconstructionism
Potter, Beatrix, 10–11
Pound, Ezra, 3
Prediction, 24
  story grammar and, 33–34
Primary theme, 66
Private meaning, 35
Propp, Vladimir, 32, 33
Protagonist conflict patterns, 60
Public meaning, 35
Publishers Web sites, 119
Puppeteer (Lasky), 253

Questions
  about *What Jamie Saw* (Coman),
    46–47
  aesthetic response and, 54

encouraging aesthetic response
    with, 48–49
  open-ended, 54–55
Quicksand Book, The (de Paola),
    125

Racial bigotry
  in Mildred Taylor's work, 230,
    231–32
Racial discrimination
  in Mildred Taylor's work,
    232–33, 235, 236, 238, 242
Racial hatred
  in Mildred Taylor's work, 229,
    235–36, 238, 240
Racial prejudice
  in Mildred Taylor's work, 230,
    235–36, 237–38, 242
Racial pride, 220
  in Mildred Taylor's work, 231,
    242
Radical theories, 39–42
Ramayana, 126
Ransom, John Crowe, 30
Raphael, T., 55
Rapp, Adam, 73
Reactions
  character development through,
    64
Reader response
  author studies as, 25–26, 34–39
  Avi's views on, 171–72
Reader response theory, 27, 35–38,
    42
  criticism of, 38–39
Readers' Theatre, 134, 185
  for *Hattie and the Fox* (Fox),
    100–102, 106, 107, 109
  for *Magic School Bus* books, 187,
    188, 191, 217
Reader-text relationship, 35, 38–39
Reading
  appreciation of, 82
  classroom, 167
  enjoyment of, 173
Reading logs, 125
Reading Marathon, 134
Reading Teacher, The, 120
Reading workshops, 84
Reception theory, 42. *See also*
    Reader response theory
Rechenka's Eggs (Polacco), 225
Reflection
  through aesthetic response, 49
Relatives Came, The (Rylant), 24
Reports
  comparison, 194–95, 207, 217
  description, 194–95, 207, 217
  sequence, 192–95, 207, 209, 217
Rereading, 84–85
Research. *See also* Animal reports
  by authors, 156
  for Mem Fox author study,
    185–86
  note taking, 205–207, 208

process, 96–99
  reports, 102
  "Researcher's Notes" worksheets,
    98–99
Resnick, Jon, 96–97
Response projects, 39
Rhetoric, 43
Rhythm, 11
Rime of the Ancient Mariner, The, 78
Road to Memphis, The (Taylor), 229,
    237–39, 242
Roll of Thunder, Hear My Cry
    (Taylor), 61, 229, 230,
    231–35, 240, 241, 242, 243
Romance, 31
Rose Blanche, 61
Rosenblatt, Louise, 27, 34–35, 36,
    38, 48, 49, 94, 171–72, 182
Rosie's Walk (Hutchins), 54
Round characters, 65, 146–49
Russian folktales, 32
Rylant, Cynthia, 10, 23–26, 28–31,
    33–34, 39, 43, 61, 66, 68–69
  use of autobiography by, 69

Sabine, Gordon, 7
Sabine, Patricia, 7
*Sadako and the Thousand Paper
    Cranes* (Coerr), 35–37
Sail Away, 78
Sam, Bangs, and Moonshine, 61
Saussure, 32–33
Scholastic
  Meet the Authors and Illustrations
    series, 115
Secondary theme, 66
Selective attention, 35
Self-reflection, 51
Sendack, Maurice, 259
Sequels
  as craft, 239–40
  by Mildred Taylor, 229, 230–40,
    242
Sequence reports, 192–95, 207,
    209, 217
Series books, 112–13, 167–68
*Shadows in the Dawn: The Lemurs of
    Madagascar* (Lasky), 246–47,
    251, 256, 257
Shakespeare, William, 2–3
Shannon, Patrick, 41
Sharks (Cole), 183
Sheeman, Angela, 177
Shepard, Becky, 125, 126
Sherlock Holmes books, 168
Sherrill, A., 114
Shiloh (Naylor), 8
Shor, Ira, 41
Sibling rivalry
  in *Koala Lou* (Fox), 88–90
  in Patricia Polacco's work, 227
Signifieds, 33, 40
Signifiers, 33, 40
Sign of the Beaver, 60
"Silver Packages" (Rylant), 68

Similes
  in works of Joanna Cole, 180, 184
  in works of Kathryn Lasky, 248–49
Simon, Seymour, 184
Singer, Isaac Bashevis, 13
"Slumber Did My Spirit Seal, A" (Guerin), 30–31
Snake's Body, A (Cole), 180
Social injustice, 220
  as theme in Polacco's work, 223–24
Social resistance
  as theme in Mildred Taylor's work, 230, 232–34, 236–37, 238–39, 242
Something About the Author Autobiography Series, 115, 181
Something Upstairs (Avi), 154, 158
Sometimes I think I Hear My Name (Coman), 74
Song of the Trees, The (Taylor), 61, 229, 230–31, 240, 241, 243
Sophie (Fox), 103, 106, 111
S.O.R. Losers (Avi), 133
  autobiographical nature of, 164
Sound devices, 11
Speakers
  for nonfiction studies, 197–99
Spider maps, 144
Squirrel Nutkin (Potter), 10–11
Static characters, 65, 151
Steig, William, 60
Stine, R. L., 112–13
Story boards, 106
Story grammar, 32–34, 60–65
Storyline, 209–211
Storymaking, 131
Story maps, 24, 60
Story skeletons
  for *Magic School Bus Goes to the Vernal Pool* (student project), 204–205
Story structure
  series books and, 113
Story syntax, 32
Storytelling
  characters as element of, 11–12
  elements of, 11–13
  instilling values through, 221
  by Patricia Polacco, 228
  plot as element of, 12
  retelling, 45
Stream of consciousness
  reader response theory and, 35
Structuralism, 26–27, 32–34, 42
Structure
  of nonfiction literature, 184–85
  of stories, 113
Student-teacher collaboration, 78–79, 109, 124–25, 126–27, 128, 181–82
Subjective response, 45. *See also* Aesthetic response

Sugaring Time (Lasky), 244, 247, 253
Summarization, 45
Surtsey: The Newest Place on Earth (Lasky), 247–48, 258
Surveys
  Fighting Ground, The (Avi), 135–37
  Mem Fox, 17–19
  nonfiction author surveys, 178
Survival stories, 60
Symbolic thought, 56–57
Symbolism, 43, 56–59
  defined, 57
  literary modes and, 31
  minilessons on, 57–59
  teaching, with matching game, 57
  in *What Jamie Saw* (Coman), 56–59
Symmetry
  in works of Kathryn Lasky, 248–49

Taylor, Mildred, 12, 61, 66, 134, 145, 220, 221, 229–43, xi
  historical fiction, 239
  life-literature connections, 240–42
  lyrical prose, 239
  racial bigotry as theme of, 230, 231–32
  racial discrimination as theme of, 232–33, 235, 236, 238, 242
  racial hatred as theme of, 229, 235–36, 238, 240
  racial prejudice as theme of, 230, 235–36, 237–38, 242
  racial pride as theme of, 231, 242
  sequels, 229, 230–40, 242
  as a writer, 242–43
Taylor, Wilbert Lee, 240, 241, 243
Teacher-led instruction, 123
Teachers
  collaboration with students, 78–79, 109, 124–25, 126–27, 128, 181–82
  knowledge about literary elements, 59–69
  knowledge about multiple response, 43
  role of, 114
Teaching power, of children's literature, 6–9
Television
  critical analysis of, 171
  Magic School Bus programs, 185, 187
  round and flat characters in, 148–49
Tell Me Everything (Coman), 44
  conflict patterns, 60–61
  flashbacks in, 62
  interview with Carolyn Coman about, 71–74, 77

point of view in, 68
symbolism in, 59
Temper tantrums, 49–50
Terkel, Studs, 7
Text
  literary experience and, 43
  reader response theory and, 35, 38–39
Thank You, Mr. Falkner (Polacco), 228
Thematic curriculum
  nonfiction literature and, 176
Themes, 65–67
  analysis of, 24–25
  child abuse, 44
  children's sensitivity to, 65–66
  in Carolyn Coman's work, 65–67
  critical analysis of, 34
  death as, 44
  explicit, 66–67
  family, 220, 221–24, 231, 234–35, 237, 241–42
  in *Fighting Ground, The* (Avi), 142
  in Mem Fox's work, 102–103, 105
  identifying, in Mem Fox author study, 102–103, 105
  implicit, 67
  intergenerational, 220, 221–24
  in *Koala Lou* (Fox), 85, 88–90
  in Patricia Polacco's work, 220, 221–24, 223–24
  in *Possum Magic* (Fox), 92–94
  primary, 66
  secondary, 66
  in Mildred Taylor's work, 229–38, 240–42
  in *What Jamie Saw* (Coman), 66, 67
  in *Wilfrid Gordon McDonald Partridge* (Fox), 99, 102–103
Think Like an Eagle (Lasky), 247
Thoreau, Henry David, 182
Thunder Cake (Polacco), 223
Tico and the Golden Wings (Lionni), 20
Time, manipulation of, 61–62
Time for Bed (Fox), 103–104
Time lines, 125–26
Titch, 66
Tompkins, G., 55
To Tell the Truth (Avi), 129
Tough Boris (Fox), 103, 104, 109, 120
Traces of Life: Origins of Humankind (Lasky), 250
Transactional reading, 35, 37. *See also* Reader response theory
Transactional theory, 48
True Confessions of Charlotte Doyle, The (Avi), 60, 129, 131
  biographical hunches based on, 154, 156, 158, 159, 160
  research for, 165

True courage
in *Fighting Ground, The* (Avi), 150–51
in *Poppy* (Avi), 152
Trumpet Club, 120
Tsuchiya, Y., 220–21
Tubman, Harriet, 246
Tuck Everlasting (Babbitt), 54, 68
Twain, Mark, 7, 10
Two Bad Ants, 61

Ukrainian folktales, 221, 224–25
Uncle Vova's Tree (Polacco), 225
Under the Blood Red Sea, 52
Uris, Leon, 256

Van Gogh Cafe, The (Rylant), 25
Veatch, Jeanette, 123
Venn diagrams, 92, 94
Videotapes
on authors, 120–22
Magic School Bus Goes to the Vernal Pool (student project), 212
student, for Mem Fox author study, 107–109
Violence
in Avi's work, 158
in children's literature, 63
Virtuous stories, 6–7, 221. *See also* Moral issues
Visual display. *See also* Artwork; Illustrations; Photographs
for *Magic School Bus Goes to the Vernal Pool* (student project), 181, 211–212, 218
in nonfiction literature, 179, 181, 211–212, 218
Vygotskian theory, 114

Waiting to Waltz (Rylant), 24
Walden (Thoreau), 182

Walker, Eula May, 226
Washington, Steward, 226
Washington, Winston, 226
Waste Land (Eliot), 30
Weaver's Gift, The (Lasky), 247, 253
Web sites
authors, 115, 119
Joanna Cole, 181
nonfiction authors, 214
publishers, 119
Welty, Eudora, 170
What Jamie Saw (Coman), 44, 172
aesthetic response to, 48–51
ambiguous ending, 62
author interview, 71–77
biographical response to, 70
character development in, 63–65
conflict pattern, 60
critical response to, 48–51
multiple responses to, 45–48, 52–53
point of view in, 68
questions to ask about, 46–47
symbolism in, 56–59
teaching literary elements in, 59
theme, 66, 67
When I was Young in the Mountains (Rylant), 24, 28, 29
Where the Wild Things Are (Sendack), 259
White, E. B., 34, 68
Whole-class discussion, 125, 126
"Who Was That Masked Man, Anyway?" (Avi), 133, 163–64
Wiesel, Elie, 14
Wildlife Fact Files, 87, 98, 106
Wilfrid Gordon McDonald Partridge (Fox), 20, 99, 102–103, 110, 120
Williams, William Carlos, 1, 2, 3, 6
Windcatcher (Avi), 156

Wizard of Earthsea, A (LeGuin), 45, 56
Wolf Rider: Tale of Terror (Avi), 133, 164–65
Word clarity, 10
Words
character development through, 145–46
deconstructionism and, 40
Wordsworth, William, 31
Writer's block, 76
Writer's notebooks, 70–71
Writing
connections through, 81–82
literary experience and, 43
Magic School Bus Goes to the Vernal Pool (student project), 207–211
passion in, 83
purpose in, 81
series books and, 113
student self-analysis of, 172
transformational nature of, 29–30
Writing process
for authors, 74–78
Avi, 154, 155, 160–63, 170
Joanna Cole, 218–19
Charles Dickens, 28–29, 218–19
Mem Fox, 109
Kathryn Lasky, 253–54
Patricia Polacco, 228
Cynthia Rylant, 29
Mildred Taylor, 242–43
Writing style
Avi, 159
for nonfiction literature, 179, 180
Writing workshops, 84

Yolen, Jane, 4, 12, 65

Zarnowski, M., 177, 180